HITLER'S COLLABORATORS

Advance praise for *Hitler's Collaborators*

'Focussing on Western and Northern countries in Hitler's Europe, Philip Morgan illustrates and assesses the captivating history of collaboration with the German occupier during the Second World War. It ranges from the appeasing and accommodating attitudes during the early phase of Nazi-occupation to the ambivalent role of state officials and businessmen, and finally, discusses the deplorable collusion and complicity in the deportation of Jews. Far from moralizing, Morgan's meticulous study explains the realities and reasons, as well as the consequences, of this equally diverse and disturbing phenomenon.'

Professor Gerhard Hirschfeld, University of Stuttgart

'In common with studies of resistance to Nazi occupation during the Second World War, the myriad forms of collaboration have largely been studied from a purely national perspective. In an overtly comparative and accessibly written approach to the subject, Philip Morgan sets out to summarize the debates on state, bureaucratic, and economic collaboration during the Nazi occupation, and provides his own distinctive analysis to explain the behaviour of all those involved.'

Professor Bob Moore, University of Sheffield

HITLER'S COLLABORATORS

Choosing between bad and worse in Nazi-occupied Western Europe

PHILIP MORGAN

OXFORD
UNIVERSITY PRESS

OXFORD
UNIVERSITY PRESS

Great Clarendon Street, Oxford, OX2 6DP,
United Kingdom

Oxford University Press is a department of the University of Oxford.
It furthers the University's objective of excellence in research, scholarship,
and education by publishing worldwide. Oxford is a registered trade mark of
Oxford University Press in the UK and in certain other countries

First Edition published in 2018
Impression: 1

Published in the United States of America by Oxford University Press
198 Madison Avenue, New York, NY 10016, United States of America

British Library Cataloguing in Publication Data
Data available

Library of Congress Control Number: 2017942094

ISBN 978–0–19–923973–3

Printed in Great Britain by
Clays Ltd, St Ives plc

This book is dedicated to my friends and colleagues, Mike and Lesley,
and their wondrous joint project, The White House.

Preface

In my last years as a lecturer at the University of Hull, I devised and taught a final year module, 'Occupation, Collaboration, and Resistance in Northern and Western Europe, 1940–1945'. Many of the students who took the module did not 'get' collaboration, despite my efforts to make civil servants interesting. This shortage of empathy was mainly, I think, because they could not envisage anyone beyond the usual suspects, fascists and Nazis, actually choosing to collaborate with such an evidently 'evil' phenomenon as German Nazism. This book is, retrospectively, and far too late for them, in the hope that they have carried on reading.

The title and concept of the module were stolen, with his permission, from my friend and ex-colleague in European Studies at Hull, Mike Smith, after he had taken the fork in the road to university management and strategy. He had taught a module with the same title, and built up in the university library an impressive collection of foreign-language primary and secondary materials. He relished, as I did, the chance offered in a European Studies programme of tackling European history with undergraduate students who also had a facility in one or more European languages. His own contribution to the field was an article on that extraordinary Dutch political phenomenon of the early period of Nazi occupation, the *Nederlandse Unie*, with the provocative title 'Neither Resistance nor Collaboration...'.[1] Mike died before he could fully indoctrinate me with his approach to collaboration, and I think he would have produced a more iconoclastic view of collaboration than the one I have in this book. So, with apologies for its moderation and caution, this book is also for Mike, and for European Studies.

All the translations from French are mine. I am grateful for the help of an ex-colleague, Esther Velthoen, in translating articles in Dutch on the two most important officials in the Dutch wartime ministerial administration; and to Wendy Burke and Rob Riemsma for kindly translating the Dutch government's instructions to its top civil servants. Thanks, also, to Keith Hill, who kept me abreast of what to read, and not read, on wartime Belgium; and to Professor Hans Otto Frøland, of the University of Trondheim, and Emeritus Professor Mark Van den Wijngaert, of the Catholic University of Brussels, for their helpful suggestions on reading for Norway and Belgium respectively. Dot Merriott, without any bidding from me, kindly tracked down the Frank Capa photograph.

I must also thank the anonymous reader of the draft manuscript for stimulating some last-minute additions to the text. I did not agree with the points that were made, but the critique enabled me to clarify and strengthen the basic argument of the book.

The greatest thanks should go to my OUP editor, Matthew Cotton, who has been patiently encouraging, compassionate, and understanding, throughout the research and writing of a book that has been rather too long in the gestation. I can only hope that he is happy with the outcome of a prolonged wait, which is as much the product of his own perseverance, as of mine.

P.J.M.

Acknowledgement

I would like to thank my editor at Oxford University Press, Matthew Cotton, for his forbearance and encouragement in bringing this book to completion.

Contents

List of Illustrations   xiii

Map   xv

Abbreviations   xvii

Introduction: Dealing with the Past   1

1. Starting at the End: Liberation and the Post-War Purges
   of Collaborators   13

2. The Nature of the Beast: The Nazi New Order and the Nazi
   Occupation of Northern and Western Europe   32

3. Collaboration with the Grain of Occupation, 1940–1942   55

4. Economic Collaboration, 1940–1942   102

5. The Collaboration of Officials, 1940–1942   154

6. Collaboration against the Grain of Occupation, 1942–1944:
   The Deportation of Jews   235

7. Collaboration against the Grain of Occupation, 1942–1945:
   The Deportation of Workers   284

   Conclusion: Officials Will Be Officials   327

Notes   335

Select Bibliography   345

Picture Acknowledgements   355

Publisher's Acknowledgements   356

Index   357

List of Illustrations

1. A post-liberation street scene in Chartres, August 1944   5
2. 'All I wanted was a single Europe'   33
3. Pétain's meeting with Hitler at Montoire, October 1940   65
4. Orderly queues of Dutch people, The Hague, August 1940   73
5. The *NSB* versus the *NU*   76
6. Alexandre Galopin   110
7. Scavenius and Best before an audience with the king of Denmark, late 1942   247
8. A grinning and relaxed René Bousquet, January 1943   276
9. Papon's release from prison, September 2002   282
10. A Vichy propaganda poster for the *Relève*, summer 1942   302
11. Laval's promotion of the *Relève* in Compiègne, August 1942   305

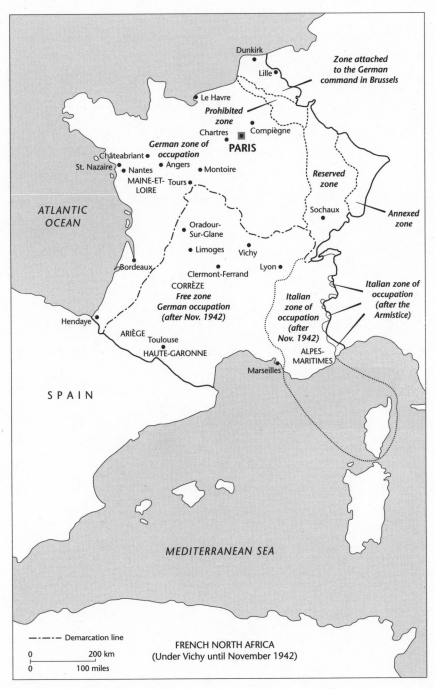

Dunkirk

**Zone attached
to the German
command in Brussels**

Lille

Le Havre

**Prohibited
zone**

Chartres ● Compiègne

PARIS

**German zone of
occupation**

Châteabriant ●

St. Nazaire ● ● Nantes ● Angers ● Montoire

MAINE-ET- Tours ●
LOIRE

**Reserved
zone**

ATLANTIC
OCEAN

Sochaux ●

**Annexed
zone**

● Oradour-
Sur-Glane

● Limoges Vichy ●

Bordeaux ● Lyon ●

Clermont-Ferrand

CORRÈZE
**Free zone
German occupation
(after Nov. 1942)**

**Italian
zone of
occupation
(after
Nov. 1942)**

**Italian zone of
occupation
(after the
Armistice)**

Hendaye ●

ARIÈGE
Toulouse
HAUTE-GARONNE

ALPES-
MARITIMES

Marseilles ●

SPAIN

MEDITERRANEAN SEA

—·—·— Demarcation line

0   200 km
0   100 miles

FRENCH NORTH AFRICA
(Under Vichy until November 1942)

Map 1. Vichy France, 1940–1944

Abbreviations

CGQJ	*Commissariat Général aux Questions Juives* (General Commissariat for Jewish Affairs: France)
CGT	*Confédération Générale du Travail* (General Confederation of Labour: France)
CNAA	*Corporation Nationale de l'Agriculture et de l'Alimentation* (National Corporation of Agriculture and Food Supply: Belgium)
CO	*Comité d'Organisation* (Organization Committee: France)
DNSAP	*Danmarks Nationalsocialistiske Arbejder Parti* (Danish National Socialist Workers Party)
EEC	European Economic Community
FFI	*Forces Françaises de l'Intérieur* (French Home Forces)
Gestapo	*Geheime Staatspolizei* (Secret State Police: Nazi Germany)
GMR	*Groupes Mobiles de Réserve* (mobile reserve force)
Nap	*Noyautage des administrations publiques* (Infiltration of Public Services)
NG	*Nederlandse Gemeenschap* (Netherlands Community)
NS	*Nasjonal Samling* (National Unity: Norway)
NSB	*Nationaal-Socialistische Beweging* (National Socialist Movement: Netherlands)
NU	*Nederlandse Unie* (United Netherlands)
OCRPI	*Office Central de Répartition des Produits Industriels* (Central Office for the Allocation of Industrial Products: France)
ONT	*Office National du Travail* (National Labour Office: Belgium)
OT	*Organisation Todt* (Todt Organization: Nazi Germany)
PPF	*Parti Populaire Français* (French Popular Party)
PTT	*Postes, Télégraphes et Téléphones* (Postal Services and Telecommunications: France)
RHSA	*Reichssicherheitshauptamt* (Central Office of Reich Security: Nazi Germany)
RNP	*Rassemblement National Populaire* (National Popular Rally: France)
SCAP	*Service de Contrôle des Administrateurs Provisoires* (Inspectorate of Provisional Business Administrators: France)

SD	*Sicherheitsdienst* (Security Service: Nazi Germany)
SIPO	*Sicherheitspolizei* (State Security Police: Nazi Germany)
SNCB	*Société Nationale des Chemins de Fer Belge* (National Belgian Railways)
SNCF	*Société Nationale des Chemins de Fer Français* (French National Railways)
SS	*Schutz Staffeln* (Protection Units: Nazi Germany)
STO	*Service du Travail Obligatoire* (Compulsory Labour Service: France)
Sybelec	*Syndicat Belge de l'Acier* (Belgian Steel Syndicate)
USSR	Union of Soviet Socialist Republics (The Soviet Union)
VNV	*Vlaamsch Nationaal Verbond* (Flemish National League)
ZAST	*Zentralauftragstelle* (Central Ordering Office: Nazi Germany)

Introduction
Dealing with the Past

This book deals with collaboration, the most contentious, uncongenial, and divisive of the responses of occupied peoples to Nazi Germany's wartime occupation of Europe. The term itself has changed in tone and meaning during and as a result of the wartime experience of cooperation with Nazi Germany in the occupied territories. We can scarcely use the term in its positive sense of working together in partnership on a common task or towards a common aim, without acknowledging its degradation into meaning a traitorous cooperation with an enemy power in occupation of one's own country. Its treasonable connotations were evident, or at least articulated, by the time of the Allied liberation of European countries from Nazi domination in 1944–5. But in October 1940, after meeting Hitler, the head of the French state, Marshal Philippe Pétain, made not quite the first public and official announcement of the term to mean simply, and positively, the cooperation between a country and its occupying power.

Some historians have even stopped using such an apparently tainted term, preferring to find alternatives, like 'accommodation,'[1] which, to my mind, indicates a form or mode of collaboration, rather than another way of expressing it. Danish resisters and collaborators used the word 'cooperation' to describe the policy of state-to-state collaboration between the Danish and German governments, and then gave different intonations to the term as they used it against each other. Both contemporaries and historians in Denmark have been reluctant to employ the term 'collaboration' at all. When they did so, it again denoted a particular mode of collaboration, in this case, active collaboration in the service of enemy, rather than the generic phenomenon of collaboration itself.[2] But, Denmark aside, 'collaboration' was the word generally used by those who resisted the Germans, and those who collaborated with the Germans, even when, towards the end of the war, the term was becoming a taunt and a mark of shame and dishonour. There seems to be no valid reason to abandon the term for a synonym, or a euphemism.

The important terminological distinction that needs to be made, however, is that between 'collaboration' and 'collaborationism', if only because so many historians continue to use the terms interchangeably. 'Collaborationists' were those people who chose to cooperate fully and unequivocally with the Nazi German occupiers, and did so out of a sense of ideological affinity with Nazism and of ideological conviction that this was the right thing to do. They were, above all, though not exclusively, local fascists, none of them of any significant or lasting political weight in the late 1930s, but galvanized by German military victories into believing that their chance had come. Given their poor political and electoral performance in the 1930s, collaboration with the Nazi occupier was probably their only route to power, after 1940.

The fascists' national enemies were also those of Nazi Germany: Jews, communists, masons, liberals, democrats. The German Nazi regime was taken by them as a model to emulate in their own countries, a leading example of what their own national fascist revolutions would achieve. It is the case that towards the end of the war, and *in extremis*, the Nazi occupiers had to rely increasingly on their ideological collaborators, as they effectively became besieged in the territories they occupied. In occupied Norway, Vidkun Quisling, the leader of the fascist movement, *Nasjonal Samling* or National Unity, was made Prime Minister of an *NS* government in February 1942. But this experiment was not really repeated anywhere else in occupied Northern and Western Europe. 'Quisling' has, unfortunately, become a concept in his or its own right, leading to an unhelpful blurring of the boundaries between 'collaboration' and 'collaborationism', to the point that 'collaboration' is taken to be 'collaborationism'.

There are good historical reasons for taking the view that Quisling is not the real face of collaboration in Nazi-occupied Europe. The local fascists clearly expected German help in bringing about in their own countries what the Nazis had themselves achieved in Germany. But their vision of a 'fascistized' Europe was one of a federated Europe of 'fascistized' and sometimes enlarged national states. The nationalism of the local fascisms, which was what defined them, cut across the prevailing German Nazi idea of incorporating Germanic peoples into a Greater Germanic empire where Nazi Germany was the core, hegemonic power. These contrasting visions of the new Europe made for often prickly collaboration between the fascists and the occupier and its agencies, and mutual frustration and disappointment. The Germans had reservations about the collaborationists on other counts, too. They were unpopular, before and during the war, which meant they could not really deliver on anything, besides repression, and certainly could not be relied on to govern the occupied territories with any significant level of popular sympathy or tolerance. What made them unpopular, of course, was their undisguised aspiration to 'fascistize' their own societies. Quisling's quasi-governmental role irrevocably shifted the balance between collaboration and resistance in occupied Norway, and made German occupation inherently unstable and contested. This book can hardly avoid mentioning Quisling again, but it is not a book about Quisling and the like.

The book concentrates on the wartime situation in occupied Northern and Western European countries, because the opportunities, or gaps, for collaboration were much more evident there than in occupied Central and Eastern Europe. Arguably the crux of the war was the German invasion of the Soviet Union in June 1941. The invasion was designed to open up 'living space' for German colonization and settlement in Eastern Europe and the Western USSR, which was Hitler's permanent solution to the perceived insecurity of Germany and the Aryan race in Europe and the world.

During the war, Hitler did, sometimes, talk privately of some colonization in Western Europe, indicating a swathe of territory from Belgium to eastern France, from where, it was thought, a Francophone population could be expelled and replaced by German farmers from south Tyrol. Parts of this area were an exclusion zone during the war, deliberately cut off from France. The French inhabitants of this zone were initially prevented from returning there after the great dispersal of the French population during the German invasion of France in the summer of 1940. The Germans set up farming colonization agencies in the area, which confiscated local farms, presumably indicating the region as a site of future mass German settlement. But, in Hitler's view of things, Northern and Western Europe were not typically and not generally seen as territory to be conquered, and then settled and colonized.

German occupation was bound to be more brutal and emphatic in areas designated for German settlement in the east than in areas that were not. There is, here, a fundamental distinction between how the Germans occupied Eastern, and then, Western Europe, which had important implications for how the occupied peoples responded to occupation. The margins for collaboration were correspondingly greater, and for resistance, smaller, in Western Europe than in Eastern Europe. In Poland, Nazi occupation, from the start, practically excluded collaboration; the aim was to destroy, for good, the Polish state and nation, and prepare a clean slate for German colonization. In Poland, as a result, organized, armed underground resistance to German occupation was almost immediate. The Nazi authorities in annexed and occupied Poland, and in Western Russia, ruled out or minimized economic collaboration by their actions. Jewish capital and management were eliminated and excluded from the economy, and Germans took over and ran large businesses. German officials, managers, and technical experts organized and coordinated production, usually through public agencies working hand in hand in a subordinating capacity with private German companies. There was no interest in reviving local economies after war, only in plundering resources for the Nazi German war effort. Even in these circumstances, the occupying Germans were capable of squeezing out some marginal economic collaboration, sometimes pragmatically subcontracting to local firms where 'Germanization' proved to be difficult. Peasants supplied the occupying forces with food, engineers and workers put their damaged factories and mines back to work, but under the severest of constraints. As a German official from the Economics ministry put it in August 1942, 'only he who works for the German war effort will be fed by us'.[3] The basic point still stands. In occupied Eastern Europe, the Nazis were not interested in collaboration, did not need it, and relied on coerced change in order to realize their ideological goal of a racial empire.

By comparison, in occupied Northern and Western Europe, existing states and nations were made up, in some cases, of those the Nazis regarded as 'Germanic' peoples rather than, in the Nazi outlook, racially inferior Slavs, and were, more or less, and in some form or another, left standing. This opened up the possibility of collaboration from the start.[4]

Although collaboration was a widespread phenomenon, it was largely undervalued in the period after the liberation of Europe from Nazi rule. During and immediately after the war, there emerged in all German-occupied countries a convincing and reassuring view of Nazi occupation, and of people's responses to it, which came to determine how post-war governments and societies regarded and judged the experience of wartime occupation until at least the 1970s. A French broadcaster, Roger Chevrier, spoke on behalf of Charles de Gaulle's exiled Free France movement in Britain in a radio series entitled 'The French talk to the French', beamed by BBC Radio London to occupied France. In a transmission of June 1943, he mentioned that, 'when we refer to the "Vichy police", it goes without saying that we are not speaking of the whole of the French police, of which, we know, the majority are behaving as good patriots, but rather of the minority of sad individuals who have deliberately put themselves in the service of the enemy'.[5] The war was not yet over, far from it, and the liberation of France would not be launched for another year. But the tide of war was clearly moving against the Germans. In this context, the broadcast was an appeal and a warning, calculated to drive a wedge into the loyalties of policemen to France's collaborating government at Vichy, with the clear insinuation that their patriotic duty now lay in not cooperating with the Germans. By deliberately assuming that the situation Free France wanted to bring about already existed, the broadcaster was attempting to induce policemen, and the French in France, to move to a line of conduct that corresponded to the desired outcome. His words were also a judgement, made from the outside and in advance of liberation, on the behaviour of France's policemen during the occupation. The framework of that judgement was to be applied to the period of occupation, and to the French people's wartime conduct, as a whole.

You can see how this view of the occupation took hold by looking at the photograph reproduced as Illustration 1, taken by the famous photojournalist

Illustration 1. A woman whose head has been shaved as punishment for her 'horizontal collaboration' with a German soldier is hounded through the streets of Chartres, in France, shortly after the liberation of the town from German occupation in August 1944.

'Frank Capa' (an assumed name), immediately after the liberation by Allied troops of a French town, Chartres. This is just to the south-west of Paris, was and is the main urban centre of its department, or administrative district, and was occupied by the Germans with a large military garrison from June 1940 until August 1944. To my eyes, now, it is a shocking and poignant reminder of popular revenge on a 'collaborator'. It would have represented something more to contemporaries. A young woman, head shaved and carrying her baby, is being paraded through Chartres to the general derision of the town's population. Her gender does not make her vulnerable, but weak, capricious, wilful, and unpatriotic. The look on her face is fearful, but not shameful. She is being publicly humiliated for 'horizontal collaboration', sleeping with the enemy, a victim of a kind of popular rough justice, which ensured her post-war social exclusion. A Norwegian woman from a small village near Narvik in northern Norway gave birth in November 1945 to a child conceived during a late occupation affair with a German army sergeant, and took the child to Sweden to escape the fate of the woman in Chartres. 'Norway's gift to Sweden', the Abba singer Frida Lyngstad met her German father for the first time in Stockholm, in 1977.

The woman in Chartres was also being punished for working for the Germans. Many of the women who had liaisons with German soldiers and officials were secretaries, hotel maids, laundresses, waitresses, women in daily, mundane contact with men of the forces of occupation, as they would then be, of course, with the men of the invading Allied armies. The man in the uniform and tin hat in Capa's photograph, taunting the woman as he walks alongside her, was a member of the *Forces Françaises de l'Intérieur* (*FFI* or French Home Forces), the umbrella Resistance 'army'. He completes the image of a town of resisters, and of self-liberation; you will notice that there is not a liberating Allied soldier in sight. A populace united in resistance to the occupiers takes its justified revenge on the lone figure of a woman who collaborated intimately with them. This is the ways myths are made.

The photograph, taken on its own, is almost bound to be misleading. Capa's collection of photographs capturing the liberation of Chartres shows that several groups of women were identified for the shaving of heads ritual. One estimate is that between 10,000 and 15,000 French women were punished for having sex with Germans in post-war judicial and professional purge proceedings, and that probably tens of thousands of French women had sexual relationships with Germans during the occupation. The German

SS estimated that there were between 50,000 and 70,000 children resulting from such liaisons.[6]

Yet Capa's image entered and helped to shape the post-war reading of wartime occupation, that a patriotic, resisting majority had liberated itself from German occupation and its handful of unpatriotic collaborators. The consensual view of an overwhelming majority of resisters and a small, exiguous minority of collaborators was an entirely understandable version of events. The war was seen in all the occupied, and now liberated, countries of Northern and Western Europe as an extraordinary, abnormal experience. The occupying force was Nazi, as much as German, which introduced an unavoidable moral dimension to people's conduct during the war. Nazism, as an ideology and totalitarian system of rule, was regarded as being so 'evil' that it *had* to be resisted. It was a question of either cooperating with an 'evil' system, which was 'bad', or resisting it, which was 'good'. There were, or could not be, any qualification of these two responses. The only choice under German Nazi occupation seemed to be accepting and, therefore, collaborating with Nazism, or rejecting it, and then resisting; either collaboration or resistance. I do not think that the concept of 'evil' has any place in historical analysis; it simply short circuits any attempt at a meaningful examination of human conduct and motivation. But Nazism was an inhumane and morally repugnant ideology, and the nature of Nazism has led to very polarized and categorical terms of reference being used to study and analyse the war years.

Again, post-war recovery and reconstruction required governments and societies to re-create a sense of national unity, bring about a social pacification and reconciliation, even foster a deliberate obliviousness to the hatreds and divisions engendered and exacerbated by wartime occupation. The point can be made in obvious and self-evident ways. Where was the utility, and gain, in investigating and punishing businesses for entering into war contracts with the German occupier, when that would damage the post-war revival of the economy? In a speech made in September 1945, a short time after liberation, the Dutch Minister of Transport attempted to draw a line under the war experience for his audience of state employees. His speech commemorated the 1944 railway workers' strike against German occupation, a significant and effective act of resistance. Workers, he said, should not be blamed for working throughout the occupation; it was their honourable duty to carry on working, since maintaining the country's transport system had salvaged the network for national post-war use. At heart, he concluded, the railway workers were 'resisters', neglecting to mention that railway employees had transported young Dutch men to forced labour in Germany, and had transferred Dutch and foreign Jews to transit camps, for deportation to the death camps in the East.[7]

The myth of a resisting nation, common to all once-occupied countries, was also a way for people in the immediate post-war period to cope with a multifaceted national humiliation constituted by military defeat, occupation, and liberation by foreign armies.[8] It was a myth enabling national redemption. The myth was essential to post-war reconstruction in a political, as well as a moral and economic, sense. The post-war political recovery of West European countries was based on a rejection of Nazism and all it represented. A post-war political consensus resting on anti-fascist and democratic foundations practically demanded that the history and memory of the wartime experience be assessed in the polarized but asymmetrical terms of a resisting majority triumphing over a collaborating minority.

Historiographically, and in terms of popular consciousness, things began to change in the 1970s, 1980, and 1990s. In part, this was down to a boom in the collection and dissemination of holocaust survivors' memories, and more generally of elderly people's memories of wartime. Accumulatively, these memories contested, fragmented, and nuanced the consensual myth of a resisting majority. Films, at another level of popular cognition and self-awareness, also changed the way people perceived life under German occupation, and the ways in which historians approached the experience of occupation.

The ground-breaking film in France was Marcel Ophuls', *Le Chagrin et la pitié* (*The Sorrow and the Pity*), commissioned by French State TV and completed in 1971. But it was banned from a TV showing for a decade, revealingly in the words of the head of the French broadcasting body, because 'certain myths are necessary for a people's well being and tranquillity'.[9] Purporting to be a documentary, Ophuls's mesmerizing four-hour-long film focuses on the town of Clermont-Ferrand, in south central France, during the war. It provides a skilful and highly manipulative mix of contemporary newsreels and interviews with both big shots and ordinary people. There is nothing in the film from or about de Gaulle. It offers a remorselessly unheroic representation of the French people under German occupation. The German ex-military commander in Clermont boasts of how well his troops were received by the local population; two secondary schoolteachers haltingly reminisce about the sacking of Jewish colleagues from their *lycée*, with nobody on the staff objecting to their removal; a local peasant complains about the *maquis* (armed resistance bands living off the land) stealing his chickens, and calling down on his community, by their presence alone, the full weight of repression of the German and Vichy police; Maurice Chevalier, France's most popular performer and a very public partisan of the Vichy regime, delivers a sickly sentimental song about how beautiful France is; a contemporary newsreel shows the trial of the head of the Pathé film production company, later deported to his death, portraying him as a Jew and a pornographer.

Louis Malle's 1974 film *Lacombe, Lucien* had a similarly deflating impact on how the French people conventionally viewed the experience of occupation. Painstakingly authentic in its staging of a typically French small town and its rural hinterland in 1944, it was apparently based on a story told to Malle by a local farmer while Malle was staying in his second home in the French countryside. The film gives us a crushingly amoral portrait of a violent, inarticulate young man on the make. Turned down for the Resistance by the local teacher, whom he later betrays, he accidently finds a literal and a psychological home in the hotel headquarters of a heterogeneous group of misfits working against the Resistance as agents of the German *Gestapo*. In Malle's film, resistance and collaboration are no longer polarized categories of behaviour, in a situation where people certainly made choices, but ones determined by the force of circumstances and opportunism, rather than any considered moral or principled stand.

The transforming power of cinema was particularly felt in the French revision of its wartime history, but its influence was experienced elsewhere, as well. In the Netherlands, for example, a rich vein of films in the 1960s, 1970s, and 1980s punctured both the heroic resistance myth and the post-war drift into obliviousness about the war. Some of them sought to convey the same imaginative truth of Malle's films about the war in France, exploring the grey areas between the apparently polar opposites of collaboration and resistance, and sceptically questioning the motivations for people's behaviour and conduct during the country's occupation.[10]

In time, the private, now public, memories of the war interacted with other revelations about the past, emerging, for instance, from the trials of Frenchmen for wartime crimes against humanity, and helped to change the official memory of the war. In 1995, the President of France, Jacques Chirac, commemorating the anniversary of the round-up of Jews in Paris in 1942, acknowledged and apologized for the role of the wartime French state in the deportation from France of French and foreign Jews.

The shift of perspective on wartime occupation is especially marked in France and Denmark among the occupied countries of Northern and Western Europe. But it is less evident in Norway, where the reasons for the survival of the post-war 'nation of resisters' story should become evident in the course of this book. A French historian of collaboration in France during the war can argue that, 'taken to the extreme, every Frenchman who remained on territory occupied by the German army or that was under its control had, to some extent, "collaborated".'[11] The transformation of France from a 'nation of resisters' to a 'nation of collaborators' is now complete.

The great majority of people, apparently, did nothing during the occupation to expel the Germans from France, an inertia that amounted to acquiescence, and functionally, 'collaboration'. An absence of 'resistance' becomes a factor of 'collaboration'. Apathy is taken, here, as passive support for the situation as it was, and represents a form of consent to German occupation. Doing nothing could equally, it seems to me, denote a resigned dislike or antipathy towards the occupier—in other words, a non-active form of dissent or opposition, and hence, a kind of 'resistance'.

This is a terminological and conceptual quagmire, from which one can at least draw one certain and one speculative conclusion. Those who collaborated or resisted by doing something, as opposed to doing nothing, 'active' collaborators and resisters, were undoubtedly minorities in the population as a whole. This might suggest that, for the great majority of people under occupation, life was neither a matter of collaboration, nor one of resistance. The problem with this rather too neat formulation is that the war and German occupation were extremely intrusive in their impacts on peoples' daily lives. There was widespread penury arising from wartime shortages and increasing German demands on the economic and manpower resources of occupied countries. People, as a result, were obliged to have often difficult and uncomfortable relations and contacts with those in authority, whether German, national, or local. If people in straitened wartime circumstances did what they had to do in order to survive, and often found themselves acting inconsistently from one encounter to the next, then it is at least questionable whether terms such as 'collaboration' and 'resistance' can convey the sense of the wide range of behaviours necessary to ensure survival in tough times. It might be more illuminating, and closer to the reality of choices people made under occupation, to assess collaboration and resistance on a continuum of attitudes and conduct, with armed resistance and collaborationism at the two extreme ends of the line. This might

work rather better than the usual collaboration/resistance axis, which pre-
sumes a once and for all choice on one side or the other of the great moral
divide between the two. We need, perhaps, to remind ourselves of the wise,
humane, and, it must be said, unpopular words of Václav Havel, the Czech
writer, intellectual, and dissident who became the first democratically
elected president of Czechoslovakia. Reflecting on life in what he called
'post-totalitarian' society, he argued that the system that oppressed people
was sustained by the people themselves, who were simultaneously its victims and supporters. The division between victim and perpetrator ran
through individuals, and was not something that separated one individual
from another.[12]

Life is often a messy affair, and historians face the occupational hazard of
failing to convey the messiness of people's conduct in the past by simply
doing their job, writing histories that are clear, coherent, rational, and have
a beginning and an end. My way out of the intricacies of wartime behaviour under occupation is to concentrate on the collaboration of two groups,
civil servants and businessmen, who were required to collaborate with the
German occupiers, and also chose to do so. In meeting this obligation and
rising to the opportunity to collaborate, they faced the most difficult choices
and dilemmas in dealing with the various Nazi authorities and agencies that
were responsible for gearing up the economies of the occupied territories
to the German war effort, and setting up a Nazi European New Order.

Concentrating on state officials and businessmen, the occupied countries'
administrative and economic elites, can be justified in two ways. As should
be clearer from Chapter 1, which considers the post-liberation purges of
collaborators, they were the most significant of collaborators: their choices
affected, for worse and less worse, the livelihoods and security of their fellow countrymen for the duration of the war. Because collaboration was a
matter of considered policy for these groups, the reasons and motivations
for their collaboration are more discernible and accessible, and more open
to meaningful rather than speculative analysis. It is certainly more productive
than, for instance, delving into the mind of the young Norwegian man who
joined the German *Waffen SS*, or of our fictional but perhaps authentic
would-be resister and accidental collaborationist, Lucien Lacombe.

Collaboration, as with the range of responses to occupation, was necessarily conditioned by the unpredictable and non-uniform ways in which
the Nazis decided to rule their conquered territories. This is why Chapter 2
examines the occupation regimes foisted on the North and West European

countries, and their relationship, if any existed, to Nazi projections of a
European New Order.

The book tries to explain the reasons for collaboration with the Nazis by
analysing it as a practice that had to be adapted over time and under the
impact of dramatically changing circumstances. It also attempts to explain
the rationale and consequences of collaboration in respect of the Nazis'
most infamous occupation and New Order policies applied across Europe
from 1942, which resulted in the deportation of tens of thousands of West
European workers to Nazi Germany, and the genocide of Europe's Jews.

The approach is broadly comparative, one of the toughest things to pull
off as a historian. But sometimes, within the basic chronological division
between 1940–2 and 1942–5 of Chapters 3–7, I have to deal with countries
one after the other, reflecting the different ways in which the Nazis occupied the countries they had conquered in 1940. There is less material on
Norway compared to the other countries. This is a consequence of the
language barrier, the relatively narrow base of published research, only now
being rectified by a big project on economic collaboration in occupied
Norway, and Norway being the country that corresponded more closely
than the others to the stereotype of a 'nation of resisters.'

I

Starting at the End
Liberation and the Post-War Purges
of Collaborators

There was a great deal at stake in the purges of collaborators that occurred before, during, and after the Allied liberation from Nazi occupation of the countries of Northern and Western Europe in 1944–5. The unavoidable settling of accounts with a harrowing recent past had somehow to be dovetailed with an immediate and longer-term future of post-war recovery and reconstruction. The tension between handling the past and projecting the future ran through the purge process in each of the newly liberated countries.

Impending liberation, and liberation itself, released popular anger, despair, and resentment at the deprivation and suffering people had directly experienced during and as a result of an increasingly harsh German occupation. Popular demands for justice, retribution, and recompense were directed at those who had aided and abetted, and were seen to have benefited from, the Nazi occupation. Internal resistance movements had both fuelled and channelled popular hostility to collaborators. They warned collaborators of all hues that they would pay for their collaboration, in the expectation that the threat would deter any further collaboration. They drew up black lists of people to be purged at liberation. Some, if not all, resistance movements saw their role as extending beyond liberation to the shaping of a new post-war society. For them, the purging of collaborators, especially of political, administrative, and economic elites, the establishment, was an essential element of the post-war recasting of politics, economy, and society on progressive and egalitarian lines. Resistance movements that felt this way were quite deliberately widening their attacks on wartime collaboration to a critique of the pre-war structures of power. The continuity between the interwar period and the war lay in the systemic failure of the country's elites to prevent the Depression, the rise of fascism, and the coming of war.

The returning governments-in-exile, and the ever-present Danish government, representative sections of the political establishment, after all, were understandably wary of the radical reforming aspirations of some resistance movements. But they conceded that it made sense to cleanse the countries of the stains of occupation that they had largely experienced at a distance. This would be the basis of a renewal of post-war political, economic, and social life on humane, anti-fascist, and democratic values. The governments-in-exile also needed to re-establish their legitimate right to govern after years of enforced absence. A purge of those who had collaborated with the enemy was a clear way of making credible their authority over liberated territory, and restoring the confidence between government and governed necessary for the recovery of a shattered national political and economic system.

These high stakes explain why the post-war purges were themselves a source of enduring political and social conflict in early post-war Western and Northern Europe. The popular verdict on the purges, as they proceeded, was that too little was being done, and too slowly. People suspected, or assumed, that this apparent leniency and delay were a matter of deliberate self-limitation by governments. The perceived softness of the purges was also a factor in the often tense post-liberation relations between returning governments and some of the resistance movements, especially those on the left. It strained the cohesion of post-war coalition governments of national unity broadened out from the anti-fascist political parties to incorporate representatives of the Resistance. Left-wing parties were for a radical and far-reaching purge of collaborators, as part of a general national regeneration. Centrist and right-wing parties were usually for a purge limited in time and scope, in order not to damage a process of national reconciliation and restored unity, and to enable public administration and business to contribute to an orderly reconstruction of their countries.

These conflicts, prevalent throughout newly liberated Northern and Western Europe, had the greatest impact on the transition from war to peace in Belgium, where continuing internal divisions over the position of the monarchy were as complicating a factor in Belgian politics as they had been at the start of the German occupation. Popular protest and discontent, in part fed by anger over the purges, persisted into the summer of 1945, and raised doubts about the suitability of entrusting the country to the returning government-in-exile rather than to an Allied military administration. The Belgian coalition government of national unity was reconstituted in February 1945, with the Catholic party effectively excluding itself because of its moderate approach to the purges. The political ramifications of the purges affected in turn the reach and duration of the purge process itself, in a virtuous or vicious circle, depending on the political perspective.

Becoming Belgian Prime Minister in February 1945 as an apparent hardliner on the purges, the Socialist Achille Van Acker later declared that 'you cannot reconstruct on the basis of hatred'.[1] His government tried to draw out some of the political and popular poison of the purges by revising in a moderate way the categorization of what were culpable acts of collaboration, and attempting to speed up the process. The Catholic party campaigned electorally in Flanders for the amnesty of wartime collaborators. It was here that Belgium's special circumstances made it difficult to close the wounds reopened by the war. Belgium had been occupied by the Germans in both world wars, and during both occupations the occupier had deliberately favoured the country's 'Germanic' Dutch-speaking Flemings over the francophone Walloons. In the Belgian case, the official post-war myth of a victimized and resisting nation strained to sublimate long-standing divisions between the country's linguistic communities, now exacerbated by the impact of Nazi occupation. But that is the point and purpose of national myths, to create a perception of events that need not be really or entirely accurate, as long as it is authentic enough to justify a country's renewed sense of itself.

Denmark was the country at the other end of the spectrum to Belgium. Here, post-war political and popular tensions over the purges were more muted than elsewhere. In part, this was down to the merger between the Danish Resistance, whose leaders formed a so-called Freedom Council, and the Danish government, from early 1945, prior to the liberation. This fusion of Resistance and governments in order to plan and prepare for the post-war period of recovery and reconstruction occurred in France and Norway, too. Partly because of the rapidity of the Allied liberation of the country in September 1944, it did not take place in Belgium, which goes some way to explaining the open conflict over the purges between the returning government-in-exile and some resistance movements. One of the reasons for, and outcomes of, the alliance between the Freedom Council and Danish government was agreement on how to handle the purges. These had to be limited in scope in order to enable a full post-war public justification of the government's official policy of collaboration sustained throughout the occupation, or at least to the German suspension of parliamentary government in the summer of 1943.

The pre-emptive agreement on the extent of the purges was reflected in the relatively organized and orderly way in which the purges were initiated. Apparently, on 9 May 1945, the day after the German surrender, special units under Freedom Council command got into their cars armed with lists and files, and proceeded to arrest and intern about 22,000 'selected' collaborators. In Denmark, the consensual myth of resistance was easily embedded into post-war popular consciousness.

In March 1947, the broad post-war anti-fascist coalition in Belgium finally broke up altogether. Those parties most opposed to how the purges had gone, albeit from very different political perspectives, the liberals and the communist party, left governing to a Catholic and socialist coalition. By this time, Belgium was part of a wider trend. The wartime and post-war anti-fascist alliances were dissolved across Western Europe in 1947–8, as its politics took on a cold-war mould. The coalescing of democratic politics around the motif of anti-communism in the late 1940s involved the exclusion from the arc of government of communist parties that had played a significant part in the armed resistance to Nazi occupation. If communists were frozen out, the coming of the cold war also contributed to the scaling-down of the purges and official amnesties for already punished collaborators, and a more general desire to forget the divisive nature of wartime occupation in face of a perceived greater existential threat to Western civilization.

The purges occurred in what can be regarded as two stages, the one merging into the other. The first stage was, as the French called it, 'l'épuration sauvage', or 'wild purge', which started more or less spontaneously as invasion and liberation by Allied armies proceeded. A form of popular rough justice, punishment was meted out by local people and by resistance groups exercising a vigilante vengeance on their behalf. It could be lethal. Figures inevitably vary, but perhaps up to about 10,000 people were lynched in France before, during, and after liberation in 1944–5.[2] The targets were mainly informers, a particularly hated kind of collaborator throughout occupied Europe, and men enlisted in the collaborationist police force, the *Milice*, set up by the Vichy government to counter and repress resistance activity.

More generally, this stage of the purges took in people who were perceived to have benefited or profited from, or been advantaged by, occupation, in any way, big or small. It extended to people who had socialized with, been familiar with, or been friendly or sympathetic to the occupier. A resistance news-sheet in the northern French port of Le Havre urged the town's population to treat as 'collaborators' all those shopkeepers who had solicited German business by placing German-language signs in their shop windows.[3] Denunciation was rife. It often led to the local resistance group arresting and detaining people who were then dealt with (and often released without charge) by more formal police investigation and court proceedings, later. But denunciation was usually enough to provoke the public outing and humiliation of 'collaborators', such as occurred in Chartres's treatment of girlfriends of Germans. Staff of a firm, or a post office, ganged up on unpopular colleagues and pressurized their employers to sack or transfer them, as punishment for their alleged wartime attitudes and conduct.

The 'wild purge' was bound to be a localized phenomenon, since it was sustained by local knowledge and rumour, and expressed pent-up popular resentment at what were condemned as contemptible and damaging attitudes and behaviour experienced in the daily small encounters of wartime life. Denunciation and public shaming ostracized unworthy individuals from the community, and, in effect, was a way of restoring what was left of communal solidarity after the divisive and disruptive impacts of war and occupation on local societies.

Some Scandinavian historians have been rather complacent about the extent of the 'wild purge' in Denmark and Norway. But, although perhaps not reaching the levels of vindictiveness of incidents in France, Belgium, and the Netherlands, it most definitely occurred, as illustrated by the treatment of Frida Lyngstad's mother in Norway.

The other stage of the purges was a more formal one. There was a legal process enacted within the judicial system, involving police investigation and courts, whether military or civilian. This overlapped with an extra-legal process where the civil service and then occupational groups (doctors, employers' associations, for example) set up their own purge commissions to investigate the conduct of public employees and professionals.

The 'wild purge' affected the formal purges in several ways. It fed popular demands for a radical clear-out of the country's administrative and professional elites, at a time when new post-liberation governments were hoping to effect an orderly transition to 'normal' life through the good services of these very elites. It filled the internment camps and prisons with people who had been fingered by popular disapprobation and accusation. They now had to be handled by a judicial or quasi-judicial procedure, inevitably slowing down a process that governments needed, for the sake of national recovery, to be as speedy and decisive as possible.

Finally, and most interestingly, at least for the historian, the 'wild purge' served to direct popular anger at perceived bad attitudes and behaviour, which might not have been criminal according to the law, but were, nevertheless, seen to be immoral and unworthy. This line was often pursued in the more formal purge investigations. The public employment and occupational purge commissions, especially, considered not only failures or inadequacies in the performance of people's jobs and professions, but also attitudes and mentalities regarded as reprehensible. People were held accountable for views and opinions that might have been aired casually in the workplace, even though they had little to do with work. Government officials could have their cases dealt with by both a ministerial purge commission, and then by the courts, and punished by both. The purge commission offered, perhaps, some kind of security for the officials. It was internal to the specific public service employing the officials, and would presumably have some empathy for the challenges faced by civil servants during the war. But the commissioners would still judge them for non-criminal attitudes and activities, for, say, remarks passed in the office on a particular occupation policy, or Allied bombing raids, or the resistance. This aspect of the formal purge process greatly extended the range of *thoughts* and actions regarded as 'collaborating', introduced a moral dimension to collaboration, and gave considerable nuance to what might have been a rigid and inflexible procedure.

The purges in each country lasted longer than the post-war governments wanted or expected. By the time they were more or less completed, the prisons were already being emptied of people who had served all or part of their sentences for various acts of collaboration. Retrospectively, to have nearly finished the legal job by, for example, late 1947 in Belgium and France, and late 1948 in the Netherlands, seems pretty impressive. The length of time spent on the process is explained by the huge number of cases to be investigated, and then tried, and the sheer complexity of the cases under investigation. These cases were handled not so much by a police and judicial system, which was being reconstituted in difficult post-war conditions, and which itself 'needed' purging. All countries had extraordinary judicial arrangements, planned for and rapidly put in place by the new governments after liberation. So, for instance, in Belgium, the government-in-exile had deliberately decided to entrust the post-war purges to a ramified system of special military tribunals, rather than the civilian courts. Here, military prosecutors were confronted by files on 405,000 people accused of collaboration, equivalent to about 7 per cent of the country's adult population; over 57,000 prosecutions were launched. In the Netherlands, the special courts had a military presence, but they and the popular tribunals were civil bodies, and the bulk of the purges were actually conducted in various purge commissions. But, even so, the workload was staggering. According to the Dutch Ministry of Justice, there were about 150,000 arrests, and 450,000 investigations.

As political and popular pressures associated with the purges began to ease, governments did all they could to accelerate and close down the process, without exposing themselves to too much criticism for doing so. Laws and decrees covering collaboration, some pre-dating the war and some composed during the war itself, were reviewed and revised even as cases continued to come to court. It became clear that they were just too tough and too inflexible to apply to complicated cases. Prosecutors bundled cases of a similar minor nature for out-of-court settlements, offering light sentences in lieu of a trial. Prison sentences were reduced, favouring those defendants who calculated that, by stringing out their cases, they might be treated more leniently.

In my tentatively held view, the figures and estimates of the number of people who were sentenced or punished for collaboration give a pretty fair indication of the extent of collaboration in each country. This is partly because, taken together, the courts and the purge commissions investigated and penalized conduct deemed to be culpable in both a criminal and a non-criminal sense. They also imposed a wide range of penalties on collaborators, ranging from the death sentence (often not actually carried out), through long and short terms of imprisonment, to withdrawal of civic rights, dismissal from employment, loss of pension, 'retirement', suspension from work, demotion, and transfer.

However, given the highly political character of the purges, it must be conceded that what the figures really show is the comparative severity of the purges in the countries involved. So, for what they are worth, here goes. According to Novick, 94 per 100,000 of population were imprisoned for collaboration in France, 374 in Denmark, 419 in the Netherlands, 596 in Belgium, and 633 in Norway.[4] The loss of civic rights, often combined with other sanctions, including prison, affected both 'criminal' and 'non-criminal' collaborators, and therefore involved people culpable of less serious acts of collaboration. Here, the incomplete figures are of 70,000 people being punished by loss of their civic rights in Belgium, 107,000 in the Netherlands, 90,000 in France, and about 30,000 in Norway.[5]

Perhaps all the figures confirm is that collaborators were a significant minority of the population, as were resisters. More can be gained from looking beyond the global numbers to consider those who were purged, and what they were punished for. The obvious targets, the 'traitors', were tried the earliest and punished the most severely. These were the leaders, ministers, and top officials of the collaborating Vichy government of France, and of the collaborationist NS government in Norway. Philippe Pétain, Vichy's head of state, Pierre Laval, Vichy's prime minister in 1940–1 and again in 1942–4, and Vidkun Quisling, NS leader and prime minister from 1942, were sentenced to death. Pétain's sentence was commuted to life imprisonment.

The concern of de Gaulle's Provisional Government was to establish its own right to govern by denying that of Vichy, regarded as a de facto state, where the official policy of collaboration with the Germans was, by definition, illegitimate. This could not apply, of course, to the collaborating government in Denmark, which remained the recognized legitimate authority throughout the occupation. Its leaders could not be held accountable, legally or otherwise, for their collaboration. The matter was hived off to a parliamentary commission in June 1945. MPs judged their own behaviour during the war in secret proceedings, and unsurprisingly concluded in 1953 that there was no reason for any legal prosecution of wartime coalition government ministers and top officials.

The other self-evident targets of the purges were people I have identified as collaborationists, collectively guilty of collaboration as leaders and members of fascist parties, or of collaborationist groups and organizations, which included police formations working with or for the German *Gestapo*, and men who joined German military and paramilitary forces, like the *Waffen SS*. The Norwegian purge was particularly hard on NS members. Irrespective of whether they were active or passive members, they were automatically indicted for collaboration, largely because NS became, uniquely in occupied Northern and Western Europe, the party of government under German supervision. Pre-war membership was seen as being more reprehensible, even though NS was a legal party, because it apparently demonstrated a degree of ideological commitment rather greater than what might have been an opportunistic wartime adherence to the governing party.

Things were less clear-cut for other groups of people. Economic collaboration beyond black marketeering proved to be the most difficult to define, whether for the courts or for the purge commissions, and, hence, the most difficult to pursue through a formal process. As a result, economic collaboration was probably the least sanctioned of all forms of what was considered to be culpable collaboration. Perhaps 150 business managers and executives were penalized in France, compared to, say, 700 schoolteachers.[6] In the Netherlands, special boards set up in autumn 1945 to investigate the conduct of business leaders during the occupation had by July 1946 handled 1,231 cases, with sanctions applied in only 40 of them.[7] In Belgium, there were about 52,400 cases under initial investigation for economic collaboration. The process was already having an effect on companies, through the consequent freezing of assets. But only about 4,000 cases came to court, representing between 7 and 8 per cent of all court cases involving collaboration. Of these, guilt was found in just over 1,500 cases.[8] In Norway, about 16,400 cases of suspected economic collaboration were investigated, and under 3,400 people were punished, in a variety of ways. Unlike anywhere else, the Norwegian prosecutors concentrated first on the 'easy' cases of small-scale collaboration. As time passed, and the process as a whole became more lenient, the big guns were generally let off the hook, for lack of sufficient evidence against them. The few business owners and managers who had joined the NS faced post-war financial ruin because their fines were punishment for being members of the country's fascist party, rather than economic collaboration.[9] In all countries, most court cases led to acquittal, and most cases never saw a courtroom and were dismissed in the catch-all phrase 'non-lieu', meaning that there was no sufficient case to answer.

Workers, whether voluntarily going to Germany for a job during the occupation or as deportees, were usually or eventually excluded from investigation altogether. For one thing, there were hundreds of thousands of them to investigate. For another, access to post-war employment and social benefits rested on their perceived status as victims of occupation. Workers were clearly also too important politically and electorally to stigmatize with the charge of collaboration. More objectively, the elements of constraint, and compulsion, in their recruitment to work in Germany were seen as sufficient to make them patriotically blameless.

A similar kind of logic worked in favour of employers and businessmen who had collaborated. Indicting them was an attack on the existing social and economic order, and put at risk the precarious process of economic recovery. This factor was quite explicitly given by the Belgian government as a good reason for revising in May 1945 the draconian article 115 of the country's penal code, which made economic collaboration a criminal activity punishable by the death penalty. The government had to tread carefully, when its predecessor had more or less approved a policy of economic collaboration before it left in 1940 after military defeat and foreign occupation. Here in Belgium, as elsewhere, general and singular national concerns interacted with each other. The severity of the Belgian penal code reflected the experience of German occupation in the First World War, and haunted collaborators of all kinds throughout occupation during the Second World War.

But the very complexity of cases of economic collaboration inhibited the purges in this sphere of activity in all the liberated countries. Most purges settled on the idea of 'offensive' collaboration, meant not so much in the sense of giving offence as in the sense of being active, taking the initiative. Manufacturing equipment and arms for the German armed forces were acts of culpable collaboration. But so were an active soliciting of German contracts, and an evident desire to profit from such projects. This denoted not only the actual profits on deals, which were unavoidable, but also their use as a means to gain a competitive advantage by increasing production, or extending and transforming the means of production. As with operating on the black market, 'profiteering' on the back of occupation was considered to have been unacceptably self-interested and unpatriotic conduct. Start-up companies, responding to the new opportunities created by occupation, were relatively severely dealt with, everywhere.

Collaboration was the official policy of the Vichy French and Danish governments. As we shall see, civil servants were enjoined by international law and convention and by the governments-in-exile to cooperate with the occupier in Belgium, the Netherlands, and Norway. To then judge public officials for carrying out official policy might appear contradictory. But it was the performance of officials, how the policy was implemented, that was being judged, especially when there was such a release of popular anger at the apparently supine way officials had done the occupier's bidding. However, the post-liberation governments' dependence on the career civil service for an orderly and organized reconstruction tended to limit the scope of the purge of officials.

Global figures on the extent of the purge of public employees are hard to come by, which is partly due to the nature of the process. Top officials were usually tried in the courts for 'crimes' of collaboration. But most civil servants had their conduct during the occupation considered, not in the courts, but in the ministerial purge commissions. The process had every appearance of being an internal disciplinary matter, where officials were judged for non-criminal activity and penalized by the usual service sanctions of suspension, dismissal, retirement with or without pension, demotion, and transfer. The proceedings were usually secret, and no overall figures on resignations or dismissals were released.

In a detailed and comprehensive account of the purges in sectors of the French administration, François Rouquet arrives at an estimate of between 22,000 and 28,000 public servants being penalized in various ways in the purges.[10] He also calculates that the purges were heaviest among 'les allemands de France' ('France's Germans'), officials holding posts in the eastern provinces of Alsace and Lorraine, effectively annexed to Nazi Germany in 1940. They had a relatively high impact on the ministries of Interior, Information, War Veterans, and Colonies, and were felt relatively lightly in the ministries of Agriculture, Public Works, Postal Services and Telecommunications (*Postes, Télégraphes et Téléphones* (*PTT*)), and Education. *SNCF*, the state-owned railway system, employed about half a million people, but only about 4,800 of them were punished. By mid-1945, the internal purge of the *PTT*, with a total staffing of over 200,000, had yielded barely 1,728 cases worthy of internal sanctions or referral to the courts.

It is, of course, open to speculation as to why these variations occurred. It would seem likely that the ministries taking the biggest, though still not very debilitating, hits contained more officials who had been strong political supporters of the collaborating Vichy regime. This was sometimes reflected in their membership of collaborationist and Vichyite organizations outside their place of work. Some *SNCF* employees had been involved in organizing and carrying out the 'job' of transporting French and foreign Jews, and political and other prisoners, to the German border, for onward transmission to German camps and prisons. The light treatment of railway staff in the purges might have something to do with the need to get the railway system operating again, or with the uncongenial fact that Jews were regarded after the war as ordinary victims of Nazi persecution.

The low figures for the *PTT* purge might reflect the essentially non-repressive and non-political nature of the service, compared to, say, the Interior ministry, which was responsible for national policing. This impression may be confirmed by the experience of purging the police forces of the Netherlands. In a significant but not severe purge, just over one in three of about 15,800 lower-rank policemen were investigated, and, of these, about 56 per cent were disciplined or dismissed. Those purged were usually policemen who combined exceeding their orders with Nazi sympathies, membership of the Dutch fascist party or the German *SS*, and working for the *Gestapo*.[11]

Even more interestingly, the Ministry of Education was arguably the most Vichyite of ministries, given its mission to regenerate French society under the auspices of the so-called National Revolution. It might have suffered relatively little from the purges, precisely because its officials were most under pressure to conform to Vichy's directives. This suggests an overall comment on the process of purging officials in France and else-where. The internal ministerial purge bodies, if only because of an *esprit de corps*, were likely to be understanding of how officials had behaved during the occupation.

The fact that most civil servants were judged in an internal disciplinary process can be considered in other ways. The tendency was to subject top officials to criminal investigation and trial in a court, leaving officials of a lower rank to be dealt with by the ministerial purge commissions. This dutifully reflected the hierarchical nature of government service, and the sense that it was the top officials who had set the tone for collaboration throughout the departments they ran. As a result, they should be held responsible for collaboration in the service as a whole. The hierarchical principle was applied in ministerial purge commissions as well. For instance, the Dutch rank-and-file policemen who had actually knocked on the doors of Jewish families to arrest them were not held responsible for their actions and were not investigated in the purge carried out by the Ministry of Justice. Their officers, however, were investigated.

The purge commissions for civil servants also considered actions and attitudes of officials that were not in themselves criminal, according to the law, but that were, nevertheless, regarded as unworthy and unpatriotic. The result was to widen the net of the purges, in order to catch conduct deemed to be 'collaborating'. The civil service purge commissions were certainly more empathetic than the courts in their treatment of officials. But they were also more comprehensive in evaluating what constituted 'collaboration' and 'resistance'.

This point is evident in the widespread sentencing of officials to what the French and Belgians called 'indignité nationale', or 'national dishonour', which usually penalized officials with the temporary loss of civil rights, including the right to vote. The use of the term 'national dishonour' in the purges indicated that there was a certain appropriate standard of conduct expected of all citizens living under enemy occupation, but especially of public servants. As public officials, they were required to demonstrate a higher level of conduct than ordinary citizens. Civil servants, in other words, were expected to be 'model' citizens, or rather 'super-citizens', in circumstances of national defeat and humiliation, and foreign occupation.

So we find that the Danish law of July 1945 intended to hit people who 'flinched from their duty to their country during the occupation', or who were 'guilty' of 'omitting to counteract the collaboration of... organisations with the occupying power'.[12] Similar provisions were made elsewhere. The Belgian purges were designed to incriminate 'those whose conduct during the occupation was not what it should have been... all those who, without being guilty, cannot be called innocent'.[13] In Norway, collaboration was something that did not correspond to the 'required reserve' of the 'loyal' citizen.[14] The new Interior minister in the partially liberated Netherlands, Louis Beel, himself a top civil servant in Eindhoven until resigning in 1943, added a separate regulation to the government-in-exile's 1944 Purge Act. This covered officials who, in good faith, had not done their patriotic duty and, hence, could not continue in office because they had lost the confidence of the public and their colleagues in the course of the occupation. You can imagine what a wonderfully flexible tool this was to streamline the civil service while preserving its sense of being a reputable national institution.

The best way to see 'national dishonour' in action is to look at an actual and emblematic case. The Dutch government followed the usual pattern of having a separate judicial procedure for 'crimes' of civil service collaboration, while delegating most cases of collaboration to an internal disciplinary process. The latter passed judgment on Karel Johannes Frederiks, arguably the most important government official during the occupation. He was Secretary General, effectively the minister, of the Interior ministry, long regarded as the major department of continental European governments because it controlled the police. Frederiks had all the self-importance and sense of worth of a top official, and clearly resented being subject to a disciplinary process for his conduct during the occupation. The investigating Interior ministry commission found that Frederiks had acted in good faith, but that he had failed in his duty as an official to oppose the occupier's efforts to nazify the country's public administration and its policies.

The result of Frederiks's *inactivity* was a loss of public and his superior's confidence in his capacity to do the job in the best interests of the Dutch people. Frederiks was dismissed from the service, with an 'honourable discharge'. It could have been worse, and in the circumstances was a pretty understanding and finely balanced verdict. A 'dishonourable discharge', which was the fate of one of his colleagues, Robert Verwey, the Secretary General for Social Affairs, would have deprived Frederiks of some or all of his pension and other benefits. There can be no doubt that Frederiks felt humiliated by the process and the verdict, and the commission's rejection of his defence of his conduct, when he saw himself as the representative and embodiment of the national interest during the war.

The judgment was clearly meant to set a standard for future cases. Frederiks's collaboration was not a crime, but a 'mistake', a 'failure', and, for an official making a mistake rather than committing a crime, the appropriate sentence was dismissal, not prison. Intriguingly, the Frederiks judgment redefined 'collaboration' and 'resistance', which happened in many similar cases across the purge process in the newly liberated countries. By not opposing the nazification of the Dutch administration, Frederiks had, according to his assessors, undermined the 'spirit of resistance' both among the population and in the administration.[15] In other words, 'collaboration' amounted to a failure to 'resist'; not 'resisting' was culpable behaviour. This was equivalent to the way some employers were castigated as 'collaborators' because they objected to, sought to prevent, or did not permit the sabotage of plant and production by their workers, whether in cahoots with the resistance or not. The Belgian government went further in late 1947, recognizing the 'patriotic deception' of civil servants who had stayed in post and had, therefore, been 'collaborating', while actually undertaking acts of 'administrative sabotage'.[16] This was really double edged, because it took 'resistance' to be the appropriate default position of officials, and more than implied that civil servants should have been using their positions of power and authority as public officials to subvert the occupation from within.

You can perhaps now begin to see how the purges subtly filled out the post-war myths of 'resisting' nations. If 'collaboration' was not 'resisting', then not 'collaborating' was 'resistance'. Doing nothing, being inactive, was, effectively, 'passive resistance'. On this basis of positive and patriotic inertia was constructed an image of a passively resisting majority sustaining the action of a militant resisting minority, those in organized resistance groups and movements.

The governments of Northern and Western Europe more or less managed to close down the purges, at least for the time being, with the amnesties, and in the Norwegian case, pardons, for convicted collaborators in the late 1940s and early 1950s. By definition, an amnesty was an act of 'forgetting'. The governments' motive was to bring about the rehabilitation of offenders into society, and, more generally, a national reconciliation that sublimated the divisions of war and occupation. The amnesty usually, though not always, involved a restoration of civic rights and the individual's return to the state of full, democratic citizenship. This meant that amnesty was also an act of 'forgiving'. One could almost say that wartime conduct was being erased from popular consciousness. The amnesties granted in France in the early 1950s made it illegal to mention the names in public of those who had been condemned for collaboration after liberation and were later amnestied.

High-profile trials continued to keep old wounds open in France during the 1950s and 1960s. But the statute of limitations, embedded in countries' legal systems, extended the dampening impact of the amnesties. The French parliament had to reinterpret the statute in 1964, to enable some ex-Vichy officials to face trial for 'crimes against humanity', not a 'crime' that had existed when the purges took place.

This chapter has treated the purges as 'history', locating them in their own time and conjunctural set of circumstances. Viewed historically, it seems to me that they rather impressively contributed to how governments and societies managed a difficult and painful transition from a Nazi war to a democratic peace. If you were to judge the purges from the vantage point of universal humane values, and whether they provided 'justice' for the victims of war and occupation, you might want to arrive at a different conclusion. It was very noticeable that, during the post-war purges, the awful singularity of the Holocaust was, if not actually denied, then certainly immersed, even submerged, in a sea of victims. This was, of course, because of the very specificity of the genocide of Europe's Jews. Genocide left relatively few survivors who returned to their home countries, important when the purges received a kind of stimulus each time a big group of other victims of war and occupation, such as POWs, political prisoners, and deported workers, were repatriated. Probably more attention was given to, say, whether officials could be held responsible for the deportation of workers to Germany than their part in the deportation of Jews. If the persecution of Jews was hardly ignored, we have to accept that 'justice' would not be done for at least another thirty years.

To my surprise, the purges turned out to be a calibrated and nuanced process. There is a gap here between the myth and official memory of the occupation, and 'history'. For the sake of the myth, the relatively limited post-war purges confirm the reassuring presence of a large, if passively resisting, majority. A study of the process of the purges reveals, rather, that collaboration was extensive, and that collaborators were treated with some sensitive regard for the difficulties and ambiguities of their position. The myth has smoothed out the rough edges of the actual process for easier consumption and acceptance.[17]

The top men, in terms of collaboration and collaborationism, were hit hard by the purges, which dealt rather more humanely with those collaborating beneath them. It can quite properly be argued that the law was a rather blunt instrument with which to judge people's conduct during the war. The courts tried certain individuals for specific and demonstrable acts of collaboration, and 'treason', rather than general conduct over time. They required a presentation and assessment of evidence that went beyond the expectations and practice of, say, historians. The courts could deliver only a verdict of 'guilt' or 'innocence', when the indistinct territory between 'guilt' and 'innocence' was perhaps more suitable terrain for evaluating how people had behaved during occupation. What the legal process did, however, was to offer a general verdict on occupation. In its targeting of a few big hitters as collaborators, the courts validated the portrayal of the great majority of the population as being 'passive resisters'.

But we have to remind ourselves that the purges flexibly allowed for the inflexibility of the legal process. The laws themselves were revised and softened. Even if the main intention was to limit the impact of the purges, the effect was also to refine what could be regarded as culpable collaboration, and to encourage a more proportionate matching of punishment to 'crime'.

More importantly, the great majority of cases of collaboration were handled not in the courts, but in extra-legal purge commissions, usually occupationally based. This enabled a wide and generous treatment of collaborating conduct that was not criminal and would not be properly evaluated in a court of law. Here, we find that investigations were thorough, sometimes over-thorough, well documented, and capable of assessing not only specific acts of collaboration, but also the attitudes and mentality of individuals, what, arguably, might have determined or influenced their conduct. The purge commissions were forums that enabled something of the complexity and ambiguity of choices and decisions during wartime occupation to emerge and be taken into account. The purge investigations also helped to define what kinds of behaviour constituted 'collaboration' and 'resistance'. We might not agree with these sometimes rather improvised and rough definitions, but they were a start, and a real contribution to the historical debate.

I am evidently moving towards some acknowledgement of what the purges can offer to the historian of wartime Europe, rather than to the historian of post-war Europe. I will try to summarize this, while also reflecting on what the historian can add to the purges in order to enhance our historical understanding of collaboration.

The purges, and the voluminous documentation they generated, provide the historian with many stories of collaboration, and reveal how those accused or suspected of collaboration defended themselves. We can ask different questions of this material from those asked by the original prosecutors and judges, and test out the validity of the case for the defence. The best defence proved to be evidence of 'resistance'. This revelation secured the release of several big guns. In the post-war climate, acts of resistance were bound to have more weight than acts of collaboration, however apparently heinous their impact.

These cases are mentioned now, because they will be examined later in the book. René Bousquet, Vichy's police chief in 1942–3, was, like other Vichy ministers and top officials, tried before a special high court, which sentenced him to five years loss of civic rights for 'national dishonour' in June 1949. In the light of what much later investigations revealed of his relations with the Germans, this was a very lenient punishment. The sentence was immediately suspended for his acts of 'resistance', which included obstructing the German deportation of foreign and French Jews. A 'resisting' attitude was indicated by his removal from office on German orders in late 1943, and subsequent house arrest in Germany after the Normandy invasion. Bousquet joined the Bank of Indochina and pursued a career in business.

Bousquet's official police representative in the German-occupied zone of France was Jean Leguay, another top official held responsible for the round-up and deportation of Jews. He was dismissed as prefect in May 1945 by the Interior ministry purge commission, as a matter of administrative rather than criminal justice. Ten years later, in 1955, the decision was reversed, in recognition of acts of resistance, enabling him to have a new career in business.

Further down the bureaucratic chain, Maurice Papon, an official in the regional prefecture of the Gironde in south-western France between June

1942 and August 1944, helped to organize the deportation of Jews. Promoted prefect immediately after liberation, having made good use of his resistance contacts and credentials, Papon became the police chief of Paris under de Gaulle's presidency in the late 1950s and 1960s, and later a Finance minister under Giscard d'Estaing. Decades later, all three men were indicted for 'crimes against humanity', in cases that blew apart the post-war Gaullist myth of a 'resisting' nation.

In Belgium, the Baron de Launiot, founder and head of one of the two huge industrial and financial holding companies that dominated the national economy, was accused of economic collaboration with the Germans. He provided evidence of big financial contributions to resistance movements across the political spectrum, made by laundering profits from black-market operations, and of facilitating the creation of a resistance group within his own business organization.

In these and other cases, we can assess the acts of collaboration independently of the acts of resistance, explore the links between them, and attempt to explain why and how the same people could be both collaborators and resisters.

What the historian, finally, can bring to the already considerable nuance and delicacy of the purge commissions' work is what historians do best, to contextualize and, hence, to explain. To some extent, the purges did this by distinguishing between collaboration undertaken in the early years of occupation and that which occurred in the later years of occupation, taking a more severe view of the latter. Advertently or not, the purge commissions of public officials did appear to avoid treating as isolated incidents specific acts or words of collaborating behaviour and outlook. They tried to determine whether the recorded individual acts actually represented a consistent pattern of behaviour over time. If the charges and accusations in the purge commission files reveal what was popularly regarded as 'collaboration' at the point of liberation, the fact that so many files were closed with an emphatic 'non-lieu', indicates that judgments were not necessarily made in the vindictive spirit of 1944–5 and liberation.

However, for the historian, the key drawback of the commissions' work remains. Many acts and attitudes were held to be worthy of investigation in the circumstances of 1944–5, but would not have been so in the circumstances of 1940–2. The complacent and self-justifying testimonies of top French officials gathered together in the US Hoover Institution's volumes published in 1957,[18] record and commemorate acts of 'resistance' carried out in 1944–5 as if they characterized their behaviour throughout the occupation. The purges more or less authorized this compressed, or telescoped, perspective on occupation, as they were bound to do. It is still evidently anachronistic to assume and expect, as the purges did, that the first duty of officials was to 'resist' German occupation. This is clearly a 1945 judgement on events that marched to the beat of a different drum in 1940, or 1941, or 1942. Retrospect is fine; it provides you with the distance from events that enables balanced assessments to be made on them. Nevertheless, 'history should be written forwards, not backwards,'[19] with an awareness of what people knew and did not know at the time they were making choices and decisions, and a sense of the imponderables in that decision-making. When context is all, 'history' can properly explain both variations and evolutions in attitudes and conduct over time. Whether contextualization as explanation removes the need and justification for universal moral judgements on reprehensible human behaviour is perhaps something to be considered as you read the rest of the book.

Empathy is required, even, perhaps especially, in circumstances where it is not easy to provide. Take those situations where officials and businessmen acted, or appeared to act, reprehensibly; when, for instance, civil servants facilitated and organized the deportation of Jews to the death camps, or employers fulfilled German orders in the full knowledge that the production of their factories was aiding the German war effort, and might help the Nazis win the war. Empathy is certainly required of a historian like myself, and his readers, who come from a European country that did not experience Nazi occupation and methods.

Empathy informing historical analysis has implicit and self-evident dangers. Empathy can imperceptibly drift into justification, an overidentification and unwarranted sympathy for people placed in difficult predicaments, when explanation and understanding are the aims. I must say that empathy was in short supply when I read the self-justifying and obfuscating commentaries of the French officials who contributed to the Hoover collections. It was more in evidence when I read some of their memoirs and pronouncements during the occupation, which struck me as, sometimes inadvertently, expressing their attitudes and approach as officials, which affected how they behaved as officials under occupation. What empathy does is challenge you to consider how you would have behaved, as an official or a businessman, in the given circumstances of Nazi occupation of your country.

2

The Nature of the Beast

The Nazi New Order and the Nazi Occupation of Northern and Western Europe

The cartoon reproduced as Illustration 2 appeared in the British broadsheet newspaper the *Guardian* in June 1994. It is a very British take on the European Union, and both confirms and subverts what are taken to be stereotypical British attitudes towards the post-war process of European integration. A bemused and outraged Hitler is in hell, of course, because his 'single Europe' was one of conquest and empire; or is it just because he wanted a unified Europe? Hitler's actions in Europe during the war, from the perspective of a European country that did not suffer the experience of occupation, apparently discredited post-war moves towards political union and federation, and justified the strengthening and reconstruction of democratic national states in Western Europe. Nevertheless, the cartoon reminds us of the extent to which Nazi Germany appropriated the idea of Europe during the Second World War.

Hitler himself was deliberately reticent about saying anything in public about Nazi plans for Europe during the war. It was not so much that he feared public exposure of Nazi aims would weaken popular tolerance of Nazi occupation. He was prepared to admit to his cronies that 'we do not want to make any people into enemies prematurely and unnecessarily'. But he felt, nonetheless, that 'one ought not to be dependent on the goodwill of other people'.[1] This was the crux of Hitler's position. His public silences were more to do with an obsessive concern not to compromise on Nazi ideological aims and their realization. There could be no hostages to fortune, no making of promises that he would not want to redeem once the war had been won. His

6 June 1994

Illustration 2. 'All I wanted was a single Europe.' A very British and ironical take on Hitler and the process of European integration. The Nazi New Order for Europe both induced and repelled wartime collaboration in the occupied territories.

general view was that, where issues could not be definitively resolved at the time, then they could be postponed until the end of the war, when Nazi Germany would be able to apply without interference or hindrance its political and military power and supremacy to the task of recasting Europe.

Hitler imposed some of his own reticence on others in the Nazi German leadership, such as Joachim Ribbentrop, the Foreign Minister, and Josef Goebbels, the Minister of Propaganda. They were willing to go public on European matters, if only to make more palatable German control of occupied territories and secure the internal collaboration necessary to sustain occupation. It is important to realize that Hitler's attitudes towards Europe and Europeans and his ideological intransigence determined his viewpoint

on collaboration in the occupied territories during the war. Not wanting
or needing to rely on the help of others was for Hitler a mark of the
Germans' racial superiority and of the absolute priority to be given to his
ideological aims: the achievement of the Nazi racial and imperialist mission
was something that Germans alone were fit to undertake. A congenital
dislike of cooperation in general was translated in wartime to a specific
distrust of collaborationism and a qualified acceptance of collaboration,
which seems rather odd, but was not, if you follow Hitler's logic. If the
premise was that nothing should be allowed to compromise in advance any
future Nazi plans for a European New Order, then the most likely challenge to this principle would come from national fascist movements that
might expect political concessions in favour of their 'nations' as a return for
their support for Nazi occupation of their countries. As extreme nationalists, even fascists could not be relied on to fight unequivocally for German
interests. Yet their identification with enemy occupation would make
them seem traitors to their fellow countrymen, and confirm their unpopularity. Non-political forms of collaboration, however, were less likely to
antagonize occupied populations, and to have as their price the limitation
of Nazi political goals.

The Nazi European New Order had a history of its own. In the 1930s,
improvised think tanks of geopolitical and economic 'experts', often associated with particular Nazi figures and agencies, produced blueprints of what
a Nazi-dominated Europe might look like. A good idea of what the Nazis
intended as their European New Order also emerged from the mainly private and unguarded discussions, meetings, and statements of Hitler and top
Nazi leaders during the war.

Extrapolating and simplifying, we can say that the Nazi mission was to
create a racially purified and reorganized Europe, built around a 'Greater
Germanic empire of the German nation'. Hitler, with his 80 million to 90
million 'Germans', and Himmler, with his 115 million to 120 million
'Germanics', disagreed quite profoundly over the extent and dimensions of
the empire's German and Germanic core. This internal subterranean dispute
affected their respective views of what could be expected of the peoples of
the occupied territories. Both were sure that the conquest, colonization,
and settlement of 'living space' in Eastern Europe and western Russia would
secure the present and future of the race in its endless struggle with rival
global racial blocs. A racially reordered Europe under Nazi German auspices
would have meant the redrawing of political and territorial frontiers on

racial criteria, and the disappearance or absorption of many of Europe's national states.

Besides the enlargement of the 'Germanic' areas of Europe and the territorial changes that would entail, the idea of a Greater Germanic empire would also involve an internal political and economic restructuring in order to align a German-dominated Europe to New Order principles. This was evident in the new economic order, the most clearly articulated and most concretely realized component of the Nazi German vision of Europe. The concept of the *Grossraumwirtschaft*, or 'large economic area', drew on the long-current idea of *Mitteleuropa*, a Central and Eastern European economic zone oriented to and around Germany. It connected, also, to Hitler's own version of 'living space', combining race and economics in a geopolitical, macroeconomic project where the German race, in order to survive and dominate, had to expand territorially so as to match land and economic resources to a growing German population.

Any *Grossraumwirtschaft* would extend much further than the Nazi Germanic empire, since it envisaged an integrated and planned European economy, a unified economic bloc capable of holding its own in a global system of competing and predatory blocs. There would be an international specialization or division of labour within the bloc, each country or territory producing what it produced best. The idea of interlocking complementary national economies, more broadly an agricultural and raw material producing South-Eastern Europe servicing an industrialized North-Western Europe, was to achieve autarky, or economic self-sufficiency, of the continent as a whole. The principle of autarky was being extended from Nazi Germany, and its wartime ally, Fascist Italy, to the rest of Europe and its Mediterranean basin.

The Nazis had also developed in Germany itself in the 1930s, and extended to territories acquired before the outbreak of war (Austria, the 'German' Czech lands), a kind of model of a non-Marxist, non-capitalist, post-liberal economic order. Its essence was the replacement of a free market, characteristic of a capitalist economy, by a state-regulated, though not necessarily state-owned, economy. This new economic model could, once again, be translated to the occupied territories.

In the summer of 1940, Hermann Göring, the head of, among other things, the Four Year Plan Office, which had overall responsibility for the German war economy and for the economies of the occupied territories, commissioned Walter Funk, the Minister of Economics, to work out a coordinated plan for the reorganization of the European economy. The setting for Funk's plan was Nazi Germany's rapid military conquest of Denmark, Norway, the Netherlands, Belgium, and now France, which made it likely that the war would end soon in an overwhelming German victory. This prospect made it both possible and imperative for Germany to plan for an economic New Order. This might explain why Funk's plan for a form of European economic union revealed practical, concrete step-by-step ways in which such a union could be achieved. Funk also clearly expected that an immediate start could be made on his plan while the war was still proceeding. Some of the measures proposed in the plan were actually introduced into the running of the occupied territories during the war, even though the prolonging of the war beyond expectations made a priority of directly exploiting Europe's economies for the German war effort.

Göring was rather dismissive of the plan he had asked for, and evidently wanted to sideline it for consideration after the war had been won, when the definitive *political* decisions about the shape of a new Europe would be made by the Nazi leadership.[2] His own advice, and practice, were what characterized the first few months of the Nazi occupation of Northern and Western Europe, which was 'pillage, comprehensively'.[3]

In August 1942, Göring summoned the civilian and military heads of the German occupation regimes in Northern and Western Europe to a conference in Berlin, to find ways of meeting what turned out to be a temporary food supply crisis in Germany and the occupied territories. In a darkly hilarious exchange between Göring and the other leaders, the continued and intensified plundering of Europe's economies was clearly in the forefront of the deputy *Führer's* thoughts and actions. Göring embarked on a glorified rant, and his harangue, and the responses to it, were a typical expression of the Nazis' entrepreneurial cowboy, target-setting mode of operating, which made them so difficult to deal with as occupiers. The Dutch, yelled Göring, were not to be treated as a Germanic people, but as 'nothing but a nation of traitors to our cause', and in terms of what could be squeezed from Dutch agriculture, he 'could not care less whether the Dutch gentlemen are Teutons or not'.[4] Göring proceeded to pluck out of the air target figures for agricultural production to be requisitioned for German consumption, revising already submitted quotas on the spot. He engaged in competitive banter with the Nazi civilian commissioners in charge of occupied Norway and the Netherlands, who shouted out that they could exceed what was demanded. This was a characteristic Nazi procedure, which served to galvanize Nazi leaders into action by setting competitive and impossible targets, in the full expectation that they would be met in a supreme and ruthless act of will.

The point was that the plundering of occupied Europe's economic resources continued at some level throughout the war. But it coexisted with, and was increasingly superseded by, overt planning and coordination of Europe's economies, made necessary by the German invasion of the USSR from June 1941, and the prolongation of the war, once the *blitzkrieg* had exhausted itself. This shows that there was no real incompatibility between longer-term restructuring of the European economy and meeting the immediate demands of the German war effort. When the war began to stall for the Germans in 1942, it was clear that the Nazi regime needed to extract more from its own economy and the economies of the occupied territories. Economic planning and integration on a European scale became more attractive as ways of making the most productive and efficient use of European economic resources. As the war effort had to be stepped up, Hitler appointed his favourite architect, Albert Speer, to be Minister of Armaments and War Production in February 1942, with the brief to increase production through the organization of the economies of a German-dominated Europe.

In the occupied territories, then, the Nazis acted to bring about perman-ent changes in the management of their economies, making it possible to discern a shape to the new European economic order. The 'Aryanization' of Jewish property and businesses occurred across occupied Europe. There were attempts, uneven in their impact, to penetrate foreign banks and companies, with German banks buying shares in those banks. Since many continental European banks held shares in businesses as security for loans and investment, buying into bank capital also brought a portfolio of indus-trial share holdings. Price- and market-fixing German cartels, which often covered entire branches of the economy, were extended into the occupied territories, along with other characteristic forms of German business organization and association. Berlin was to become Europe's new trading and financial centre, and the 'clearing house' for transnational economic activity. The deliberately overvalued German currency, the *Reichsmark*, was the official European currency for these transactions.

In the 1930s, Nazi Germany lacked sufficient reserves of gold and hard international currencies to pay for the goods it was importing from Central and Eastern Europe. In a series of bilateral arrangements, it created a kind of barter system with an exchange in goods rather than currency. Extended across the continent of Europe during the war, Nazi Germany's clearing system was an ingenious and cost-free way of endlessly exploiting the European economies. At the European clearing house of Berlin, the German importer of goods and raw materials from the other countries paid for the imports by depositing cash with German banks, enabling the German government, in turn, to use these funds to pay the businesses exporting to Germany.

In theory, the system was meant to balance out the economic exchange between Germany and its dependent territories. In practice, once Germany had started to demand more goods and raw materials than it could possibly pay for from its exports, then clearing was a device by which Germany became a permanent creditor in its economic relations with other countries. Germany was enabled to purchase goods and raw materials from the occupied territories on credit, against future repayments in the post-war period. It was a limitless IOU scam, delaying payment for goods received until, and only when, the war had been won. In a cruel turn of the clearing screw, the creditor territory had a choice between two evils, either delaying payments to its own people for exports to the debtor, Germany, or paying its own people in advance of German 'payment' from its own revenues and resources, in order to keep it afloat. Even the NS Norwegian Finance Minister recognized that this was a win–win situation for the occupier, who presided over the uncompensated transfer of economic resources from the occupied territories. As he remarked to Quisling, 'if Germany loses the war she will not be able to pay, and if she wins the war it is questionable whether she will want to pay'.[5] The centralized clearing system run from Berlin was also a perfect illustration of the dual purpose behind Nazi economic policy. Clearing was both a means of credit funding for the German war effort, and a step towards the incorporation of dependent European economies into a German-dominated continental economic system.

As it turned out, Norway, uniquely among the occupied territories of Northern and Western Europe, was a net economic beneficiary of German wartime occupation. Norway paid disproportionately high occupation costs, because the country's strategic position necessitated the stationing there of German armed forces of half a million men. But the costs to Germany of attempting to incorporate the Norwegian economy into the *Grossraumwirtschaft* were evident in high food imports to feed the Norwegian people and the occupation forces. Also, bauxite had to be imported from other parts of Europe to sustain and expand the aluminium industry, which, like Norway's hydroelectric power potential, required German capitalization and inward investment. The outcome was that for both, in the shorter term, the war effort, and in the longer term, the *Grossraumwirtschaft*, Nazi Germany had to subsidize Norway as an occupied territory.

The exploitative nature of German occupation is laid bare in the requisitioning of European economic resources throughout the war, and the blatantly partisan operation of the clearing system. But we cannot assume that businesses in the occupied territories would be put off by the *Grossraumwirtschaft* and its partial realization during the war. The Nazis' entrepreneurial political dynamism and their ruthless getting-things-done pragmatism were applied to everything they touched; and, as totalitarians, they intended to touch everything. Their adventurous, risk-taking way of operating appealed to what remained of the capitalist spirit among Europe's captains of industry, as it did to some disaffected politicians and union leaders who despaired of the slow workings and poor outcomes of interwar parliamentary democracy. As we shall see, those firms that had operated and exported across national borders, sometimes in multinational cartels, and were already organized in business associations to lobby governments, had little to fear and much to gain from involvement in the Nazi *Grossraumwirtschaft*. They could regard the occupation quite plausibly as an opportunity to consolidate and extend markets and market share.

The Nazis made no attempt to hide the unequal relationships that would persist in the *Grossraumwirtschaft*, nor the fact that its realization would be down to German conquest and hegemony in Europe. But the economic bloc could certainly be portrayed with some degree of conviction as a kind of European economic community or partnership of European countries, each contributing in its own way to the economic independence of Europe as a whole. Göring, in words and action, was always contemptuous of the need for collaboration when he could simply seize economic resources. But his was not the only voice, and his views became increasingly less influential as control of the economic exploitation of the occupied territories passed from the Four Year Plan Office to other agencies. Others recognized that dictating things exclusively in German economic interests was not enough to mobilize Europe's economic assets, and that collaboration was both necessary and desirable if the *Grossraumwirtschaft* was to be realized. In a gathering of major German industrialists in October 1940, one of the Economics Ministry's top officials, Gustav Schlotterer, who was Funk's man on the economic New Order in Western Europe, emphasized that 'we are not alone in Europe and we cannot run an economy with subjugated nations'. He encouraged German companies to interact normally with businesses in the occupied territories, so that there was a 'healthy mixture between German interests and those of other nations and countries in Europe'.[6] This was the message that Schlotterer had taken to his meetings with French, Belgian, and Dutch industrialists in the summer of 1940, anticipating a long-term economic cooperation between them and their German counterparts. The official's view was that it was possible to induce a kind of 'voluntary compulsion' from European companies. As we shall see, this was a principle shared by the Nazi political authorities in the occupied Netherlands.

More generally, the various versions of a Nazi European New Order stimulated, in a sometimes competitive, usually hostile wartime dialogue, some imaginative rethinking about the shape of Europe in the post-war world, whoever actually won the war. The study commissions set up by the wartime West European governments-in-exile concluded that some form of regional economic union should be set up after liberation. Practically all of Western Europe's non-communist internal resistance movements developed programmes, or visions, of a federal post-war Europe, first separately, and then collectively, rather hopefully assuming that Nazi occupation had created a clean slate for a fundamental institutional change. Both prongs of the wartime anti-Nazi resistance in Western Europe promoted union largely for the same reasons, to do away with interwar conditions of economic crisis and rampant nationalism, which had enabled the rise of fascism and the rush to war. The post-war impetus to West European integration, the full realization of which ran aground on the victorious Allies' basic commitment to the restoration of national states, came as a result of, and as a counter to, the Nazi European New Order.

This was also certainly the case for the collaborationists, the national fascists and Nazis who rallied more or less unreservedly to support and profit from Nazi occupation. Interwar and wartime fascist leaders in Northern and Western Europe always 'thought European'. They placed their own national revolutions against the threat of Bolshevism in the context of a general struggle to rescue and regenerate European civilization facing its nemesis in Asiatic barbarism. They saw the war as a European ideological civil war, fought between Bolshevism and fascism over the corpse of democracy, held responsible for the decadence of European civilization.

Leon Degrelle, the Belgian Rexist leader, went totally 'Eurofascist' during the war. He moved opportunistically from the idea of reviving a Low Countries–Burgundian empire bridging the historic racial and cultural frontier between 'Northern' and 'Southern' Europe, and bought into the SS-inspired idea of a 'Germanic' Europe. He spent much of the war fighting on the Eastern Front in a German uniform, with regular stopovers in Berlin. There, he persuaded Himmler to recategorize the Walloon francophone Belgians as good 'Aryans', and managed to find a common racist strand in the ideologies of all European fascist movements that could be the basis of a post-war European racial community.

Other fascist leaders in the occupied territories took, or already had taken, the first of Degrelle's steps, if not the second. They all envisaged some kind of supranational political and territorial form to a Europe liberated from parliamentary democracy, communism, capitalism, and Jews as a result of the war, in which the 1939–40 boundaries of national states would disappear. They usually proposed regional sub-European entities, like the 'Greater Netherlands' idea of Anton Mussert, the leader of the Dutch *Nationaal-Socialistische Beweging* (*NSB*), or Quisling's Nordic Union. The new 'historic' configurations were conceived as having a confederal relationship with each other and with a 'Greater Germany', in a European-wide confederation of federations. These fantasies reserved far too much autonomy to the peoples of Europe for the German Nazis to stomach, which partly explains Hitler's suspicion of his most committed collaborators.

Again, it would be mistaken to assume that the Nazi New Order for Europe appealed only or mainly to collaborationists. The Nazi wartime slogan propagandized in the occupied territories was 'Europe united under German leadership in the struggle against Bolshevism and plutocratic powers, alien to Europe'.[7] These motifs had some real resonance for the occupied peoples to whom it was addressed. There was an appeal to Europe and Europeans as the location and embodiments of a historic civilization, a cultural force and entity under threat from alien materialisms, Anglo-American capitalism, and Russian collectivism.

It was no wonder that the Nazi occupiers' most suggestible appeal in occupied Europe was for all European peoples to join and support, in what ways they could, the 'anti-Bolshevik crusade' being fought on Europe's behalf by German armed forces in the USSR. The most independent of the governments in occupied Europe, in Denmark, was induced by a very hands-off German occupier to sign the Anti-Comintern Pact in 1941, and to ban the communist party internally. The Pact might not have amounted to much, representing from its invention by Nazi Germany in 1936 a common international ideological front against the Communist International. But it had, after all, laid the ideological and diplomatic ground for a formal political and military alliance between Nazi Germany and Fascist Italy in 1939. In the context of the war, it was a symbolic alignment of a nominally still neutral country, Denmark, to the Nazi German war against the USSR. The signing was accompanied by caveats to the effect that Denmark had not committed itself to waging a military war against the Soviet Union. Nevertheless, the Danish government could no longer claim that Denmark was a neutral non-belligerent; it was on the German side, and wanted Germany to defeat the USSR. The French Vichy government, in its turn, deployed anti-Bolshevism to justify to its own people the economic and other collaboration it gave to Nazi Germany. As we shall see, government officials across occupied Northern and Western Europe were influenced by an ingrained anti-communism in some of their acts of collaboration with the Nazi occupier. Anti-communism, as we well know, was the political and ideological cement of democratic parliamentary coalitions in cold-war Western Europe.

Anti-Bolshevism was clearly a means of broadening the consent of occupied peoples for occupation and the New Order beyond the narrow and self-limiting confines of the collaborationists' ideological affinity to Nazism. As well as being a bridge connecting the Germans to collaborators of all kinds and the occupied populations as a whole, the anti-Bolshevik crusade was also used to disorientate, if not dislodge, national state patriotism. Bolshevism was plausibly identified as the enemy within and the enemy without, across Europe; you were defending your own country in Europe, if you supported Nazi Germany against Asiatic Bolshevism. The inducement was to cooperate with the 'enemy' power occupying your own country, which you might otherwise assume you should resist in order to protect the interests of your own nation.

The approach so far has been to analyse the Nazi European New Order in general terms of the collaboration it invited and could expect from governments, officials, businessmen, and populations at large in the occupied territories. A similar approach will be taken in considering how the Germans occupied countries that they had defeated militarily in Northern and Western Europe. We self-evidently need to determine what people were collaborating with, and the conditions under which collaboration took place. Collaboration has historical meaning only in relation to Nazi occupation regimes and occupation policies. Such an approach is also one way of imposing some kind of retrospective order on a situation in 1940 where no discernible pattern to occupation was evident. The defeated countries in Northern and Western Europe were occupied in ways that reflected a range, or a mix, of military, strategic, economic, and racial–ideological concerns.

Given Nazism's *modus operandi*, it seems pointless to say that occupation need not, or should not, have happened in this fashion. The final decision on the form of occupation was always Hitler's, and he directly mandated each occupation authority. But every important party and state agency of the Third Reich had a view on how conquered countries were to be occupied, and lobbied intensively for that view to prevail. It was, for Norway, almost literally the case that the kind of occupation was determined by whoever Hitler had spoken to, and listened to, last.

There was a default position, and it was a military administration. The Army command had certainly planned for this to be the norm, having been promised by Hitler in November 1939 that Nazi agencies would be excluded from the preparations for occupation. That Hitler made such a promise under pressure from his military men was a sure sign of the competitive spiral that was typical of Nazi practice. Military occupation was also a logical consequence of invasions that took place largely for militarily strategic reasons, as was the case for Denmark and Norway in April 1940, and probably also Belgium, in May 1940.

Military administration was, again, a natural outcome to the way Nazi Germany had declared war. The small states of Northern and Western Europe—that is, all of them, with the big exception of France—were presented with a German ultimatum that also contained a choice: if there was no military resistance to German invasion, then Hitler would respect the political and territorial sovereignty of the invaded and occupied country. This was a very sensible and potentially appealing offer to countries that were neutral and pacifist, did not have strong enough armed forces to be more than a presence in the event of German invasion, and could not rely on the League of Nations to provide them with collective security. The offer raised the interesting possibility of the invaded countries themselves determining the form of German occupation, dependent on whether they capitulated immediately to the Germans, or not. The foreign and military policy of the small West European states in the late 1930s was also the seed of wartime collaboration with the Germans, though this is a controversial thing to say. The only effective deterrent to German invasion would have been massive rearmament and functioning military alliances. These countries did and had neither, accepting that they could do little to prevent or combat a German attack. Their resignation to certain defeat in the event of war, and that in itself seemed inevitable, was a prior acceptance of German domination that was something they could not resist, only come to terms with.

In the event, of the invaded Northern and West European countries, only in Denmark did the king, government, and military command accept the German offer. Denmark surrendered after a few hours of combat with a few casualties, under threat of the German bombing of the capital city, Copenhagen. The German military commander joked seriously that Denmark could now be taken over by a march past of his forces' brass band. At least until the summer of 1943, Nazi Germany had formal state-to-state relations with Denmark and allowed a democratically elected Danish government to continue to govern the country, all state institutions intact, including the monarchy. There was a 'peaceful' and consensual military occupation enjoying the broad support of the Danish people, confirmed in the free parliamentary elections of March 1943, when over 80 per cent of those participating voted for parties making up the collaborating coalition government of national unity. Collaboration with the Germans was official government policy, and a matter of negotiation between nominally sovereign states.

There was another reason for military administration of occupied territories not being normal. Hitler was politically and temperamentally averse to trusting the military with anything important. They were a still powerful non-Nazified component of the German conservative establishment whose safe, legalistic, and cautious ways were always perceived as a restraint on Nazi revolutionary dynamism, and made them unsuited for the carrying-out of 'political' tasks. Hitler was always open, then, to alternative 'political' solutions that could give full expression to Nazi *élan* and drive.

In Norway, the initial German offer of an uncontested invasion was rejected, the Norwegian armed forces, stiffened for a while by Allied military assistance, put up a fight, and the king and his government eventually fled the country for exile in Britain. The determining element in the form of occupation adopted in Norway was the persistent presence of the Norwegian Nazi party leader, Quisling, in both pre-war thinking about any invasion and the period of the invasion and conquest itself. He had the patronage and protection of Alfred Rosenberg, German Nazism's semi-official ideologue with a special interest in 'Nordic' racism, and of the head of the German navy, Admiral Erich Raeder. As a Nazi, ex-army officer, and ex-Defence Minister, Quisling had been consulted before the war on the military planning for an invasion of Norway. He had offered to stage a coup in Norway, and 'invite' a German invasion in order to protect Norway's neutrality against Britain and to prepare the country for full political incorporation into the Greater Germanic Reich. The coup played no part in the actual planning and execution of the invasion. But the indefatigable Quisling staged an abortive coup, anyway, at the point of invasion, which was effectively disowned by both the Norwegian people and the German invaders.

As the Germans literally thrashed around, looking for a body of representative Norwegians with whom to deal with during the invasion and, then, occupation, Hitler got himself out of a fix by taking Göring's advice to appoint a *Gauleiter*, or regional Nazi party leader, Josef Terboven, as *Reichskommissar* of occupied Norway. His immediate task was to troubleshoot his way out of what was for the Germans a fast deteriorating situation, and fill the country's political and administrative vacuum. Protracted and inconclusive negotiations with various representatives of what remained of Norway's establishment led Terboven to what was the defining moment of the occupation. He eventually decided to abolish parliament, all political parties except for NS, and the monarchy, and appoint a so-called Council of Commissioner Ministers to govern the country under his direction. Quisling, meanwhile, had reignited his influential contacts with Nazi luminaries in Berlin and made his availability known to Terboven. The new 'government' of Norway contained a majority of NS 'ministers'. Quisling remained NS party leader, and formally became Prime Minister of a national government in February 1942.

The formation of a mainly NS government was an incredible outcome, which had taken five months to be reached, from the invasion in April 1940 to the creation of the Council in September. Uniquely in occupied Europe, a national fascist party was in power under the direction of a German Nazi party boss as Reich Commissioner. His intention was clearly to 'Nazify' Norwegian society through the agency of the Norwegian NS party, and so enable Norway's absorption into the 'Greater Germanic empire'. It scarcely needs saying that this was bound to have an impact on the willingness, or not, of Norwegians to collaborate with the Germans in a process of self-Nazification. Terboven's decision to eliminate Norway's institutions for an *NS* government marked the point at which the German occupier abandoned its attempt to co-opt the country's established elites in 1940, its initial tactic throughout occupied Northern and Western Europe. It was now certain that the Norwegian people would regard the new government as being illegitimate. As a result, resistance was guaranteed from the very start of the occupation.

If Belgium was invaded mainly for military and strategic reasons, then the likelihood of the country remaining a war zone, either as a launch pad for the invasion of Britain or as the probable site of any Allied landing in continental Europe, tended towards the establishment and retention of a German military administration there. The attachment of the northern French departments of the Nord and the Pas-de-Calais to the jurisdiction of the German military administration in Brussels was part of the territorial dismemberment of France. It was probably, as well, an attempt to create a natural heavy industrial zone in North-Western Europe that would facilitate German exploitation of the area's economic resources. There was even a hint of political and racial New Ordering, since the association of northern France and Belgium indicated that a 'Germanic' Flanders could be on the horizon. But the presence of two separate linguistic and 'racial' communities in Belgium, the francophone Walloons and the 'Germanic' Flemings, complicated the picture.

Where no definitive decision was yet forthcoming on the territorial and racial boundaries of a future 'Belgium', a neutral military administration both allowed the occupation and economic exploitation of the country, while keeping open all options for the future. A military, rather than 'political', occupation regime was likely to put the tasks of occupation before any active promotion of the New Order, and more likely to abide by the conventions of international law on the rights and obligations of the occupier. This perception in itself, even though it was gradually undermined by some very 'political' measures taken by the military government during the occupation, eased the way towards cooperation with Belgian institutions and authorities, at least initially.

You might expect that Nazi occupation regimes would be directly geared to the realization of the big New Order ideas of the 'Greater Germanic empire' and the *Grossraumwirtschaft*. All the German occupation authorities, whatever their form, were instructed to secure conditions of social peace and public order that would enable the economic exploitation of the occupied territories. The concern was primarily, of course, to sustain the German war effort and to maintain the consumption levels of the German people. But, as we have indicated, it was also the aim to bring about a German-dominated European economic bloc. It was, and is, significant that only France of the occupied countries in Northern and Western Europe was not initially included in German thinking about the *Grossraumwirtschaft*. This suggests that, in common with other New Order conceptualizations, France quite literally had no viable or certain place in the future new Europe.

The Germans agreed to the French government's request for an armistice in June 1940, which effectively ended the war as well as the fighting, whereas the governments and monarchies of Norway, Belgium, and the Netherlands had gone into exile to continue the war against Germany. As in Denmark, a legitimate national government remained in place. It had nominal sovereignty over all French territory. But metropolitan France was now divided into a so-called free zone in the centre and south of France, which was actually administered by the French government located in the small, pleasant spa town of Vichy, and an occupied zone under German military administration encompassing the most strategically important and economically productive areas of western and some of northern France.

The division and dismemberment of France were clearly designed to humiliate and weaken Germany's traditional and hated enemy, and the only Great Power in Northern and Western Europe. A rump territory and government could then be manoeuvred into contributing to the war against Britain, if only by defending France's African empire, which it retained, against Britain and the Free French forces of General de Gaulle ,who had rallied to the continuation of the war against Nazi Germany. The military defence of a German-dominated Europe lay behind the German decision to create yet another demarcation line from March 1941, this time subdividing the occupied zone to the west and cutting departments in two, in a 'forbidden coastal zone'. This covered a narrow strip inland extending from Dunkirk to Hendaye, and was the location for the construction of the Atlantic Wall and submarine shipyards and bases.

The German treatment of France after its defeat could not be taken as a definitive resolution of Franco-German relations. But the signs for the future of France in a German-dominated Europe were hardly benign, especially when Nazi Germany's ally, Fascist Italy, was allowed to occupy a small zone in south-eastern France, almost as a marker of Fascist Italy's territorial claims on metropolitan France and the French empire. The

French, or most of them, were hardly 'Teutons'. As Hitler recognized in his rhetorical questioning of the future of France and the French in 1942, 'can we absorb them with advantage? Do they by blood belong to our race?...One must act in accordance with the answer one gives oneself.'[8] Quite understandably in the circumstances, the concern to ease the armistice terms, to end or overcome the division of France into occupied and unoccupied zones, and to find a meaningful place for France in the New Order lay behind the Vichy government's decision to collaborate with the German occupier.

The territorial dismemberment of France also showed some signs of intent towards creating the 'Greater Germanic empire'. The exclusion zone of north-eastern France ostensibly extended Germany's racial borders westwards, and was designated as an area of German settlement. The eastern provinces of Alsace and Lorraine, which had been German between 1871 and 1914, were *de facto* annexed to Nazi Germany, and placed under the *Gauleiters* of neighbouring German regions, who were mandated by Hitler to 're-Germanize' them within ten years. German law applied, and Alsatian young men were conscripted into the German army. Some of these *malgré-nous* ('in spite of ourselves') soldiers were tried in the 1950s for their part in the massacre of French civilians at Oradour-sur-Glane by a retreating *Waffen-SS* company in June 1944, a trial that kept open the deep wounds inflicted on French society by the occupation. As a first step in the ethnic cleansing of eastern France, over 80,000 people regarded as unassimilable— that is, French-only speakers, anti-German francophiles, Jews, gypsies, foreigners, criminals, a-socials—were expelled from Lorraine and dumped across the border in Vichy France. The *Gauleiter* in Alsace, with a less rigorous view of the possibilities of 're-Germanization', nevertheless expelled 24,000 people, some to Germany, some to Vichy France.

Perhaps the clearest or least ambiguous statement of German intent came in the occupied Netherlands, where the initial plan to install a military administration was superseded by Hitler's decision to appoint Arthur Seyss-Inquart as *Reichskommissar*. His role was indicated by his political background and pedigree. He was an Austrian Nazi leader, who brought in fellow Austrians to run his German civilian administration, and had been involved in bringing about the *Anschluss*, or union, of Austria with Germany in 1938. The Dutch, whatever Göring might say, were regarded by the Nazis as a good 'Germanic' people who, like the Austrians, but more so, had to be helped over a period of historical territorial separation from the motherland. Seyss-Inquart was to 're-Germanize' the Netherlands, from below and by inducement and encouragement, if at all possible, and not necessarily through the local fascist party, the *NSB*. This, of course, was the case in Norway, the other country with a Reich Commissioner whose job was to prepare the occupied territory for incorporation into the 'Greater Germanic empire'. That Seyss-Inquart was open to the Dutch people's voluntary self-Nazification by other means and agencies raised some very interesting possibilities for collaboration in the early phase of occupation.

We are left with a situation in late summer 1940 in Northern and Western Europe that appeared exceptional only if you fail to take into account the dynamic and improvised ways in which the Nazis approached governance. Belgium–northern France, and the western and northern parts of France were the only occupied areas to be under a German military administration, when that might have been the norm. Denmark was the only country that was occupied by 'consent', and, as a result, retained its king, parliamentary government, and national institutions. This, again, might have been the norm if other countries had not chosen to continue to resist the German invasions, and, while surrendering, remain at war with Nazi Germany. France was the only country that secured an armistice, effectively an end to the war, and a temporary arrangement that in due course would be superseded by a peace treaty between France and Germany. Because France was the only serious military power in continental Western Europe, it was the only country to be seriously dismembered by the Germans, and divided into occupied and unoccupied zones. Both Norway and the Netherlands were placed under Nazi civilian Reich Commissioners, a clear enough statement of probable inclusion into the 'Greater Germanic empire'. But, in an unforeseen sequence of events, Norway was the only occupied country in Northern and Western Europe where the local Nazi party was in power, almost from the start.

Some common ground existed across the occupied territories in Northern and Western Europe, which both clarified and confused an already fragmented reality. Whether civilian or military, the German occupation authorities were never intended to be more than supervisory administrations. As far as possible, the Germans expected and wanted to rule through the existing national and local administrative and executive bodies, from governments (in Denmark and France) to central ministerial, and municipal officials and bureaucracies. The Reich Commissioners certainly established their own commissariats, made up of central departments covering the economy, politics, and propaganda, which employed German personnel. Their role was not to govern or administer directly, but to direct and supervise the work and activity of central, regional, and local administrations staffed by officials of the occupied territory. The military governors in Belgium–northern France and occupied France set up a central German-run military administration, and decentralized this structure to the regional and local levels so that they corresponded to, and cohabited with, the various levels of the occupied country's state system. So, in occupied France, under the central military administration in Paris and four regional military administrations, there were *Feldkommandants* (Field Commanders), one in each department, the basic territorial and administrative unit of France, opposite the prefect, the central government's representative and executive power holder. At a rung below were the *Kreiskommandants* (District Commanders), one in each *arrondissement* or electoral constituency, opposite the sub-prefect.

Governing through already well-established administrations, a system of 'indirect rule', has generally been the practice of most imperial and colonial powers. The Nazis adopted it for broadly the same reasons as others did. It was economical on the occupier's own material and human resources, and kept to a minimum the costs and bother of administering things itself. It gave a semblance of continuing legality, and a sense of business as usual, to traumatized, or at least shocked and fearful, conquered populations. Existing governments, or bureaucracies, provided a ready-made channel for the transmission or execution of the occupier's directives, as if they had not actually come from the occupier, at all. Willy nilly, officials in the newly occupied territories became the first and most important collaborators of the occupying power.

We have already seen that the initial decisions about the form of occupation reflected the sometimes convergent, sometimes conflicting, aims and intentions of top Nazi leaders, the Nazi Party, the SS, state ministries, and the armed forces. These internal conflicts intensified during and as a result of occupation, as the Nazi regime exported the organized chaos of their system of rule in Germany itself to the *tabula rasa* of the occupied territories. Whatever the type of occupation, a plurality of Nazi agencies and organizations set up shop in the occupied territories. Depending on how effective they were on the ground, they coalesced into more or less discernible alternative centres of power. Coexisting with military commands in an unstable constellation of forces were the ideological policing presence of the *SS*, Nazi Party-related agencies and their support staff, state ministerial representatives and their staff, and state and Party newcomers, like the Todt organization, formed in 1938 as a provider of civil and military engineering projects, and the wartime sectoral agency for labour recruitment under a Nazi Party *Gauleiter*, Fritz Sauckel. In theory, these organizations were hierarchically answerable to the occupation authorities. But, in practice, they had cross-cutting lateral chains of command and accountability to ministries and agencies with their headquarters in Berlin.

The competitive radicalizing pressures inherent to the way the Nazis operated resulted in a changing of minds over how the territories were to be occupied. In Denmark, for instance, the 'peaceful' occupation of the country, which left intact democratic parliamentary institutions, self-evidently held back the Nazification of a 'Germanic' people. During 1942, Hitler shifted from regarding Denmark as the 'model protectorate' to demanding that the country 'become a German province', with a 'puppet government which will do everything he requires of it'.[9] The fresh approach was confirmed in the appointment of new men in the autumn of 1942. The military commander, General Hermann von Hanneken, formerly head of the raw materials division of the Economics ministry and iron and steel plenipotentiary in the Four Year Plan Office, was verbally briefed by Hitler to treat Denmark as hostile territory. The Foreign Ministry diplomat Cécil von Renthe-Fink was replaced as plenipotentiary for Denmark by Werner Best, an *SS* officer who had earlier run a department of the military administration in occupied France, and was now expected by Hitler to behave like the Reich Commissioners in Norway and the Netherlands. Again, the military governor of Belgium–northern France was, from the start, destabilized by the constant harassment and criticism of Himmler and the *SS* over what the latter regarded as his technical and overly legalistic approach to occupation. He held out for most of the occupation, partly because he ran a tight ship, and mainly because of the persistence of the conditions that made military government the preferred option in the first place. But he was eventually replaced by a Nazi Reich Commissioner in July 1944, very much *in extremis*.

In the volatile and unstable world of Nazi politics, what mattered more than any formal changes in the approach and structures of occupation were the shifting power relationships between the German agencies operating in the occupied territories. By the end of the war, the most powerful Nazi organization in the occupied territories was Himmler's *SS*, the 'army' of

National Socialism. The *SS* saw itself as both the embodiment and catalytic agent of the New Order. More than any other Nazi body, it had the organizational capacity and expertise to distribute itself in force around Europe. Of all the Nazi agencies, the *SS*, in particular, behaved as if it was organizationally and operationally independent of the German occupation authorities, accountable only to Himmler and the mandates he gave to his officers in the occupied territories. Many top officials of the German state and Party organizations were also ranked honorary or serving *SS* officers, and, while this did not always happen, they were expected to demonstrate a loyalty to the *SS* before any other body.

The *SS* had a generally hostile relationship with the military occupation authorities in Belgium–northern France and in occupied France. The dealings of the *SS* with the Reich Commissioners in Norway and the Netherlands were symbiotic rather than antagonistic, and alliances were possible. Terboven and Himmler were personally and ideologically close enough for the Reich Commissariat and the *SS* to be mutually supportive in occupied Norway. Some tension was caused by the undermining by the *SS* of Quisling's position as *NS* leader by patronizing the *NS* Chief of Police, Jonas Lie. But the ultimate aim was the same, to induce the Norwegians to be 'Germanics' and integrate them into the 'Greater Germanic empire'. Seyss-Inquart was more tolerant than supportive of a growing *SS* presence in the Netherlands, and disliked the deliberate attempt by the *SS*, as in Norway, to challenge the political monopoly and representation he had eventually conceded to the Dutch Nazi Party, the *NSB*. But he thought it was futile and counterproductive for the Reich Commissariat to be at loggerheads with the *SS* as the coming Nazi organization, and preferred a tacit alliance with it rather than perpetual contestation of its increasing influence.

The *SS* was both a security and police organization, and the Nazi agency responsible for racial policy, a really lethal combination of policing and ideological drive. It ran the colonization and settlement programmes in occupied Europe.

Both its policing and racial roles were enhanced by the prolongation of the war beyond 1941. In occupied Western Europe, growing violent resistance to Nazi occupation was a consequence of the German invasion of the USSR, which released European communist parties from the restraints of the 1939 Nazi–Soviet Pact. A greater concern for the security and protection of occupying troops in turn provided the wedge for wider *SS* involvement in policing the occupied territories, not only in the commitment of German personnel, but also in the direction of national police forces.

The January 1942 Wannsee conference of state, Party, and SS representatives, which met to organize the systematic genocide of European Jews, explicitly recognized the role of the SS in coordinating and managing the operation and its primacy in the implementation of racial policies. The meeting's purpose was probably to ram that point home to other interested parties that had a competitive relationship with the SS in the Reich and the occupied territories.

Besides the security situation, the other foothold for the SS in the occupied territories was the recruitment of suitably 'Germanic' young men to the *Waffen SS*, its combat units, who were trained to fight on the Eastern Front in Europe's crusade against Bolshevism. This kind of *entreé* to the politics of the occupied territories was particularly significant in Belgium, where the military governor tried to contain and even squeeze out Nazi organizations. Here, the Flanders SS units served an internal political purpose as well, since the intention was to build them up as the unifying core of fascist collaborationist groups in the region.

This strategy was repeated elsewhere in occupied Northern and Western Europe. The SS sponsored and promoted local Nazi organizations, sometimes from within existing fascist parties, and usually against already established movements, in the expectation that they would constitute the future racial elites when their territories were incorporated into the 'Greater Germanic empire'. The growing presence and weight of the SS in the occupied territories of Northern and Western Europe, in pursuit of their self-appointed task of re-educating racially defined 'Germanic' peoples in and through the medium of SS-inspired Nazi organizations, denoted a New Order that was not just being contemplated, but in the making.

The export of Nazi polycentrism to the occupied territories was marked by sometimes contradictory or contested decision-making, and jurisdictional and competency disputes between incoming and already established German agencies, and had a destabilizing and de-legitimating impact on the German military administrations, especially. Its likely or possible outcomes for collaboration were mixed, to say the least. Collaborating governments and officials could, perhaps, hope to extract some marginal gains and advantages, to portray as the 'fruits' of collaboration, by exploiting or playing on the differences and conflicts between competitive German agencies.

Doing so would deliver what appeared to be more than insignificant or symbolic gains in the arena of economic collaboration with the Germans. But being the middleman in wrangles between ideologically driven Nazi organizations was an extremely risky and dangerous game to play, and led to the enactment of what might be called the historical law of unintended consequences. If nothing else, such collaborative playing with fire raised questions as to whether those who collaborated should be held or judged to be responsible for the consequences, as much as for the motivations of their actions.

It might be reasonable to expect that collaborating with a German military administration would be different in tenor and outcomes to collaborating with a Reich Commissioner, or with the SS. But, whatever the form of occupation adopted in each occupied territory, common occupation policies were applied across occupied Northern and Western Europe. The military governments in Belgium–northern France and in occupied France, as well as the Reich Commissioners in Norway and the Netherlands, enacted and implemented measures that discriminated against and persecuted Jews. The military administrations had no option but to accept and enable the organization by the SS of the deportation of foreign and national Jews from the summer of 1942. Genocide was never a problem for the Reich Commissioners. The odd one out, as always, was Denmark, whose unique status as an occupied country was reflected in the non-application of anti-Jewish measures until the summer of 1943. Again, all German occupation authorities, whatever their ilk, moved from the 'voluntary' recruitment of local workers for employment in Germany, to their round-up and deportation under the direction of Sauckel's labour agency.

The effect of Nazi polycentrism being transplanted to the occupied territories was, as in Germany itself, a competitive intensification and radicalization of Nazi policies. This required collaborators to make ever more agonizing and difficult choices about how to respond to such policies.

3

Collaboration with the Grain
of Occupation, 1940–1942

There was an almost perfect symmetry between occupation and
collaboration in the summer of 1940, a situation that lasted, broadly
speaking, for a good year, until the autumn of 1941. The needs and interests
of the occupier converged naturally with those of the occupied, because of
the immediate circumstances of the war in 1940. The war also catalysed and
opened up opportunities for the enactment in practice of minority currents of
thought developing in West European countries during the 1930s. The only
premeditated collaboration came from fascists, and a few other political figures
who had moved closer to fascism before the war. But the collaboration of
1940 was, nevertheless, no bolt from the blue; nor was it simply an aberrant
response born of defeat and occupation.

In 1997, the British historian Robert Gildea interviewed a man who
had been a member of a mainly Catholic peasants and workers *maquis* band
operating just before the Allied landings in the Châteaubriant area of
occupied western France. During the occupation, the man had also been an
official of the Vichy government's peasant corporation, and had apparently
got on well with the local occupying German military authorities. He had
evidently chosen to collaborate and, then, to resist, at very different stages
of the German occupation. But he remembered rather ruefully that, in
June 1940, he greeted the news of Pétain's request to the Germans for an
armistice with an exclamation of relief, 'ouf!'[1] There was a collective 'phew!'
being exhaled across Western Europe in the summer of 1940. Paul Struye, a
Belgian Catholic lawyer and jurist, and later in the war the founding editor
of an underground resistance newspaper, wrote a diary and a series of regular
reports on public opinion in the country throughout the occupation. The
milieu he moved in, and whose views he in some sense represented, was that

of the well-off francophone professional middle classes of the capital city, Brussels. He recorded that the German occupation of the city was received there as 'soulagement physique', with a feeling of 'physical relief.'[2] The capitulation and surrender to the invading German forces were seen throughout Western and Northern Europe, except perhaps in Norway, where armed resistance was more prolonged, as a wise and sensible move that avoided further devastation being inflicted on civilians.

The suddenness and enormity of military defeat were, quite literally, a shock to the system. The humiliating conquest of their countries was so crushingly definitive that people assumed that the war was practically over and that German dominance of the continent would be permanent. There seemed to be no way back, and to be no alternative to dealing with, and coming to terms with, the occupier. In the face of such an indisputable and irresistible victor, it appeared both necessary and proper to rally around the new guarantors of order. In the immediate trauma of defeat, there was a will or a propensity to collaborate with the occupier, a general if not universal phenomenon in the summer of 1940.

A military defeat of such dimensions also served to discredit the pre-war political systems that had demonstrably failed to defend the nation's sovereign independence. Popular antipathy to the old political order, swept away by German military purpose and might, was most keenly felt and expressed in France, Belgium, and the Netherlands in 1940. Here, awareness of the collapse and breakdown of national institutions was a matter of personal and vicarious experience. In these countries, monarchs and heads of state, government ministers, government officials at all levels, and a multitude of people fled before the invading German forces. The withdrawal of governments and some top officials in the event of invasion had undoubtedly been planned for. But what happened was far from being an orderly evacuation. In some cases, the hasty, unannounced departure of local mayors and officials was the impromptu signal for local people to get on the move, as well. The mass exodus in Belgium meant that at the point of military capitulation there were around two million refugees outside the country, mainly in France, with many more stranded in Belgium itself, and the majority of officials no longer at their posts. It was perhaps even more chaotic in France, with millions of people leaving their homes and jobs in Paris, the north and east of the country, in order to reach an imagined sanctuary from German invasion across the river Loire in western France.

The mass evacuation, if that is what we should call such a panicky and disorganized flight from invasion, suited the Germans down to the ground. They, as the occupier, could now quite plausibly pose as the restorers of peace and order. They could also use the exodus as the reason for a preliminary purge of local elected mayors and other municipal officials, knowing that these men who were now returning to their localities were disgraced in the eyes of an abandoned population as a result of their flight, which was justifiably perceived as a dereliction of their public duty.

Struye, again, evoked the prevailing mood of the time. He wrote that many Belgians, meaning bourgeois like himself, saw in the German occupiers 'merits and qualities which appeared to be the antithesis of vices and abuses blamed on our democratic system'. The Germans were models of 'order, discipline... civic sense, responsibility, solidarity between classes', compared to the anarchy, disorder, egoism, and panic of the Belgians at war.[3] Later, in December 1940, he mentioned the widespread criticism in his big city circles of the country's pre-war party political system, held responsible for the defeat, and the sense of disappointment felt at the emigration of the Belgian government after the defeat. He concluded that 'perhaps three quarters of the Belgian people were largely resigned to the New Order or actually in favour of it'.[4]

The feelings of disillusionment with a democratic parliamentary system that had failed to defend the country adequately did not immediately, or even necessarily, lead to the conviction that something new should be put in its place. Probably the most widely felt reaction to defeat and occupation was one of apathy and inertia, and a sense of impotence and resignation in the face of the rapidly accomplished and apparently irreversible fact of German conquest. Naturally enough, the mood was reflected in a concern to get on with things as best one could, to concentrate on mundane but pressing demands of day-to-day existence, and to return to conditions of normalcy to the extent that this was possible. Henri Frenay was a professional soldier who rallied to the Vichy government after the armistice, remaining an army officer in France's greatly reduced post-armistice armed forces. He then went underground in 1941, founding Combat, one of the earliest and most significant of resistance movements within France. Writing in autumn 1941 of life in the unoccupied zone of France, Frenay remarked that people felt that the war was over, and that the important things were 'to have enough to eat, something to wear, and a roof over one's head'.[5]

The concern for business as usual in 1940–1 corresponded exactly with the initial goals of German occupation, which were to restore order, provide security for occupying troops and the civilian population, and get the economy up and running for the German war effort. Reich Commissioner Seyss-Inquart's first report from the occupied Netherlands in late July 1940 recycled what Hitler had mandated him to do in May, 'securing public order and public life for the protection of the Reich's interest'.[6]

It should be clear that the interests of the German occupier and of the occupied peoples converged in 1940–1, in the shared concern for the normalization of conditions of life in the occupied territories. Here was the grounding for a deal between the German occupation authorities, whatever their nature, and government officials whose public duty was to protect their fellow citizens and represent their interests. If the occupier wanted to secure conditions of social peace and public order, essential as bases for the economic exploitation of the occupied territories, then these were, in the circumstances, bound to be the priorities of public officials, as well. Now the war was over, the people of the occupied territories needed to get back to work. Officials at all levels were ready to cooperate with the occupier to ensure a resumption of economic activity.

The arrangement in 1940 was that the German occupiers would rule through indigenous officials, allowing them a degree of autonomy as long as their actions and decisions worked to guarantee order and a ready supply of economic resources. It was self-evident to both sides that producing goods and services for the Germans and for themselves required order not chaos. Both sides needed and wanted the same things, and, to secure them, wanted and needed good mutual relations. The model of indirect rule, where the occupier supervised local administrators, proved to be both economical and effective, delivering what the occupier wanted in a way that helped to bed in the occupation. In the circumstances of the initial period of occupation, the natural, logical, sensible response to occupation was to cooperate, not to resist or do nothing.

If the end to fighting was received with overwhelming relief, then for some, also, German military victories were a matter of deliverance, even redemption. Defeat and occupation encouraged the emergence of what might be called authoritarian collaboration in 1940.

The most evident and vociferous critics of the West European model of parliamentary democracy and a capitalist economy in the 1930s were the fascist movements. But there were other movements, both political and intellectual, which occupied the same ground as fascism, and for the same reason: to find viable alternatives to what appeared to contemporaries to be the systemic malfunctioning of democracy and capitalism in face of the Great Depression. These movements often used the same kind of language as fascism in their concern for a spiritual regeneration of individuals impoverished both materially and morally by a heartless and impersonal free-market capitalism. But they offered essentially non-fascist and non-communist solutions to the perceived crisis of parliamentary democracy and capitalism, initially intended to keep the middle classes from fascism.

On the socialist left in pre-war France, Belgium, and the Netherlands, there developed new currents of thought and action, stimulated by the ideas of a Belgian socialist leader, Hendrik de Man. His programme to reform and humanize a dysfunctional capitalism anticipated state-level macroeconomic planning and regulation of a mixed part-public, part-private economy; a corporate cross-class organization of the economy and society; and Keynesian infrastructural public spending to stimulate self-sustaining economic growth capable of bringing full employment and collective well-being. It was, more or less, the approach adopted by West European social democratic and Christian democratic parties after 1945. It had some, limited, resonance in pre-war politics, as well. De Man's programme was echoed in that of the 'neo-socialist' *Parti Socialiste de France*, which split from the mainstream French socialist party in 1933–4, and in some of the policies of the socialist-led Popular Front coalition governments of 1936–8. It was adopted by the Belgian socialist party, which participated in coalition governments between 1935 and 1940, where De Man himself became Minister of Public Works, and by the Dutch socialist party, which entered a coalition government for the first time in 1939. De Man's views were far from being implemented as a package before the outbreak of war, because of the compromises required in coalition politics, and of an economic recovery from the Depression that occurred without the restructuring envisaged by De Man and those who shared his ideas.

How some of these left-wing reformers of the 1930s responded to German victories in 1940 was very significant. Marcel Déat, leader of the French 'neo-socialists', and an appeaser who believed in Franco-German reconciliation, completed his transition to fully-blown fascism and collaborationism. He founded a new political movement, *Rassemblement National Populaire* (*RNP* (National Popular Rally)), which aspired to be the single party of the Vichy regime. He was eventually appointed at German behest Minister of Labour in the Vichy government in March 1944.

De Man's evolution was less spectacular, but no less important. For him, as for Déat, 1940 saw the final shots in the interwar European ideological civil war between parliamentary democracy, communism, and fascism. Nazi Germany, and the superior 'national' form of 'socialism', had 'won'. Since it had proved impossible to realize his 'third-way' solution to the crisis of capitalism within the now decrepit parliamentary system, it might yet be possible to reorganize society and the economy in a German-dominated Europe where Nazism's anti-capitalist and anti-communist ideology would prevail. So we find De Man not becoming a fascist, but nevertheless capitulating morally and politically to the Germans as military victors. In the political vacuum momentarily created by German occupation in 1940, he started working with the king of Belgium to arrange an authoritarian replacement to the departed government-in-exile.

The intellectual stream of the 'third-way' thinking of the 1930s sometimes overlapped, or intertwined, with the political sphere, and was no less important to the development of collaborating tendencies in occupied Western Europe in and from 1940. Although the new, nonconformist thinking about the reordering of capitalist economies and democratic politics had its party political outlets in the 1930s, it was mainly conducted by intellectuals as a matter of intellectual debate in a myriad of officially sponsored and informal study groups and think tanks in France and the Low Countries. These networks brought together clever, highly, one could say over-, educated, usually young, university academics, top government officials, those officials recently graduating from the elitist training schools who would expect to be the top officials of the near future, business and corporate managers and lobbyists with similar educational and work-experience backgrounds. These experts, all with a sense of being or becoming their country's natural elites, talked about the same things inspiring the political activity of Déat and De Man. They reached broadly similar conclusions: a rejection of the existing capitalist disorder for a more efficient and at the same time more humane economic and social 'order', built on planning, corporatism, and a stronger, but not totalitarian, state.

Some of these young Turks held, or were promoted to hold, top public positions in the wartime administrations of the occupied territories. As public servants and employees of the state, they were emboldened in very dark times for their countries by visions of a better future, which gave a positively enhancing moral and institutional role to the state in the forging of a new economy and society. With the removal of the personnel and the systems of democratic parliamentary politics, which had arguably been the obstacles to reform in the 1930s, they had before them a realistic opportunity to realize the modernizing changes they had discussed and formulated for themselves before the war. These highly trained, professional and expert officials and managers will feature throughout the story of wartime administrative and economic collaboration. If not yet the obvious protagonists, they were certainly in 1940 the active background supporters of the moves made in the occupied territories of Northern and Western Europe towards a more authoritarian order following defeat and occupation.

Defeat and occupation in 1940 made the themes and motifs of the often subterranean critique of democracy and capitalism in the 1930s immediately and concretely relevant, and matters of supreme national importance. The *tabula rasa* created by conquest and occupation was a frightening and bewildering prospect. But it also gave life and opportunity to those harbouring ideas for, or realizing the need for, profound change in the ways they were governed, and in how the economy and society were organized.

Authoritarian collaboration did not emerge in Denmark in 1940, because the discrediting of the pre-war political and economic systems was not as evident as elsewhere. The democratically elected government chose to collaborate with the Germans from the start, and did so on the understanding that existing institutions would not need to change. However, given the circumstances, an authoritarian internal realignment of Danish wartime politics did occur in the course of the German occupation. In part, this was due to wartime government regulation of the economy, which, as elsewhere, brought out the corporatist tendencies of some businessmen who looked to the Portuguese dictator Antonio de Oliviera Salazar rather than Hitler as the bearer of a new social and economic order. A lobby group of conservative nationalist business leaders called on the Danish King, Christian X, to get rid of the socialist and left liberal ministers in the coalition government, and appoint non-political experts in their place. The government reshuffle of July 1940 probably did not owe everything to these back-room pressures. But three non-party men entered the government then, and two of them were businessmen, both employers in the cement industry, which was already beginning to profit from a German military construction boom in the newly occupied country. Later on, the outcome of a serious crisis in relations between the Danish and German governments in November 1942 was the appointment as Prime Minister of the 'German' preference, Erik Scavenius. He was a career diplomat, who, as Foreign Minister since July

1940, had conducted relations with Germany and took a proactive, or pre-emptive view of collaboration. He felt, rather against the majority view in the cabinet at the time, that, if you could anticipate German concerns and accommodate them even before they were made, then you avoided any German bullying or pressure at a later stage and so better protected Danish independence and sovereignty. The risk, self-evidently, was that you undermined that independence even as you sought to defend it by giving the Germans what they wanted in advance. Even before Scavenius's promotion, the Danish government had, under German pressure, limited the pluralism of a fully democratic polity by introducing press censorship, taking action to suppress anti-German activity and propaganda, banning the communist party, a legal party in the Danish system, and interning communists, including elected parliamentary deputies.

Authoritarian collaboration existed in Norway, however, and revealed itself during the prolonged interregnum of April to September 1940. The Reich Commissioner, Terboven, tried to work through a provisional administrative council cobbled together, with judicial endorsement, by some ministerial officials and parliamentary deputies in Oslo, to ensure some continuity of administration in the areas of the country coming under occupation as the German invasion proceeded. The council had some pretensions to become, with German blessing, a more permanent apolitical national administration, capable of taking over from the king and his government. It was clearly open to and was involved in Terboven's negotiations with remaining figures of the Norwegian establishment, mediated by a prominent member of that establishment, the country's most important legal officer, the President of the Supreme Court.

Terboven apparently wanted to get the administrative council to transform itself, legitimately, through approval by the Norwegian parliament, into a nominated State Council with both legislative and executive powers. This would clearly mark the end of the monarchy and of the democratic parliamentary system in Norway. It was notable that Terboven was quite prepared to exclude Quisling from these arrangements. Indeed, he used his possible exclusion as a negotiating tool, or threat, in order to persuade his establishment contacts of the sincerity of his attempt to arrive at a conservative authoritarian, rather than Nazi, solution to the problem of who would administer the country under German occupation.

What transpired in Norway was similar to developments elsewhere in the defeated and occupied countries of Western Europe. The outcome was, however, very different in Norway. The rump parliament eventually rejected Terboven's State Council proposal, undoubtedly stiffened by the king's implacable defence of his own constitutional position during and after the German invasion. From London, he broadcast to the Norwegian people, making clear his commitment to the country's democratic constitution, and to the parliamentary mandate of April 1940 giving him and his government the full powers, which Terboven was now claiming for his State Council. The king played his hand brilliantly; and Quisling managed to reinsert himself into the game, now that other avenues were being closed off. A furious, exasperated, and impotent Terboven abandoned his preference for an authoritarian Norwegian regime, and, *faute de mieux*, went for the Nazi option.

The phase of authoritarian collaboration found its fullest expression in occupied France, Belgium, and the Netherlands, rather than occupied Denmark and Norway. After the German occupation of Paris, the final government of the French Third Republic was entrusted to Marshal Philippe Pétain, the octogenarian First World War military hero of the battle of Verdun in 1916, who had been brought into the government as Deputy Prime Minister a month earlier. His task was to negotiate an armistice with Germany, which led to the partial German occupation of the country, leaving the French government nominally sovereign in all of France, but effectively so only in the unoccupied southern zone. The armistice presaged the end of the Third Republic. In July 1940, the National Assembly, now located in Bordeaux, voted by a large majority for a government motion that gave Pétain full powers to draft a new constitution. Pétain became 'head of state' with the authority to exercise all executive and legislative powers without the need to consult parliament, except for the declaration of war.

This was not a coup, nor was it a provisional government. The Vichy government was legitimate, the result of the legal self-dissolution of the Third Republic's parliamentary democracy, whatever was said to the contrary by another less-well-known military man, Charles de Gaulle, the self-styled leader of the 'Free French' in exile in London. Persuading the French parliament to abolish itself was down to one of the Third Republic's quintessential politicians, Pierre Laval. Originally a socialist, Laval had moved to the classic centre ground of Republican politics, and was Foreign Minister five times and Prime Minister four times in the 1930s. Always a pacifist and anti-communist, he was, by extension, consistently Europeanist and supported Franco-German reconciliation and appeasement of the fascist powers. Out of office from 1936, and bitter about it, Laval had also rethought his position on Republican democracy, along with other politicians in France and the Low Countries. As Deputy Prime Minister in July 1940, this was how he induced the turkeys of the French parliament to vote for Christmas: 'since parliamentary democracy wished to enter into a struggle with Nazism and Fascism, and since it has lost that struggle, it must disappear. A new regime—one that is bold, authoritarian, social and national—must take its place.'[7]

The Vichy regime, and the so-called National Revolution that it committed itself to implement, were definitely not fascist. But Vichy was xenophobic, nationalistic, racist, clerical, corporatist, and authoritarian, aiming to bring about the political and moral regeneration of the country on the basis of traditional national values. Its appeal and relevance in 1940 were its explicit systemic repudiation of the Third Republic, condemned as the embodiment and cause of national decline, consummated in defeat by Nazi Germany. In particular, the National Revolution was sweet political revenge on the France of the Popular Front governments of 1936–8, run by socialists led by a Jew, anti-clerical Republicans, and communists, who were not in government but gave it parliamentary support. All the political flotsam of the 1930s, the political opponents of the Popular Front, and the critics of parliamentary democracy as a system, both on the right and on the non-communist left, rallied to Vichy and served in it. Some fascists, or ex-fascists, notably belonging or once belonging to the *Parti Populaire Français* (PPF (French Popular Party)), found a place in Vichy, especially in Darlan's government. The fascist presence increased in the final months of Vichy's existence. But many of them sulked in Paris, from where they criticized Vichy for not being fascist at all or not being fascist enough in newspapers, magazines, and movements funded by various German agencies. If these fascists and fellow-travelling collaborationists had any use for the Germans at all, it was to pose as a standing threat to Vichy: if you do not collaborate as we wish, then we have Frenchmen who will. In the event, it was a threat that was not carried out until 1944.

The famous, or notorious, photograph of Pétain's handshake with Hitler (see Illustration 3) after their meeting at Montoire on 24 October 1940 was intended to symbolize a new collaborating relationship between France and Germany. It was, of course, used to discredit Pétain and the Vichy regime during and after the war. The symbolism was important, but there was far more to Montoire than a photo opportunity. For one thing, as a Vichy minister, Yves Bouthillier, artfully reminded everybody, there were two

Illustration 3. Pétain commits Vichy France to 'the path of collaboration' after this handshake and meeting with Hitler at Montoire in October 1940.

Montoires, not one.[8] Hitler also met Laval, Vichy's Prime Minister, on 22 October, before travelling to Hendaye, near the Franco–Spanish border, for largely fruitless talks with the Spanish dictator, Francisco Franco. Laval's was arguably the more significant meeting in terms of relations between Vichy France and Nazi Germany.

Both sides wanted and needed to meet. Hitler hoped to involve both France and Spain in the Axis war on Britain. Pétain was chafing after four months of Germany's rigorous application of the terms of the armistice, and was keen to assert France's standing as a nominally independent state, which would in some sense be confirmed by a leader-to-leader meeting.

From other people's reports of the meetings, largely based on what Pétain and Laval said to them, there was a discernible difference in approach between the two men. The difference lay, perhaps, in their respective backgrounds. As a military man who had fought the Germans in two wars, Pétain had to respect German military dominance in Western Europe, and deal with its consequences for the status of France. But respect did not mean that Pétain had to like or trust the Germans after an age of Franco–German hostility. According to Bouthillier, Pétain said that he merely acquiesced in collaboration with the Germans, which he defined rather prosaically as having 'some tasks in common'.[9] Henri du Moulin de Labarthète was even closer to Pétain as the head of his civilian secretariat, and he reported that Pétain envisaged collaboration with the Germans as a matter of neighbourly co-habitation, a way of reaching a *modus vivendi*.[10] It was, in other words, a route to a getting-on that implied no real intimacy or meeting of minds.

Pétain apparently said very little during his meeting with Hitler, which was perhaps inevitable, given Hitler's verbosity and Pétain's deliberately cultivated reticence. He was understandably unwilling to make any promises to Hitler. But, according to Paul Schmidt, Hitler's interpreter at the meeting, Pétain even held back from the usual compliments and pleasantries you might expect to be exchanged at such a first-time meeting between leaders. Pétain's demeanour would suggest that he was quite happy to get Hitler talking, partly because this allowed him to stay non-committally silent, partly because the point of the meeting, for him, was to discover what Hitler's intentions were, and what threats or opportunities these represented to Vichy France. Schmidt thought that Pétain's reserve and silent obduracy had won out against Hitler's habitual garrulousness and neediness, in pursuit of French help in the war on Britain.[11]

Something of Pétain's caution and nuance was detectable in his momentous radio broadcast to the French people about the Montoire meeting, on 31 October 1940. But it was doubtful whether these qualifications would necessarily have been picked up by his audience, who listened to their leader asserting that France had chosen to engage in a policy of open and voluntary collaboration with the enemy power occupying the best half of the country. 'It is', declared Pétain, 'with honour, and in order to maintain French unity—a unity of ten centuries standing—in the framework of the constructive development of the European New Order, that I enter today the path of collaboration'. If the armistice required France to collaborate with Germany, then Montoire transformed an obligation into an offer. In return for such collaboration, Pétain said that he expected to be able to relieve the country's sufferings—that is, to soften the sharp edges of the armistice agreement. Then came the cautious disengagement from something he had just promoted as his government's policy: 'the modalities of collaboration' are yet to be determined.[12] In private, Pétain said that these would be studied 'at leisure',[13] as if the Germans would wait on the implementation of his commitment to the principle of voluntary collaboration.

Laval clearly regarded himself as a politician and statesman of class and experience, both his strength and his flaw. Throughout his political career, he continued to believe in his own powers of persuasion, and was genuinely convinced that, in a personal, face-to-face meeting, he could secure what he wanted, and gain his audience's approval and endorsement of what he wanted. The Hoover collection of the highly selective wartime memories of French officials are full of admiring appraisals of Laval's personal techniques of what today we would call man management.

Who would not be anxious about meeting Hitler for the first time, or, indeed, any time? On learning in the car that he was being driven to meet Hitler, Laval was reputed to have said, 'merde alors!'[14] The rather inadequate translation of these words as 'Oh, shit!' does not really convey the resignation, trepidation, and also wonder and admiration of the French phrase. Laval was travelling in fear, but also in anticipation. Laval was also, clearly, to some extent susceptible to what Alan Clark said of the charismatic appeal of power personified in relation to his boss, the one-time British Prime Minister, Margaret Thatcher, 'Führer Kontakt'.[15] Laval informed Bouthillier after his meeting with Hitler that 'my impression is a good one. Hitler is a really great man who knows what he's doing and where he's going. He is confident of victory...', and was someone who believed himself to be 'marked by destiny'.[16] There is an even-ness, a matter of factness, even an element of insouciance, to Laval's remarks. These were terms that Laval applied to himself; the meeting, to him, was one between national leaders who both had a mission, and a vision. Bouthillier, an austere career financial official turned Vichy government minister who disliked Laval for his Republican politician's ways and supported his sacking in late 1940, again unsympathetically recorded for post-war posterity Laval's sense of importance and indispensability. 'I know Stalin', he reported Laval as saying after Montoire, 'I know Mussolini, I know Hitler. Could any other Frenchman, faced by them, defend France better than me?'[17] Laval's vision was consistently held and pursued, from his support for the then Foreign Minister Aristide Briand's imaginative plans for a form of European integration in the late 1920s, to his backing for 'appeasement' in the late 1930s, and now with collaboration in 1940. To Laval, the only prospect for a secure and lasting European peace rested on Franco-German reconciliation. This is not to be sniffed at. The process of post-war West European integration was embarked on as a way of absorbing permanently the long-standing hostility between France and Germany, and arguably, was the EEC's signal and lasting achievement.

The only problem was that, in 1940, it was Nazi Germany with which Laval was expecting to do a deal.

This clearly did not intimidate Laval. After meeting Hitler, he was confident that he had divined what Hitler wanted, and how Hitler expected collaboration between the two countries to proceed. He told du Moulin de Labarthète that 'Hitler wants to provide France with a chance to escape from her defeat',[18] which might appear a staggering judgement until you realize that this Lavalian gloss on his meeting with Hitler was written into the secret Montoire protocol, a record of the Hitler–Pétain meeting. Apparently, Hitler 'expressed the will to guarantee to France the place that is due to it in a newly-constituted Europe, and to the French people the right to participate in the cooperation of European peoples so indispensable for the future'.[19]

Whatever you might feel about hope replacing reality here, Laval carried his perspicacity further. Hitler's reply to Laval's generic offer of Franco-German reconciliation in return for France gaining an 'honourable peace' was to say that France's attitude would be decisive in kickstarting such a process.[20] In other words, this was an opportunity for France to demonstrate France's value to Germany and the New Order. Laval claimed that, in both his own meeting and that with Pétain, Hitler had indicated that collaborating within the framework of the New Order would have a return for France in the easing of the terms and application of the armistice, that French concessions and guarantees to Nazi Germany would be paid for in a relaxation of the burdens of occupation. Hitler's negotiating position was, apparently, donnant–donnant![21] That meant 'give and take', certainly France 'giving' and Germany 'taking', reflecting the power imbalance between the two countries, but not an empty exchange, nevertheless. There would definitely be real somethings being exchanged for real somethings, as long as France made the initial cash-down payment to initiate the exchange. This was risky, because the French concession would be made in return for a promise of German action in the future. The weaker partner had to commit itself to do something, and then do it, in the expectation that the stronger partner would reciprocate with a compensating concession, and also do it. But, in the circumstances, the risk of Nazi Germany reneging on its promises, or not making concessions in return for actual French initiatives that were already being carried out, appeared to be within Laval's self-perception of his political nouse and negotiating skills. And, anyway, nothing ventured, nothing gained.

The net outcome of the two Montoire meetings was to make Laval into an enthusiastic, pro-active collaborator of Nazi Germany, while confirming Pétain as a cautious, rather more passive collaborator of Nazi Germany. While the French government remained open to collaboration, it was scarcely a wonder that the Germans practically froze their relations with Vichy France for a period after Pétain's dismissal of Laval as Prime Minister in December 1940, precipitated by the latter's willingness to offer a greater degree of military collaboration in the war against Britain. The Germans agitated for Laval's return to office, finally realized in April 1942.

The impact of Belgium's military defeat in May 1940 was exacerbated by a huge, unseemly row between the king, who was head of state and nominal commander-in-chief of the armed forces, and the country's coalition government. This did not occur in Norway or the Netherlands, where monarchs and governments departed together into exile in order to continue the war against Nazi Germany. The dispute served to deepen popular disaffection with Belgium's parliamentary system. It cast a very long shadow over the period of the occupation, and, indeed, post-war recovery, since liberation required the country to confront and resolve as best it could the position of the monarchy in Belgian public life, as divisive an issue in 1945 as was in 1940. Whatever popular goodwill the king accrued as a result of staying on in 1940, was largely dissipated by the realization that the king intended to collaborate with the occupier.

The ostensible cause of the row was whether to continue the war or not. This was real enough, but it soon became clear that what was at stake was how the country was to be governed during the German occupation, and, even more important, who was the legitimate authority in the country, the king or the elected government. This constitutional conflict confused the lines of responsibility of Belgium's civil servants, who were expected by all sides, the Germans, the government-in-exile, and the king, to continue to administer the country under occupation.

The king had consulted De Man before the outbreak of war over the possibility of avoiding war through further 'appeasement' of Nazi Germany. He was being closely advised by De Man throughout the developing crisis in relations between king and government. You could say that De Man had been consciously preparing himself for such a role, and for the realization of an outcome that was intended to be pretty close to what happened in France, later. The hope was for an armistice to suspend military hostilities, negotiated by a new royal government that, like the Vichy regime, would become the legitimate, and collaborating, Belgian authority under German occupation.

In the 'phoney war' period between the outbreak of war and the actual German invasion, De Man used a forum provided for him by a circle of pro-German Belgian figures in Brussels, to publicize his views on a compromise peace with Nazi Germany. This would, according to De Man, enable a neutral free-standing Belgium to remain independent in a German-dominated Europe and equip the country with a new authoritarian and corporatist royal government capable of governing in such circumstances. His programme was very close to one put forward in the late 1930s by a Belgian think tank, the Study Centre for Reform of the State, which brought together a select group of prominent businessmen, conservative politicians, officials, university professors, and jurists. The group consciously excluded left-leaning and socialist thinkers like De Man, but there was a natural alignment between them in the circumstances of 1940. De Man pursued this line consistently through the invasion and early occupation. As president of the Belgian socialist party, he issued a manifesto in July 1940, which envisaged 'the Belgian people united in its fidelity to the king', who had, after all, not followed the government into exile, but remained to share and mitigate the sufferings of his people. The manifesto also attributed the military victory of the German army to its superior sense of national and social unity and respect for authority. These attributes were, for De Man, a good enough reason to abandon parliamentary democracy for a Nazi-lite version of a corporatist 'socialism', a 'community of labour' to be realized through new agencies such as his own recently formed Union of Manual and Intellectual Workers.[22]

De Man's programme for change struck a chord with other influential corporatist apologists in what was a summer of glorious possibilities for authoritarian collaboration. René Goris, one of the leaders of the Flemish Catholic employers' association, published a corporatist 'manifesto' in September that was practically a verbatim repeat of the association's call in the early 1930s for a system of single, compulsory employer and labour organizations, the latter to be enfeebled by a ban on the right to strike. The affinity of De Man's and authoritarian Catholic ideas to Vichy's National Revolution is clear. De Man intended to regenerate the country from within as well as position Belgium for its survival as a state in a Nazi European New Order, by installing an authoritarian government that would collaborate with the Germans.

On 25 May 1940, three days before the Belgian surrender to Germany, the king met a group of government ministers, who clearly expected the king to join the government in exile and continue the war on the side of the Western Allies. But the king refused to do so. Since the government had effectively rejected his earlier proposal that it stayed on in Belgium, he insisted that the government offer its collective resignation so that he could form his own government to arrange an armistice with the Germans. The Belgian cabinet, then located in Paris, recognized this demand for what it was, a royal coup to set up a rival government that would collaborate with the Germans in occupied Belgium. A very public formal rupture occurred. Chased by the German invasion of France to Limoges, in central southern France, a group of parliamentary deputies, on 31 May 1940, endorsed the government's decision to continue the war, and refused to approve any new royal government to end the war.

This was a constitutional crisis, and left public officials in Belgium unsure of who their legitimate masters were, and, as we shall see, of the extent of the powers vested in them during the occupation—and legitimacy was a really important matter for civil servants required to exercise the executive powers of government. The constitutional stand-off, or stalemate, between the king and the government-in-exile continued for much of the war. But it ceased to have much of an impact on how things went under German occupation after the autumn of 1940. The king, as a self-declared POW, was holed up in his royal palace in Lokeren by the Germans, who treated him as an unwelcome guest in his own country whose presence was tolerable only if the king said and did nothing.

What settled things down, constitutionally, was the king's inability, despite De Man's advice and promptings, to form a government of his own that would be recognized as a legitimate authority by the Germans, let alone his people. It was interesting that our partial observer of the Belgian scene, Paul Struye, sympathized, as did most Belgians, with the king's decision to stay in Belgium, but did not share De Man's hopes that the king should put together a new government.[23] The point where both the king and the Belgian people realized that the king's presence could do nothing to affect Belgium's situation as an occupied country came when Leopold held his first and last meeting with Hitler at Berchtesgaden in November 1940.

Leopold rather forlornly hoped that a personal dialogue with Hitler would be Belgium's equivalent of the meeting at Montoire in October, which had concluded with Pétain's formal commitment of the Vichy government to a policy of collaboration with the Germans. No meeting with Hitler was exactly a dialogue, and Hitler remained true to the instructions he had given to the German military administration of occupied Belgium in July 1940: that the king should not be allowed to engage in any political activity. For Hitler, the king's presence in Belgium was a nuisance. Although Hitler had not yet decided on Belgium's eventual place in the New Order, if indeed it would have one, the king's staying on raised yet another obstacle and complication to making those decisions. To put it brutally, Hitler did not want or expect the king's collaboration, and was certainly not about to concede anything to a figurehead of Belgian national independence whom he wanted out of the way. Leopold, whenever he could get a word in, simply drew a blank on his requests for an easing of occupation, an end to the deliberately discriminatory German repatriation of Flemish before Walloon POWs, and better food provision for the Belgian population. In the end, it was Hitler who rejected the offer of authoritarian collaboration in Belgium. One suspects, however, in light of the initial German manœuvres in other occupied countries, that, if such collaboration had not been channelled through the person of the king, the reception might have been different. De Man was told to shut up by the Germans in early 1941, and went to occupied Paris, where he moved in similar pro-German circles to the ones he frequented in Brussels, but had no further influence on events in Belgium.

In the interwar period, the Dutch political system had evolved in a way that to its exponents provided stability by successfully accommodating the divisions in Dutch society, and to its critics simply deepened those divisions and undermined any sense of national unity. Political parties in the Netherlands formed around religious denomination, and its absence. Three confessional parties, two Protestant and one Catholic, represented religious communities or 'pillars', which were kept together by separate networks of civil society organizations, from unions to schools, sports clubs, and professional associations. Cooperation between the 'pillars' occurred at the national political level, where coalition governments dominated by the confessional parties packaged policies serving the interests of each 'pillar'. The alternative secular 'pillar' to the liberal party, the socialist party, was politically excluded until 1939, when it entered a coalition government for the first time. The only challenge to this rather cosy 'pillarized' political life came from the Dutch Nazi Party, the NSB, which claimed to be a national and nationalist party representing all Dutch people, but was unable to dent the 'pillars' to any significant extent.

Political leaders of the 'pillars' were inadvertently self-critical in 1940, when defeat and occupation put an end to and discredited this particular version of parliamentary democracy. Hendrik Colijn was leader of the conservative orthodox Calvinist Anti-Revolutionary Party, and five times Prime Minister in the interwar period. He now attacked the queen and her government for their 'disgraceful flight',[24] made clear to the Reich Commissioner, Seyss-Inquart, his willingness to cooperate with the German occupier, and was the driving force behind the formation of a committee of leaders of the largest parties in July 1940. The intention was to create a new movement, a 'National Front', which accepted the reality of a German-dominated Europe and would represent the Dutch people in its relations with the occupier.

Very significantly, the actual initiative to form a new national movement came, not from the old political parties, but from outside those parties, and without their involvement. The *Nederlandse Unie* (*NU* (United Netherlands)) was set up in late July 1940. Its founders and leaders included a top official in the Education, Science, and Culture ministry, an ex-royal commissioner or governor of the Dutch province of Groningen, a university academic who worked for the government on employment matters, and the police chief of the major industrial port city of Rotterdam. These were conservative establishment but non-party figures, who were drawn from an extra- and anti-parliamentary movement called *Nederlandse Gemeenschap* (*NG* (Netherlands Community)), formed in January 1939 in reaction to what the

Illustration 4. Orderly queues of Dutch people gathering for the first public meeting of the *Nederlandse Unie* at The Hague, August 1940.

group saw as the party political induced factionalism and division of the Netherlands in the 1930s.

The NU manifesto and programme were an understandably vague and non-specific version of the NG's agenda, carefully worded and adapted to the current circumstances of German occupation. They had, in fact, been submitted to and approved by the Reich Commissariat. There was a promise of loyal cooperation with the German occupiers. At German insistence, the programme left unsaid any concerns about national independence and the retention of the monarchy, an absence of comment that could be construed as a delegitimation of the monarchy, but was probably more a concession to ensure publication. The manifesto offered instead a 'new Dutch sense of solidarity... respecting traditional spiritual freedom and tolerance', and the programme a working towards 'the preservation and strengthening of father-land and people's community'. The German Nazis used similar terms, and, for them, 'fatherland' had Germanic as well as national connotations. 'An organic construction of the Dutch commonwealth under strong and reso-lute leadership'[25] amounted to a conservative nationalist, authoritarian, and corporatist alternative both to the fascism of the NSB and a now defunct democratic parliamentary system.

These developments, both Colijn's National Front committee and the NU, occurred with the knowledge, supervision, encouragement, and endorsement of Seyss-Inquart and his political staff in the Reich Commissariat. Again, there was a natural match between occupier and occupied, between Seyss-Inquart's search for a suitable Dutch vehicle for the bottom-up, 'voluntary' self-Nazification of the Netherlands, and the calls in the country for a more authoritarian system of rule. Behind this lay a broader concern of the Dutch people and its leaders to preserve and protect some semblance of Dutch identity and values in a situation that put at risk the very existence of the Dutch nation and state. Seyss-Inquart was only too pleased to enable the growth and development of a movement that represented a clean break with the old parliamentary parties, and sidelined the NSB, the evident unpopularity of which in the Netherlands made it a risky and unreliable accomplice in any process of self-Nazification. At its extraordinary peak in late 1940, the NU had about 800,000 members, this in a country of a total population of about nine million; about one in six of the country's adult population had joined the movement in a matter of a few months. It seemed that the NU recruited people from across and outside the 'pillars', to a lesser extent from the Protestant 'pillar'.

After *NU*'s foundation, a strange kind of courtship dance occurred, as the Reich Commissariat probed and tested out the movement's suitability for the task of Dutch self-Nazification from below, and the *NU* sought to preserve an authoritarian and national Dutch presence in the Nazi New Order. Some of the tests were met, just. The *NU* was basically monarchist and could not really reject such an important and popular national institution if it was to be a national movement. This was a real sticking point for the Germans, who at least obtained the exclusion of any specific approval of the monarchy in the *NU* programme.

The *NU* came out publicly against any popular resistance to the occupation, though this stance was compromised and strained by the harsh German repression of the February 1941 strikes against the early anti-Jewish measures carried out in the Netherlands. In May 1941, the *NU* eventually excluded Jews from membership, and expelled existing Jewish members in November.

Fritz Schmidt, head of the department of Special (that is, political) Affairs in the Reich Secretariat, to whom Seyss-Inquart delegated relations with the *NU*, was a member and leader of the German Nazi Party and effectively their representative in the occupied Netherlands. He preferred a merger between the *NU* and the *NSB*, a smart way of subsuming the latter's unpopularity into the former's popularity, providing the *NSB* with a ready-made mass movement, and offering a secure way of infiltrating and Nazifying the *NU*. But the *NU* evidently saw itself as a Dutch national movement, which pre-empted the need for the *NSB*, and much of its popular appeal lay in the fact that it was not the *NSB*. So Schmidt's cleverness was bound to be suspect to the *NU*'s leadership. Schmidt changed his mind too, as time went on, since the *NU* membership grew so rapidly that it threatened to become a kind of Frankenstein monster, devouring the *NSB* rather than being taken over by it.

The turning point came with the German invasion of the USSR, accompanied by Seyss-Inquart's call for the Dutch to 'look to the East'[26] and rally to the European anti-Bolshevik crusade, which took the *NU* into areas of policy that were beyond its own remit. The *NU*'s careful statement in early July 1941 confirmed the Dutch people's backing for the struggle against communism. But it could not adhere to the Anti-Comintern Pact and make any decision on declaring war on the Soviet Union, because it was not a government. Such policy decisions could 'only be made in complete freedom and by our own government',[27] and that government-in-exile was, of course, still at war with Nazi Germany, and, therefore, an ally of the USSR. This was a studied, almost technical response, and implicitly referred to international law, which permitted only a legitimate government to make decisions on war and peace.

It is difficult to work out whether the *NU* was, in effect, challenging the Germans to make it their collaborating government, or was demonstrating its ultimate loyalty to the still legitimate government-in-exile. It seems more likely that the *NU* was, as usual, in defensive mode, walking the tightrope of relations with the Reich Commissariat, saying enough to please, or not offend, the Germans, while seeking to avoid the political over-commitment that would damage its standing with the Dutch people.

The *NU*'s statement was not sufficient for the Germans, exposing the probably insuperable problems arising from collaboration with them, or, at least, with a thoroughly Nazi Reich Commissariat. The Nazis were only really interested in cooperation on their terms, and, by nature, were not content

Illustration 5. A demonstration of the gulf between collaboration and collaborationism: a uniformed member of the Dutch fascist movement, the *NSB*, stands provocatively in front of premises of the *Nederlandse Unie*, most likely prior to its ransacking.

with middle-ground compromises, only either/or positions; ultimately, they would collaborate only with those who gave them all of what they wanted. The *NU* certainly failed to pass this test and was dissolved, as a result, in December 1941. The day after, Seyss-Inquart recognized the *NSB* as the only legal party in the occupied Netherlands. From this position of monopoly, it was expected to bring about the Nazification of the Dutch people, with the backing of the power, resources, and direction of the Reich Commissariat. Later on, in October 1942, Seyss-Inquart, on Schmidt's instigation, petitioned Hitler to make Anton Mussert, the *NSB* leader, Prime Minister of a Dutch fascist government. Hitler, as always distrustful of the capacity of national fascist leaders to deliver what the Germans wanted, demurred in December, but allowed Mussert to call himself *Führer* of the Dutch people, and set up a kind of consultative shadow government to advise the Reich Commissioner. While never enjoying the wide range of powers exercised by Quisling in Norway, Mussert nominally presided over the intended Nazi realignment of Dutch society, to be realized through the steady appointment of *NSB* men to public positions and the spread of monopolistic and Nazified professional and occupational associations.

So, by late 1941, Seyss-Inquart had reached the same position that Terboven had in September 1940, banking on the local Nazi party. To put it from another perspective, if the point of the *NU* was to see off the *NSB*, then its only palpable achievement was to delay its rival's political primacy in the Netherlands by about eighteen months, which was something, or nothing. The prevention of worse, even if only temporarily, was a common self-justification of collaboration at the time, and retrospectively. It would be a harsh retrospective judgement to say that the fate of the *NU* showed that collaboration had 'failed'.

The official post-war inquiry into the occupation naturally enough investigated the *NU*, and concluded that it was a 'resisting' organization, presumably based on the fact of its dissolution by the Germans, and the resistance activity of some *NU* leaders and local groups after the *NU*'s dissolution. The verdict fitted the context of liberation, but is plainly ridiculous in the light of its own context of 1940–1. The *NU* was a collaborating organization, if only because it accepted and dealt with the consequences of defeat and occupation, explicitly ruled out any resistance to the Germans, and never attempted to reverse that defeat and occupation. Everything that happened in the occupied territories needed the explicit approval and consent of the occupiers. This was why the top ministerial officials told the

NU leaders, when approached, that the first step was to contact Seyss-Inquart. Only collaborating organizations could possibly survive, let alone flourish, under the conditions of German occupation. Collaboration was the minimum price to pay for being allowed to exist, and the leaders of the *NU* knew and recognized this.

The *NU* was an extraordinary wartime phenomenon. But it is less remarkable when one understands its place in the wider setting of the initial period of German occupation of West European countries. In 1940, what connected the Vichy regime in France, King Leopold and De Man in Belgium, the President of the High Court in Norway, the *NU* in the Netherlands, and even the Danish government, was the common acceptance of defeat and occupation as being definitive, and, by extension, the shared recognition that Nazi Germany would dominate Europe now and into the future. Accepting and recognizing Nazi hegemony made cooperating with the Germans a matter of unavoidable necessity, made more palatable by the glimmer of opportunity. There was also a common fear that defeat and occupation could well entail the disappearance by elimination of national states in a Nazi European New Order, and, whatever happened territorially, the eventual Nazification of their countries. The people and movements behind the authoritarian collaboration of 1940–1 were articulating a defensive response to that prospect, hoping to stave off both the destruction of national states and internal fascist governments that would then be the instruments of Nazification. In each of the occupied North and West European countries, with the exception of Denmark, defeat and occupation provided the occasion for some critics of interwar democracy to rebuild and regenerate their countries on the ruins of failed and discredited parliamentary systems. The evidence suggests that the Germans had a mixed response to these initiatives for national reform. They did not really interest themselves in the content of Vichy's National Revolution, but were certainly very interested in the programme and outlook of the *NU*. This, in itself, tells us something about how the Nazis assessed the likely or possible places of France and the Netherlands in the New Order. But whatever they thought of them, these exercises in national renewal depended on at least German tolerance and approval, and, as a consequence, required collaboration with the occupier.

It is still possible to say that, uniquely in France, there was a major reshaping of the country's political system as a consequence of military defeat, and that it took place under conditions of occupation. But the equivalents of Vichy's

National Revolution were seriously envisaged in Belgium, the Netherlands, and Norway, as well, and with the same rationale. It was felt that their countries' future in a German-dominated Europe depended on the restructuring of government in an authoritarian direction; not totalitarian, because that would remove what was 'national' about their reforming intentions. A reshaped polity was regarded as the best way of securing a place for their country in the New Order. And, as even the odd one out, the Danish government, discovered, to continue to collaborate with the Germans in Denmark required a certain authoritarian realignment of Danish politics and policies.

There is one further point to make about the authoritarian drift in the occupied territories in 1940. Each German occupation authority, whether military or more self-consciously Nazi, applied at some stage of the occupation the Nazi 'leader principle' to existing indigenous administrations. It also informed the running of any new organizations and agencies that were set up under the occupation, whether established by the Germans themselves or at their behest, by the national and local administrative bodies of the occupied territories.

Much of the force and dynamism of the German Nazi Party before it came to power in 1933 derived from the practice, which became a principle, of charismatic leadership. Leaders were not so much appointed from above as self-selecting: leaders by dint of their demonstrating by doing and achieving that they had leadership qualities and a hold over their followers, allied to an unstoppable sense of mission. The 'leader principle' was then applied to German institutions after 1933, and clearly it could operate only by appointment. But the point was to impart the same mentality of validating one's position of leadership by performance on the job. The dynamism inherent in the Nazi system was retained, because the appointees had to justify and enhance their status as leaders by taking the initiative and being effective and successful in what they did, often in competition with other leaders heading organizations operating in the same sphere of activity.

The Nazis expected that the 'leader principle' would have the same energizing effects on the performance levels of national administrations in the occupied territories. They also used it as a weapon to 'Nazify' what remained of the popular and collegial basis of local administration. The Dutch themselves were already halfway there in applying the 'leader principle', since the over 900 mayors were the kingpins of municipal affairs, appointed not elected in order to ensure that they represented the centre in the periphery and hence bridged national and local government. They already headed the local administrations and presided over a body of elected councillors. Seyss-Inquart's application of the 'leader principle' to Dutch local government from August 1941 completed the centralization of local power. It involved the elimination of municipal councils where a combination of mayor and councillors ran local affairs, and the installation of a single figure as 'leader', the mayor, now responsible to the Reich Commissioner, not the people or the crown. The intention was to then to appoint as mayors men from the *NSB*, or other identifiably pro-German officials. The application of the 'leader principle' was clearly ideological; it was the extension of Nazi ideas and practice to the occupied territories. But it was also what the occupiers regarded as the optimum way of getting the most out of indigenous administrations, and of supervising and checking on the performance of local officials. *One* man was to be responsible and accountable for the activity of the administrative agency or unit he headed. It was seen as the most effective way of ensuring that the occupiers' orders and directives were carried out rapidly and efficiently. You only had to harangue one man, for him to harangue his subordinates so that the job was done.

It became very noticeable that the German occupation authorities often went directly to one official on the ground for a decision, or a chat. These meetings were not necessarily confrontations, at least in the early stages of occupation, and were routine. Much of the contact was, after all, between one German career official and his counterpart, another local career official, who spoke the same executive language. It was certainly much more confrontational when national officials faced the ideological bureaucrats of specifically Nazi agencies, such as the *SS* or Sauckel's labour organization, who were driven with a zeal to carry out their Hitler mandates, which career officials found difficult to cope with or resist.

The German habit of picking out the local officials to work on in order to get things done was a matter of some sensitivity in all occupied territories, since it had the potential for disrupting the usual chains of command within the national and local administrations. This was particularly felt in France, where, say, the prefects' superiors in the Interior Ministry were very concerned to affirm the sovereignty of the Vichy government, practically its *raison d'être*.

But it mattered elsewhere, as well. The Dutch Secretary General at the Interior Ministry, our man Frederiks, had been looking after local government affairs for a decade by 1940, and in that capacity had been in regular contact with mayors and councils. He formally protested against Seyss-Inquart's implementation of the 'leader principle', and went on giving guidance to mayors and councils, as if the hierarchical link between centre and periphery had not been broken by the German measure. He had a very nuanced position. Some mayors resigned, or wanted to resign, at the Reich Commissioner's attack on local decision-making. Frederiks advised them not to do so, and to remain in post. Why? Self-evidently, to halt or at least slow down the infiltration of local government by *NSB* members, a poor second best to direct German administration; preventing worse was thereby confirmed as one of the major justifications for continuing collaboration. You could say that this worked, to the extent that by the summer of 1944 just over a third of Dutch mayors were *NSB* members, though they administered well over half of the population.

But Frederiks also wanted to get the Germans out into the open, and provide some kind of cover for his collaboration. The 'leader principle' measure clearly breached entrenched practice, undermined the democratic legitimacy of local government, and stepped all over Frederiks's own toes as the official with legal jurisdiction over local administrations. He felt that, if the Reich Commissariat was demonstrably seen to be imposing the measure by insisting on the sacking of mayors, rather than simply accepting their 'voluntary' resignations, then it assumed the formal responsibility for the measure, rather than himself as Secretary General at the Interior. Accepting the measure was then a justifiable retreat in the face of a *force majeure*. It is perhaps difficult to see what else Frederiks might have done. He could argue that he was behaving in the letter and spirit of the 1937 guidelines, which obliged him to protest against the occupier's unnecessary changes to existing regulations and practice, but not to refuse to cooperate in their implementation if required by the occupier to do so.[28] He ruled out his own resignation, even though the threat of it featured in his formal protest against the measure, for the same reason that he recommended his mayors not to resign. He had also avoided a decisive confrontation and break with Seyss-Inquart, which might have induced the Germans to remove him from office, and brought nearer the prospect of an *NSB* member at the Interior or direct German control of the ministry. The price was to reduce still further the room for manœuvre for collaborating officials. He had to accept a measure that was illegal under Dutch law and practice, and confine his efforts to influencing, as best he could, the practical application of the German-inspired measure. This, again, was a decent or a derisory return on collaboration, depending on your perspective, and when you were making the judgement.

The German occupiers were undoubtedly offended by and opposed any attempts by national officials to mute or absorb the impact of the application of the 'leader principle'. In both occupied Belgium and the Netherlands, the secretaries general, the top ministerial civil servants who under occupation ran the government ministries in the absence of elected politicians, re-established collegial links between themselves, forming committees that met regularly to take decisions affecting their own departments and those of their colleagues. This was cabinet government in all but name, and put collective before individual responsibility. The Germans had to put up with it, and find ways around it. They still insisted on dealing directly with individual secretaries general on matters involving the departments they ran, and sometimes got them to act in areas of their specific ministerial competence without consulting or seeking the endorsement of their colleagues on the committee. There were also officials who were more pro-German than their colleagues, and, indeed, whose appointment the Germans had solicited, and these men were usually the conduit for the occupier's viewpoint in committee meetings. One has to say that this arrangement came to suit both the Germans and the committees, as the occupation tightened its grip from 1942. The pro-German secretaries general became intermediaries between the committees and the Germans, carrying the views of each to the other, sometimes working to soften the demands made by the occupiers, sometimes to ensure that German demands were met by the committees.

The routine nature of regular contacts between the occupier and responsible national and local officials provides some sense of the direct pressures exerted by the occupation authorities at all levels on collaborating officials, whatever the nominal margins of autonomy allowed by the occupier to local civil servants. Constant German scrutiny and interference were the norm throughout the occupied territories, with the usual exceptions—Denmark, and for a while, anyway, unoccupied Vichy France. Seyss-Inquart in the occupied Netherlands equipped himself with a relatively well-staffed and ramified secretariat, employing about 1,600 German officials by mid-1941, made up of four separate and specialized departments entrusted with the job of supervising the activity of Dutch officialdom, and, in addition, appointed German special commissioners to monitor and direct the Dutch administration at the provincial and municipal levels. Such a degree of bureaucratic control was impossible and irrelevant in Denmark, reflecting that country's unique status as an occupied territory. What governed the collaboration of the Danish government with the Germans was the diplomatic relations between the two states. A German staff of less than 100 mainly Foreign Ministry officials was sufficient for that task and managing other state-to-state contacts, leaving the Danish administration, public bodies, and judiciary still under the full control of its own government.

Perhaps it would be fairer to say that any direct, unmitigated German pressure would fall on the Danish government, rather than on Danish officials, who would, however, still have to deal with their German counterparts on the intergovernmental working groups set up to handle, say, economic collaboration between the two countries. What differed, then, was the extent and degree of German supervision or guidance, at a relatively high level in the Netherlands and Norway, made more necessary by the Reich Commissioners' task of Nazifying Dutch and Norwegian society from below; and at a relatively low level in Denmark, where no such expectation inspired the work of the German Plenipotentiary in Denmark in the first year or so of occupation. So, with the relative exception of Denmark, the German occupation authorities in all other occupied West and North European territories, whatever their form, exercised a supervisory control over internal administrations. This management, in practice, amounted to local officials having to report back to their German 'controllers', the occupiers making recommendations and giving instructions to officials in leadership positions, extending or refusing their approval of officials' measures and initiatives, and intervening in the appointment, promotion, and removal of officials.

As an authoritarian regime that wanted to strengthen the power of the executive and provide strong government, Vichy, on its own initiative, centralized functions in fewer hands, replaced elected officials by appointed ones, and empowered representatives of state authority in France's considerable periphery, such as the prefects, appointing cross-departmental regional prefects from April 1941. In Vichy's new conceptualization of state authority, the prefect was the epitome of administrative power, which was to be both concentrated and de-centralized. Marcel Peyrouton, Vichy's Interior Minister, was a career official whose own upward progress in the colonial service before the war had been eased by the patronage of Republican politicians. He now condemned the paralysis of state officials because of their 'politicization'. In a circular to prefects in November 1940, he urged them to behave less as functionaries, and more as 'leaders who must know how to command and organise'.[29] A rather more important Interior Minister of the

Vichy regime, Pierre Pucheu, later made explicit the latent totalitarianism of his predecessors' remarks, and, incidentally, Pucheu's own incipient collaborationism. He saw the prefects as the spiritual leaders of their communities, shaping and guiding public opinion.

It was, of course, a moot point as to whether prefects did as they were instructed by these ministers, when the Vichy regime remained authoritarian rather than totalitarian. Nevertheless, the application of the 'leader principle' in the occupied territories certainly corresponded to the authoritarian tendencies emerging not only in France, but throughout the occupied territories in 1940. It also resonated with reforming officials who in the 1930s had wanted to make government and administration more efficient and streamlined. In occupied Belgium, for instance, the Germans' concern to appoint officials to replace elected mayors implemented an idea recommended in a minority report of a government think tank in 1937, which meant, at the very least, that Belgian civil servants would have appreciated the intrinsic value of the German measures to do away with local democracy.

These tendencies, and the Nazi 'leader principle', had a discernible impact on the outlook and conduct of top officials required to collaborate with the Germans during the occupation of their countries. One is stretching a point to say that top officials welcomed occupation because of the enhanced status and powers accorded to them by the 'leader principle' and the authoritarianism of the initial responses to German occupation. But for those elite officials who had in the 1930s circulated among themselves ideas for a more efficient, managerial, technocratic administration of the nation's affairs, accepting and participating in a more authoritarian order of things would have been something of a liberation, rather than a constraint.

Two of France's top officials turned wartime Vichy ministers exemplify attitudes shared with their counterparts now wielding real governmental authority across occupied Western Europe. Both men were graduates of the elite higher education professional training schools that provided the country with its top civil servants, engineers, and industrial managers. Both men claimed at their post-war High Court trials that they were merely 'technicians' managing technical and non-political economic ministries. In reality, they became committed Pétainistes who believed that authoritarian rule would enable France to remake itself after the humiliation of the French Republic in defeat and occupation. Even though they distrusted and despised Laval for being a hangover from a discredited parliamentary regime, they shared his belief in the possibility of Franco-German reconciliation, to be realized through a policy of collaboration with the Germans. Yves Bouthillier, as an Inspector of Finances, the driest and most austere of officials you can imagine, and Vichy's Minister of Finance, declared in 1941 that

> I have always been *dirigiste* (that is, a proponent of a state-directed economy). But I never made this clear under the preceding regime... I thought that if we went for a planned economy, that would mean granting huge opportunities to governments which would end up abusing them. I did not wish to strengthen this kind of regime.

These were the words that Bouthillier used earlier, in September 1940, to inspire his officials in the Finance Ministry: 'The party game has led the country to disaster. From now on, there is only one party, that of the public interest... Our great corps must be homogeneous and sound; it must become a bloc without any cracks, in a renewed France.'[30]

His friend and colleague Jean Berthelot was appointed Vichy's Minister of Communications in September 1940 after an interwar career as head of France's regional railway networks. His advancement on the eve of war to deputy director of the *SNCF*, the state majority owned national railway service, owed a great deal to his stint as head of the cabinet office of a Republican Minister of Communications. Berthelot left us with the most inadvertently reckless of statements on the sense of impregnability and rectitude of officials, who from men were now gods, beyond accountability: 'under Pétain, the government can legitimately... give the force of law to its decisions, without any other restraint than that which men can exercise over their own acts. How could it be otherwise?'[31]

Even those officials who had not previously thought of ways to modernize and streamline the running of the country, and who pragmatically accepted the need for collaboration as their duty as public employees, would have been susceptible to a climate that clearly favoured and encouraged civil servant initiative and more authoritarian government and administration. State officials worked in hierarchical organizations, and in a hierarchical environment. They were used to imbibing and passing on the models of conduct set by their superiors. If they were listening to Bouthillier's pep talk, the Ministry of Finance's officials would have felt empowered by their boss's vision of the civil servant as the embodiment of the state with a monopoly on the national interest. Officials have always felt like this, since governments come and go, but the state remains. However, now they were the government, and in charge of the national interest as defined and determined by them. And who better?

Civil servants in the occupied territories had guidelines and instructions on how they were to conduct themselves in the event of occupation by an enemy power. There was a body of international law on the obligations of occupiers and occupied in the 1907 Hague Land Warfare Convention, to which all the countries involved, including Germany, were signatories. The Convention was appended to the Dutch government's 1937 directives on occupation to officials in the Netherlands, and informed those instructions. The Belgian government produced its own primer for public officials in 1936. The Hague Convention was buttressed by specific national laws and decrees formulated beforehand, which were then enacted by the parliaments at the point of or during the German invasion. The terms of the French government's relations with the German occupiers were set by the Armistice of June 1940, which brought an end to the fighting in France. The Vichy government circulated the armistice terms, the Hague Convention, and a commentary on the powers of the occupier to its prefects.

The Dutch government-in-exile revised its 1937 guidelines to officials in May 1943, and communicated them in a broadcast transmitted to the Netherlands on Radio London. Both the revisions and their publicizing must have exasperated officials on the ground who were dealing with the ever greater pressures exerted on them by the Germans. They also put the fear of God into them. The new guidelines dealt with specific and contentious issues of collaboration, notably the deportation of Jews and workers and the extent of Dutch economic support for the German war effort, which Dutch officials had been grappling with for nearly a year. They emphasized that individual officials could not hide behind any collective institutional responsibility, but would be held personally responsible for their actions. One wonders what could possibly be the point and value of publicly reminding officials that the deportation of workers was a breach of international law. The new guidelines were an unhelpful, retrospective, and damaging judgement on officials' conduct during the occupation, and opened officials up to being penalized for their actions at the end of the war. Given that the war was moving against the Germans, this was probably the intention of the broadcast, to induce officials to change their behaviour. But saying this was what you should have done, when you have already done something different, was hardly good for morale, or an incentive to carry on in challenging circumstances. The Dutch government's changes to its own directives also indicated that the original ones did not cover or allow for occupiers departing from the Hague Convention script. So, it as well to establish, if we can, what civil servants were expected to do as invasion turned into occupation.

The certain things that emerged from international and national laws and guidelines were that officials were bound to cooperate with the occupation authorities, that they were bound to continue to run public services, and that they were bound to remain at their posts in order to collaborate and administer. Was this enough for top officials? What mattered to them, above all, as public servants, was that they had a clear legal authority to act, a legitimacy that would be recognized by, and govern their relations with, the German occupiers, the governments-in-exile where they existed, and the public administration at lower levels of function and command.

But, whatever the laws and guidelines, there was an insuperable problem for officials. The occupiers were in charge, and what really mattered was how the German authorities viewed collaboration, and the relationship between themselves and officials. This was especially the case where Reich Commissioners were at the helm. As good Nazis, they could be relied upon to follow the mandate to govern personally bestowed on them by Hitler at the point of taking up their positions, even if—one could say, especially if—fulfilling the Hitler mandate involved breaching or exceeding the limits of domestic and international law. Right from the start, then, officials were in a kind of bind, obliged to negotiate their way between what internal and international law accepted as correct behaviour, and what the Germans might demand of their collaboration, unconstrained by any regard for law as a regulator and guide to conduct.

It is no surprise to find that the most unequivocal statements on collaboration came from the German authorities. The Franco-German armistice, an agreement dictated by the victorious power to its defeated rival, clearly stated that, 'in the occupied parts of France, the German Reich exercises all rights of an occupying power'. This was sufficient to require the French government 'to support with every means the regulations resulting from the exercise of these rights and to carry them out with the aid of the French administration'. As a result, 'all French authorities and officials of the occupied territory are to be promptly informed by the French government to comply with the regulations of the German military commanders, and to cooperate with them in a correct manner'.[32]

Hitler's decree mandating Seyss-Inquart as Reich Commissioner for the Netherlands in May 1940 was no less emphatic. The Reich Commissioner not only could 'legislate by decree', but also 'may call on the Netherlands authorities to enforce his orders and to assist…with the discharge of his administrative functions'. With a nod to article 43 of the Hague Convention, which urged the occupying power to respect, 'unless absolutely prevented, the laws in force in the country', the Hitler mandate confirmed that Dutch laws 'shall remain operative in so far as (they are) compatible with the purposes of the occupation'.[33] Seyss-Inquart's later decree on how he would exercise his governmental authority was formulated after meeting the Dutch secretaries general, and primarily addressed to them. It was a catch-all synthesis of the Hitler mandate and the Hague Convention. Article 43 stated that legitimate power passed to the occupier, and Seyss-Inquart claimed to exercise all the constitutional powers vested in the monarch and government, and could enforce his directives through both Dutch authorities and direct action by German authorities. The secretaries general were responsible to him for public administration, and could issue 'rules and regulations implementing Netherlands laws and orders of the Reich Commissioner'.[34]

The implications could not be clearer. Seyss-Inquart regarded Dutch civil servants as agents of the occupying power, and, if they failed, or refused, to do his bidding, then the Germans would do it themselves. This was not as fearsome as it appeared, because even direct German action, to succeed, required some degree of cooperation from Dutch officials, and could potentially overstretch the German personnel resources at the Reich Commissioner's disposal. One would naturally expect the secretaries general to be cute and daring enough to detect that behind the rather brutal portrayal of the subordination of Dutch officialdom to the occupier's will lay, in fact, a regime of weighted but mutual interdependence. Seyss-Inquart wanted, needed, and preferred Dutch officials to collaborate.

According to Seyss-Inquart's decree, public order was a matter for the Dutch police, who were, nevertheless, under German police supervision and 'required to comply with its orders'.[35] Again, though, the Reich Commissioner could get the German police to enforce his orders, and he decided how, and for what 'crimes', Dutch citizens could be tried in special courts under German military or police jurisdiction. The existence of a parallel policing and judicial system removed people from the reach of Dutch law and legal procedure. The eventual exposure of Dutch police and citizens to the full force of Nazi ideological policing by the SS was practically unavoidable.

Seyss-Inquart explicitly recognized the independence of the Dutch judiciary, important for guaranteeing the occupier's respect of the rights to property, family life, and religion under article 46 of the Hague Convention. It was also necessary for the testing of the constitutionality of the occupier's measures and their conformity, or not, to current Dutch and international law. The Dutch government's 1937 guidelines authorized civil servants to protest against any measures of the occupying power deemed to be illegal under international law. Officials were required, in other words, to question and evaluate constantly the integrity of the occupier's directives. Such protests could, or should, lead to the measures being validated or nullified in a court of law. However, the Dutch Supreme Court, at the apex of the judicial system, left officials to stand alone, declaring in January 1942 that it was not competent to attest to the legality or not of specific occupation measures in relation to the Hague Convention, and, therefore, that Dutch judges and courts could not challenge the validity of the occupier's measures. Playing Pontius Pilate could perhaps be seen as a supine abdication of the Court's legal and patriotic duty, and, at the very least, as being singularly unhelpful and undermining of the secretaries general. But, again, things were not quite that simple.

The specific case at issue involved the punishment of a Dutchman by a German 'economic' court for violating food rationing regulations, a pretty significant 'crime' at a time of shortages and austerity and a burgeoning black market. The Supreme Court regarded the 'crime' as a 'political' matter, which was exclusively within the competence and authority of the occupation powers. This, you might say, was highly convenient; but it reflected the legalistic, apolitical approach of the Dutch secretaries general themselves in their dealings with the occupier. The Supreme Court's judgment also illustrated the classic self-justifying circularity of officials' collaboration. If the courts were to challenge the legality of occupation decrees, then they could expect the occupier to retaliate and interfere in the judicial process itself, undermining the independence of the judiciary and the right of Dutch citizens to be tried in Dutch courts for infractions of Dutch law. Was that better, or worse, than leaving things as they were?

You could argue that officials and judges were constantly and mistakenly assessing their own actions in the light of a potential or imagined future threat, that they were trying to second-guess how the Germans would react to any decision they took, which was a severe inhibition on them doing anything at all. But they actually had a point, because the 'worse' did happen.

In Norway, the resignation of Supreme Court judges in late 1940 over what they regarded as Terboven's undue interference in the country's judicial system opened the way for the appointment of more pro-German candidates. There occurred in Belgium in spring 1942 a full-blown legal and constitutional crisis over the independence of the judiciary, and its 'right' to make judgments on the legality of measures undertaken by both the secretaries general and the German occupation authorities. For a while, the country's administrative and legal systems were paralysed by the dispute, and the relationship between occupiers and occupied was at breaking point. It was not just that officials were being prevented by the crisis from running the public administration and public services, and thereby meeting the needs of the population under occupation, which was the basic reasoning behind collaboration. Everyone in occupied Belgium thought they knew what the consequence of a definitive rupture would be, the installation of a different and more severe occupation regime from that of the German military. You can, in retrospect, regard this as an exaggerated sense of future risk; you can even say that the risk was worth taking, that it was an opportunity to call the occupier's bluff and confront it with the implications of the removal of collaboration. But you cannot deny the hold of these fears at the time, and how the contemporary perception of what might be worse than the already terrible situation induced people to behave as they did. It did not require much imagination for the Netherlands' top judges to realize what was at stake in making their judgment, and withdrawing from the fray into a kind of technical neutrality at least kept things as they were, and did not make anything worse. Once again, averting the 'worst case scenario' was the main rationale for continuing collaboration.

In one respect, at least, Seyss-Inquart's May 1940 decree on his powers breached the Hague Convention, which ruled out, in article 45, any compulsion to 'swear allegiance to the hostile power'.[36] In an attempt to make a statutory obligation into a solemn personal and moral commitment, he demanded that judges, officials, public employees, the heads, teachers, and lecturers in schools and universities make a 'declaration in lieu of an oath' that they would 'comply conscientiously with the general and other orders of the Reich Commissioner and the German authorities subordinate to him', and 'will refrain from any action directed against the German Reich or the German armed forces'.[37]

This requirement deliberately put public officials on the spot, and encapsulated the question of sovereignty and legitimate power, and the very real issue that sprang from this for civil servants, of having to serve, simultaneously, two masters. The German interpretation of article 43 of the Hague Convention made officials the direct executive agents of the occupying authority. By this interpretation, officials had all the power, and none of the power. They could issue decrees and laws of their own, and the German occupier actively wanted them to have such powers, because, as the overarching legitimate authority, they could supervise, and if necessary bypass, the exercise of these powers. Any decree of the secretaries general in the Netherlands and Belgium had to have the prior approval of the German authorities if it was to be enacted. If the Vichy government in France wanted its laws to apply also in the occupied territories, and it did, because this demonstrated its sovereignty over all of France, occupied and unoccupied, then, again, the Germans had to approve the laws beforehand. If officials were reluctant to issue decrees requested or demanded by the occupier, then the latter could publish its own directives, which officials would be expected to implement. The occupier could either work through existing law and that enacted by officials, or supersede these with its own decrees.

As you might expect, the Dutch government, both before and during the war, contested this extreme German interpretation of article 43 and the issue of sovereignty. The 1937 guidelines distinguished between 'sovereignty', which was permanent and lay with the Dutch government, and 'control' or the 'exercise of that sovereignty', which was temporarily held by the occupier. The conclusion was that 'every resident of the occupied territory, whether a civil servant or not, is . . . required to follow strictly the orders of the Dutch government during the occupation'. The 1943 revision of the pre-war code of conduct made a point of reiterating the government-in-exile's claim on the loyalties of officials. It had the grace to acknowledge that the 'dual relationship' of officials with the occupier and the government 'will obviously cause difficulties' (as if it had not already done so). But it insisted that the government retained its constitutional authority 'to give instructions to civil servants so as to determine the boundaries which they will not be allowed to cross if they do not want to be guilty of treason or in violation of their official duties in exercising their responsibilities'.[38]

This was a mouthful. The communication restated the basic problem of whether officials should regard themselves as primarily the agents of the occupying power or of the constitutional state and its laws. The answer seemed to be that officials were both. If this was the case, whom should officials obey in the event of a clash between the two 'legitimate' calls on their obedience and loyalty? The Belgian government's 1936 guidelines allowed officials to resign if the occupier was intent on imposing measures incompatible with their duty of loyalty to the country and its interests. But exactly how did this square with the requirement under the law of May 1940 that officials stay on in order to 'protect' their fellow citizens and mitigate the effects of the occupation on the population?

The Dutch government's 1937 guidance devoted many words to the key matter of resignation, and actually provided specific advice to specific groups of public employees, as well as a general principle on which officials could base their 'independent' decision as to whether to resign, or not. It was necessary advice, since, in the event, Seyss-Inquart, the Reich Commissioner for the Netherlands, in common with other German occupation authorities, was entirely relaxed about officials resigning and told the secretaries general so in his meetings with them shortly after the occupation began. He emphasized that officials could resign without any fear of reprisal if they disagreed with or could not accept his measures, clearly expecting that he would be able to determine or influence the appointment of more amenable candidates. The sting was in the tail: if they chose to stay on, then he demanded loyal collaboration from them. The government's advice turned out to be an early version of the 'lesser evil' premise. The point of considering resignation was reached, apparently, only when the official 'by remaining in office would provide such services to the enemy that would be deemed to outweigh those benefits for the population' that would accrue from him staying at his post.[39] This was as complicated a judgement for the official to make as it was for him to read. If resignation could be triggered only when the official by staying in his post was of more help to the occupier than the population, the onus was on the official to work out whether he had crossed such a fine line. The natural tendency would be to find reasons to stay, rather than leave. The 'principle' had the effect of making the official feel indispensable, and it was difficult to imagine a better way of getting him to remain in his job.

The 1943 statement seemed to remove the possibility of resignation altogether, on the grounds that 'others have so often shown themselves to be prepared to fill vacant posts and obediently follow the directives of the enemy', a clear reference to the *NSB*. So, because the alternative to the official was 'worse' than the official continuing, the duty of the official was to refuse to implement any unacceptable measure, but 'only in the case of dismissal may he leave his post'.[40] The official could not resign; he could only be sacked.

Having absorbed all this, the official would have realized that he was between a rock and a hard place, faced claims on his loyalty that could not really be reconciled, and had to evaluate and measure his conduct during the occupation against these contradictory pressures. Above all, his government seemed to want him to remain at his post, for as long as humanly possible, because the likely replacement would be worse for everybody. The assumption that it was their duty to stay put, regardless, carried many top officials through the occupation. After he became Prime Minister again in April 1942, Laval returned to the old Third Republic ways, where politicians often developed close relationships of a patron–client kind with government officials. He often made a point of meeting personally prefects he was appointing or transferring to difficult departments, and they were all testing locations in 1943–4, and even before. In these amiable conversations, he, perhaps counter-intuitively, usually refrained from giving specific guidance or advice, more than implying that they had the wit, expertise, and experience to handle things themselves. He always leaned heavily on their sense of the dutiful thanklessness of their task, reinforced by his sometimes gnomic remarks on the personal suffering and torments he was experiencing on the nation's behalf at the centre of things. It was not always a game for Laval, and, although the level of self-delusion was high, he realized that dutiful patriotic misery resigned officials to their jobs, when, in the circumstances, it was evidently difficult to enthuse them with and about their appointment.

Frederiks, after all, stayed on, as secretary general at the Dutch Interior Ministry, for the duration of the occupation of the Netherlands, and justified his longevity in office on the grounds originally supplied by his government superiors. He advised his mayors according to his interpretation of the 1937 guidelines, including the recommendation to avoid resignation. No wonder he was so deeply offended by being held to account for his behaviour during the occupation after the liberation, specifically on the charge that he had failed to prevent the Nazification of municipal government.

Although the Belgian government had made the customary preparations for invasion and occupation, the transition from invasion and defeat to occupation was a difficult one, and in this, as in many other aspects, Belgium was a special case. What was specific to Belgium in 1940 was the experience of German occupation of the country in the First World War, and Belgian responses to it. The Germans, then, had favoured Flemings over Walloons, deliberately engineered the fragmentation of the country, and begun to introduce their own administrative and judicial apparatus while the Belgian civil service went on working to Belgian and international law. In response to industry's refusal to produce for the German war economy, at the cost of high unemployment throughout the war and a huge state, voluntary, and charitable welfare effort, the Germans had closed and dismantled factories, and deported workers to Germany. The government was nearly present, located in a territorial enclave in the French port of Le Havre, and the king controversially issued a stream of emergency decrees, the constitutionality of which was confirmed legally only after the war had ended.

This was quite a legacy, and was imperfectly dealt with. It meant that considerable strains and stresses began to show, with a second German invasion in May 1940, over the nature and range of powers to be delegated by fleeing politicians to the civil servants and businessmen who were obliged to remain in or return to conquered and occupied territory. The clarification of their role, so crucial to the sense of legitimacy and purpose of the Belgian secretaries general, was not really settled during the hastily arranged and conducted meetings and exchanges between ministers and officials. This happened elsewhere during the occupation, of course. But, in the Belgian case, there was a particular sensitivity to the amount of time and energy the top officials expended during the occupation deciding whether they had the powers and authority to act. The lack of clarity spilled over into the conflict over Belgium's central bank in 1941 and the 1942 judicial crisis, both of which threatened to undermine the administration of the country by the secretaries general, and into bitter post-war legal disputes between officials, judges, and the government returning from exile.

The Belgian parliament passed a law on 10 May 1940 to coincide with the German invasion. In the event of the normal process of government proving impossible to maintain, government ministers were enabled to delegate their ministerial powers to the secretaries general, who could act, effectively, as ministers in their individual areas of departmental competence and jurisdiction. The delegation occurred so that officials could 'protect' the population during any occupation through, among other things, keeping public services going. The delegation also made an important point of principle, at least for the Belgian government. The authorizing source of the transfer of powers was a *Belgian* law, passed by the national parliament and enacted by an elected, legal government. Sovereignty, and the right to govern, remained with the Belgian state. Government by the secretaries general was legitimated by Belgian law and institutions, not by the occupier and the powers it assumed under the Hague Convention.

But serious questions remained. Could the secretaries general act collegially, in a kind of cabinet, or did they have to restrict their activities to running their own individual ministries? Could they issue decrees or laws, as if they had legislative as well as executive powers, and were there any limits to such potential lawmaking powers? What if, as in the First World War, the Germans started tinkering with the constitution and the territorial integrity of Belgium? Most officials seemed to prefer operating within the framework of another law, that of September 1939, which effectively derogated the Belgian constitution and gave the king extraordinary powers to issue decrees in conditions of war. Having powers delegated to them under this law apparently offered officials the capacity to act more flexibly and more widely, since decrees could be justified by a catch-all state of 'necessity' and 'urgency'. The final showdown between the government and the king did not occur until 25 May 1940, a few days away from military surrender. But, given the emerging conflict between king and government over whether to continue the war or not, and stay in the country or not, raising the 1939 law as a preferred option to the May 1940 law was waving an official red rag at a government bull.

Anyway, the secretary general for the Interior Ministry asked the Interior Minister on 15 May, the day before the government left Brussels for the coast, for advice on how to behave during occupation. He received a pretty standard reply, which, nevertheless, contained an important and interesting injunction. Everything was covered by the Hague Convention, the Minister stated; officials knew exactly what their rights and duties were and should ensure the smooth functioning of public services. Officials could not, however, change or allow any change to the way the country was administered, as established by Belgium's constitution and laws. This reference to the current status of the Flemish and Walloon linguistic communities in Belgium scarcely needed decoding; it was the essence of the existence of the Belgian state. The issue was significant enough to warrant yet another communication for further clarification. The secretaries general wanted to know whether *any* administrative reform was ruled out, even that in conformity with Belgian law. This time Hubert Pierlot, the Prime Minister himself, responded on the same day, 15 May. His tetchy and superficially unhelpful reply probably indicated the stress induced by the rapid advances of the invading German army. The 'principle', wrote Pierlot, was not to allow the enemy to determine any changes to the existing balance between Flemings and Walloons, since this would further enemy plans and weaken the national state. Any such proposed changes would be acceptable, however, if recommended by sovereign Belgian authorities. If the situation arose, continued Pierlot, 'it will be a matter for...the secretaries general to be vigilant' about the application of such measures 'in the best interests of the country'. He concluded, rather dismissively, that 'it is impossible to be more precise on such matters. I cannot anticipate here the various instances of its application which may arise. They will have to be resolved in the spirit which I have just invoked.'[41] The tenor of Pierlot's hasty reply to the secretaries general owed everything to its stressful context. 'Why are you bothering me?' Pierlot was saying, 'you work it out'.

It was, I suppose, a moot point as to whether officials preferred to comply with precise, specific laws and guidelines, or with more general ones. The former would not require them to think too much or worry too much about what they did, because they were sufficiently covered and reassured by the detail of their directives. The latter would enable interpretation, a certain flexibility of response, the exercise of discretion and intelligence, even the taking of initiative. Elite officials, already about to assume the position of ministers, and later in the occupation to be designated as 'leaders', tended naturally to the latter approach, if only because it reinforced their own sense of their standing and importance, and played to their professional training and expertise. From this perspective, Pierlot's reply was inadvertently perfect. It provided a 'principle', however shaky, on which to act in circumstances and on occasions that could not yet be predicted, and gave the secretaries general some leeway in interpreting how the 'principle' was to be applied in different and various conditions. Pierlot had effectively given the secretaries general *carte blanche* to prevent a repeat or an equivalent of what had been initiated by the Germans from early 1917, the administrative separation of the Flemish from the Walloon provinces, hence dismembering the Belgian state.

After these rather unsatisfactory exchanges between the government and its top officials, it was, one suspects, with some hope of resolution to their questions that the secretaries general went to their first meeting with the German military command in Belgium on 22 May 1940. This was very much a preliminary meeting, indicating that both sides wanted and needed to collaborate over practical and urgent matters of food and money supply, and economic recovery, as well as the officials' own role and status in an occupied country. At this meeting, the then secretary general for Public Health and Food Supply, Raymond Delhaye, explained in German on behalf of himself and his colleagues how they expected collaboration with the Germans to proceed, on the basis of serving the people's interests and in accordance with current Belgian and international law. This preliminary encounter was followed up by a more official meeting on 5 June 1940 between the secretaries general and the head of the German military administration in occupied Belgium, Eggert Reeder. He had certainly helped to plan the German military's invasion and occupation of Belgium. But he was not a career army officer, rather a lawyer and career civil servant who had become the head of various provincial and city governorships in Germany, joining the Nazi Party in 1933, and the SS in 1939. The lateness of his membership of these two Nazi organizations suggested that his adherence was nominal rather than ideological, and that they were more interested in co-opting him than he was in joining them. He respected in both form and practice Himmler's placing of SS personnel and organizations under the aegis of the occupation authorities, the usual compromise that enabled the SS to operate at all in the occupied territories. After this meeting, both sides worked towards agreement on a protocol that would determine relations between the occupying power and collaborating officials.

The need to reach a formal and workable agreement with the occupier certainly concentrated minds. There were intense discussions involving the secretaries general, ex-ministers, jurists, and German officials, and the arguments went back and forth over the key issue of whether the secretaries general, as well as applying current Belgian law, were also authorized to issue decrees of their own—that is, exercise lawmaking powers. There was a not too subtly placed German trap in these consultations. Some secretaries general were evidently keen to ensure that they gave themselves as full and as wide-ranging powers as possible to administer the country. Otherwise, it was thought, the Germans would realize that they could not run the country effectively through officials who did not equip themselves with sufficient powers to do so, and would install a direct administration of their own. But this was precisely the situation that the Germans wanted to avoid through collaboration, and so they also had every interest in ensuring that the secretaries general had full powers to act. The officials and the Germans were on common ground, the former in order to forestall a situation that the latter did not even contemplate. In fact, the Germans actually suggested to the secretaries general that their powers should be extended, and artfully wanted to know whether that would be acceptable to them. The German proposal took up a whole meeting of the secretaries general on 10 June, and was dealt with in a way that confronted the issue mattering most to officials, legitimacy and sovereignty.

The meeting decided that legally the Germans could not delegate to them the occupier's powers under the Hague Convention, and certainly could not extend that delegation to sensitive 'political' matters. Anyway, the secretaries general thought that they could grant themselves wide enough powers to administer the country using the May 1940 Belgian law and pointing to the exceptional conditions of war and occupation, in a kind of intellectual fusion of the 1939 and 1940 laws. It must have been satisfying for these officials to have hammered out a legal position for themselves, even if they had needed a German stimulus eventually to reach a stance that the Belgian government had thought, mistakenly, was crystal clear from 10 May 1940. They ended up with the argument that they wanted and needed to equip themselves with as much power as possible, and to be able to exercise that power across as wide a range of the nation's activities as possible, and that it was safe to legitimate this power by reference to Belgian, not German authority.

If the secretaries general had detected the German trap of them taking full powers to be exercised on German authorization, then their formulation evidently bypassed it. But their interpretation was, self-evidently enough, not without its problems. Reeder, in a generally conciliatory address to the secretaries general on 5 June, had offered the poisoned chalice of autonomy in return for the occupier's confidence, and sympathetically recognized that officials were in an unenviable political and constitutional position. But, and it was a big 'but', he drew attention to the fact that, in exceptional wartime conditions, there was a need to move beyond the simple application of current laws, and warned them that 'the duties incumbent on the head of the military administration cannot be paralysed by obstacles of pure form. I presume that you, as well, in the interests of your fellow-citizens, are fully aware of your moral responsibility.'[42] In terms of actual, day-to-day, issue by issue, collaboration with the German military authorities, the secretaries general faced the problem that they were merely putting form before substance, and that the only likely gain of collaboration was securing the form, rather than the substance, of the administration of the country's affairs. Something of this constant dilemma can be discerned in the protocol itself, eventually drafted and submitted by Reeder, and then approved by the secretaries general on 12 June 1940.

The protocol empowered the secretaries general to act over wide, non-'political' areas, and appeared to reconcile the dual claims on the loyalty and obedience of officials. The secretaries general recognized that German decrees issued within the framework of Hague Convention regulations would have the same force as Belgian laws, and that they would have to implement German decrees in the same way as they did Belgian laws. The clash would obviously come if, or when, a German decree violated either international or domestic law, or both. One would not necessarily have expected the German view that its decrees superseded Belgian and international law to be included in what was, after all, a document summarizing what both sides were agreeing to. The secretaries general could themselves issue decrees having the force of law in areas where they individually had ministerial competence and jurisdiction. On more general matters involving several ministries, the officials could act collectively and issue common decrees. This represented something of a German concession to the idea of collegial decision-making, and, in practical terms, potentially inhibited 'divide-and-rule' tactics, and the Germans being able to bring pressure to bear on individual officials to get a decision on a matter within his exclusive departmental area of competence.

The concession to cabinet government was compensated for in the protocol's enabling of the centralization of powers in the hands of the secretaries general, which was bound to limit the autonomy and power of local mayors and councillors. The secretaries general could now issue binding decrees on local administrations even in areas that had previously been a matter of local decision-making. Here was concrete evidence of the 'leader principle' being applied in all but name, from the start.

Political affairs were consciously excluded from the lawmaking remit of the secretaries general in the protocol, meeting Belgian officials' and government sensitivities on Fleming–Walloon relations. This was, in effect, the officials' own political self-denying ordinance, since it was unrealistic to expect that the German occupation authorities, even though a military administration, would reciprocate by not interfering themselves in 'political' matters. When one thinks about it, this was a case of officials, true to form, adopting a technocratic, neutral, and non-political stance to their work as professional administrators, and was, in its own very official fashion, a way of interpreting the application of Pierlot's 'principle'. Their removal from political issues could not prevent 'politics' being raised by the occupier. The

German occupiers would realize that its 'political' interventions and measures would probably provoke protests from the secretaries general, and might well threaten the collaboration they relied on to run the country. This awareness could make them think twice about introducing 'political' changes and reforms, and as such constituted a kind of leverage for collaborating officials, who were, however, as afraid of the consequences for the country of ceasing to collaborate. The other point of political self-denial was, of course, to maintain the purity of the officials' legal position. They were not to be held responsible for or accountable for 'political' decisions and actions, which would be the responsibility of the occupiers alone, who would have to issue their own decrees and implement them with their own resources, if necessary. What was this, but conceding on the substance of the power to act in order to preserve the form of the officials' authority to act?

There was another hastily convened meeting during the invasion of the country that had a significant impact on collaboration in occupied Belgium. On 15 May 1940, Paul-Henri Spaak, the Foreign Minister, and Camille Gutt, the Minister of Finance, called together businessmen and financiers. Only three of them could attend, the heads of two major Belgian banks, and Alexandre Galopin, chief of a huge industrial and financial conglomerate that dominated the Belgian economy, the ubiquity and hold of which was indicated by its anodyne title, *Société Générale de Belgique* (General Company of Belgium). Spaak appeared to be overwhelmed by events and susceptible to making the grand gesture, and he was almost certainly aware of the role played by the banks and big business in funding and organizing a huge social welfare initiative for the Belgian people during the First World War German occupation. He melodramatically informed the group of three of their mission: 'Gentlemen, we entrust Belgium to you!'[43]

Quite what this 'mandate' meant became a little clearer in the course of the conversation. Spaak expected the country's economic elites to be the government's eyes and ears on the ground, and to act as the government's and people's advisors during the coming occupation. He also expected them to maintain economic and administrative activity, urging the banks to pay the wages, salaries, and allowances of state employees in return for post-war reimbursement, and industrialists to get production rolling again. Galopin had just asked whether industry should repeat the First World War policy of passive abstention from production, which, in his view, had made a 'cemetery' of the country. Here was the government's emphatic answer, the one he wanted to hear: economic production must be restarted in order for the country to survive occupation, and that could only involve economic collaboration with the occupier. One can imagine the liberating impact of Spaak's message on businessmen living under the shadow of article 115 of the Belgian penal code, which envisaged penalties up to and including the death penalty for those aiding the enemy in the form of soldiers, manpower, food, arms, and munitions. Economic collaboration was now official policy. This departure from the practice under the previous German occupation perhaps explains why Spaak constantly downplayed the significance of the meeting. He denied that he had 'mandated' economic collaboration both during and certainly after the war, in order to evade responsibility for it taking place and to remove the cover for collaborating employers that the government might well intend to penalize on liberation. But Spaak's words were certainly taken by Galopin as prior endorsement of the 'policy of production' that he initiated and developed for the duration of the occupation.

4

Economic
Collaboration, 1940–1942

From the summer of 1940, officials and businessmen in the occupied
territories collaborated with each other, and with the Germans, in
order to restart economic activity and end the scourge of mass unemployment in countries that had barely recovered from the effects of the Great
Depression by the time of the outbreak of war. Economic recovery and the
absorption of unemployment were the mutual concern of governments,
government officials, and German occupation authorities. They shared the
same broad perspective that, by removing a likely source of popular discontent, they could help to re-establish 'law and order', restore social calm and
stability, and secure a 'peaceful' occupation.

Economic recovery in France was also severely constrained by the
Germans' territorial dismemberment of the country. The military demarcation line separating the German-occupied north and west from the
unoccupied Vichy zone to the east and south acted as a human and economic frontier that could be alternately tightened or eased by the Germans;
the same problems of access affected the north-eastern 'forbidden zone'.
Much of France's heavy industry was now located either in the 'annexed'
provinces of Alsace and Lorraine, or in the northern departments, which
were placed under the control of the German military administration of
Belgium–northern France.

In the summer of 1940, governments and officials did what they could to
restimulate the economy by putting the state's money into a swathe of public
works and infrastructural repair and restoration projects, which amounted
to, and in some cases became, a formal labour service for unemployed
workers. Precisely in order to put gangs of young unemployed men to work
on a variety of works for the public good, the Vichy government in France

set up a special task force in the Ministry of Industrial Production and Labour, the *Commissariat à la lutte contre le chômage* (Commissariat for the Struggle against Unemployment). The new unit, with a suitably activist and rather fascist or Bolshevik-sounding name, was run by François Lehideux, a bright and energetic young official who had managed Renault before the war (and married the owner's niece). It later morphed into a permanent planning body within the ministry when Lehideux was its minister from July 1941. After the war, Lehideux defined his work as head of the Commissariat as 'administrative resistance'[1] in the national interest. He had apparently rejected German demands in 1940–1 that unemployed French workers go to their own construction projects, and sought to disguise unemployment when his agency could not end it, in order to shield workers from having to work for the Germans. This is simply incredible as a defence, in the circumstances of 1940–1. Sure, the Commissariat 'disguised' unemployment by encouraging French employers to introduce short-time working, which was clearly intended to share around the work that was currently available, not to hide workers from the Germans. The job of his agency was to get people back to work, not to prevent them from doing so. The only accurate and authentic aspect of his post-war testimony was the recognition that his own agency was incapable of solving France's unemployment on its own.

So, while these initiatives made some difference, they were never enough. Far more significant funds, with a greater impact on job creation, came from German occupation spending on the repair of bridges, roads, and railways, and on the building or refurbishing of military installations, such as airfields, barracks, arsenals, and shipyards. The German occupations in their own right ignited a construction boom across the occupied territories that lasted well into the war, with much of the business and employment coming to local businesses subcontracted to German companies and organizations. The largest number of start-ups during the occupation was in the building and construction sector, 'mushroom' companies that became the particular targets of post-war purges because of their very close association with the presence of the occupying power.

The immediate and lasting impetus to employment generated by construction for the occupying forces confirmed what government officials and businessmen across occupied Western Europe realized and accepted from an early stage. There seemed little possibility of restoring national markets and internal demand to a level capable of absorbing mass unemployment.

The French general Charles-Léon Huntziger, fresh from the defeat of his army at Sedan and looking back on developments in the previous few months, acknowledged as much in September 1940 to the commander-in-chief of the German army, Field Marshal Walther von Brauschitsch: 'the few companies which resumed production were working for Germany. The French government wanted to put all French industry at the disposal of the German war economy, as long as raw materials were made available in sufficient quantities. The government realised that otherwise, France would collapse.'[2] These remarks were much more than idle banter between military men who for past and present reasons both feared that military defeat precipitated social revolution. Huntziger was a really important figure in the Vichy regime then and later, and had made the comments as head of the French governmental delegation at the Armistice Commission in Wiesbaden, where Franco-German relations were thrashed out in the first few years of the occupation. His sentiments were echoed and repeated by the secretaries general in Belgium and the Netherlands, and elsewhere by officials throughout occupied Europe. The uniquely 'French' dimension of Huntziger's commonplace words lay in the bundle of contradictions behind the collaboration of these early Pétainist leaders. Huntziger, who became Minister of War under Laval and retained the position under his successor, Admiral Jean-François Darlan, was incensed by the recent British attack on the French navy at its Algerian base. He managed to be both anti-British in his current eagerness to offer French economic aid to the German war against Britain; and later anti-German in his eventual reluctance to countenance joint military action with the Germans against Britain in the French African empire and the Middle East.

The early and continuing construction boom in the occupied territories was the first concrete initiative of economic collaboration between the occupying power and the leaders and officials of the occupied countries. There were legal problems to it, but these were brushed aside by both sides, given the convergence of interests in providing work for idle hands. The Hague Convention declared that the occupied populations should not have to work on purely military projects of the occupier. The Germans, or at least the German Nazis, were never really bothered about the Convention as a guide to conduct, unless it suited them. In the delicate very early stages of occupation, observance did suit them, for the obvious reason that good behaviour would win the tolerance of the population. Both sets of lawyers advised both sets of officials to the same, desired effect. It was permissible to allow workers to be recruited to build, repair, or extend military installations because they were essentially a shelter for the maintenance of occupying troops. You could see how this interpretation would apply to the construction of a military barracks; it was used to justify the employment of local and relocated men on airfields for the German air force, too. It must be said that Max Hirschfeld, the Dutch secretary general of the country's economic ministries throughout the occupation, objected to the majority decision taken by the committee of secretaries general. He apparently told building contractors who sought his approval that working on airfields could be punishable under Dutch law. But even he provided a way out for aspiring Dutch contractors for German orders. Employers needed to show that they were under some kind of duress to work for the Germans, that they were pressurized by the occupiers to work for them—that it was unavoidable, in other words. They should not simply be responding to the German military's request for local labour. It did not seem to matter one way or the other. By August 1940, about 50,000 Dutch workers were employed on German airfields, presumably being prepared for the invasion of Britain, among other things.

Belgium and Denmark, in particular, were, or had been, strongly exporting nations, and there was certainly even less prospect of renewing multilateral international trade to boost employment. The Allied economic blockade of continental Europe, and the closing-down of much overseas and colonial trade in conditions of war, defeat, and occupation, effectively left available only German markets and those of countries and territories allied to or in the orbit of Nazi Germany. The German markets progressively restricted by the Nazi regime's pursuit of autarky in the 1930s were now opening up for the distressed economies of newly occupied Western Europe. If economic production was to revive in the occupied territories, then business had to be done with the Germans, in servicing both the German military occupation of their countries and the German war economy.

The need for German orders dovetailed naturally with the Germans' intention to exploit the economies of the countries they had defeated and occupied. The intention became a need as the war in the West did not end imminently, and Hitler initiated preparations for the invasion of the USSR from late 1940. The Nazis exported to the occupied territories what they were best at, organized chaos, and getting things done. On the coattails of the invading armies, representatives of German big business, sectorally organized under the Nazi regime into 'Business Groups', poured into the occupied territories, jostling alongside the staff of the armed forces procurement bodies, and of the usual mixed bag of state and Party-affiliated economic ministries and agencies. They were formally under the jurisdiction of Göring's Four Year Plan Office, enabled by Hitler's mandates to claim overall responsibility for the German war economy, and, by extension, the economies of occupied Western Europe; and of the economic departments of the military administrations in occupied Belgium and France and the Reich Commissariats in Norway and the Netherlands.

In many cases, these agents of private German industry and German military and civilian public bodies made direct and immediate contact with individual companies, which they had clearly earmarked for economic collaboration. These approaches were often made within days of the occupation and while the occupation authorities were still setting themselves up. The latter would certainly have admired their drive and initiative, but they caught local officials and the Vichy government in unoccupied France on the hop. Their actions provoked responses of what might be called 'wild' collaboration. The German military procurement agencies naturally targeted big companies manufacturing arms, armaments, vehicles, and aircraft. Their owners and managers were clearly concerned to get an official seal of approval, which was usually given retrospectively. But they were willing to accept German orders and the presence of a German commissioner in the factory on the evident grounds that they could carry on making what they had been making up to this point, and hence avoid a potentially painful and uncertain transition to peacetime civilian production. And, of course, accepting orders enabled them to keep a skilled workforce together. Renault workers at the company's huge mass-production factory, really a complex or city of factories at Boulogne-Billancourt on the outskirts of Paris and now in the German-occupied zone, had made tanks, trucks, and aircraft components for the French government in 1939–40. Now they pragmatically accepted the consequences and implications of defeat and occupation. Some of them on their return to work were reported as saying: 'we're off to work for the Boches, but what the hell! We have to live.'[3]

There were many cases of such 'wild' collaboration, and they gave a crucial impetus to the establishment of a system of economic collaboration, in much the same way as the 'wild purges' at Liberation induced returning governments to systematize that process. Organized and authorized economic collaboration often amounted to government officials intervening in contractual negotiations between German and local companies in the occupied territories, and registering and confirming the continuation of these initial unilateral contacts and contracts between them. But at least these initiatives were now subject to a degree of control from above, at a governmental or ministerial level. The involvement of officials meant the assertion, or reassertion, of some sense of the wider interests of the national economy in the servicing of the German war economy, over the all too evident self-interest of individual companies to restart their businesses.

The German incomers merrily participated in the Göring-championed requisitioning and plunder of plant, machine tools, vehicles, and rolling stock, and the remaining reserves of raw materials and semi-finished and finished goods built up by both state-owned and private companies to sustain the war effort of the now defeated countries. Short-term plunder, if it had continued unabated, would have had damaging long-term consequences for the future German exploitation of the economic resources of the occupied territories. You could, after all, plunder only once. The Four Year Plan Office soon had to live up to its name and purpose. Plunder was accompanied and then superseded by medium- and longer-term planning to sustain the German war economy and move towards the incorporation of the economies of the occupied territories into a putative *Grossraumwirtschaft*. Funk had already indicated that it was possible, and desirable, to build some of the infrastructure of a future European economic union at the same time as fighting a European war.

In the late summer of 1940, the Germans—that is, Göring, the Four Year Plan Office, and the Economics Ministry—decided to follow a policy of *Auftragsverlagerung*, or 'order displacement'. The idea was to increase manufacturing in the occupied territories, which would replace production in Germany and so release additional capacity for military goods in Germany itself. In some cases, the policy would involve the transfer and diversion of orders for civilian goods in Germany, and of production servicing the German occupation forces, to factories in the occupied territories, enabling German firms to concentrate on military orders. The policy would also entail raw materials available in the occupied territories being used *in situ*, rather than being exported, or plundered, to Germany. In Göring's mind, it was 'safer' to manufacture military materials in Germany, using German managers and workers, than rely on the untrustworthy natives of the occupied territories.

Perhaps unsurprisingly, the decision did not go down well with some German manufacturers, who faced losing orders to potential competitors in the occupied territories, closure, or a costly transition from civilian to war production. The delays that occurred in implementing the policy were down to foot-dragging on the German employers' side, rather than any reticence among companies in the occupied territories, who were only too willing to restart production and end the plunder by fulfilling German orders.

Delivering on the policy gave an added impetus to bringing about a semblance of order and system to the German wartime exploitation of the West European economies. The arrangements put in place in the summer and autumn of 1940 largely prevailed until the spring and summer of 1942, when there occurred another major reorganization of the German and European war economy under Albert Speer. The German occupation authorities, as well as Reich agencies, developed in tandem organizational mechanisms that would control and regulate the absolutely crucial supply and distribution of industrial raw materials and energy, the key elements in managing both the volumes and the kinds of industrial production in both Germany and the occupied territories. Göring superimposed a body known by its acronym, *ZAST*, *Zentralauftragstelle*, or Central Ordering Office, as a kind of stadium roof to an already pulsating arena. Its job was to ensure that raw materials reached companies working on German orders, and to coordinate, filter, and prioritize German orders to producers in the occupied territories. As a real statement of intent, *ZAST* offices were set up in occupied France, Belgium, and the Netherlands, but not in Denmark, where Danish–German relations always took a different form, or Norway. One can only speculate about its absence in occupied Norway. Perhaps Göring trusted his *protégé*, the Reich Commissioner, Terboven, to deliver without the encumbrance of another Reich agency. More likely, there were less rich economic pickings to be had in Norway, and it soon became clear that the Germans would have to invest in the Norwegian economy before they could begin to exploit it. Anyway, in the places where it was located, *ZAST* more or less functioned as the official German conduit for German orders to the occupied territories, an essential stopping point in the circuit linking German purchasers to West European suppliers.

 Once officials and employers in the occupied territories realized, and accepted, that their national economies could revive only with German orders, then they had every interest in working with and through the systems and organizations created and imposed by the Germans to exploit the economic resources of the occupied territories. They had themselves been responsible for their own national state's economic mobilization for war from the late 1930s into the outbreak of war in 1939 and its operation during 1939–40. They recognized the need for the continuation of top-down and formal structures appropriate to planning and managing the economy in wartime conditions of bottlenecks and shortages. They positively welcomed the establishment of some kind of order in the Germans' economic exploitation of their own countries. It was the best way of easing down and replacing the initial German ransacking of national economic resources, the kind of one-off asset stripping which, if it lasted, would cripple the country's future productive capacity and potential.

The installation of a centralized, rational, and planned war economy, to the extent that this was ever possible in Nazi polycracy, was clearly in the mutual interests of both occupier and occupied in the summer of 1940. Participating in, cooperating with, and thereby influencing the operation of German wartime economic agencies were the only serious and workable option for officials and businessmen in the occupied territories. If in a very real sense this was the only sensible option available to them, as one imposed by the occupier, it was still the best move to make. It is worthwhile reflecting a little on the significance of this. The Dutch secretary general for Economic Affairs, Hirschfeld, had already suggested to employers that they should cover and justify their cooperation with the Germans by emphasizing the constraint imposed on them by the Germans to induce that cooperation. Much of their self-defence before investigatory commissions after the Liberation rested on the argument that their actions were not freely taken, but constrained. In reality, the only constraint faced by employers in the occupied territories was the one shared by each and every one of their fellow citizens, the hard fact of occupation and war. In these circumstances, most employers made a choice to collaborate with the occupier, which was as free and willing as it was possible to make in an occupied country. Employers were not press-ganged against their will to collaborate; they willed that collaboration.

ZAST was there to coordinate the German side of the economic exploitation of the occupied territories. It worked with other organizations that represented, as it were, the side of the occupied territories. Their form was determined, in part, by the way the occupied countries were administered. In Belgium and the Netherlands, the organizations were imposed by the occupying authorities—hardly a surprise. The German military administration set up *Warenstellen*, or 'Goods Offices', for each sector of the Belgian industrial economy. They were primarily responsible for fixing the market in the various sectors, and distributing German orders among companies in the sector and allocating raw materials to them. The German decree on the *Warenstellen* was then adopted, with some slight modification, by a separate decree of the Secretary General for Economic Affairs. This, of course, made their installation legal and 'Belgian', and enabled the involvement of Belgian officials and businessmen in an agency of German occupation. The secretary general, on German approval, appointed the directors of the *Warenstellen*, along with their advisory committees. Both were usually drawn from top officials in the Economic Affairs Ministry and/or the leading businessmen or business managers in the sector. The committees were the small, Belgian amendment to the German insistence on the 'leader principle'. Each office had a German commissioner attached to it.

Illustration 6. A formal portrait of Alexandre Galopin, governor of Belgium's most important business corporation, *La Société Générale*, and the architect of the policy of economic collaboration in occupied Belgium.

The other, less formal Belgian component was Galopin, or rather the Galopin committee, which formulated in July 1940 a 'doctrine' or set of criteria for managing the economic collaboration of the country's businesses. The basic premise and justification of the Galopin doctrine was that, since the country could meet only about half of its raw materials and food needs, Belgian industrial exports to Germany would be exchanged for raw material and food imports from Germany and German-dominated Europe. The truth of the word according to Galopin was that Belgian trade with Germany met its patriotic limit in the nourishment of the Belgian people.

Legitimated to act by the retiring government-in-exile's 'mandate', the Galopin committee was, in practice, the Belgian economic and professional establishment at work and play. The secretaries general fully approved of Galopin's 'policy of production', and regularly consulted Galopin and his colleagues. In turn, the country's top lawyers, prosecutors, and judges, and this included Struye, were consulted by the committee and the secretaries general to advise on the legal ramifications of economic collaboration, especially with regard to the notorious article 115 of the penal code.

If the Galopin committee was from the start the intellectual and operative hub of economic collaboration in Belgium, then the secretary general for Economic Affairs, Hirschfeld, was the one-man equivalent in the Netherlands, the essential fulcrum of cooperation with the Germans. As the Allies feared, the Dutch government had over-prepared for the coming of the war, building up big stockpiles of food, raw materials, and finished industrial products, which were then seized by the Germans on occupation. The agricultural agencies set up to protect Dutch agriculture during the Great Depression, and then ensure a wartime food supply, were already moving the country's farmers from export to internal production, from dairy to arable. The whole apparatus of Dutch governmental regulation of the war economy was working so smoothly that the Reich Commissariat simply co-opted the existing so-called *Rijksbureau*, or 'National Offices'. All it had to do was attach a German economic official to each of these public, sectoral bodies, responsible to the Dutch Ministry of Economic Affairs for the supply and distribution of raw materials and industrial goods, and economic collaboration was up and running.

In both the Netherlands and Belgium, later in 1941 and 1942, the Germans reformed the *Rijksbureau* and the *Warenstellen* so that they mirrored even more closely the German corporative business organs. This indicated that the export of Nazi German models of economic organization to the occupied territories was integral to the making of the *Grossraumschaft*. But these changes were never really necessary, in terms of facilitating economic collaboration. Certainly, in the Netherlands, both sides continued to organize the Dutch economy through the familiar and well-tried bodies created in 1940. Neglecting to implement reforms is hardly uncommon practice in any bureaucracy. But the remodelling of Dutch economic organizations was clearly seen as another step towards the Nazification of the Dutch economy, and, as such, a potential entry point for *NSB* members. On the grounds of economic competence alone, the appointment of *NSB* members would have disrupted the smooth running of the economy by technically equipped officials and businessmen. Even a Nazi Reich Secretariat was willing to limit the development of Nazi economic bodies to secure the continuing collaboration of trusted and proficient Dutch officials, in itself a nice example of the give and take possible in a collaborating exchange.

The Vichy government rushed through a law establishing *Comités d'Organisation* (*COs* (Organization Committees)), which were compulsory state groupings of employers in the various sectors of the industrial economy. They were not only set up to help to manage the wartime economy. They were also the first steps towards the creation of a new authoritarian social and economic order, and the planned economy. There was a preemptive element to their rapid growth across the sectors of the French economy. René Belin, the new Minister of Industrial Production and Labour, claimed that the German military administration disliked the *COs*, because they were 'French' not 'German'. It certainly delayed its approval of the new bodies, probably to remind the Vichy government that German endorsement was needed to secure their application in the occupied zone. But there was nothing to fear from them. Belin also admitted that it was on the polite suggestion of the economic department of the German military administration that he set up the really important government economic agency. This was the *Office Central de Répartition des Produits Industriels* (*OCRPI* (Central Office for the Allocation of Industrial Products)). Its subsections did exactly the same job as the Belgian *Warenstellen* and the Dutch *Rijksbureau*.

The Danish system differed because it reflected the still democratic nature of its polity, which the Germans had to respect in order to ensure their continued 'peaceful' and consensual occupation of the country. As during the Great Depression, the Danish government fostered a joint agreement between employers and unions on the wartime regulation of the national economy. Everywhere else, free unions were dissolved, their assets and members shunted to compulsory single 'front' organizations, or, in the Vichy case, to a promised future corporative reorganization of society and the economy.

The outcome was that the Danish government was able to exercise a far greater degree of control over the nature and extent of economic collaboration, and conducted what could pass as normal trade relations with Germany. Business was settled and managed by a co-chaired Danish–German intergovernmental committee. The major figures on the German side were an official of the German Ministry of Food and Agriculture, and a representative of the powerful Armed Forces purchase and orders agency, both responsible to the German Foreign Ministry and its Reich Plenipotentiary for Denmark, Renthe-Fink. Negotiations for the Danish government were handled by a top official in the trade department of the Foreign Ministry, Matthias Wassard. He was answerable in turn to the Foreign Minister, Scavenius, whom he met for a daily discourse on economic collaboration in the ministry cafeteria. Wassard was aided by a Danish Industrial Council of prominent businessmen, who often acted as behind-the-scenes intermediaries and 'facilitators' in the official negotiations.

Clearly, the Danish settlement affected economic relations between the occupied country and the occupying power. It put the Danish government in a far better position to protect the country's economic independence, if it decided to do so. The Danish government was able to abort discussions about a possible customs and currency union in late 1940. This was forced through by the Reich Commissariat in the Netherlands at about the same time, leading to the resignation of the Secretary General for Finances, who had previously (and secretly) acquiesced in German financial controls on foreign-exchange transfers. There was relatively little plunder, no Nazi economic organizations were set up, and the 'leader principle' did not apply. But there was no avoiding the German clearing system, which, as in all other occupied countries, effectively required the national bank to fund exports to Nazi Germany through the accumulation of credits to its account. Given Wassard's (and Scavenius's) key role in the intergovernmental committee, the Germans were, in effect, negotiating with a single recognizable and authoritative 'leader'.

The Germans could not formally push for measures that would integrate Denmark into the *Grossraumwirtschaft*. But they could, as they did elsewhere, encourage the formation of an economic Trojan Horse, a new Danish business association with some fifty members by mid-1942, benignly called the '1940 Study Group'. Its aims couched the *Grossraumwirtschaft* in acceptably neutral public relations terms. In order to bring about 'the adaptation of business to the demands of the time', the group would familiarize its members with 'the newest principles and ideas in the field of business, including the organisation of businesses at home and abroad, and the newest principles of international trade'.[4] The *Grossraumwirtschaft* could clearly be promoted effectively as the next big thing, and that undoubtedly resonated with business across occupied Europe.

Certainly, the Danish government could negotiate its own terms. In doing so, it protected, for instance, domestic consumption levels, and, by extension, internal social order, in a way that was beyond the Belgian secretaries general. They were obliged to confront Seyss-Inquart's team with the consequences of inadequate food supplies for the country, in early 1941. But Danish agriculture could feed its own people, and a good proportion of Germans, too. German officials did not have to press very hard on Danish economic capacity in order to secure what they wanted for the German war effort, and, indeed, for the *Grossraumwirtschaft*. An efficient and productive animal and dairy sector supplied Nazi Germany with food imports throughout the war, along with the specialized industrial products it wanted, including ship engines and machine tools. The Germans secured, through negotiation rather than imposition, the virtuous circle of collaboration, exactly what they needed from the Danish economy, both for the war, and for the future. They did so, because the Danish government was willing to provide what they required. Their approach was determined by the inescapable fact of life in all occupied territories, however they were occupied, that Nazi Germany was the only serious market available for Europe's products. What was also common ground in the war economies of the occupied territories was the high level of business and official economic self-management and self-administration under state auspices. Both companies and officials welcomed the establishment of an economic system that they staffed themselves, and that replicated the organization of the German war economy. Whatever the forms of German occupation in Western Europe, the symbiosis between a market dependence on Nazi Germany and a joint business and state organization and planning of national economies ensured a long-lasting economic collaboration between occupier and occupied.

The discussion has centred on the creation of official wartime markets in the occupied territories, and will continue to do so. It is, nevertheless, important to recognize that both sides participated in the various shades of an informal black market. This had the effect of making it part of the economic system of occupation, to the extent that black-market transactions were sometimes recorded officially. German purchases of black-market goods in Belgium went through clearing. The black market was never really a problem for the German authorities, or at least for those who purchased goods from the occupied territories. Recourse to the black market was an effective way of securing the additional goods they wanted, at the expense, once again, of the occupied territories. Such a market rather suited the entrepreneurial, go-getting approach of German agencies and individual businessmen. They opportunistically exploited the volatility of the supply of raw materials supply, which could lead to unexpected, one-off windfalls, in turn passed on to an available and willing local company.

National and local officials always treated the black market as a problem, since it worsened shortages and pushed up prices for the ordinary consumer, with evident, or feared, repercussions for public order and social peace. But they had to accept it, while being unable to eradicate it. Its existence was systemic, a near-unavoidable outcome of the penury and shortages that made necessary the establishment of official systems of market regulation in the first place. The black market was also next to impossible to police, and, indeed, undesirable to police, since it came to involve large swathes of the population as both producers and consumers.

The Germans did not make similar demands on all sectors of the national economies. They were, naturally enough, interested in production that contributed directly and indirectly to the German war effort. But the ripple effects of German demand went beyond the companies receiving German orders for military or related purposes. The policy of 'displacement' in the occupied territories broadened out the reach of German purchasers to include consumer goods producers, as well as producers for the military war. Many big companies in receipt of German orders subcontracted out to smaller firms and traders, as did the German companies working on construction projects for the Todt Organisation. Firms that produced for domestic consumer markets faced worsening shortages of energy and raw material resources, which were diverted to priority German contracts. This led to underused productive capacity, the threat of closure, short time or lay-offs for workers, who could find themselves seeking work, or being directed to work, in the war industries. Economic collaboration was in its own way a process that stretched all of the national economy.

Employers could choose not to accept German orders. A few did so, fully aware of the likely economic consequences for their company. But nearly all employers who were approached did accept German contracts, and, we must assume, for broadly similar economic and social reasons. The basic reason was, however, 'political', in both a specific and a broader sense. The reason is so self-evident as to be banal. But it must be emphasized again and again, nevertheless. Economic collaboration was government, or official, policy. It was encouraged, sometimes required, by governmental authorities in the occupied territories, and in exile.

It was certainly the case that the governments-in-exile became increasingly restive about the economic collaboration they endorsed in summer 1940. They were, after all, the legitimate authority of countries that were still at war, who had fled abroad in order to continue the war against Germany. The host to their exile, Britain, was their ally in the war against Germany, and expected both the governments-in-exile and the occupied peoples to play an appropriate part in the war. As the war went on, and expanded with the German invasion of the USSR in June 1941, that Allied demand for a contribution to the war effort became more insistent. Under pressure from their Allied host, the governments-in-exile had to assume a default position of resistance, and somehow induce this kind of response among their peoples in the occupied territories.

This was not something easy to achieve in practice, even allowing for the evident difficulties in communication with the occupied territories, which diminished their understanding and awareness of what was actually happening there. A policy of resistance to occupation obviously ran counter to their own initial acknowledgement of the need to collaborate, enshrined as it was in international law and in their guidelines to officials. The task was easier, or, perhaps, less difficult, for the 'Free French' of de Gaulle, a movement, rather than a government, in exile. They had called for resistance to the German occupier from the start, and could claim that they represented the 'real' France against a usurping Vichy regime that was collaborating with the Germans. The Norwegian king and government had, as a result of their behaviour during the German invasion, managed to communicate a spirit of resistance to their people even as they were leaving the country for exile. The government-in-exile immediately committed to the Allied cause its only remaining war asset, the country's mercantile marine and its crews, which had largely avoided being quarantined in foreign and home ports. Civilian and military resistance organizations were established early on during the occupation, with British help. These organizations did not do much active resisting until the point of liberation; but that is another story. The combination of a German policy of Nazification to be realized through a government of the Norwegian Nazi party, and a king who made a stand against the Germans in the name of a democratic constitution, was sufficient to induce a greater degree of reticence towards occupation among public officials than was apparent in other occupied countries.

The Belgian and Dutch governments-in-exile straddled collaboration and resistance, without really knowing how to resolve the choice between them, until the course of the war moved irrevocably against Nazi Germany. Until then, their attempted interventions in the affairs of their occupied countries only served to make life extremely uncomfortable for those officials who were busy collaborating, as a matter of government policy. Galopin was obliged to defend the 'policy of production' against the rumblings from abroad, to the point of actually demanding a clarification of the government-in-exile's position.

A letter of reply from Gutt, the Finance Minister-in-exile, reached the Galopin committee in May 1941. The government-in-exile had grudgingly, or shamefacedly, depending on how you want to look at it, come off the fence. You Belgians have to produce to sell, and eat, conceded Gutt. It was best not to produce war materials in order to survive, but 'everything has to do with the war'. He concluded in the same dismissive tone he had used in 1940: 'it's down to how you handle this, and to relations with the Germans.'[5] One rather doubts that Galopin was someone who whooped at receiving long-awaited good news. But he was probably someone who took a kind of grim satisfaction at being proved correct, yet again. The letter was a vindication and a validation of the Galopin doctrine, and also of the officials' right to make judgements based on what was actually happening on the ground. Economic collaboration was still official policy, though, as we shall see, Gutt's letter was hardly a definitive end to the story.

The broader 'political' reason for economic collaboration lay in a general employers' perception of the role of government and the state in the economy. It is easy, and perhaps even accurate, to see employers as natural authoritarians in the workplace, and in politics and society. This might explain why many bosses in wartime Vichy France publicly endorsed *Pétainisme* and *Pétainiste* values in their company house bulletins. But most employers were capable of separating the overriding concern for the success of their businesses from their political preferences. They certainly had to do business in whatever kind of polity they belonged to or were located in. The owner and head of *FIAT* in Italy, Giovanni Agnelli, famously said of his company's relationship with Mussolini and the Fascist regime that 'we are government supporters, by definition'.[6] This was the case in the most obvious of senses, since *FIAT* was a major government contractor before, during, and after the Fascist period in Italy.

But Agnelli's remark indicates something more: an adaptability to the situation as it actually was; a propensity to rally to the state, any state, as long as it was capable of providing a suitable legal and social framework for business activity. And, by 'social', I mean a basic public order. 'Order' in the summer of 1940 was restored by the occupier, acting in tandem with collaborating government officials.

Economic collaboration being official policy was a clear incentive for employers. It covered them legally and morally in their relations with the Germans. Producing for the Germans was self-evidently good for the business, and, since collaboration was official policy, it was also clearly judged to be good for the country, a seamless meshing of private and national interest. It apparently removed from the calculation of future risk to the business the fear that those who contracted with the Germans would be regarded as unpatriotic and traitorous, and prosecuted as such, and that any profits made from business dealings with the Germans would be confiscated. It became embarrassingly evident in post-Liberation investigations that a great many employers had collaborated with the Germans, and had been encouraged to do so because it was policy. We have here at least a plausible explanation of why so many files were subsequently closed.

Part of the legal and moral cover for business relations with the Germans involved military production for the German war effort, something excluded by international and domestic law. The Galopin doctrine attempted to moderate the extent of economic collaboration by ruling out military contracts, and insisting that its sole purpose was to export civilian industrial goods in return for the import of sufficient food supplies to feed the Belgian people. However, Vichy France wanted to revive its own defence industries, in order to restore some sense of France being a militarily independent great power. It could do this only as part of a manufacturing programme that produced combat aircraft for the German air force as well as for their own armed forces.

Both the legal and practical position on military contracts had to change, if only because the Germans were primarily interested in military production.

All kinds of legal and other devices were employed by the Germans, companies, and officials together, to meet or deflect the sensibilities over manufacturing arms, armaments, and military materials for the Germans. Vehicle manufacturers made military ambulances rather than armoured cars or tanks. Shipbuilders and engineers made patrol and customs vessels rather than navy destroyers. So, for instance, Danish shipbuilding contracts were negotiated with the German navy, for non-combatant vessels, but, in the same deal, repairs were carried out on fighting vessels as well, including U-boats. Aircraft manufacturers made training and transport planes rather than fighters. Subcontracting on military orders was disguised as 'civilian' production. Companies would accept military orders from German firms or civilian agencies, while turning them down if they came from military procurement bodies. Components manufacture was generally justified on the grounds that finished weapons were being assembled elsewhere. Military orders were circuited in mysterious and logistically extraordinary ways. As one example of many, three Belgian steel manufacturers in mid-1941 'exported' steel ingots to a German company across the border in Aachen, which 'imported' them back on German railway wagons to be made into shells at a Belgian firm in Liège requisitioned by the German state-owned arms manufacturer that had made the original order. The ingots were accounted in clearing as German exports to Belgium. Some companies manufacturing arms agreed 'voluntarily' to having all or a section of their factories and equipment requisitioned by the Germans for explicitly military production. There was nothing constrained or involuntary about any of this; all the players were complicit in the process.

While all this went on, it was also the case that companies in the occupied territories manufactured on German contracts armoured trucks, fighter planes, submarine bases, naval ships, machine guns, shells, artillery, gunpowder, military uniforms, and boots, ad infinitum. The reason, or justification, was that, in the total war being fought by the Germans, it was all but impossible to distinguish between production for civilian and military purposes, and pointless to do so, as Gutt recognized in his letter to Galopin. The officials, rather than individual businessmen, had a better and more-informed sense of how production in the occupied territories contributed to the German military war. Secretary General Hirschfeld in the Netherlands deliberately ignored the 1937 guidelines on producing military materials for the Germans, and made no attempt to disguise the fact that civilian production contracts also aided the German war effort by releasing German capacity for military production. It would have been excessively punctilious for an official to recommend that a company turn down a German contract because it 'displaced' production in Germany.

Since so many firms in the occupied territories produced for the Germans, it is possible to make some rather self-evident generalizations about the reasons and motivations behind economic collaboration. These sustained that collaboration throughout the occupation, but especially in the 1940–2 period. Individual employers were, naturally enough, concerned to keep their businesses going, and retain an experienced and skilled workforce, which, if dispersed by unemployment or relocation to work in Germany, would take an age and considerable investment to train and recruit again.

In their negotiations with German agencies, officials were also keen to ensure that workers not only remained in employment, but remained in the country. Deportation to work in Germany, which had happened in occupied Belgium during the First World War, was a constant fear. From this official perspective, continuous employment on an income capable of sustaining a worker and family was the most effective way of 'policing' and protecting working-class communities, and ensuring 'public order'.

For those of us who do not own or run a business, and have never done so, it is perhaps easy to underestimate the fierce proprietorial attachment of a person to a company founded by himself, his father, or grandfather, especially when it has been built up from scratch into a going concern through individual and family graft, innovation, and entrepreneurship. For such owners, the firm was literally one's life, to be protected and nursed at all costs. Keeping it in the family, and being managed by the family, were paramount. For owners whom the French called *patrons*, the business also rooted them in their communities, gave them social status, and power and influence that went beyond a paternalistic concern for the welfare of workers and their families. From the *patron*'s perspective, if the firm collapsed or struggled, then the whole community that depended on it suffered, together with the owner's standing and position in society.

Not all employers were owners, and not all owners were *patrons*. Capitalist economies were increasingly marked by the separation of ownership and management. The sense of loyalty and attachment was different for a manager who in the course of his business career might well have moved from one highly capitalized enterprise to another. But being accountable to anonymous shareholders did not dilute a managerial commitment to sustain and improve the business. Both patronal employers and industrial managers had the interests of their businesses at heart, and regarded those interests as ones overriding all others.

All I am arguing here is that a company patriotism determined the economic choices made by employers in response to the straitened circumstances of war and occupation. This can best be illustrated by taking two rather extreme cases in France. The first is the Michelin tyre-manufacturing company, which had factories located in the unoccupied zone of Vichy France. The Germans were very keen to exploit the rubber industry. In view of uncertain raw material deliveries from French Indochina, they could offer Michelin replacement supplies of artificial rubber, or 'buna', to keep tyre production going. The Vichy government was also very interested in Michelin's future. It was not only a matter of protecting 'national' tyre production. It was an opportunity for Vichy to demonstrate its economic sovereignty, and, more generally, its sovereignty over national territory and its resources. The Vichy government also intended to commit Michelin to participation in an overall deal to be negotiated with Germany on the development of the rubber industry.

The stakes, as they were in all such negotiations on Franco-German economic collaboration, could not have been higher. The Vichy government wanted to negotiate its way to a place in the Nazi European economic New Order, the *Grossraumwirtschaft*, as a valued partner of Germany in the realization of a common European enterprise. The deal agreed between the two governments was that the German side would supply 'buna' to the French tyre industry, which would manufacture tyres for Germany, and enjoy, after the war, a share of a European market. In return, the Vichy government would enable German companies to buy outright or purchase a stake in Michelin factories located in other parts of occupied Europe, in Belgium, the Netherlands, and the Czech lands. It was an unequal exchange, as one would expect in any deal reached in these circumstances. But it was an exchange, nevertheless, and a version of *donnant–donnant*, give-and-take collaboration.

Despite the direct pressure of the French government, which could argue that this was an agreement made in the national interest, Michelin refused to oblige, even though the allocation of 'buna' would enable tyre production to continue. In August 1941, the company called off the sale of its foreign assets, and the deal sank as a result. It made its reason clear to both French and German officials: 'to sacrifice the present in order to save the future.'[7] In other words, Michelin made a business decision not to collaborate on the basis that the company's long-term interests were best served by retaining its foreign investments, so that it could continue to exert and benefit from a European presence in a European post-war market. Given that its decision was made in 1941, it must be assumed that it contemplated operating in a post-war *Grossraumwirtschaft*.

This, then, was a rare case of a major company refusing to collaborate as a way of continuing current production, because its own cost–benefit analysis led to the calculation that its potential post-war market position was more important to its long-term prosperity. As interesting was the coda to Michelin's story. At the same time as Michelin was aborting the Franco-German rubber deal, two other French companies were busy resurrecting it. Ugine and Rhône-Poulenc were in talks with the German chemicals giant, IG Farben, brokered by Jean Bichelonne, a top official in Vichy's Ministry of Industrial Production, later to become the minister. These negotiations were for a joint enterprise to construct and run a factory manufacturing 'buna' in the unoccupied zone. The factory would not start production until 1945, and, hence, was yet another commitment of French companies to the *Grossraumwirtschaft*.

The Michelin case, despite its rarity, was a demonstration that to collaborate economically with the Germans was still very much a *choice* for employers. The affair also showed that organizing company bosses was rather like herding cats—or grandchildren. It made an even stronger case for officials negotiating a single, collective agreement for a sector's or an industry's economic collaboration. That individual bosses were prepared to put their own company interests before those of a perceived national interest is also evident in the second extreme case, this time of a collaborating industrial employer.

Marius Berliet, aged 75 in 1940, was a self-made autodidact motor vehicle engineer and designer, a typical *patron* who owned and ran with his sons a company employing 8,000 people before the war. The company was innovative, pioneering diesel motor manufacturing, continuous mass production, and the application of US Fordist and Taylorite management practices. Berliet specialized in the production of a standard model heavy truck, and the company was France's third largest heavy vehicle manufacturer, behind Renault and Citroën. After the Liberation, Berliet was investigated for obstructing the Republican government's industrial war mobilization plans in 1939–40, and the charges stuck. He thought the government should commission his company to make trucks, which his factory was set up to do.

The government eventually requisitioned one of his plants to manufacture shells, not trucks, sent in its own engineers to manage the factory, and banned Berliet from entering the factory while it was running.

It was hardly surprising that such a cussed and independent-minded employer was one of the early 'wild' collaborators after the German invasion. With one of its components factories in the occupied zone, and one in the unoccupied zone, Berliet's company did a local deal with the German commissioner of his factory in the occupied zone. This enabled parts to be transferred from one zone to the other, and so allowed a start-up of production on German orders on both sides of the demarcation line. When Berliet was asked by his post-war investigator whether it might have been better if he had kept on his workers, but not accepted German orders, he thought the question was nonsensical, which it was.

When the *Comité d'Organisation* for automobile manufacturers was formed, Berliet was obliged to accept its decisions on how many vehicles he should produce, and for whom. The quota system meant that he actually made fewer vehicles than he wanted, whether for the Germans or for the domestic French market. The company remained a thorn in the flesh of both Vichy officials, who were trying to organize a planned economy while negotiating collaborative economic deals with the Germans; and of the Germans, who were very keen to get more from their own productive relationship with the French automobile industry. To both sides, Berliet insisted that he would manufacture only what his company was best at, heavy vehicles, because otherwise he would have to invest in new plant, change his production methods, lay off some workers, and retrain and recruit others. As a *patron* who brooked no interference in the way he ran his company, he refused to collaborate with a German company in a joint Franco-German scheme, which had Vichy backing, for the development of vehicles that were fuelled by gazogens. The Germans eventually managed to check the distribution of orders and raw materials, which prevented Berliet from unilaterally manufacturing gazogene vehicles, if not trucks running on petrol and diesel.

The Berliet family paid dearly for collaborating in a way that, from their perspective, protected the ownership and management of the company Marius *père* had created. As a result of the post-Liberation investigation of their wartime conduct, Marius Berliet was sentenced to two years' imprisonment, and a lifetime removal of his civic rights. Two of his sons were handed down sentences of five years of hard labour in prison. Perhaps worst of all, their assets were confiscated, while the factories were requisitioned by the post-war government and experimentally run by the workforce for a period. A Berliet son re-entered a company factory in 1952. Only Renault, another family firm, was sanctioned as severely for its wartime collaboration in France.

Berliet's story reads like a Greek tragedy—at least, if you are a businessman. To the investigating magistrate in 1945, he gave what for us historians is the standard declaration of employers approaching the prospect of undertaking production for the Germans during wartime occupation: 'I saw things exclusively as a *patron*.'[8] Rather more mournfully at his trial, he confessed that, 'if I have lived too much for my factory, I don't think this amounts to a crime'.[9]

I have portrayed Berliet both as an individual and as a representative case of economic collaboration. That Berliet prioritized the continued existence of his family business was, in my view, the basic explanation of his economic collaboration. You may want to argue that this is unduly reductive, a limitation on the reasons and context for his choices. Were there any other personal and individual characteristics in Berliet's make-up and outlook that might have induced a willingness to collaborate?

Berliet was apparently an extremely conservative and sectarian Catholic, who politically would probably have preferred a Catholic legitimist monarchy to the democratic parliamentary Third Republic. This rather unusual mindset would have reconciled him to Pétain, but hardly to the radical, secular, anti-establishment, and totalitarian ideology of Hitler and the Nazis. We can surely rule out any trace of collaborationism. Berliet's personal and religious views certainly contributed to a patronal and paternalistic concern for the welfare of his workers and their families, as well as his insistence on being the master in his own factories. They did, admittedly, sit rather oddly with his proven stance as a pioneering and technically progressive vehicle manufacturer, which might owe something to his being very much a self-made man.

But exploring these connections, I would argue, is unnecessary. Berliet was undoubtedly a contrarian; he fell out with everybody. But the reason he did so was, in his eyes, to protect and promote the best interests of his business. This, to him, was paramount, whatever he felt personally (and religiously) about Pétain, the *Comité d'Organisation*, or the Germans. It was demonstrable in his words and, above all, in his actions. Berliet's idiosyncratic political and religious views were unlikely to have affected his stance as a businessman keen to do business on his terms, whether with the Vichy government or with the German occupier. This most individual of employers displayed the rather more general characteristics of collaborating businessmen during the occupation.

The officials, or businessmen as officials, who were responsible for implementing the policy of economic collaboration were bound to be motivated by a sense of national and collective interest. In their view, this had to prevail over company patriotism, especially when that was expressed by such individualistic employers as Michelin and Berliet. The broad motivation of collaborating officials who ran the economies of the occupied territories was to protect national economic production and consumption, both now and in the future. In conditions of occupation, this amounted to creating, and then retaining, a reasonable balance between producing for the Germans and producing for domestic consumption. The concern to ensure decent living standards for their people was behind the emphasis officials gave to moderating the extent of economic collaboration. Such moderation had to be applied, if necessary, against both the Germans, only too keen to exploit the economies of the occupied territories, and the country's own employers, usually as keen to meet German demand. If either, or both, were uncontrolled, then internal consumption would be excessively disadvantaged. Too many German orders entailed an endless inflationary spiral, a distortion of the national economy, and the damaging undersupply of basic popular needs.

The defence of the national economy in circumstances of occupation also involved a wages and prices policy to control or curb inflation and the black market, however futile that was in practice. It meant the avoidance of deportation of workers to Germany, essential for securing the social and economic fabric of the country. Such concerns flowed naturally into the preservation of what the French called the national economic 'patrimony'— that is, the economic infrastructure of the country, its inbuilt economic assets, to be regarded as the 'property' belonging to the country as a whole. This became the fundamental justification for economic collaboration. The idea of 'patrimony' embodied the continuity of the nation and of a national economic life and activity. It dignified and gave a sense of national and moral purpose to what, in banally economic terms, might be construed as maintaining the country's productive capacity and potential both during the occupation and, even more importantly, for the post-war period.

With this in mind, we can begin to understand the mode of economic collaboration adopted by officials across the occupied territories, whatever the form of occupation, and the dynamic of that collaboration. Given that officials saw economic collaboration as in and for the national interest, it was really important to them that they presented a single, unified approach to economic relations with the occupier. Collective discipline among employers was at the heart of the Galopin doctrine. A unified stance assumed by officials on the nation's behalf would not only prevent or minimize differences and rivalries between government ministries, and between employers, which the Germans would naturally exploit. It would also expose and exclude individual, rogue contracting of the 'wild' collaboration kind. It would serve to moderate the demands made on the national economy by the Germans, and curb the enthusiasm of employers seeking German contracts, which were detrimental to the balanced economy they aspired to run in the national interest. It would appeal to employers, because a collective approach reduced the chances of one employer, or group of employers, using the opportunities of economic collaboration to secure a competitive advantage over their business rivals, in both internal and external markets, and both currently and in the post-war. Galopin was sometimes confronted by Belgian employers, including his own most serious business rival, Baron Paul de Launoit, head of the Brufina holding company, who were reluctant to accept his principle of collective solidarity and keen to deal with German contractors unilaterally. He always reminded them that a centralized system of economic collaboration would not only ensure a fair distribution of orders among companies during the war itself, but also give a competitive advantage to the Belgian industrial economy as a whole, once the war was over.

You could say that the officials' concern to ensure no unfair competitive advantage ensued from economic collaboration matched employers' concern to remain competitive in the post-war world. It was certainly an issue that rumbled on throughout the post-Liberation inquiries into economic collaboration, with investigators keen to expose cases of businessmen 'profiting' from the occupation. But the issue of competitiveness, apparently so dear to employers concerned to secure the future of their companies, played out in many different ways in the course of the occupation.

For one thing, economic management during the occupation involved allocating scarce resources among employers working on German contracts. The distribution of orders, and of the raw materials required to complete them, was clearly a very effective lever of control for officials running the country's war economy. But, by its very nature, the process of delivering a German order privileged those companies on German contracts; access to raw materials provided an inbuilt competitive advantage. Such preferential treatment was enhanced once the Germans, in face of continuing shortages in supply of raw materials, started to designate and prioritize favoured companies for the receipt of raw materials. By late 1941, ZAST was actually turning down applications for orders, and closing down companies, in order to ensure raw materials reached the preferred provider.

The big players in an economic sector dominated the French *Comités d'Organisation*, the Belgian *Warenstellen*, and the Dutch *Rijksbureau*. The system of distribution and allocation of wartime contracts froze the existing power relations within the sector, usually at the expense of small and medium-sized companies, and always of newcomers to the sector. To give one example of a very common practice across the occupied territories, the head of Sybelac, *le Syndicat Belge de l'Acier*, or Belgian steel association, the recently formed steel production cartel set up at German instigation, became the head of the *Warenstelle* for steel in the Belgian Economics Ministry. The management of the wartime economies in the occupied territories naturally strengthened the position of the larger companies in relation to the smaller. The latter complained, or their representatives did. But only in Vichy France, ideologically committed to the small man against the 'plutocrats' of the banking and big industrial sectors, did their complaints resonate at all.

Again, occupation itself provided other competitive advantages to some employers rather than others. The 'Aryanization' of the economies of the occupied territories occurred under Vichy auspices in unoccupied France, and under German auspices everywhere else. But it did not happen in Denmark, because of the independent status of the Danish government. The drive to eliminate a Jewish presence and influence in West European economic life led to the confiscation, sale, or liquidation of Jewish businesses, property, and assets. This was self-evidently to the commercial advantage of enterprises, big and more often small, competing in those areas of the economy where Jewish-owned firms were well represented. 'Aryanization' reinforced what happened anyway in economic systems built on the allocation of scarcity. A lack of orders, with no prospect of a supply of raw materials to continue business activity, precipitated company closures, mergers, and takeovers. Such a concentration and rationalization of the economy were actively encouraged by the German occupier, and deliberately engineered by the economic planners and officials of Vichy France as an essential element of the 'modernization' of the French economy.

Finally, German penetration of the economies of the occupied territories during the war led to a double-edged offering of actual and potential commercial advantage and disadvantage. On the whole, economic officials of the occupied territories were wary of German attempts to acquire a stake in their country's economy, in defence of the national economic 'patrimony'. Actual German purchases or takeovers of companies in the occupied territories were few. Businessmen and officials put too many obstacles in the way of the process. They bargained and negotiated their way out of the danger of a significant German presence in their national economies, in a classic demonstration of 'give-and-take' collaboration. The foreign assets of local companies located in other parts of occupied Europe were sold off to German predators, in return for a kind of immunity from German penetration of the mother company. In August 1940, Galopin was approached by the German Dresden Bank, which wanted to buy shares in the *Société Générale*. He stonewalled on the request, indicating that the approach was premature; and, in the event, the bank was permitted to acquire shares held by his companies in Central European and Balkan banks. Minority German shareholdings were allowed, in order to stave off or postpone the purchase of a majority stake or a full buyout.

Some German companies and cartels wanted to buy into local companies in order to limit the latter's competition to a national rather than a European market, which they intended to dominate. These attempts to purchase what was effectively a commercial advantage to German companies were an evident risk to the firms targeted for a German approach. After protracted negotiations at the Armistice Commission, IG Farben was allowed to purchase a majority stake in a new Franco-German dyestuffs company, Francolor, set up in November 1941, the most high-profile takeover of a French industry during the occupation. The German chemicals giant's aim was to exploit the war potential of the new company, since its products had a military use as components in the manufacture of explosives. It was also probably to confine the new company to the French market. Part of the trade-off was Francolor being given a shareholding in IG Farben; any kind of partnership with such an important and expansionist company was crucial to post-war business, even as a subcontractor in the domestic market. Whatever the risk, partnerships with German companies were still of obvious appeal to local businesses, opening up prospects of a bigger external market and a keener competitive edge gained through technology and patent transfer and the adoption of German business, commercial, and working practices. Pierre-Louis Brice was the head of a family-owned construction firm, *Sainrapt et Brice*, and every bit as abrasive and self-centred a businessman as Berliet. He disliked working as a subcontractor for the Todt organization, and avoided work on German submarine bases, mainly because he wanted to balance German with domestic orders. But, as a pioneer of reinforced concrete production, he was drawn into cooperating on other projects with Todt and the German companies that worked for Todt in France, attracted by access to German technology and innovation and the opportunity to parade his own firm's attributes. His was a view shared across the industrial economy. When the head of the *Comité d'Organisation* for the mechanical and electrical industries wrote in late 1941 to Jacques Barnaud, the official handling economic relations with Germany, that the Germans wanted to create the 'bases of a European organization inspired by the German model', he regarded it not as a threat, but as an opportunity. The process of collaboration with the Germans was an 'extremely valuable school and stimulant'.[10]

So economic collaboration in the occupied territories had mixed, even paradoxical, effects. Negotiations with the Germans over economic collaboration were usually conducted at an official, governmental level, in order to present that common-front approach that would enable officials to regulate competition among companies. But economic collaboration opened up all kinds of avenues for big business (and small, in the case of 'Aryanization') to gain a commercial advantage over others. This served to strengthen the general consensus of the business community behind the policy of economic collaboration. Industrialists understood very quickly that, when they worked and delivered for the Germans, they would receive more orders, be paid and in good time, and have preference in the supply of energy and raw materials.

The European dimension to economic collaboration is usually underplayed, when it was, in fact, a significant factor in explaining the ubiquity and persistence of collaboration throughout the occupation. Government officials were generally enthusiastic about the prospect of their national economies' participation and integration into a post-war *Grossraumwirtschaft*. Their enthusiasm was shared by businessmen, as well. Many national companies with international markets had, in the interwar period, enjoyed productive and mutually beneficial economic relationships with their German counterparts, and had entered European cartels together. Joining German-dominated cartels and partnerships during the occupation was not seen as an imposition, simply as an extension of existing, sometimes well-established contacts.

You could say that the iron and steel manufacturers in Belgium, Luxembourg, the northern departments of France, and the eastern French department of Meurthe-et-Moselle had no option but to join the German-run consortium set up on his government's orders by Otto Steinbrinck, a retired army officer and board member of a major Germany iron and steel company. The arrangement was clearly designed to ensure German control of Western Europe's heavy industry during the war, as a prelude to possible full German ownership of this international cartel after the war. But it was a transaction conducted between businessmen, and in the language of business. In business terms, no West European iron and steel company could actually afford not to cooperate in the establishment of a regional transnational cartel.

Coal-mine owners and traders in the occupied northern departments attached to Belgium felt abandoned by a Vichy government that struggled in its attempts to reassert any kind of meaningful sovereignty in this detached part of France. In one sense, they did not need German orders to continue production, because they were producing an essential industrial and domestic fuel in a wartime situation where demand always exceeded supply. But they certainly needed to join the German-run coal cartel set up to run the industry in Western Europe, under the auspices of a German plenipotentiary for coal in the annexed and occupied territories appointed in January 1942. They did so to escape the isolation and bottlenecks in trade caused by the wartime division of France that Vichy strained to overcome; and to ensure a place and a say in the post-war organization of Europe's coal industry. It was no pain to his conscience or his pocket for a steel manufacturer or a mine owner to translate something that had arisen as a result of Nazi political and military domination into sound business sense and opportunity, and to become a 'European' operating in a European market.

Baron De Launoit was a controversial figure during the occupation of Belgium. He behaved like a *patron*, and considered himself to be one, which was rather incongruous given the dimensions of the financial and business empire he headed. But the core holding company of what was an agglomeration of holding companies was family owned and directed. He courted unpopularity by socializing with the German officials and company bosses with whom he was doing business. While certainly on the political right, like most employers, he was not a fascist nor a collaborationist. His funding of the Belgian fascist party, Rex, before and during the occupation was more the usual businessman's hedging of bets or playing the political field. Unlike Galopin and the Société Générale, and probably reflecting the wider European export markets and investments of his own company, the baron was openly enthusiastic about economic collaboration in a European framework, including Belgian–German partnerships to tap a European market and German investment in Belgian companies.

He struck a deal with a German company so early on in the occupation that it constituted yet another example of 'wild' collaboration. De Launoit made an agreement with Otto Wolff, a German steel trading and investment company, for the latter to sell in Germany and in Eastern and South-Eastern Europe the products of the largest steel manufacturing plant in Belgium, Ougré-Marihaye, owned by one of De Launoit's holding companies. In return, the Belgian steel company would market German steel products in Belgium. The deal would become fully operational in the event of what was assumed to be an imminent German victory. De Launoit's intention was clearly to secure a place for his manufacturing companies in post-war European markets.

The deal was an early victim of the Galopin doctrine and its principle of collective solidarity and discipline among employers. De Launoit resented the restraint imposed on his business activity by Galopin's policy. Later on, he was reprimanded by Galopin for not initially wanting to take on a German order, and was told to do so. The 'uncrowned king of Belgium', which was what the Germans called him, overrode De Launoit's declared fear of article 115 of the penal code, and his undeclared concern to quieten the animosity in Belgium provoked by the Otto Wolff deal and his clear German associations. His European ambitions were eventually realized through the Belgian iron and steel cartel, Sybelac; Ougré-Marihaye went on to produce barbed wire and anti-submarine nets for the German armed forces.

For some businessmen in the occupied territories, 'Europe', in the shape of the Nazi European New Order, seemed to offer something more than simply being cartelized. Even De Launoit's enthusiasm for European projects was surpassed by the raptures experienced by Lehideux, ex-Renault manager and head of the Comité d'Organisation for the French automobile industry. What European car salesmen would not be carried away by a meeting with

Hitler himself, and then regular consultations with German economic officials and engineers, to cook up a plan for the continent to be interconnected and unified by a vast motorway network carrying mass-produced motor cars and trucks manufactured in France and sold in car showrooms in all the major cities of Europe? A protected expanding market on the continent of Europe was the best possible defence against US competition, a major concern for the French automobile industry.

Lehideux's involvement in long-term European transportation and communication projects was certainly encouraged by the Vichy government. Danish involvement in related New Order initiatives was also 'official'. As a result of intergovernmental negotiations and agreements, Danish construction companies started work on improving rail, motorway, and ferry links between northern Germany and Copenhagen. For Todt, the man behind Nazi Germany's public works projects across occupied Europe, this link was but a step towards realizing a much larger scheme for European security and defence, a connection between Germany and a planned future German naval base at Trondheim in western Norway. A major Danish construction firm, which had helped to build the German motorways in the 1930s, went to Norway in 1940 to erect a new aluminium factory for the Todt organization and the German air force. This New Order project, bringing together the economic resources of three different Germanic countries in a productive and cooperative way to achieve something beyond any one of them, was almost the *Grossraumwirtschaft* in formation. We need to remind ourselves that the bauxite required to make the aluminium was mined in unoccupied France.

After the German invasion of the Soviet Union in June 1941, the European anti-Bolshevik crusade and the Danish government's signing-up to the Anti-Comintern Pact provided the opportunity and justification for the German Foreign Ministry to open talks with Danish government officials over Danish companies getting involved in the economic exploitation of occupied Eastern Europe and western Russia. The prompting came from the top. Hitler told the newly arrived Danish ambassador to Berlin in September 1941 that the recently conquered areas of western Russia were a 'common European field of expansion for Germans and Danes'.[11] He must have meant agricultural colonization as well as industrial development.

The initial German contacts over potential Danish involvement in the New Order in Eastern Europe were with the Danish Ministry of Public Works, the minister of which happened to be the managing director of

Denmark's biggest cement manufacturer and trader. He had the good sense and decency to keep quiet about these early talks, because of the evident encroachment on the government's policy of neutrality. But the 'Working Committee for the Promotion of Danish Initiatives in Eastern and South-Eastern Europe', after arranging business trips to the occupied Baltic States, came under the aegis of the Danish Foreign Ministry in mid-1942. The ministry was, of course, responsible for all formal negotiations with the Germans. Things did not progress much further, but this was hardly down to a lack of interest from Danish officials and businessmen. It had more to do with the internecine rivalries between Ribbentrop and Rosenberg over the exploitation of those areas most exposed to New Order restructuring. Not for the first time, Nazi polycracy got in the way of collaboration.

There was an undeniably sinister aspect to this level of state-sponsored economic collaboration. Danish companies who had contracted for public works with the pre-war Polish government were allowed by both the Danish and the German governments to continue those projects, and employed slave labour, including Polish Jews, on them. The kind of economic collaboration envisaged by the Danish Foreign Ministry was a sign of a willing involvement in the *Grossraumwirtschaft*. This was significant in itself, given the nature of Denmark's 'peaceful' occupation and Nazi Germany's recognition of its neutrality in the war in 1940. It certainly made a mockery of Scavenius's post-war justification of economic collaboration as an 'unavoidable evil'.[12]

There were similar schemes hatched in the occupied Netherlands to involve Dutch business in the Nazi New Order in the East. The employers concerned were associated with the *NSB*, which helped to set things up with the Germans. The initiatives were encouraged and facilitated by the appointment in April 1941 as Secretary General of Finances and President of the Dutch National Bank (both posts were held simultaneously) of Rost von Toningen. He was the leader of the SS-inclining wing of the *NSB*, an alternative to Mussert, not least because he was happy to see the Netherlands annexed to a Greater Germany and the country's full incorp-oration into the *Grossraumwirtschaft*. It was indeed telling that economic opportunities in Eastern Europe were offered only to businessmen from good 'Germanic' countries. In the Dutch case, anyway, the projects were also a small part of the campaign to Nazify the country from below, through the promotion of *NSB*-related business activity. In both countries, the economic action stimulated by East European New Order projects was relatively very small. But it marked the point where, for some businessmen at least, collaboration crossed the line to collaborationism, intentionally in the Dutch case, probably inadvertently in the Danish case.

The ideological element was arguably missing from the Vichy government's tentative moves towards involvement in the economies of occupied Eastern Europe, which came late on, in the summer of 1943. The Minister of Industrial Production, Bichelonne, urged employers in the construction, chemicals, and hotel industries to explore the possibilities of expansion into the region, and a few fact-finding visits by officials and businessmen took place, with unproductive results. The timing of Bichelonne's initiative was revealing: it coincided with very productive meetings with the German economic supremo Speer over the exploitation of French labour, and enabled Bichelonne to indulge his long-held hopes of integrating the French economy into the post-war *Grossraumwirtschaft*. It was almost touching that Bichelonne still retained his belief in a German victory at this stage of the war, but he was not the only one.

I have constantly emphasized that economic collaboration was conducted, as far as possible, from a single point with a single approach, primarily to control the process in what was perceived to be the national economic interest. This was an especially important factor in Denmark and France, where independent, or quasi-independent, national governments existed. For both governments, the simple fact that agreements to collaborate economically were negotiated with the German occupier rather than imposed by them, on a state-to-state basis, was a daily, ongoing demonstration of their right to exist and their legitimacy to govern. The Danish government defined collaboration as the 'policy of negotiation'.[13] For the Danish and Vichy governments, economic collaboration was bound up with the survival and integrity of the national state and its institutions.

This meant that, despite any appearances to the contrary, economic collaboration was, essentially, also highly political in Denmark and France. In turn, awareness of what was at stake gave an added intensity and sensitivity to negotiations over economic collaboration, even when conducted by officials on both sides at a technical level that apparently indicated the exclusion of political considerations. Officials, even when working in areas where they had both experience and expertise, and even when dealing with officials with similar attributes and expectations, had to be 'politicians', as well. This, indeed, was what was also required of the secretaries general in the occupied Netherlands and Belgium, when, as officials, they assumed ministerial roles previously held by elected politicians. Despite 'political' issues being off limits, the secretaries general had to marry their administrative and technical skills with the kind of human touch usually associated with the despised politicians. As we shall see, there was some doubt as to whether officials as ministers even thought that intuitive skills were necessary to their jobs, or actually had any effect on the way they behaved.

There was, of course, a huge difference in international power and expectations between Denmark and France. This went some way towards explaining the relative ease of collaboration between the Danish government and the Germans, and the relative pain and stress of the collaboration between Vichy France and Nazi Germany. Negotiations on Danish shipbuilding and repair contracts for the German navy took four months, between January and May 1941. Franco-German negotiations on French companies repairing and manufacturing aircraft and aircraft engines for the German air force took ten months, between the autumn of 1940 and July 1941. German reports on Danish delivery of their shipbuilding contracts described the process as 'frictionless and punctual'.[14] The German air force (Göring, again) complained about the level of French delivery of German aircraft, and, in September 1942, effectively scrapped the second year of the agreement, insisting on production for Germany as the absolute priority.

It was not all down to the dimensions and capacity of their respective industries, and the size of their respective contracts. The Danish government recognized that Denmark was a small country with no great power pretensions, and that its position in the world would be largely determined by the country's more powerful European neighbours. The point of capitulating so quickly to the German invasion was to retain for a while, anyway, the small amount of international manœuvrability allowed to small countries. Whether Denmark kept its parliamentary democratic system clearly depended on who won the war, and the chances of that happening in the event of a German victory were remote. So a 'peaceful' occupation allowed a breathing space, minimized the disruption to the way the country was governed while the war lasted, and did not irrevocably tie the future Denmark to a German victory. The purpose of governmental collaboration was, then, to keep things as they were, as far as this was possible.

The Danish government could hardly avoid a steady incorporation into the *Grossraumwirtschaft*, and showed no desire to evade this completely. Danish agriculture and fisheries ended up supplying between 10 and 15 per cent of German wartime food consumption. Denmark was clearly being lined up to provide pork, butter, and fish in a future autarkic Nazi-dominated Europe. Its niche industries were also exploited by the Germans, as military needs arose. But this was all done with a degree of moderation on both sides. The Danish government could not escape the trawl of the *Grossraumwirtschaft*, nor of the intrinsically exploitative German clearing system. It did, nevertheless, avoid the payment of occupation costs, the overt penetration of the national economy by German banks and companies, and a customs and financial union with Germany. The Germans, in other words, respected the semi-independence of the Danish government and its economic sovereignty. It did so deliberately, in order to set up and maintain the virtuous circle of collaboration. This meant that collaboration was rewarded with collaboration, in a perpetually self-reaffirming process. The Germans got what they wanted from the Danish economy, precisely because they did not press too hard on it, and did not interfere too much in the country's economy and polity. As a result, economic collaboration was low key, normal, routine, and rather boring.

There was nothing dull about Franco-German relations during the war. All Vichy governments, whether under Laval, Darlan, or Laval again, wanted to restore France's great imperial and maritime power position after the traumatic defeat of 1940, and secure a decent role for France in the future European New Order. All Vichy governments banked on a German victory in the war. The government set up a very high-level delegation in February 1941 to handle intergovernmental economic negotiations with the Germans. Its head, Jacques Barnaud, was the identikit Vichy technocrat of the Darlan era, and a member of an informal cabal of young, enterprising officials and businessmen turned ministers who pushed for closer collaboration with Nazi Germany, in order to guarantee France's place in the New Order. In April 1941, this group—that is, Barnaud, Jacques Benoist-Méchin, along with Lehideux, Pucheu, then Minister of Industrial Production and soon to be Interior Minister, and Paul Marion, later promoted to head of propaganda services in the Vichy government—signed a 'Plan for a New Order in France' and submitted it to Otto Abetz, the German ambassador to France. It was a preliminary shot in the internal battle to move Vichy towards collaborationism.

The driving force of Vichy's collaboration in 1941–2 was Benoist-Méchin, a writer and military historian, with a German mother, and one-time member of a French fascist party, the *PPF*. He was well educated, but rather outside the charmed circle of overeducated elite technocratic officials who dominated the Darlan government—a brotherhood he, nevertheless, came to share and lead. He advanced what he saw as a proper strategy of collaboration from his strategic position as secretary of state to the vice-president, who was Darlan. He was, effectively, the minister servicing the cabinet of ministers, at the political high command of the government.

What characterized Vichy's economic collaboration in 1941–2 were its nakedly political dimension and the practice of *donnant–donnant*, 'give-and-take' collaboration. Prompted by Benoist-Méchin, the Vichy government under Darlan negotiated economic agreements that were not just for economic ends, such as preserving the national economic 'patrimony' in order to enable France to compete in wartime and post-war markets. Economic collaboration was meant to strengthen Vichy's position in relation to general, political negotiations over France's place in the New Order. Specific economic agreements were seen as steps along the way to a comprehensive political settlement between France and Germany. Economic collaboration was the 'give' of the 'take' of a more general strategy of collaboration.

Perhaps the best way to illuminate this process is to look at and contextualize the negotiation of one of the most important economic partnerships between Vichy France and Nazi Germany, for the manufacture of aircraft and aircraft engines in France. Naturally enough, the aeronautics industry in France was the recipient of heavy state investment and planning. Although way down on its pre-war status and dimensions, at its production peak during the occupation in early 1944 the industry employed 95,000 staff in 200 factories in both the occupied and unoccupied zones. It had a self-evident military and political importance for both sides. The Germans wanted to mobilize the industry to produce planes and engines for the war effort, and according to German models and specifications. The desire became a need in early 1941, as the German air force tried to make good the losses incurred in the 'Battle for Britain', and prepare for the invasion of the USSR. The negotiations also coincided with temporary difficulties faced by the Axis war in North Africa and the Middle East in the spring of 1941. The Vichy government sought to exploit the fluctuations of war, in its endless search for a concerted and comprehensive political and military settlement with Nazi Germany. The Germans were also keen to involve in their war effort the manufacturing base of unoccupied Vichy France, and thereby extend their economic influence from the occupied to the 'free' zone.

The aeronautics industry had obvious political and military clout for both the Laval and the Darlan governments in 1940–1. Vichy France was naturally concerned to recover and retain a national French arms industry, as the basis for the relaunch of the French armed forces, in turn, the essential muscle of Vichy's claim to be a major imperial great power that merited a place in the New Order. Importantly, negotiations over the industry would take the Vichy government's relations with Nazi Germany beyond the terms of the Armistice, and into areas of wartime strategy likely to enhance France's standing with Germany. The Armistice, after all, limited French arms production to providing for national defence. This effectively meant no new arms production, simply the recovery and repair of existing stock, and ruled out the continuation of research and development in the arms industry.

The Armistice had also divided France territorially. The demarcation line fragmented a vital national industry, with some companies having factories in both zones, or the administrative offices in one zone and factories in the other, or components factories in one zone and assembly in the other. The negotiations provided a great opportunity for the Vichy government to re-create a national industry, and thereby assert its economic sovereignty over both zones. Vichy, as much as the Germans, was able to use the division of France into occupied and unoccupied zones to its own negotiating advantage. If the Germans intended to exploit the economic resources of the unoccupied zone, then they would have to accept the creation of a national industry and a national market that cut across the internal barriers to production and trade erected by the divisions of occupation. More than that, a revived and functioning aircraft industry would enable Vichy France to offer active military aid to Germany in Africa and the Middle East, where its own great power aspirations naturally lay.

The negotiations for an agreement on aircraft and engine manufacturing began in the autumn of 1940. Initially, on Vichy's side, the concern was to put an end to, or regulate, the 'wild' collaboration of the summer between the occupier and individual companies. The aim was to ensure that the industry as a whole could be deployed as a bargaining tool in Vichy's policy of collaboration with Germany. The early negotiations were inhibited by the inherent German anxiety about allowing the speedy rearmament of a defeated enemy. The Germans were also worried by the patriotic and technical risks of having German planes built by French manufacturers.

The negotiations were complicated by the Vichy ploy of extending the reach of the talks beyond the economic to the political and military. Nearly all the German authorities, from Hitler and the Reich Economic and Armed

Forces ministries downwards, disliked and distrusted this approach, because it required them to take decisions about France that they had intended to postpone until the end of the war. The Germans, with few exceptions, wanted to make the agreement sectorally specific, rather than wide-ranging. It was scarcely a few months from the signing of the Armistice. It was hardly unexpected to find out that the German side was sensitive and impatient when confronted by French officials negotiating on the basis of aircraft production in return for a raft of concessions, which were not directly related to the matter in hand. Easing the demarcation line, releasing French POWs, reducing occupation costs, opening up the 'forbidden zones' to Vichy France, detaching the northern departments from the German military administration in Brussels—these would have returned France to more or less its pre-Armistice standing in Europe, through the actual as opposed to virtual re-establishment of Vichy sovereignty throughout French territory.

Göring usually lost his temper when dealing with inferior foreigners, and indeed, anybody, and did so again when he met Pétain in December 1941. In response to Vichy's blanket presentation of the usual list of returns for continuing collaboration, the head of the German air force, among so many other things, literally exploded at what he saw as the German 'give' and the French 'take': 'this is madness...anyone would think that you won the war!'[15] It was, in purely negotiating terms, unrealistic to expect German leaders and officials to sign away every aspect of the leverage they, as occupiers, could exercise against Vichy France. The stalling of talks in late 1940 probably had the effect of making French officials realize that moderating their negotiating demands, or, at least, separating out their demands, would conciliate rather than antagonize their German counterparts.

What had developed into something of an impasse was relieved in January 1941, when the Vichy negotiators apparently abandoned their global strategy and settled on straight 'give-and-take' discussions, leading to a specific economic agreement on aircraft manufacture. The apparent change in approach was probably induced by the fallout from Laval's dismissal as Prime Minister, and Vichy's understandable concern to unfreeze its relations with Nazi Germany and resume some form of collaboration. Even though henceforth no political concessions were to be traded off in the negotiations, General Huntziger gave the decision an authentically political gloss: it was for reasons of 'high politics'[16] that the negotiations were to be specific, not general. This just about made sense, even to Huntziger. A search for a comprehensive political and military settlement with Nazi Germany was being temporarily shelved in order to restore the principle of Montoire— that Vichy should collaborate with Germany.

It is admittedly difficult to work out whether the change was a general one, affecting other aspects of Franco-German collaboration, and whether it took place for the same reason. There is an indication, perhaps, in the decision of Vichy's Minister of Finances, Bouthillier, to resume payment of the 400 million francs a day for German occupation costs. He had unilaterally suspended these payments in late 1940, intending to lever the Germans into negotiating a full settlement with Vichy France, including occupation costs. Coinciding with Laval's dismissal, the move only alienated the Germans further. However, if there was an overall change in Vichy's negotiating position on collaboration, it was theoretical rather than actual, even for the talks on the aircraft agreement. In practice, over the spring of 1941, Vichy continued to link its demands for concessions, acting in the belief and expectation that it could trade off an economic concession for a supposed equivalent political and military concession. The continuation of the practice was encouraged by the circumstances in which collaboration was being revived. When it appeared that the Germans needed and would benefit from French cooperation in the Axis war in Africa and the Middle East, then surely this improved the chances of them accepting an exchange of concessions in unrelated areas of collaboration.

The return to specifics did not necessarily make collaboration any easier. The German aircraft manufacturer Junker wanted French factories to construct German-designed planes. German negotiators requested that Junker receive shares in French companies as a kind of collateral for completion of the contract, and a way around the problem of a foreign manufacturer making German planes. The French officials demurred, as they always did when faced by a possible German penetration of the French economy. The Germans then made a virtue of necessity. In return for withdrawing the request for shareholdings, they demanded a say in the appointments to the heads of French companies executing German contracts, and a single French official in Paris (the 'leader principle') to be responsible for delivering the contracts. This ploy might have been normal negotiating tactics. It was certainly characteristic of the way German officials negotiated similar deals across occupied Western Europe. A side issue would be raised, only to become a bargaining chip in the negotiations; the Germans wanted something substantial in return for something they had merely proposed.

Hitler would have been proud of these officials, since they were collaborating in exactly the way he had envisaged in his earlier conversation with Laval about *donnant–donnant*. It was up to you Frenchmen to demonstrate your good intentions and will to collaborate, German officials were saying, by giving us something in advance in return for nothing. This would create the trust necessary for negotiations to continue. Reflecting the unequal balance of power between the two sets of collaborating officials, this kind of exchange was exasperating and time-consuming for French officials, who had to be really tenacious and resilient in negotiations with their German counterparts. You could say that this was what officials were trained to do: conduct high-level negotiations with equally committed and qualified civil servants. But it was a treadmill, nevertheless. German officials were very adept at working the modalities of a specific agreement in a way that practically undermined or changed the principle of the agreement. So, for instance, if they apparently agreed to concede the release of some French POWs, they would then raise endless questions about the exact numbers, timing, and kind of POWs to be repatriated (officers, men, First World War veterans, farmers, miners, engineers).

And politics kept on intruding. The French aircraft agreement negotiators continued, despite Huntziger's pledge, to request impossible counter-concessions in areas unrelated to the current economic talks. With the arrest of Frenchmen in the occupied zone for acts of resistance, or for violating food and rationing regulations, officials asked that the German military administration be prevailed upon to transfer the arrested men to French courts rather than have them face German military tribunals. This time it was German officials who rolled their eyes and threw up their arms in exasperated despair. As members of the economic delegation to the Armistice Commission, they could hardly decide on matters outside their expertise and jurisdiction, and they rather resented the possibility of the negotiations passing into the hands of other German bodies and agencies.

The eventual agreement, signed in July 1941, was to run for two years. The original German proposal for a 5:1 ratio in the manufacture in France of planes for Nazi Germany and Vichy France was whittled down to one nearer 2:1. Most of the production in the first year of the agreement was of French planes for French service, understandable for technical as much as for patriotic reasons, since French production methods had to be adapted to work on German models. But the German negotiating principle, that French production was conditional on production for Germany, was retained.

In the end, 90 per cent of aircraft engines and 87 per cent of aircraft produced in France during the occupation went to Germany. These figures reflected the collapse of the agreement in its second year, finalized after the German invasion and occupation of the 'free' zone in November 1942, which served to prioritize production for Germany.

There were monthly targets to meet on delivery of German planes, annual ones for French production for French use, another demonstration of how attentive the Germans were to the modalities of an agreement. Vichy could choose the models it manufactured for its own deployment. French companies manufacturing the aircraft, and engines were paid for from French credits advanced by French banks. Apparently this was something on which the French side insisted, and on which the Germans were only too ready to concede: the appearance of national economic sovereignty was exchanged for the substance of actually paying for what was manufactured. The programme, on the French side, would be managed by the French *Comité d'Organisation* for the aeronautics industry, which would distribute the raw materials and energy kindly conceded by the Germans in order to ensure production on German planes went ahead. The huge gain of the agreement, from the French viewpoint, was that it was negotiated, not imposed, and could be portrayed as a joint programme to be realized by a Franco-German partnership in an industry essential to the present and future security and military power of the European New Order. It both provided a niche for France in that New Order, and justified the means by which it had been brought about, through state-to-state collaboration.

Over the spring of 1941, there was an evident conjuncture between negotiations for a Franco-German partnership agreement on aircraft production, the evolution of the Vichy's government's general strategy for Franco-German collaboration, and the Axis war in North Africa and the Middle East. Despite Vichy's apparent decoupling of specific agreements from a more general agreement in January 1941, the connection of mismatched concessions still went on. In May 1941, in order to support an anti-British rebellion in Iraq, the Germans requested that Vichy enable the transit of German military aid to the rebels through or over the French League of Nations mandate of Syria. Vichy obliged, and clearly expected some movement in the constant negotiations over occupation costs, as a result. The German delegation to the Armistice Commission was blind to the linkage, because it could handle economic and military matters only within the framework of the Armistice. But it duly accepted Bouthillier's proposal to reduce daily occupation payments to 300 million francs, careful to explain that it did so on the economic grounds put forward by Bouthillier himself—that excessive occupation costs were fuelling price inflation in France.

The exchange of unrelated concessions was something that existed in the minds of French ministers and officials, not in those of their German counterparts. As was often the case, the workings of what was proving to be a flawed strategy of collaboration were painful and unsatisfying. The Germans got what they wanted: French aid to support Axis machinations in Iraq. Vichy received nothing more substantial than a building-up of potential credit with Germany that might, or might not, be useful in facilitating future Franco-German cooperation. With a fantastic sleight of hand, the Germans scuppered the proposal for reduced occupation costs by, once again, manipulating the modalities of the apparent agreement. The German delegation insisted that, in return for conceding lower occupation costs, the Vichy government should pay a significant proportion of the costs in gold, hard foreign currencies, and French shares in foreign firms. This was angrily rejected by the French delegation, because it was clearly a disproportionate and damaging 'give and take'. Vichy would actually end up paying more in occupation costs, and could not countenance any further German encroachments on French companies nor any draining-away of the country's gold and currency reserves. And, of course, occupation payments remained at 400 million francs a day.

As was the case in occupied Belgium, the Vichy government felt that the only way to rescue an increasingly untenable and unproductive strategy of collaboration was to press for a clear-the-air meeting with Hitler and the top Nazi leaders. Benoist-Méchin rather doubted that this was a good move. He thought that his boss, Darlan, as a navy man and official, lacked the charisma, political skills, and self-confidence to take on Hitler, attributes that Laval had claimed for himself at Montoire. Benoist-Méchin preferred to work through the German ambassador to France, and a kind of Nazi plenipotentiary in France, Otto Abetz, who at least said things that the young minister wanted to hear. Abetz had been long committed to Franco-German reconciliation at all levels, including, at this juncture of the war, a military alliance between France and Germany.

It was, perhaps, understandable that so many illusory expectations were raised by the prospect of a face-to-face meeting between the country's leaders. This, after all, was how the Nazi system operated. Access to Hitler was essential in order to secure the *Führer*'s endorsement of the line of policy you wanted to follow. The problem was that such a meeting removed Vichy's leaders and officials from the much cosier and generally civilized and cooperative relations with the German military administration in France itself. A deliberate testing-out of Hitler's intentions towards France risked exposing the gaps that existed between the Reich authorities' view of collaboration and that actually practised by the military government in Paris. In other words, a meeting would only be the forum for the exchange of some pretty brutal home truths about the nature and future of France's collaboration with Nazi Germany.

And so it proved in the meetings of May 1941. Hitler simply reiterated the position he had adopted with Laval a few months earlier. Darlan started off by saying that Vichy needed concessions from the Germans to justify its policy of collaboration to an increasingly sceptical and overburdened French people. Because of the essentially propagandistic and populist nature of what was required, such concessions could be 'more spectacular than profound'. This must have appeared a wise approach at the time. Vichy was not actually asking for much from the Germans: only an easing of occupation, which would enable the government to show the French people that collaboration brought positive results.

Hitler responded in typical fashion. He deliberately minimized the likely contribution of Vichy France to ultimate German victory in the war, the means by which Vichy, of course, hoped to secure a place in the New Order. So there would be no prior commitment on Germany's part to France's role in the new Europe while the war continued. If France could not win the war for Germany, it could certainly help to shorten it. The way to do this was by operating *donnant–donnant* according to Hitler's rules. 'It's not haggling', insisted Hitler; 'it's an indispensable precaution. Franco-German relations are, above all, a matter of confidence. It's up to you to show you deserve it.'[17] In other words, Germany 'takes' first and, maybe, 'gives' later. Vichy France 'gives' first and, maybe, 'takes' later. France gives now in the hope, never the guarantee, of future reciprocity in Franco-German relations. For Darlan, Hitler was simply confirming the bad faith already displayed by his officials and agents over the Syria–Iraqi 'deal'. In his view, and from his experience, Germany should pay for Vichy concessions in advance, to demonstrate *its* trust and confidence in future collaboration between France and Germany. To demand of Germany the very thing that it was demanding of you (trust) was to behave as if France and Germany were equals, if not partners, and made a cul-de-sac of the policy of collaboration.

Pétain, at least, had Hitler's number. When he met Darlan after the meetings in Germany for a debriefing, he affected to be pleasantly surprised by Hitler's endorsement of *donnant–donnant* collaboration, because it accorded with his own cautious view of what could be expected from any collaboration with Nazi Germany. He professed himself very happy with what Hitler had apparently offered Darlan: a 'step-by-step' approach of specific concessions, which should, in the circumstances, be 'small concessions... very *small* concessions—the war isn't over'.[18]

Benoist-Méchin, who had accompanied Darlan to Berlin but not attended Darlan's meeting with Hitler, was understandably enraged by Pétain's interpretation of the meeting and its consequences for the policy of collaboration. It ran counter to his own strategy of arriving at a comprehensive political and military settlement with Nazi Germany. It undermined the significance of the 'political' supplement he had managed to squeeze into the 'Paris Protocols', signed off in May 1941, which were a summary of France's limited military engagement with the Axis war in Africa and the Middle East. The 'political' protocol carried only the signatures of Abetz and Darlan, a sign of the Nazi leadership's reluctance to commit itself to what could be an embryonic Franco–German alliance, if followed up.

Benoist-Méchin counter-attacked furiously, arguing that the German invasion of the USSR in June 1941 had transformed a military war into an ideological war for the 'soul' of Europe, and that Vichy France had to associate itself ideologically with the anti-Bolshevik crusade. He was, quite consciously, moving from a policy of collaboration to one of collaborationism, a stance consistent with his own recent fascist attachments. He persuaded Darlan to submit a memorandum to Abetz, for onward transmission to Ribbentrop and Hitler, in July 1941. This document not only urged Nazi Germany to abandon the Armistice for a fully-fledged Franco–German alliance. It also promised an internal ideological and political alignment of Vichy's practices and institutions to those of Nazism, as a part, and a guarantee, of that alliance.

Benoist-Méchin was committing Vichy France to a process of totalitarian 'coordination' in terms that had already been expressed by Mussert, Degrelle, and Quisling. The Nazi leadership, true to form, was not interested in an alliance with France, nor was it really interested in a 'fascistized' France. The memorandum fell into the deep, silent pit of German indifference. The silence, which meant rejection, was eventually broken by Göring's brutal reminder to Pétain a few months later of exactly where Vichy France stood in Germany's estimation.

There was what might be called a 'logic' of collaboration that applied to all collaboration, but especially to economic collaboration. The 'logic' was that, once someone was collaborating, it was well-nigh impossible to withdraw that collaboration. This 'logic' can be illustrated best by looking at the first big crisis of the Galopin doctrine in occupied Belgium. It occurred in 1941, rather than, as for economic collaboration elsewhere, from 1942. As ever, Belgium experienced and lived through earlier, and with greater cost and intensity, the great dilemmas of collaboration with the German occupier.

The rationale of Galopin's 'policy of production' was that Belgium's industrial exports to Germany would pay for the food imports from Germany and German-dominated Europe necessary to sustain the Belgian population. Food supply was occupied Belgium's major problem, and constantly exercised officials and policymakers because of its self-evident effect on popular morale, social order, and workers' productivity. Galopin expected there to be a direct equivalence between industrial exports and agricultural imports. This, in 1940–2, meant Belgian industry *increasing* its production for Germany, and led to a touting for more German contracts. Galopin, a German speaker, himself toured the German economic ministries and agencies in Berlin in January 1941, canvassing more German orders for Belgian industry.

If the Belgians were to increase production for Germany, then they had to supply what the Germans actually wanted. As a result, there was an almost immediate slippage on the legal principle, now no more than a preference, of not manufacturing war materials for Germany. Galopin expected that the German clearing system would operate in a direct and transparent way, so that an equivalent exchange of industrial goods and food supplies could take place. The Germans, of course, had no intention of allowing an occupied country to determine the terms of exchange of their own clearing system. They did from the start what they did to the end of the occupation, accumulating huge credits at the expense of the exporting country and its banks. In the Belgian case, the credits built up in clearing industrial exports to Germany were never used to meet the level of demand for food imports. You might want to say that Galopin should have anticipated Germany's conduct, and not risked so much on the occupier running its own trading system in a more equitable way. But this was the very nature of 'give-and-take' collaboration with Germany. You had to initiate the exchange with no guarantee of reciprocation. In Belgium's case, Galopin had to set in motion a collaborative exchange in order to ensure that Belgians were fed; it was as imperative as that.

By the spring of 1941, it was pretty clear to everybody, the Belgian people, the Galopin committee, the government-in-exile, and even the German military authorities, that the 'system' was not working. It was not the case that starvation was stalking the land. But Belgians were not adequately fed during the 1940–1 winter. Struye reported that it was difficult to get hold of butter and potatoes, rations were meagre, and that 'nearly everyone is getting thinner'.[19] The government-in-exile, now in what could be regarded as 'resistance' mode, called into question the validity of Galopin's 'policy of production', which was clearly not producing the expected results. Galopin thought hard, and consulted widely among members of the Belgian establishment. Some of them wanted to ditch the policy, or at least lever more food out of the Germans by, for instance, refusing to pay the next instalment of occupation costs unless the food-supply situation improved.

After the government-in-exile's grudging endorsement of the policy in May 1941, Galopin took stock, and revised it, in his memorandum of June. As a response to the government's criticism of the policy, Galopin now spoke of the Germans as the 'enemy', of the government-in-exile as the 'government' to which he was accountable, and of a German victory in the war as being one of several possible scenarios rather than a certainty. The now uncertain outcome of the war was, however, used by Galopin to argue for a continuation of the 'policy of production', since the Belgian economy needed to be in a state of competitive readiness, whoever won the war. Indeed, he emphasized that the driving force behind the policy was the preservation of Belgium's economic patrimony for whatever kind of post-war was in store. This was the only moral purpose he could inject into the policy, since the highly patriotic one of ensuring the Belgians consumed enough could not now, through bitter experience, be met. The continuation of the policy was to be henceforth justified as a matter of 'necessity'—that is, a freely taken but nevertheless constrained decision to make do with a lesser evil.

The revised policy read more like an extension than a revision. Industrial production for the Germans had, yet again, to be increased over the coming years in order to activate the exchange of food imports, insufficient though that might, yet again, prove to be. The Reich ministries and agencies had reacted unfavourably to the secretaries general's efforts to find alternative unilateral solutions to the country's food-supply shortages, and continued to do so. Reeder, recognizing that Belgian economic collaboration required some compensatory return for the Belgian people, supported the secretaries general's initiative to import cereals from the USSR in the winter of 1940–1, only for the scheme to be stymied by Berlin. The secretaries general also tried to negotiate separate deals with Vichy France for the import of food from both the occupied and the unoccupied zones. The military governors of Belgium–northern France were generally sympathetic to Belgian officials securing more food supplies, because they shared the same wider concern as those officials, which was public order. But too many entrenched positions were challenged for the officials' campaign to succeed: the deliberately exploitative way the German Economic Ministry chose to operate the clearing system; and the objections of both the Vichy government and the German military administration of occupied France to northern France being run from Brussels.

Some one-off deals were allowed, and passed through the clearing system (Belgian coal for French fats; French West African fruit for Belgian fertilizers). But a secure and lasting exchange was impossible to arrange, in the face of the biggest obstacle, which remained: the Germans controlled Belgian–German clearing and, hence, the purchasing of food imports to Belgium.

The German military administration certainly backed the constant calls for a more effective and repressive policing of the black market that came from the Secretary General for Agriculture, Emile De Winter. Through a system of agrarian organizations as ramified as that for the country's industrial sector, his job was to ensure the production, purchase, and distribution of essential food supplies. But De Winter's campaigns against his own countrymen's evasion of food rationing and regulation counterproductively tackled a symptom rather than the cause of the food-supply crisis. It was hypocritical of Reeder to support De Winter when the military commands and agencies were enthusiastic buyers on the informal markets.

It was at least clear to the Galopin committee that they had won over the German military occupiers to their cause, and that the people they really needed to convince of the need for a more equitable exchange were the German Reich authorities. Inordinate expectations were raised for a visit to Berlin of a Belgian economic delegation, including Galopin and a couple of the secretaries general, in March 1942, which hoped to negotiate a general and permanent settlement of economic collaboration between Belgium and Nazi Germany. This was despite the omens not looking good, at least on the Belgian side. Galopin's renewed consultations outside the committee were inconclusive, leading Struye to remark in his diary that, 'when the economic and financial life and future of the country are at stake, one should cast aside the spirit and style of the official'.[20] This was less a call for 'resistance' than an appeal for some *political* leadership. He had earlier spoken of the 'demoralizing' policy of backing the secretaries general simply on the grounds that they were a lesser evil to the alternative of a Reich Commissariat, saying that 'the people want to be led'.[21] And, if Galopin could not be expected to rise to the occasion, then who else? The king, quarantined in his royal palace, who had no pull with Hitler at all? Or De Man, a similarly discredited and exiled figure? Perhaps they should have asked about Laval's availability.

The need for leadership was not being met from abroad. Gutt, the Minister of Finance in the government-in-exile, having approved the Galopin doctrine in the spring, now reverted to type in the autumn. On the separate issue of a disputed appointment to head of the Belgian National Bank, he blasted Galopin and the secretaries general publicly in a Radio London broadcast on 27 November 1941. It was an extraordinarily unhelpful and demoralizing statement for businessmen and officials preparing for a long-awaited summit meeting with Nazi leaders and officials in Berlin. According to Gutt, it was the 'same war...same Germans', and any measures implemented in Belgium under German pressure were automatically invalid. 'To save the country', one had to resist, 'passively' in Belgium, 'actively' from abroad.[22]

The meetings, when they came, were a severe disappointment to the Belgian delegation. They received not food, nor the promise of more food, but a worsening of the harsh current reality. Göring chose to lead and preside over the talks. The Belgian delegation's heads must have dropped immediately at the sight of this corpulent epitome of Nazi intransigence and bullying. The man formally in charge of the economic exploitation of the occupied territories simply refused to consider or discuss the economic arguments that his own officials and those of the Belgium delegation put forward as the basis for negotiation. Instead, he talked exclusively Nazi politics. How on earth was Galopin to respond to Göring's startling opening gambit—that he would ensure Belgians received more food in return for Belgian, presumably Flemish, peasants helping to colonize the Ukraine? Nothing in his briefings with Reeder, or among the Belgian establishment, would have prepared him for that.

Göring then heard out the Belgian delegation's reasoned economic case for greater industrial exports in return for greater agricultural imports. His reply, paraphrased and with expletives deleted, went as follows: a war for the survival of European civilization was being fought by German armies in the USSR; the anti-Bolshevik crusade entailed Germans sacrificing their lives for West Europeans who were merely contributing their products and restricting their consumption; this was clearly already such an inequitable exchange that occupied Western Europe had no right to make any demands on Germany; rather, it should give more for less. In summary, Göring said that the role of the Belgian economy was to service the war Germany was fighting for all Belgians (or the 'Germanic' ones, anyway) in the Soviet Union.

The prolonged crisis of the Galopin doctrine ran for nearly a year from the spring of 1941 to the early spring of 1942. The detail of this rather grim story is important, because only a contextualization of events enables us to understand how collaboration actually worked, as it were, on the ground. With retrospect, and without proper contextualization, we can make rather easy judgements about Galopin's policy. It failed on its own terms, it led to an excessive German exploitation of the Belgian economy, it should have heeded the government-in-exile's injunction to 'resist' 'passively'. The fact was that Belgian agriculture became more productive, rather successfully moving from pasture to arable as the Dutch agrarian economy had done. The result was that Belgians were largely fed throughout the war on home-grown produce. There were shortages, and malnourishment, but not famine. This might suggest that not only did the Galopin policy fail; it became redundant and unnecessary, and an alternative could, therefore, have been found that would at least have slowed down the German exploitation of the Belgian economy.

There can be no doubt that Galopin and the secretaries general were under extraordinary pressure in the spring of 1941, as the bad winter of 1940–1 made it doubtful that the 'policy of production' could continue. In a sense, that pressure, exerted on them by the expectations of the people, of the government-in-exile, and of the German occupation authorities, was abnormal, but it became normal. In occupied Belgium and the Netherlands, collaborating was a daily plebiscite for the secretaries general of both countries. It was a matter of constant dialogue and negotiation with the occupation authorities, and of difficult, sometimes anguished, decision-making. It really made a difference with whom that perpetual dialogue was conducted. The crisis showed, as if they did not already know, that it was more congenial to deal with Reeder than with Göring.

With Reeder, it was official to official, usually speaking the language not of politics, but of economics and administration, the practical stuff of running the country and meeting its needs. The principle of collaboration was open to challenge during the handling of each and all of those daily and specific issues. But managing them, in turn, was a daily affirmation and validation of the worth of collaboration to both sides. The German military authorities were, and remained, an integral element of the collaborating exchanges. The consensus behind collaboration held up and was reasserted during and as a result of the crisis of the Galopin doctrine. Reeder could not, and did not want to, run the country with his own staff. He needed local officials to cooperate in the realization of a shared concern for public and social order. This was essentially why Reeder did his best to facilitate the manœuvres of Galopin and the secretaries general to ease what was perceived by both sides as an ongoing crisis in food supply for the Belgian population. Reeder also knew that there were limits to their capacity and will to continue collaborating. This was evident during the crisis of the Galopin policy in 1941–2.

In summer 1941, Oscar Plisnier, Secretary General for Finances and the chair of the secretaries general's committee, effectively the acting Prime Minister, threatened to resign if the promised German supply of cereals did not appear. On other occasions, Reeder would not have blinked. He had, after all, culled three secretaries general between January and March 1941. Both in occupied Belgium and the Netherlands, some of the most serious attritional disputes between the occupation authorities and the secretaries general were over appointments to the top official positions. Usually the Germans got their way. In Belgium, only three of the original eleven secretaries general in post in 1940 were still there in 1944, and the new appointments were not Francophone, but Flemish nationalists; the proportions were exactly the same in the Netherlands.

In *this* event, Plisnier stayed, and the cereals turned up. De Winter was promised the entire proceeds of the current Belgian grain harvest, apparently enough to meet bread rations until the following spring. Collaboration had worked, in the way it was meant to work. The operating relationships between the officials and the military administration had not been disrupted by Plisnier's removal. The secretaries general had deployed, effectively this time, their only real leverage with the occupier, the withdrawal of collaboration, in order to gain a significant concession benefiting the Belgian people.

The crisis faded with the confirmation that the German Reich authorities were the real barrier to concessions on the food-supply problem. They were immovably against any long-lasting and systematic arrangements on food supply that would come anywhere near to the ideal equivalent

exchanges envisaged by the Galopin doctrine. But the crisis also showed
that ad hoc sticking-plaster solutions were resorted to *in extremis*, through
the good offices of the military administration, rather than the Reich
authorities. Galopin et al. had every reason to continue collaborating to
good effect with Reeder and his officials, if only as a way of holding the
Reich authorities at bay.

This was why 'resistance', 'passive' or not, was just nonsensical at such a
juncture. Resisting would have demonstrated the fallibility and 'weakness' of
the military government to those Reich agencies who preferred a Reich
Commissioner, as in Norway and the Netherlands. So, for Galopin and the
secretaries general, it was just good sense, and in what they perceived as the
national interest, that, even, or especially, after the disastrous meeting with
Göring, they decided to plough on with the 'policy of production'. The
Belgians had to produce more in order to secure food supplies that, if not
sufficient, were nevertheless necessary. If they refused to collaborate economically, then the only result was the risk of losing what food supplies
there were and would be in the country, a total economic shut down, and
direct German rule, an almost exact replication of what had happened
during the First World War.

Galopin, after his spasm of self-doubt in the spring of 1941, very creditably
held his nerve, and was confident enough to berate Gutt for interfering in
a situation that he could not, or would not, fully comprehend, precisely
because he was in London, not Brussels. Galopin's rebuke was written in
June 1942. It reached Gutt in August 1943; but the silence between them
was already deafening, and not really down to the difficulties in communicating from occupied Europe.

It is important to realize that the reasons and motivations behind economic collaboration remained constant throughout the occupation. This
helps to explain the continuation of collaboration in the 1942–4 period,
even when the context for that collaboration had dramatically changed.
Employers still needed to keep their businesses going on German contracts;
their workers still needed employment on delivering those contracts.
Officials still needed to manage their countries' economies in times of
worsening scarcity of economic resources. If it was logical and rational to
accept work on German orders in 1940, then it was still logical and rational
to do so in 1944. The post-war for which businessmen and officials were
preparing themselves and their companies was evidently different in nature
and outlook. But the business challenges and imperatives to survive and

prosper in an Allied post-war were not markedly different from those confronting the same businessmen earlier on in the shape of the Nazi *Grossraumwirtschaft*.

It was certainly not incongruous to catch Bichelonne, the French official minister of Industrial Production, being photographed gazing at town planning exhibits in May 1944; nor was it bizarre to find him chairing meetings of his ministry's planning committees in the summer of 1944, after the Normandy invasion. He was hardly fiddling while Rome burned. He was simply doing what he had done throughout the war, planning the national economy for a French future in the post-war world. His world view was summed up in the comment he apparently made to the head of his cabinet office in the Ministry of Industrial Production: 'it's more damaging for a country to lose its strength than for it to choose the wrong side.'[23] The post-war Monnet Plan for the modernization of France's industrial economy explicitly and unashamedly drew on both the planning exercises and personnel of a collaborating wartime ministry.

5

The Collaboration of Officials, 1940–1942

Once it had been clarified in the summer of 1940 that collaboration with the German occupier was policy, and that it was dutiful and legitimate to collaborate, then government officials across occupied Western and Northern Europe duly collaborated. It was almost as simple as that; perhaps the chapter should end here. The people who needed to be convinced of the requirement to collaborate were the top ministerial officials, the 'functionaries'. Government offices were as hierarchical as factories. The top men set the tone for the conduct and outlook of subordinate colleagues all the way through and down the bureaucratic chain of command.

Officials operating in the periphery were expected to report back to their superiors at the centre on the implementation of policy, and to do so in terms of reference established by their superiors. I am always struck by what I think is the universal capacity of officials to say exactly what their superiors expected to hear, or, to put it another way, to reflect back at the centre the preoccupations of their bosses. It was not just a question of confirming to your superiors that things were satisfactory to brilliant on your patch. It was also reassuring to both sides, conveying the sense that the job was being done in the right way, an expression of solidarity between officials, the reaffirmation of an *esprit de corps*. We need to enter what officials themselves treated and protected as a rather private and rarified world, in order to enhance the mystique and standing of being an official. We can then begin to understand the outlook that informed their conduct and behaviour as collaborators. Such an approach might even enable us to explain something of what most people would regard as the uncongenial and unacceptable outcomes of collaboration. To put it more neutrally, the decisions taken by civil servants in the course of their collaboration had a discernible impact on the lives and livelihoods of the people of the countries they administered; and so we need to understand how and why those decisions were made.

Officials were, and are, by their nature, impersonal and faceless, even when they physically interact with the public they serve. For most of us, these attributes of the official are the way they choose to project themselves in order to avoid being held responsible for the decisions they take and implement. To the officials, their anonymity was a mark of their objectivity and impartiality in handling matters of public interest and concern, part of what it was to be a good official. Of course, some officials did have personalities, and, like anyone else in a workplace, they gossiped about each other in that particularly catty vein of office 'politics'. Diaries and memoirs of wartime officials allow us to put some personal and anecdotal flesh on these otherwise suited and rather staid and uniform figures. But we have to accept that officials are best studied and analysed, not as individuals, but as a group with a group mentality, almost as an institution with institutional ways. This, of course, makes studying them easier; but, as a result, it is also more authentic history.

There will be a relative focus on top officials in wartime France, because they had perhaps the most entrenched and developed mystique of the official of anywhere in continental Europe. But it was clear from the post-war apologias of functionaries from other occupied countries, and from the demeanour, tone, and content of their appearances before post-war purge and investigatory commissions, that these officials shared much of the same outlook or group mentality.

Continental European officials saw themselves, and were seen, as an entitled elite, in a rather different way from the privileged standard products of a private-school and Oxbridge education who occupied the top positions in the British civil service. The so-called *grands écoles* existed outside and beyond the French university system, and their graduates in both technical and administrative fields moved seamlessly into the top jobs in the private and public sectors of the economy, the state service, and academia. There were about 3,000 'high functionaries' in the French civil service, less than 0.5 per cent of the total population of public employees. The elite of the elite in the financial sector of government were the Inspectors of Finance, who took and passed what were reputed to be the toughest of civil service examinations, to qualify as such. Bouthillier, who from a position of director of the budget in the Finance ministry became Vichy's Minister of Finance, was one of these austere overachievers. Officials with this kind of educational pedigree were intellectual heavyweights, and were a meritocratic elite. They possessed the same self-absorption and self-confidence as the Oxbridge graduate, but had the ability to go with them. As Lucien Petit, an Inspector of Finance, remarked of himself and his colleagues in early 1944, 'being a shrinking violet is not what elites are about; for the sake of the general interest, they must be able to assert themselves'.[1] They saw themselves as both technocrats and all-rounders, able and fitted through their training, skills, learning, and experience to manage society and the economy.

France's technocratic officials were held in awe, and sometimes even enthralled politicians. René Belin was the new Vichy government's choice as Minister of Industrial Production and Labour in July 1940. A former clerk in the state postal and telegraph service, he had worked his way up through the bureaucracy of the postal workers' union, and then was a director of the national union confederation, the *Confédération Générale du Travail* (*CGT*), representing its moderate anti-communist wing. He was one of several socialist and Catholic union leaders who rallied to Vichy, and saw the National Revolution's corporatism as the most appropriate vehicle in the circumstances to protect workers' interests in a necessarily authoritarian framework. He quite consciously decided that only Pétain could restore a sense of national unity and community after the humiliating victory of Nazi Germany, having swallowed with his compatriots the Pétainist myth that the Republic had destroyed itself in defeat in 1940.

Very much outside the charmed circle of government and its technocratic officials, he remembered being 'dazzled' by Bichelonne, a young official and mining engineer trained in the *École Polytechnique* and *École des Mines*, whom he met for the first time in the office of Raoul Dautry in September 1939. Dautry was then Minister of Armaments in the Republican government, and appointed Bichelonne to his inner cabinet office. The ministry became something of a transmission belt for the young technocrats who staffed the economic and financial ministries of the Vichy government. To the stage-struck Belin, Bichelonne, a burly, stooping, smooth-faced man with a huge head, which made him the butt of offensive remarks from his later colleagues in government, appeared 'to know everything, to have anticipated everything, and to hold in his fingers all the threads of the ministry . . .'.[2]

Belin was impressed enough to co-opt Bichelonne into his own enlarged Vichy ministry. Together with a friend and fellow *Polytecnicien*, Barnaud, who went on to even greater things as Vichy's chief negotiator on economic relations with the Germans, he concocted in express time one of the most important initial laws of the Vichy government, the setting-up of the *Comités d'Organisation*, the basis for the reorganization of the French economy. Belin had chosen as his top officials men who shared, indeed had anticipated, his ideas for a *dirigiste* economy. As the new minister himself rather laconically observed, 'the simple idea of an increase in the power of the administration appealed to them'.[3]

Getting to know him better as his minister, Belin remarked on the contrast between Bichelonne's disordered office, with open files all over the place, and his disordered physical presence, always in a hurry and late for meetings, banging into doors as he went, and the brilliance of his mind and the order and coherence of his thinking.

Laval liked Bichelonne as well, promoting him from his post as Secretary General for Commerce and Industry to acting and then full Minister of Industrial Production, after his return to power in April 1942. With Laval, however, it was always pretty clear who was in charge. Peyrouton, a career official who became Vichy's Interior Minister, said of his boss: 'In M. Laval's eyes, we were innocents. We could be valuable technicians, but we could never be politicians...'.[4] Belin had reported a colleague's assessment of Bichelonne as being 'like a performing dog, a little too inclined to display his talents to those who wanted him to do so...'.[5] This was how Laval paraded him, teasing his cabinet ministers about Bichelonne's legendary powers of memory and knowledge. With Bichelonne in tow, said Laval, you do not need any files when you go to a meeting, because he already knows it all—just as well, one can say, given the state of his filing system. Laval apparently once asked his cabinet to name the capital of Nicaragua. When, as Laval expected, only Bichelonne replied, with 'Tegucigalpa' (actually the capital of the neighbouring Central American country, Honduras), Laval affectionately congratulated the teacher's pet: 'Oh, vous!'[6]

At this point, one is inclined to say that Bichelonne's excess of knowledge, or presumed knowledge, was a dangerous as well as a useless thing. As history students are constantly warned, it is not a matter of how much you know, but how you deploy what you know. One of Bichelonne's ministerial colleagues, Joseph Barthélemy, recorded in his memoirs the uncomplimentary remark of one of his professors at the *École des Mines*: 'he knows everything, but that is everything.'[7] Pucheu, who clearly thought that he was a proper politician by comparison, commented that Bichelonne knew 'more of things learned than experienced',[8] as if his own pre-war career in business had equipped him to be a Vichy minister. All those around him in government, sympathetic or not, noted that Bichelonne was impetuous and impulsive. This does not sound very bureaucratic, until you realize that they were referring to his workaholic nature, his willingness to take on difficult tasks and to present himself as the one with the knowledge and expertise to tackle them.

Barthélemy, in his late sixties when appointed a minister, of Justice, clearly resented being surrounded by callow youths in the Vichy government. His sarcastic remembering of their antics was a kind of retrospective revenge on younger and leaner colleagues who teased him for his age and for his corpulence. Darlan nicknamed him '35,000 tonnes', the weight of France's biggest naval cruiser. Barthélemy was bitter, too, because he felt sidelined by Pucheu at the Interior Ministry in the government's repression of early communist resistance to Nazi occupation. This was obviously a convenient *ex post facto* justification of his lack of responsibility for the repressiveness of the Vichy police and judicial system. But not being one of the boys, and actually having some hands-on political experience as a right-wing parliamentary deputy in the 1920s, and then as a French representative at the League of Nations in the 1930s, gave some distance and perspective on his colleagues' lack of political standing and grip. He was expressing acidly what others were expressing more benignly.

Laval's patronizing view of officials was telling, because it essentially corresponded to the rather kinder reflections of du Moulin de Labarthète, who, from his position as head of Pétain's civilian cabinet, had every opportunity to observe the ways of the tigerish young technocrats running the most important ministries in Darlan's government between February 1941 and April 1942. He suggested that officials were only equipped to be the 'auxiliaries' of politicians, and that an official or a businessman did not necessarily make a good politician or political leader. In his view, a country could not be run like a private enterprise, nor according to the scientific, rational approach of the trained, technically proficient professional official. Officials, and here I am extrapolating from his commentary on the performance of Darlan's technocratic ministers, were good at tactics, but not at strategy. They were equipped to work out the modalities of implementing a political agreement, and good at negotiating a compromise that satisfied both sides, or neither of them. Indeed, du Moulin de Labarthète appeared to be saying that, for officials turned government ministers, negotiation, which they excelled at and were trained for, was an end in itself, not a means to an end. A friend and colleague said of Bichelonne that he was always intelligent enough to grasp very quickly the essence and rationality of the case being made by the officials on the German side of the table, which meant that he was often able to bring negotiations to a speedy conclusion while being inclined to agree to an outcome more favourable to the other side. In other words, the tidiness and coherence of the package they were negotiating was ultimately more satisfying to them than the actual terms of the agreement and its likely consequences. It sounded as though du Moulin de Labarthète was already regretting the fall from power of the master politician, Laval, and his replacement by Darlan and the technocrats, or at least pining for Laval's return.

I am not sure that you can apply du Moulin de Labarthète's critique in all its aspects to the way officials and businessmen conducted themselves as Darlan's ministers, or, indeed, the way the Belgian and Dutch secretaries general behaved as, effectively, ministers. What we can be reasonably clear about was that these top officials assuming ministerial positions thought that they would be able to do a better job than their former political masters, elected politicians. Max Hirschfeld, who became the dominant figure among the secretaries general who ran the Netherlands during the occupation, apparently remarked to a colleague, the then Secretary General for Foreign Affairs, as the Dutch government went into exile: 'Thank God they've left; what on earth would we have done, with them?'[9] Hirschfeld was, of course, referring to the government's conduct during the invasion. But his recall of the anecdote way after the end of the war indicated that he still thought that the best possible outcome had been that national affairs would henceforth be handled by officials, rather than by departed politicians.

This was common ground for all the top officials in the occupied territories. They felt that they embodied in their persons and offices the continuity of the national state, and always regarded themselves as representatives and defenders of the national interest, as opposed to the partial political concerns of democratically elected politicians. The self-awareness that they were the indispensable custodians of the state and the national interest was enhanced by the chaos of summer 1940, and the need for national recovery and reconstruction after the trauma of invasion and defeat. All top officials felt this, none more so than in France. The country, to a far greater extent than any other conquered in Western Europe, was disunited and divided, making its officials, quite literally, the major national institution still standing. They were the people who could keep France and Frenchmen together. They embodied national sovereignty, or rather, in conditions of occupation, the aspiration to national sovereignty. They felt, without equivocation, that their relations with the occupier were essential to the assertion of the Vichy government's sovereignty over French territory. Civil servants in the occupied territories felt the same way about their national role in post-liberation recovery and reconstruction.

We can safely rule out Jean Jardel's conventional collective justification of his position at his trial in 1947: 'I was a functionary; it was not my job to approve or disapprove a policy.'[10] Jardel himself was a career official in the Ministry of Finance, seconded to Darlan's vice-presidential cabinet as Secretary General for Administrative Affairs. He had the reputation among his peers of being the typically upright, neutral, and objective official. It is perhaps not very surprising to find a similar disclaimer being expressed by a more significant figure. Jacques Guérard occupied a very similar position in Laval's government, and was one of Laval's main advisors and 'fixers' while he was Prime Minister between 1942 and 1944. At his High Court trial in 1958, having been sentenced to death *in absentia* in 1947, his lawyer understandably said of the department he headed that 'it is not a decision-making body; it's an executive body. It cannot be said that Guérard determined policy. He administratively applied political decisions, and he did not approve of all of them.'[11] By all accounts, he was as committed as Laval to Franco-German collaboration. You rather doubt that the convenient separation between the politician who made policy and the officials who executed it really existed in the days of democratic Republican politics. But it certainly did not exist in an authoritarian state, and Jardel and Guérard could hardly have been closer to decision-making in the Vichy government. The top officials expected to make policy as well as implement it, and rather appreciated the opportunity to do so in their ministerial and quasi-ministerial roles.

Many of the top officials had moved to the top because of the pre-war patronage of elected politicians, who staffed their inner cabinets with young officials on the way up. Some would move with their patrons when they were appointed to other ministries. However apolitical they were, whether in theory or in practice, officials were often 'political' appointees. While patronage was part of a system that was now either abolished or discredited, the officials who benefited from it could hardly deny that it was worth having sharp enough elbows to play the political game.

Officials, of course, as citizens, had political views, usually of a conservative nature, even though they were dutifully kept in the background while at work. Now, in an authoritarian framework and climate, they could freely express them as ministers. All of France's top officials were *Pétainiste*, in the sense that they implicitly supported a man who had restored and enhanced the authority and powers of the state. Some of them were ideologically authoritarian, if not totalitarian, as in the case of Pucheu, an ex-member of a fascist party, the *PPF*, who was the Minister of Industrial Production, and then Minister of the Interior. Among those ministers who actually believed in the National Revolution and Franco-German reconciliation, which went beyond wartime collaboration, were Bouthillier, Minister of Finance; Abel Bonnard, Minister of Education from April 1942, whom Laval described as 'sometimes more German than the Germans';[12] Berthelot, Minister of Communications from 1940 to 1942; and Fernand de Brinon, a close associate of Abetz in a pre-war Franco-German cultural organization and during the war, who was effectively Vichy's ambassador to Nazi Germany.

Burrin estimates that perhaps one-third of France's more important officials were collaborationist, measuring this by pointing to the presence of about 90,000 officials in collaborationist organizations, from the cultural forum *Collaboration*, to fascist movements and their militias. The Ministry of Education, reputedly the most 'collaborationist' of government ministries, and numerically one of the state's largest employers, had an estimated 4 in 1,000 employees who were members of such organizations. At the Liberation, about 900 of the ministry's employees were sanctioned for membership in these organizations, quite a large figure when you take into account the purge commission's leniency towards nominal rather than active membership.

Again, prefects in Republican France, as the national government's representatives in the departments, were accustomed to swimming in the provincial political pool, and were expected to establish good relationships with local notables and power-holders. In the 1940–2 period, they were seen by central government as the bearers of the National Revolution, who were meant to break with the compromising and corrupt alliances of officials with the local big shots. They rarely did, because it was evidently in the state's interest to co-opt and engage all the local forces of 'order'. From 1942, Laval encouraged them to recultivate local elites who would help to steady Vichy's position in the periphery.

We can point to top officials who, lacking democratic accountability, were 'political' in a way that was stimulated by operating in an authoritarian framework and climate. Jacques Barnaud, a technocratic official who was also director of a private investment bank, the *Banque de Worms*, managed to combine intellect and a down-to-earth pragmatism, and was one of Vichy's 'grey eminences', politicking and manœuvring behind the scenes. The friend, advisor, and confidant of fellow officials such as Bichelonne and Lehideux, he had all the right connections to influence policy and appointments. As a measure of his subterranean hold on Vichy during the period of the Darlan government, those close to Pétain and his 'small man' version of the National Revolution liked to place Barnaud at the centre of a 'Synarchic' conspiracy, which was allegedly subordinating the regime to a capitalist clique of self-interested bankers and industrialists.

As representatives and agents of the national interest, wartime officials could, perhaps justifiably, say that they were not political in a party-political sense. But this hardly meant they did not assume political roles. The secretaries general in the Netherlands and Belgium exercised ministerial functions, and made and implemented policy in their area of ministerial jurisdiction. Their collegial body effectively duplicated the cabinet of ministers. They had to deal with political issues, not least because the occupier made occupation a very political and ideological matter. In Norway, officials were accountable to a German-nominated fascist government, intent on 'fascistizing' them and the rest of society. In France, officials now operated within the framework of a new authoritarian state, which they generally welcomed as officials, and were expected to implant the National Revolution as well as administer the country. This placed them in a rather contradictory and difficult position. Pétain's government alternately distrusted them and tried to purge them, because they had been formed as officials under the Third Republic, and elevated them, because they played such a central role in an authoritarian state.

It is worthwhile thinking about the consequences of putting the power to make and enforce policy in the hands of largely unaccountable officials. Being unaccountable to nothing greater than their own understanding of the national interest was, in one sense, liberating. It enabled bureaucrats to act unbureaucratically—that is, decisively and speedily, without the usual checks and balances on their conduct. So, unpopular and uncongenial things got done, because they were necessary and because officials did not feel that public opinion mattered enough for them to hold back on taking measures that they regarded as essential. And, during wartime occupation, there were plenty of unpalatable decisions to take.

Paradoxically, this situation also encouraged over-bureaucratization in an already overly regulated wartime society. In a system of top-down management, a constant stream of circulars and instructions gushed from the centre to the periphery on the implementation of policy, binding on officials further down the food chain. You can imagine this happening in a situation of war and occupation, where the central control of society's resources was necessary and unavoidable, and you can imagine its effect on people's everyday lives, built around surviving in difficult times. Too many laws and regulations, too little observed, was the outcome.

But it was hardly all that dysfunctional. For both the French and the Danish governments, negotiation per se was the alpha and omega of their collaboration with the Germans, because of what it said about the government's independence and sovereignty. Surely, then, the best people to conduct negotiations in the national interest were officials, who were, by nature, good at it, and could prolong the talking when procrastination and post-ponement served that national interest. The French departmental prefects were always politically attuned, and an integral part of their job was to assess 'public opinion' and popular responses to central government policies. In their reports to the Interior Ministry, they did not usually misrepresent the situation in their departments, rather cloak it in the language and ter-minology of one official communicating with another, his superior.

However, officials did tend to view politics as administration, or to seek to transform politics into administration, as if it was a neutral value-free zone. This was the essence of the technocratic outlook, that complex problems were both comprehensible and solvable if treated as technical matters. This was perhaps what du Moulin de Labarthète was driving at in his friendly critique of Vichy officials as ministers. It meant, I think, that top officials relied on reason, not revelation or intuition, and regarded no problem as being beyond their powers of rational resolution. From their perspective, being run by reasoning and reasonable experts made govern-ment intrinsically more efficient and effective, because each issue could be dealt with on its own technical merits, and would not, as in a democratic system, be influenced to the detriment of its resolution by popular or party political considerations. Top officials saw themselves as troubleshooters or problem-solvers. Almost alone, this explained their overwhelming and self-deluding sense of confidence and entitlement, which they brought to the handling of difficult and complicated problems. They departed from the stance of presumed omnipotence, that they alone were the people with the training and expertise really to understand things; just leave it to us. The natural inbuilt arrogance of the official seemed to exclude the humility or touch that might have come from what today are called 'life experiences'. The lack of those, among other things, made them less likely to allow for the consequences of decisions illuminated solely by reason. Whether officials were technical to a fault, and prone to the historical law of unforeseen consequences, obviously need to be tested out in how they collaborated in the first half of the Nazi occupation.

Law and order was an area where the interests of the occupier and those of officials and governments converged. Both sides willingly collaborated in its maintenance. But the Nazi invasion of the USSR in June 1941 changed things. The communist parties of occupied Western Europe unequivocally moved towards a stance of organized resistance to the German occupation authorities. Such resistance was deliberately violent, involving the sabotage of infrastructure and military installations and attacks on military personnel belonging to the occupying forces. The purpose of violent resistance was to expose the basic repressiveness of occupation, alienate the population from it, and expand the popular opposition to it. 'Terror', which was how the German authorities described communist-inspired resistance, was, and is, hardly mindless and indiscriminate. It was designed to spread unease among both the occupiers and the occupied, and push people into making choices about how to respond to occupation.

The development of armed resistance following the invasion of the Soviet Union put both the German occupation and Reich authorities in a real bind. The numbers of occupying troops were reduced in order to release them for active military service in the Balkans and the USSR. In France, the size of the occupying forces was down by two-thirds in late 1941. This was possible because of the collaboration of the police forces of the occupied territories in keeping order. The drawing-down of German military forces provided a ready-made justification of the basic premise of the occupation regimes, that, as far as possible, they ruled through existing state organs and personnel. In France, especially, the withdrawal of occupying troops for service on the Eastern Front occurred simultaneously with attacks on the German military in the occupied territories.

Officials and police departments in the occupied territories had no problem at all in organizing themselves against communists and other leftists. They had long been identified as anti-national subversives, and policed as such, in the interwar period and during the 'phoney war' of 1939–40. Officials also had no problem in publicly decrying resistance to the occupation, and in a way that was likely to resonate with the people. Their stance caused many problems for them at the Liberation, when resistance was the expected norm.

This was from the text of a proclamation signed by the three secretaries general of the Dutch ministries of Justice, Interior, and Economic Affairs, which appeared in the newspapers and on wall posters, on 28 October 1941. Such a declaration had been demanded of Jacobus Schrieke, the Secretary General for Justice, by Hans Albin Rauter, a Higher SS and Police Leader and Reich Commissioner for Security. It was the duty of the Dutch people, the proclamation ran, to obey 'without reservation' the laws and decrees in the occupied territory. Acts of sabotage 'only damage *the interests of the Dutch people*' (highlighted in the text). And why? Because the German authorities will repress 'incorrect conduct', and hence, 'the life of many people is brought into great danger by the reckless behaviour of a few...criminal elements'.[13] We have to remember that the Dutch people had already witnessed and experienced German repression in response to acts of opposition and resistance. This was no empty warning about something that might happen, but a warning of more to come unless the Dutch people complied with the German occupation authorities, and ceased being complicit in acts of resistance by remaining silent about the perpetrators. The fact that opposition brought down on the population as a whole the full repressiveness of the Nazi system was exactly what the resisters wanted, since it would make the occupation even more unpopular. The proclamation was explicitly highlighting the risk of such a strategy, that violent resistance and its violent repression would deter people from opposing the occupation because the personal and collective costs were too great.

The authorship of the two Secretaries General for Justice and the Interior was to be expected, since they policed and judged crime in the country. Hirschfeld's signature as Secretary General for Economic Affairs was clearly meant to stiffen the proclamation, since he was by far the most high-profile secretary general, and the top official most trusted and respected by the Reich Commissariat. He, in fact, drafted the proclamation, and his name on it reflected his obsessive concern with public order as the essential prerequisite for undisturbed economic production and, hence, economic collaboration with the Germans. He shared with his fellow secretaries general the common tendency of officials to regard what was really political and ideological resistance to the occupier as 'criminal' activity. As we shall see, this reduction of politics to policing occurred in other areas, too. One has to say that it was not an attitude born of the circumstances of occupation, but one held by officials with regard to communist activity before the war.

Although Hirschfeld usually gave a broad interpretation to the 1937 guidelines, on this occasion the secretaries general had kept exactly to the script. They were required to 'educate the public on the attitude they had to assume regarding the enemy and its organs...', and this they had done. The guidelines explicitly forbade citizens from 'engaging in any act of violence or resistance', and provided the same reasoning as the secretaries general in their proclamation, the risk of exposing others to retaliation, and inducing repression, even 'a reign of terror.'[14]

All of the same themes and prejudices, even the same terminology, appeared in the public proclamation condemning sabotage and resistance, which was signed by Belgian secretaries general, Gérard Romsée, at the Interior, and Gaston Schuind, at the Justice ministry. This was in December 1941, after a series of attacks, the most significant being the murder of a collaborationist Rexist leader in Tournai, which also involved the killing of two of his German military escorts, and the wounding of another. German reprisals included hostage-taking. With this in mind, the public appeal called the resisters 'terrorists' and 'the worst enemies of the country', and explained that 'it is vital to prevent innocent people suffering the tragic consequences of the reprisal measures.'[15]

The mention of 'prevention' was a significant one. Here, it explicitly referred to the need to take action to avoid the community paying for the 'crimes' of the few. But this implicitly meant that policing had to be 'preventive' as well as 'repressive' of crime, which was the constant refrain of authoritarian and totalitarian systems. In a democratic rule of law system, people were 'free' to commit crimes that were then retrospectively repressed following legal procedures that required the prosecution to prove guilt, and according to the legal principle that there could be no punishment where there was no law. But, if a system of policing 'prevented' crime before it 'repressed' it, then transparent and accountable process went out of the window. People could be arrested and detained for their 'suspicious' attitudes and conduct, and on suspicion of preparing or conspiring to commit a crime. You could be locked up pre-emptively, to prevent the risk of you actually committing the crime.

This suspension of the democratic rule of law was a natural consequence of the coming of the national emergency of war; it occurred in 1939–40, before the countries were invaded and occupied. The preventive character of policing under occupation was, also, the consequence of collaborating with the agents of the policing and judicial system of the occupier. In Nazi Germany, all the vestiges of what we normally understand as the rule of law had already been eliminated by the Nazi regime. Including the term 'prevent' in the Belgian proclamation was a kind of terminological but consequential victory of Romsée over Schuind. Their battle had been fought within the confines of the secretaries general committee, though it strongly resonated in Belgian judicial circles, as Struye's diary made clear. The conflict raised an important matter of difference affecting the conduct of the police and judiciary in occupied Belgium and the Netherlands.

Romsée was a pro-German Flemish nationalist whom Reeder had 'recommended' to the secretaries general, and saw as the lynchpin of collaboration in the German interest in occupied Belgium. He took the straight authoritarian line, that you had preventively to police actual and potential resisters in order to protect Belgian citizens against the perpetration of the 'crime' and its provocation of German reprisals. Schuind was now the only francophone secretary general left standing, an indication of how seriously the German military government had taken Hitler's instructions to favour Flemings in the country's public life. He stood by established legal procedures under Belgian law. If a 'crime' was committed, then arrests were a matter for the investigating magistrate and his small corps of judicial policemen. It was not the job of the Belgian authorities preventively to arrest communists identified and pursued by the German police, and then hold them as a pool of hostages liable to German reprisal.

In the Netherlands, the Dutch police and courts were required by Seyss-Inquart under the terms of the 1940 'understanding' reached with the secretaries general, to enforce the decrees of the Reich Commissariat. In occupied Belgium, the German military administration had a less draconian view of collaboration, and more or less respected the arrangements broadly laid down in the Hague Convention. So it was usual for the Belgian police and courts to apply Belgian law in respect of crimes committed by Belgian citizens in violation of Belgian law. It was up to the German military police to investigate and judge before German military tribunals crimes committed by Belgians against the occupiers and the German interest.

The usual practice was bent by the military government when violent communist resistance started up. In June and July 1941, Belgian police and magistrates in Liège, an industrial city with a large working-class population that proved very uncomfortable for the Germans to police, had refused to arrest local communists when told by the *Gestapo* to do so. The military administration then directed Romsée to tell the police that they had to arrest Belgians on German orders, even if it meant disregarding Belgian law and legal process, because the occupiers were the *de facto* 'legal' authority. This directive came very close to what Seyss-Inquart had insisted on from the start of the occupation in the Netherlands, which the Dutch police authorities had accepted. In Belgium, the question as to whether the Belgian police should behave as the executive arm of the German police, or remain nominally independent, was not conclusively settled. This was despite the fact that individual events occurring on the ground were constantly referred to a higher authority for 'clarification'.

The clash of jurisdiction and competences, so crucial to the way Belgium was policed, produced a very complicated law-and-order situation there, compared to the Netherlands. In Belgium, the disputes ran all ways. There was not only conflict between the Germans and the Belgian judiciary. There was also internal conflict between the Interior police (Romsée) and the judicial police (Schuind), hindering Romsée's (and the Germans') plans to centralize Belgian police forces in the Interior Ministry; and between Romsée and Schiund together, and the judiciary. These internal and external conflicts exploded into the open, finding expression in a lacerating judicial and constitutional crisis in 1942, which temporarily paralysed the country.

Ignoring what the government's own 1937 guidance had said, the Dutch parliament's post-war inquiry slated Hirschfeld's proclamation as a very serious mistake, constituting a failure of duty (to resist, presumably). The proclamation, properly located in its time, was, rather, an indication of the still smooth-running collaboration with the Germans over law and order, and the Dutch secretaries general's respect of the government's guidelines on collaboration.

The challenge to that collaboration came from the extreme repressiveness of the German Nazi response to any opposition and resistance. This was evident in the brutal and effective repression of a general strike in Amsterdam called in March 1941 to protest at the enactment of the first measures against Dutch Jews, and police and *NSB* harassment of the Jewish community in the city. Worse was to come in occupied France, after the killings by communists of the German military commander in Nantes, in western France, and of an armed forces official in Bordeaux, in south-west France, both in October 1941. An enraged Hitler initiated a policy of reprisal and collective punishment, including hostage-taking and execution, which violated the terms of the Hague Convention. This did not worry Hitler, but it did worry officials in the occupied territories, both German and national.

Hitler had a simple and single-minded view of occupation. For him, occupation 'worked' effectively as long as the occupier had the standing and respect to ensure the compliance and tolerance of the population. The occupier lost face if it responded leniently to attacks on its personnel. A 'counter-terror' to punish and intimidate the population was the best way to deter future opposition, because people would always have to contemplate the consequences of resistance for themselves and everybody else. Deterrence by terror also restored the original rationale of collaboration, since it compensated for manpower shortages in the occupied territories. Terror induced people to police themselves, and to exercise self-censorship and self-restraint.

Hitler personally instructed the German military governor in France to execute nearly 100 hostages as revenge and punishment for the killings, and to prepare for the execution of another 100 hostages if the perpetrators were not captured or handed in. By making the community at large accountable for individual acts of sabotage and violence, the German Nazi leadership intended to intimidate people into breaking their natural *omertà*, protecting the perpetrators by keeping silent about their whereabouts and contacts. Hitler's notorious 'Night and Fog' decree of December 1941 covered all of the occupied territories in Northern and Western Europe in its call for civilian offenders against the occupation authorities to be 'disappeared', so that they effectively ceased to exist.

This was a very serious development. It opened up the occupied territories to the exercise of a truly Nazi system of policing. This emerged, as in Nazi Germany itself, in parallel with, and eventually superseding, both the enforcement agencies and processes of the occupied countries, and the German military courts that were set up to deal with crimes and offences against the occupying power. Citizens of the occupied territories were now exposed to preventive arrest and internment, and to deportation to prisons and concentration camps in Nazi Germany itself. This pretty effective method of 'disappearing' marked the extension to the occupied territories of forms of detention and punishment that were clearly disallowed under domestic and international law.

There was a clear difference in approach to the repression of opposition and resistance, between, on the one side, the military administrations in occupied France and Belgium–northern France, and even the Reich Commissariats in the Netherlands and Norway, and, on the other side, Hitler and the Reich authorities, both civilian and military. The former were hardly prepared to tolerate attacks on German military personnel and premises. But they argued that collective punishment was counterproductive and disproportionate, since it alienated the public and made further attacks more, not less, likely. It also threatened the whole rationale of occupation through collaboration. A consensual law-and-order policy conducted by local police forces and judiciary not only kept the peace, but did so without requiring the excessive investment of German police and military resources. If you criticized officials and police for being too lenient in the repression of resistance activity, then you were obliged to rely increasingly on direct German policing of the occupied territories, again undermining the reason for collaboration in the first place.

These were cogent arguments, born of a practical experience of what it took to occupy a country 'peacefully'. But they cut no ice with the Reich leadership. The German military governor of occupied France, General Otto von Stülpnagel, was removed in February 1942 for his opposition to the taking and killing of hostages. Werner Best, an SS officer and its legal expert, had been sent off to be the military government's head of administration after falling out with his Reich boss, Reinhard Heydrich, effectively Himmler's deputy. There he became something of a theorist of the Nazi modes of occupation, and a committed exponent of the system of indirect rule through local officials largely adopted in occupied Western Europe. In the fallout from the law-and-order crisis of late 1941, he was transferred to be the German plenipotentiary in the remaining backwater of consensual occupation, which was Denmark.

The late 1941 law-and-order crisis was a real turning point in the occupation, at least in terms of the occupied people's tolerance and acceptance of German occupation, which, revealed in its nakedly repressive guise, became unpopular. Repression drove resistance underground, where it actively involved fewer people but which made it more difficult to be detected and extinguished. This initiated a recurring cycle of reprisal and counter-reprisal, terror and counter-terror, which made occupation and life under occupation increasingly unstable and dangerous. Rather paradoxically, the crisis drew together the two sides committed to consensual and cooperative law and order policies in the occupied territories, the German occupation authorities and collaborating officials and police. In tandem, they rather desperately worked to lighten the repressive load imposed on them and the occupied peoples by Hitler and the Reich authorities, and thereby reasserted and reaffirmed their collaborating relationship. Negotiation was still possible at the local level, to soften the impact of the Reich's repressiveness. Here, relations between German officials and national officials were usually stronger because of habitual day-by-day contact. This was a tangible gain for the occupied populations of the collaboration of officials with the occupier. Even in Norway, which had the most Nazified police force in occupied Northern and Western Europe, the *NS* mayor of Stavanger could advise the German police not to arrest minors involved in demonstrations. A timely intervention by the *NS* mayor of Kristiensund prevented the taking of hostages after an act of sabotage.

But there was now a new dimension to that relationship, which crucially damaged the standing of collaborating officials among the people they administered and policed. Occupation became unpopular, and collaboration became unpopular, increasingly so with the popular perception that officials were carrying out the occupier's business, and in ways that aligned them to the occupier. The new dimension was a change in policing and policing methods, accelerated by the late 1941 law-and-order crisis.

The growth of opposition and resistance to occupation was the eagerly grasped opportunity for the *SS* to influence and take over policing in the occupied territories. So, in occupied France, the outcome of the conflict over the kind and level of repressiveness with which to tackle communist 'terrorism' was not only the removal of leaders who fundamentally disagreed with Hitler's brutal approach to resistance in the occupied territories. In late 1941, the German military administration leant more heavily on the *SS* to police France. It did so in the knowledge that the law-and-order crisis was self-induced and that the presence of the *SS* would only prolong and intensify the cycle of repression and resistance. As a recognition of its inability to keep public order using previous methods, the military governor 'delegated' to the *SS* the policing of communists, Jews, masons, and refugees. In spring 1942, Himmler was allowed to appoint a Higher *SS* and Police Leader to France. He was Carl-Albrecht Oberg, fresh from his duties as a police chief in occupied Poland. His appointment meant that, finally, the *SS*, rather than the German military police, was responsible for law and order in France, including the supervision and direction of the French police forces. Oberg did not exactly reproduce Poland in France, and he proved himself to be a more subtle policeman and politician than his experience in the East might have suggested. But his arrival in France definitely opened a new chapter in the story of Franco-German cooperation in policing.

The SS assumption of policing responsibilities in the occupied territories from late 1941 overlapped with the internal reorganization of the police forces in the occupied territories, being carried out by the relevant secretaries general and their ministerial officials. The SS backed, encouraged, and advised on the restructuring. The outcome was a heightened cooperation between the SS and the revamped national police forces, a fresh convergence of interests on a new plane between occupier and collaborating officials.

Basically, the reorganization of the police involved simplification and centralization in a series of moves towards the creation of a single national police system. This was never entirely achieved during the occupation, but significant steps were taken on the way. In the Netherlands, Rauter, the SS officer in charge of policing in the Reich Commissariat, worked through a young lawyer in the Dutch police, Leo Broersen, whom he appointed as 'Plenipotentiary for Police', and the Secretary General for Justice, the NSB member Jacobus Schrieke. Between them, they managed to move from a situation where five separate police forces were responsible to three different ministries to one where a revamped criminal and investigative state police and the municipal police, formerly beholden to mayors and the Interior, were placed under the auspices of the Ministry of Justice. In occupied Belgium, a merger of the national gendarmes with the specialized judicial police never quite came off. But the creation of so-called grandes agglomérations, or large metropolitan urban areas, in 1941–2, involved the absorption of a city's suburbs and outlying areas into a single urban authority. This enabled the city-wide rationalization of police forces, even if it did not realize the ultimate aim of a national state police force.

The reorganization of the police forces met two connected aims. The modernization and greater efficiency of the police was to be realized by the amalgamation of still semi-autonomous communal forces that retained some democratic accountability, with elected local mayors being responsible for the police in their areas. Officials implemented reforms that had been mooted by them and their colleagues before the war, only to be blocked by the politicians' respect for local democratic autonomies. What they did in the interests of improved operational efficiency and direction aligned with the New Order aspirations of the occupation authorities and the SS. Recruitment to the police was stepped up, in occupied Belgium deliberately encouraging Flemings to join, and new training centres were established. Police forces acquired, or extended, their intelligence capabilities in particular, and equipped themselves with specialized units for the policing of Jews, masons, and communists. Again, the orientation towards political and ideological policing, exactly the role and function of the SS, was striking.

In some places, the Germans managed to induce quite spectacular transformations in police conduct, as they did in other areas of state administration. The Germans had a knack of identifying and honing local talent, individual officials occupying key positions or being capable of doing so, as 'leaders' and exemplars of the new ways. They first turned them, and then dealt directly with them for the execution of certain tasks, bypassing the normal bureaucratic chains of command. The Germans often 'recommended' officials for appointments who were fascist party members or leaders, and they did not need much turning.

The Germans' application of the 'leader principle' worked extremely well, from this perspective, in the case of the policing of the major Dutch city of Amsterdam. Disturbances and a general strike in the city in early 1941 arising from popular protests against the introduction of anti-Jewish measures were put down by *German* police. Seyss-Inquart imposed a clean sweep of city administrators who had failed to prevent or repress the protests. The new Amsterdam police chief was Sybren Tulp, an ex-colonial army officer and recent *NSB* member, who was accustomed to dealing with the 'natives' and enforcing discriminatory policies. Tulp developed close personal relations with the man Tulp always regarded as his superior, the Reich Commissioner for Security, Rauter—or should we say it was the other way round?

Tulp joined the Dutch SS, and set up a political intelligence and investigation department and a Jewish unit, largely staffed by *NSB* members or fellow Dutch SS members, drawing on the expertise and model of the *Gestapo*, with which he worked in tandem. He was clearly impressed by the range, competence, and efficiency of the German police, and sought to emulate them, if only to demonstrate that his section of the Dutch police could be relied upon to continue the policing of the Dutch people under the occupation. Quite ready himself to apply anti-Jewish measures, he developed a style of leadership that endeared him to his officers and men and enabled him to overcome or ease their reluctance to persecute Jews who were Dutch citizens. Being matey and comradely with his staff, often joining them on police operations, was his way of transferring something of the military discipline and *esprit* of his colonial service to the streets of Amsterdam. But it was also, consciously or not, an exercise in 'charismatic' leadership on the Nazi model.

The outcome of the Germans' careful cultivation of Tulp was that the *Gestapo* could approach him directly so that the Dutch police carried out some unpalatable operations against Dutch Jews. Tulp sometimes acted unilaterally in this respect. In September 1941, he instructed his men to enforce a German decree excluding Jews from public places, even though the Secretary General for Justice had stood back from applying it, judging it to be both unenforceable in policing terms and counterproductive in its impact on popular consent for policing. Tulp's intervention was partly induced by his personal esteem and support for Rauter, engaged at the time in a 'friendly' struggle for the primacy in anti-Jewish policy of the SS, where he was a top officer. This was against the claims of the Reich Commissariat, where he was the policing Commissioner. One should never be surprised by the complicated inter-service rivalries that characterized the Nazi system of rule. But Tulp's involvement was important, because it worked in exactly the opposite way to the possibility that collaborating officials could mitigate occupation policy by exploiting the competition between rival Nazi agencies. In this case, at least, his initiative served to involve Dutch police in a radicalization of anti-Jewish policy in the Netherlands, which corresponded to the way in which Nazism's internecine rivalries usually worked themselves out.

Tulp's conversion into a police 'leader' was matched on a national level under the other Reich Commissariat in Norway. Here, the new national chief of police from 1941 was Jonas Lie, the collaborationist leader of the Norwegian SS, and deliberately promoted by the German SS as a rival national leader to Quisling. Lie led a Norwegian police unit into the *Waffen* SS, the pan-European military arm of the SS, and fought with them on the Eastern Front in 1942-3. Back home, he worked closely with the *Gestapo*, and directly copied its systems and structures to facilitate cooperation with the German SS police, and, it must be said, to run for the leadership of the Nazi wartime government, which would put him in a position to realize the wider aim of the SS, the annexation of Norway to the Greater Germanic Empire. Over half of the Norwegian police force were NS or SS members by the end of the war. That the German Nazi penetration of the respective police systems can be measured at the national level in the Norwegian case, and at the city level in the Netherlands, reflects the fact that Terboven policed Norway through an *NS* government, while Seyss-Inquart worked through the Dutch secretaries general.

What should be clear is that the occupation authorities, whether Reich Commissariat or military administration, shared with officials a dislike of a level of repressiveness that was counterproductive. They all feared that such repression would simply help to realize the aims of the communist resistance, which were to drive a wedge between the people and the occupier, and the officials who collaborated with them. But officials could not really distance themselves from hostage-taking and collective punishments, if only because they wanted to mitigate their impact. This self-evidently raised the unavoidable bind of all collaboration, that it provided such poor returns for the massive effort expended in salvaging and extending collaboration.

However, in the domain of law and order, one has to say that the 'price' paid by governments and officials for continuing collaboration was not regarded by them as being excessive. In reality, collaboration was confirmed, indeed reinforced. It was perceived as achieving real gains in, for instance, the enhanced managerial efficiency and operational competence of the national police forces in keeping law and order. It also apparently ensured that citizens went on being policed by their own national forces, and judged in their own courts under national laws.

This process is best illustrated in Denmark and Vichy France, where the government's protection of national sovereignty was the very reason for its existence, and for its collaboration. It was especially imperative that the Vichy government found a solution to a law-and-order crisis that had occurred in German-occupied France, where its remit was nominal rather than substantial. The Danish government did not confront the particular pressures placed on Vichy by the division of France and a divided sovereignty. It took a similar position on resistance to German occupation as the secretaries general in occupied Belgium and the Netherlands. But there was an added edge and explicitness to its public denunciations of acts of violent resistance.

Attacks on German military personnel in the summer of 1942 had led to the perpetrators being tried and imprisoned by German military courts, as was the occupier's right. The Danish Prime Minister, Vilhelm Buhl, took to the airwaves in September, to give the Danes a lesson in wartime citizenship. The broadcast included the familiar lament that resistance simply exposed Danish citizens to severe German repression. Here the intention was clearly to deter any future resistance, and choke off any popular sympathy for resistance, by playing on the fear of consequences, which were real enough. But Buhl then raised the stakes. It was bad enough that others might well suffer for an individual's actions. Danes should not remain passive in the face of acts of sabotage; it was their patriotic duty to denounce saboteurs to the *Danish* police. Anyone who carries out sabotage, abets sabotage, and does not denounce sabotage 'acts contrary to his country's interests'.[16]

So the community should take action against the resister, precisely the outcome intended by the Nazi reprisals policy employed elsewhere in occupied Western and Northern Europe. If it was unpatriotic to connive passively at resistance, then the Prime Minister was attaching a very large weight to a very small act, in fact, something amounting to no action at all. The association was in itself an indication of just how polarized 'resistance' and 'collaboration' were made to be, at a point that was barely halfway through the occupation.

The reason for the Prime Minister's unequivocal condemnation of resistance, and his widening of the definition of resistance to include not opposing it, was, of course, that collaboration was the official policy of the Danish government. Resistance against the occupier was also opposition to the Danish government and state, which meant that the government was bound to collaborate with the Germans in repressing resistance. Since the official policy of collaboration was designed to protect Danish sovereignty and independence, any act of resistance, passive or not, was a risk to that. An essential aspect of the exercise of Danish sovereignty, of its very existence as a state, was that Danish citizens were subject to Danish laws enacted by a democratically elected parliament. It was, then, in the name of the country's legal sovereignty, that the Danish police and judicial system should act against resistance, rather than the Germans. Throughout the occupation, the overriding concern of the Danish authorities was to defend its sovereign law and order functions against what might be called German encroachments on the democratic rule of law.

As early as December 1940, in pursuit of a case against a Danish officer who had been arrested for recruiting pilots to the British air force, Renthe-Finke asked the Danish government to introduce the death penalty for acts of resistance against the occupier. This was a kind of blackmail. If the officer was tried in front of a German military tribunal, then he could face a death sentence. So the Germans were 'offering' a trial in Danish courts, as long as the government changed its own laws on capital punishment. The government responded by conceding on the detail in order to protect the principle of legal sovereignty and jurisdiction. It agreed to increase the maximum penalty for offences against the Danish state to life imprisonment, which effectively guaranteed that the officer would be tried in a Danish court.

Everybody was happy with the outcome. Indeed, it was a classic demonstration of how collaboration was meant to work, leading to a compromise that suited the interests of both sides. Renthe-Finke had successfully tested the Danish government's resolve to outlaw resistance and safeguard the country's 'peaceful' occupation. He had not insisted on the case being tried in a German military court according to German law and procedure, and had respected the government's legal sovereignty. The mutual interdependence, if not the equivalence, of occupier and collaborator had been demonstrated, with neither the Danish government nor Renthe-Finke resorting to measures that could endanger the continuation of that collaborating relationship.

In retrospect, it is possible to be critical of the Danish government's position on law and order. After the invasion of the USSR, the Danish government willingly cooperated with the Germans to take both preventive and repressive police action against communist party leaders and members. These measures would hardly have disturbed anyone across occupied Northern and Western Europe, given the already existing hostility towards communists, as subversive and anti-national. But they discriminated against, and penalized, Danish citizens, and undermined the principle of the rule of law and equality before the law. Anti-communist measures, together with other wartime laws that punished opposition to government policy, made dissent a matter of resistance. They made Danish neutrality in the war, again a mark of its sovereign independence, a bit of a nonsense. The blanket justification given by the Danish government and every other belligerent democratic country was that it was normal and necessary to suspend citizens' freedoms in face of the national emergency of war. But this simply ignored the fact that Denmark was democratic, but also occupied. The prevention and repression of resistance were justified by the policy of collaboration, and what that policy was intended to defend, national sovereignty and independence.

The issues of sovereignty raised by law and order played out in similar ways in France, with one essential difference. The Vichy government was clearly intent on asserting its legal sovereignty over all French territory. But it was interested not in defending a democratic rule of law, where individual rights were paramount, but in extending the reach of a new authoritarian state in the making. It was not so much a case of Vichy officials doing the Germans' dirty business in repressing dissent and opposition in occupied France, as if this was an unforeseen and inadvertent consequence of collaboration with the Germans. Repressing opposition *was* the business of an authoritarian government. As the prefect of police for Paris was to put it: 'You kill the people who would kill you.'[17] Vichy's own increasing repressiveness with regard to communist resistance after the invasion of the Soviet Union did not entirely match the imposition of harsher occupation methods by the German authorities. But it corresponded to the German position, and coincided with the decisive shift of responsibility for policing occupied France from the military government to the SS.

The growing collaboration in repressiveness (one could almost say, competition in repressiveness) started before the hostage crisis of October 1941, which served to clarify and accelerate the process. In August 1941, Darlan's government set up so-called special sections, hastily attached to central and regional appeal courts, and to military tribunals. These sections were there to apply a rapid and summary justice to 'terrorists'—that is, primarily communists and anarchists. Arrested alleged offenders were tried immediately; there was no appeal against a guilty verdict; and punishments, from imprisonment to death, were carried out straightaway. There was undoubtedly strong German pressure on the French government to take a more repressive stance against communist resisters. According to Barthélemy, the Justice Minister, who clearly wanted to disassociate himself retrospectively from the whole episode, the new courts were agreed on by a cabal of collaborationists, including the prefect of police for Paris; Pucheu, the Interior Minister; Jean-Pierre Ingrand, Pucheu's representative in the occupied zone; and de Brinon, Vichy's 'ambassador' to Nazi Germany. The Ministry of Justice was excluded.

The move was not really pre-emptive. It certainly preceded the crisis precipitated by the killings in October 1941. But it did not precede the German recourse to hostage-taking and collective punishments, which became, as it were, official policy as a result of the October attacks. In August 1941, for instance, the regional prefect of the northern departments attached to occupied Belgium, Fernand Carles, had protested against the German military's arrest of hostages following sabotage of a railway line. His protests had some effect: the Germans promised that hostage-taking would be confined to communists and fellow travellers. The decision to create the courts was, hence, more extensive than pre-emptive. Vichy wanted to step up its police action against enemies of the state, while at the same time assert its right to police all French national territory. This not only involved closer cooperation with the German authorities, but also enabled French police to arrest and intern communists across occupied and unoccupied France, and to try them in French courts.

It is really important to know how Vichy's greater repressiveness played out on the ground. It was clear from Carles's reaction that most prefects were opposed to taking hostages as reprisal for attacks and deterrence to future attacks. Many regional and local German military commanders felt the same way. Both sets of departmental officials feared the consequences for a consensual occupation, and for their own settled and relatively civilized way of collaboration, of the public anxiety and instability generated by a recurrent cycle of violence and counter-violence. The Vichy's government's commitment to a greater repressiveness showed that it was not really listening to its own peripheral representatives, any more than the German armed forces High Command was listening to its own military governors in the occupied territories.

In October 1941, after Ingrand had met German counterparts, he instructed his prefects and police chiefs to release to the Germans lists of all prisoners already interned by French police in French internment camps, and to highlight those arrested for communist activity. In other words, *German* hostages could be chosen from among *French* communist internees held in *French* camps. This directly contradicts Pucheu's claim, in the memoir written after his flight from Vichy France to Gaullist 'France' in North Africa in 1943, that he had told prefects in the occupied zone not to hand over any information leading to the execution of hostages.

We are on the edge of one of the most contentious episodes that occurred in wartime France. Châteaubriant, a small town in occupied western France, was the site for a French internment camp. Initially used by the Germans as a camp for POWs, it imprisoned from early 1941 a mix of common criminals, 'a-social' gypsies, and communists from across France, many of them arrested under Republican decrees of 1939–40. After the killing of the German military commander in Nantes in October 1941, the nearby Châteaubriant camp was an obvious choice for the selection of interned communists and anarchists who were to be executed in reprisal, according to the Armed Forces High Command tariff of fifty to a hundred hostages for each German soldier killed. The German military commander in France reluctantly ordered the immediate execution of fifty communist hostages, with another fifty to be executed in a few days if the local community in Nantes did not cough up the attackers.

Pucheu, at the Interior Ministry, took charge of the operation, heading a team of ministerial officials and policemen, together with their man on the ground, Bernard Lecornu, the sub-prefect for the Châteaubriant area. One of Pucheu's officials and Lecornu drew up a list of sixty names, which then passed through the district military commander, and through Pucheu, to General von Stülpnagel. The Germans then passed back a list of internees to be executed, which included twenty-six communists imprisoned at Châteaubriant. Lecornu had apparently secured the removal of one internee from the list, and also intervened on behalf of three others. He desisted after being told by the German district commander, with whom relations were good, that, if he wanted to remove those three from the number to be executed, then he would have to find replacements from among the other internees. Lecornu handed over twenty-six communist internees, who were executed in a quarry by the SS on 23 October 1941. He recorded the views of the German district commander, who was not unsympathetic to Lecornu's position but nevertheless obliged him to supply the prisoners for execution. My family lives less well than you do in France, he said, and I have two sons fighting on the Eastern Front. This was Göring speaking, albeit with a human face.

The concerted efforts of French and German local, regional, and national authorities to placate Hitler and those in the Reich who had insisted on taking and shooting hostages, and persuade them of its counterproductive impacts, had some effect in mitigating the disaster. There was a delay, and then an indefinite postponement, in the execution of the rest of the hostages. This amounted to a suspension, not yet an abandonment, of the policy. Following the killing of a German soldier in Tours, again in occupied western France, in February 1942, a similar pattern of events unfolded, with an added twist: the arrest of fifty hostages, this time including some Jews, as well as communists; the prefect's negotiated release of fifteen of them; an eventual agreement between the prefect and local military commander to put imprisonment before execution; the sentencing to death of six prisoners by the 'special section' court, and their execution by the Germans.

There were endless disputes over who actually compiled and edited the lists from which the Germans chose the definitive list of those to be executed from Châteaubriant camp and elsewhere. Du Moulin de Labarthète, for instance, claimed that Pucheu had reduced one German selection submitted to him by removing hostages who were decorated war veterans, and then accepted another list composed purely of communist party members. Lecornu was later promoted prefect, and joined the Resistance. Imprisoned and charged with responsibility for the execution of hostages at Châteaubriant, he was released in August 1945, decorated for his resistance activities, and returned to prefectural service. Pucheu, after deserting Vichy, was tried and executed in March 1944 in Gaullist North Africa for his part in the execution of communist hostages.

It was Pucheu who assumed control during the crisis of October 1941. When Pétain offered himself as a hostage to replace the fifty hostages lined up for execution, Pucheu opposed the initiative. He did so partly because it would over-dramatize an already tense stand-off between German and French authorities, and would strike the Germans as a challenge to their reprisals policy. The gesture would also complicate Pucheu's intended outcome. He preferred not to concentrate on the French government's involvement in the taking and execution of hostages. Instead, he made his own the case being made by the Germans (and, indeed, by the secretaries general in Belgium and the Netherlands) that the fear of reprisals would dampen resistance in the future. 'These attacks', he was quoted as saying, 'are down to Jews and foreigners: Spaniards, Poles. Decent Frenchmen repudiate them. They know that they will be, sooner or later, the victims... I'm one of the people. I know the workers. I know what they are thinking.'[18] His conflation of Jews and foreigners was really significant, as we shall see. But only the Poles were 'foreign' Jews; the Spaniards he referred to were the leftist Republican exiles who had come across the border to seek refuge after Franco's victory in the Spanish Civil War in 1939. Neither group, although always stigmatized as Vichy's 'enemies within', was responsible for the October killings; but that hardly mattered to Pucheu. His intention was to blame everything onto Jews and foreigners.

In his view, both the French people and the communists operating in their midst had to 'pay' for the attacks on German military personnel. They had to be made to stop resisting the occupier, since such resistance was damaging the desired collaborative relationship of Vichy France with Nazi Germany. French officials and police should cooperate with the Germans in the repression of communist-inspired resistance. Once Pucheu had made it clear that he expected French officials to comply with German demands for lists of hostages for execution, then Lecornu was bound to draft a list drawing on inmates of the Châteaubriant camp, while pursuing local negotiations with German officials he knew and even trusted for a mitigation of those demands at the margins.

It is worthwhile reproducing a conversation reported by du Moulin de Labarthète, between the masterful and decisive Pucheu and a rather more thoughtful colleague, Lucien Romier, a *Pétainiste* who was a junior minister with responsibility for drafting a new Vichy constitution.

> PUCHEU: I have done what had to be done, being fully aware of the responsibilities of my position as Minister of the Interior. I could not and should not allow the shooting of forty good Frenchmen (a reference to the war veterans apparently removed from the original German list for execution).
>
> ROMIER: But how on earth did you get involved? How could you, yourself, nominate the hostages?
>
> PUCHEU: I didn't nominate them. All I did was allow the Germans to replace the original list with a new one.
>
> ROMIER: You didn't have the right to do that, my poor friend. Whether they were war veterans or communists, they were all good Frenchmen. You didn't have to make a choice between them. You didn't have to take sides. The Germans had to be made to take responsibility for this massacre. You, now, share that responsibility with them. How come you didn't see all this?

Du Moulin de Labarthète concluded that 'Pucheu appeared thunderstruck by a sudden realization of what he had done'.[19]

If that indeed was Pucheu's reaction, then it would have been momentary. A marked disingenuousness was on display on both sides of the exchange. Pucheu could not really deny his active involvement in the drawing-up of the lists, as if it was the Germans who compiled the original lists of potential executees and then submitted them to Pucheu for revision and approval. Romier could hardly have expected Pucheu not to exempt war veterans. He would have done the same, and so distinguished between 'good' and 'bad' Frenchmen. Both the late Republican and Vichy governments had persecuted communists as a matter of policy, and Vichy especially regarded communists, along with Jews and masons, as enemies of the French state. Romier's stance was, in fact, the one adopted by most officials in the occupied territories when confronted by German measures they disagreed with or did not wish to enact. You protested against the measure, usually official to official, usually in writing, even though you knew that you could not prevent the measure being applied, and even if you and your colleagues might have to participate in its implementation. This was not just covering your back, as an official. If a measure could not be prevented, then it was your duty to avoid responsibility for the measure, not only to make it clear to the population that the measure was being imposed by the occupier against your will. The aim was also to protect yourself against any post-war investigation as to the legality of your collaborating conduct during the occupation. This was bound to happen more as the war dragged on, and the initial certainty about Germany winning the war gave way to doubts about the outcome. But it was a concern from an early stage, as well, if only because the governments-in-exile assumed quite rapidly at a distance that passive resistance was, or should be, the default position of collaborating officials.

The conversation did, however, reveal something about the nature of collaboration as practised by an official (or, as in Pucheu's case, a businessman) rather than a politician. Pétain's grand gesture, making himself a martyr for the nation, was intuitively correct in the awareness of its popular and political impact. The French people were alarmed and offended by the German reprisals and the carrying-out of collective punishments, whether it was fines or the arrest and execution of people not directly implicated in the acts of violence and sabotage. This, of course, did not stop them thinking that violent resistance would make them its 'victims', as Pucheu surmised.

Pétain's potential protest, coming from the head of the French state and the grandfather of the nation, would have channelled and reassured that popular resentment at the occupier who was turning brutal. It would have demonstrated that the government itself was seeking to defend its people against a repressive occupier. It would have shaken the occupier up, required it to confront an unpredictable situation, and made the Germans take collaboration less for granted. Whatever the impact of the proposed gesture on the resolution of the crisis, Pétain's stance would have ensured that national sentiment was being represented by the Vichy regime, and would, as a result, have helped to ground the regime in the nation. Not doing it, or something like it, practically ensured that one of the most important outcomes of the law-and-order crisis of October 1941 was to make the occupation more unpopular, and collaboration with the occupier unpopular.

An official took decisions that he thought were in the national interest, because he thought such decisions were 'right', not because they were popular or not. Pucheu did think of himself as a man of the people, a plebeian. He was the son of a member of a very identifiable and rather special group of Frenchmen, the *pieds noirs*, or French settlers in Algeria. They were hardly the average blokes in the street; they were nationalists, a minority in their own piece of national territory, and more French than the French. He did also rather set himself up as a model 'totalitarian', a member of a 'new' elite who had a populist touch and a sense of 'crowd' politics. In this instance, avoiding the big gesture, his judgement of the popular mood was awry, and his political instincts demonstrably far less developed than Pétain's.

Both before and after the crisis, he remained unshakeably committed to a line of policy that he pursued throughout his term of office at the Interior Ministry. This was to bring the country's police forces under the full control of the Interior Ministry at the centre and of the prefects in the periphery, in order to make them more manageable and more efficient. These centralizing reforms would make them more capable of taking on the policing of all French territory, and so extend the practical exercise of sovereignty by the Vichy state. This was bound to involve a more effective level of cooperation with the German authorities across French territory, because it made sense to take coordinated as well as unilateral action against common enemies of the state. Greater and more integral collaboration in policing France was the primary aim of Pucheu's reforms, which, in my view, stretched Vichy, in this area anyway, from authoritarianism to totalitarianism, from collaboration to collaborationism. That is a judgement of Pucheu that is probably still open to debate. What cannot be denied was that, before, during, and after the law-and-order crisis of autumn 1941, collaboration in policing the country was intensified to a qualitatively higher level of repressiveness than had existed only a year before. The awful consequences of this heightened collaboration would be felt in the remaining years of the occupation.

The issue of workers going to work in Germany is perhaps best dealt with as a matter of economic collaboration. It is being discussed here because the decisions were made by officials, rather than businessmen. Those decisions affected the movement and deployment of people rather than of things, which raised the wider concerns of officials for social and economic stability and for the fabric of society and family life.

We should remember that it was in the interests of both the occupier and officials that the high numbers of unemployed workers in the summer of 1940 were put back to work. Unemployment levels in the occupied territories did fall steadily in the course of 1940 and 1941. This was the happy result of the German construction boom in the occupied territories, and the decision taken at Reich level that some German orders should be diverted to the currently underused or redundant manufacturing capacity in the newly conquered territories. The idea was to release German labour and industrial capacity for priority war production. In theory, both sides could collaborate economically and to mutual benefit on the basis of workers being employed in their own countries, either on German military and civilian construction sites in the occupied territories, or in factories meeting German export orders.

In a sense, it worked out this way. In late 1941, for instance, about 250,000 French workers were employed on German construction projects, either employed directly or subcontracted by local firms. This was a very significant contribution to national economic recovery and employment. These figures are to be compared with the peak of about 75,000 French workers employed at any one time in Nazi Germany; the average, before mid-1942, was about 40,000. The Germans effectively created their own internal labour market. The Todt organization, above all German employers in the occupied territories, offered much higher wages than those prevailing in the local economy, a natural pull factor for both unemployed and employed workers.

But officials could not really be reassured by the relative preponderance of German internal, as opposed to external, demand for labour. This was because the numbers of skilled workers going to work in Germany was steadily rising, in part attracted by contracts apparently offering them better wages and conditions, and generous home leave. The migration of skilled workers was already affecting, and would continue to affect, the economic performance and viability of national industries. It was in everybody's interest that workers found work locally, and not in Germany, while the national economies recovered.

Once that began to happen, a skilled labour shortage emerged, both in Germany and in the occupied territories, from around the spring and summer of 1941. German demand for foreign labour to work in Germany was self-evidently increased by the preparations for the launching of the invasion of the Soviet Union in June 1941. From early 1942, the need to replace German losses on the Eastern Front by the call-up of workers was an additional pressure to step up labour recruitment in the occupied territories. So, out of a natural convergence of interests that facilitated and fostered economic collaboration emerged a natural divergence of interests that put a strain on collaboration, as both sides wrestled for control of the country's labour force.

The policy adopted by officials throughout the occupied territories in 1940–2 was to keep, as far as possible, workers employed on German orders in their own countries. This was both to maintain a semblance of social and family cohesion, and to protect their country's economic 'patrimony' and its most valuable economic resource. It was also policy to ensure that, if workers did work in Germany, then it was a voluntary, uncoerced process. Officials fought very hard to protect the voluntary principle behind employment in Germany, in full awareness of what the likely alternative was. They might have felt that they were defending workers' legal rights to free movement and employment, perhaps even the vestiges of a free, democratic society—though as natural authoritarians and *dirigistes*, attributes heightened by their assumption of powers in the national emergency of war and occupation, that probably mattered less than the overall defence of the national economy.

The economic *dirigisme* of most top officials complicated their task of keeping employment in Germany voluntary. They wanted to control and direct the country's economic resources, including labour, but had to move very carefully in case their *dirigisme* served that of the occupier. That dilemma was felt and experienced everywhere, but especially in Vichy France, because it was also the policy aim to rationalize and concentrate French industry in order to create a modern, efficient industrial economy capable of holding its own in the post-war world—whoever won the war. The Germans were only too happy to allow and encourage such modernizing economic reforms. Mergers and the closure of inefficient and outdated factories improved productivity, simplified the management and supply of raw materials and energy to French industries, and released labour onto the 'market' for their recruitment by German firms, whether operating inside or outside the occupied territories. It also became clear that the German demand for skilled labour could not be met by those on the unemployment registers. Many of those out of work were unskilled and/or long-term unemployed with personal and social problems that made their employment difficult. These groups of workers were regarded by both sets of labour officials as feckless 'a-socials'.

Although the labour shortage emerging in 1941 sharpened up the German recruitment drive in the occupied territories, the drive had always been there. The Germans did not observe their own agreement to locate production for Germany in occupied countries. From the start, they exerted pressure on both officials and workers to squeeze labour out of the national economies. They requested the release of categories of skilled workers of particular interest and value to them—that is, railway drivers and mechanics, skilled workers in the mining and metallurgical industries. French officials would have noted with alarm that, in the industrial northern departments of France now attached to occupied Belgium, where they had no real clout, the Germans had effectively deported Polish miners working in French coalfields to the Ruhr in the summer of 1940. They did the same to metallurgical workers in December 1940. It is worth pointing out that the Belgian secretaries general did not agree to nor undertake a similar transfer to the Reich of foreign nationals working in Belgian mines. But the transfers occurred, nevertheless.

In the occupied zone of France, the German military administration's economic department insisted that workers complete a minimum of forty-eight hours a week, and an extraordinary fifty-four hours if they were miners. This measure was not only meant to increase the demands on French workers to produce more. It was also a deliberate attempt to create unemployment, a pool of surplus, reserve labour into which it could dip, as required. In seeking ways to shake out workers from French companies who would then be available for work in Germany, the occupier was already moving from a system of voluntary recruitment to one of induced recruitment. French officials responded as best they could, in attempting to negotiate a better, or less bad, deal. The legal maximum working week remained at forty hours, which meant that officials and employers could employ workers below the maximum if this was necessary to absorb unemployment, and retain control over the movement of labour. But they were obliged in early 1941 to agree to a decree that allowed increased working hours above the legal maximum in certain designated industries or regions.

The Vichy government insisted formally that French workers were free to choose whom they worked for, and would not itself do anything to enable workers to go to Germany for work. This was neutrality or indifference of a sort. Officials still had to recognize that employment in Germany was one facet of the solution to unemployment, and could not object to German recruitment offices operating in both zones for the voluntary hiring of labour.

This was also the default position of the Belgian labour officials, as shown by their response to a German request in the spring of 1941 for 5,000

Belgian railway fitters and drivers. These men were employees of the state railway company, the *Société Nationale des Chemins de Fer Belge* (*SNCB*), who would be sent to Germany to work for the *Reichsbahn*, the German national railways. Like French, and indeed German, railways, the *SNCB* was state owned but operated like a private company with its own management and accounting structure. It was convenient for the secretaries general to pretend that they had no hold nor influence over the running of the railways, while advising the *SNCB* that it should have nothing to do with the German recruitment of its staff. Whether a Belgian railway driver went to work for the *Reichsbahn* was a matter between the worker and the German railway company alone. Both they and the *SNCB* were 'étrangers à cette affaire'.[20] It was extraneous and irrelevant to them.

The Germans could certainly publicize the vacancies in Belgian labour exchanges, but the *SNCB* would not encourage or facilitate recruitment by guaranteeing the pension and promotion rights of staff during any period of work in Germany. As the negotiations dragged on, the Germans asked in September 1941 that at least the *SNCB* could grant leave of absence, which was another way of getting the same things. The reply was again a restatement of the secretaries general's fictional neutrality in the free movement of labour between neighbouring countries. If a worker requested leave of absence, then the *SNCB* was entitled to grant it, or not, and, if it was granted, there was, again, no guarantee of the worker's Belgian rights while he was away working in a foreign country.

The secretaries general were pretty good at finding different ways of saying 'no' that did not endanger the abiding principle of collaboration in general, and the specific principle of voluntary recruitment of labour. It took a little nerve, because the two elephants in the room, to which the Germans were not reticent in drawing their attention, were enforcement by German decree, and the threat of an escalation from induced voluntary recruitment to actual deportation. This was the greater evil, which had to be prevented for as long as it was possible to do so. The fear of deportation haunted every negotiation in the occupied territories over the employment of workers in Germany. It was again no fantasy, to be easily dispelled by officials poking it and exposing it as such. The deportation of Belgian workers to Germany during the First World War had been one of the most shocking and resented measures of the earlier German occupation. It was really quite striking, and yet at the same time routine, that, at this stage of the negotiations, the Germans were as trapped by their need and desire to continue and not endanger collaboration as were the secretaries general. For both sides, collaboration was the preferred outcome of collaboration.

There were differences of opinion among the Belgian secretaries general over the extent to which the purity of the voluntary principle should be adhered to, in the recruitment of Belgian workers to Germany. Plisnier, Secretary General for Finances and, from April 1941, chair or president of the secretaries general committee, was for strict neutrality. The Belgian authorities should allow recruitment, but not cooperate in it, nor promote it in any way. He also argued against the use of the sanction of the withdrawal of benefits and welfare payments against unemployed workers and their families, the usual way of inducing the workshy back to employment. But existing Belgian labour regulations allowed the discretionary removal of benefits for people who refused an offer of employment in Belgium. The secretaries general had already decided on a temporary monthly suspension of benefits in the cases of unemployed workers refusing job offers in both Belgium and elsewhere, including Germany. This decision just about preserved Plisnier's position, since the loss of benefits was temporary, not permanent, and was taken unilaterally without any particular German pressure at this point, as part of a package of measures to get the unemployed back to work. The German military administration then used the existence of the regulation to say that the secretaries general should apply the full set of inducements and penalties they already had, to encourage, pressurize, and incentivize workers to choose to go to Germany.

The particular sanction of the loss of benefits obviously did not make any difference to the resolution of the problem of German recruitment of skilled railway workers, who were in employment, and in a sector that was an essential component of the country's economic infrastructure. Their loss would damage the Belgian economy and society. The impasse was broken in a characteristic way. In October 1941, six months after the initial German approach, the Germans tightened the screw, and directed *SNCB* to place its workers at the disposal of the *Reichsbahn*. They had effectively decreed the transfer of staff from one railway system to another, a threat made at the beginning in the hope that it would encourage compliance. The carrying-out of the threat was enough for the Secretary General for Labour and Social Welfare, Charles Verwilghen, to urge that they should now cooperate in the recruitment of railway staff, on the grounds that induced or pressurized voluntariness was at least preferable to, and one step away from, deportation. The Secretary General for Transport and Communications,

Gaston Claeys, was doubtful that Belgian railway workers would submit to this, which was an attempt to remind the occupier of the risks *it* faced in relying on coercion rather than cooperation.

In the end, Claeys apparently refused to facilitate the transfer. The task was quietly handled in February 1942 by Verwilghen and, especially, Victor Leemans, the Secretary General for Economic Affairs. Both men had come to Reeder's attention when they were, respectively, the head and deputy head of the Belgian Ministry of Labour's special 'Commissariat for Reconstruction', specifically set up to tackle Belgium's chronic unemployment of summer 1940. Reeder had insisted on Leemans's appointment as Secretary General for Economic Affairs in August 1940, when the secretaries general themselves had wanted to recall the current office holder, who had only just returned to the country after leaving with the government in the face of the German invasion. Although he had been required to evacuate, the Germans contended that his absence constituted a dereliction of duty. Reeder prevailed in his usual firm but charming way. If you reinstated your man, he told them, then 'you will have created an unfavourable situation'.[21]

Reeder had chosen his preferences well, as critical observers like Struye realized only too well. Struye constantly railed in his diary against what he saw as the hordes of unpatriotic Flemings being parachuted into government ministries. His remarks on meeting Leemans have all the francophone snobbishness that the French-speaking Belgian elites habitually threw at their Fleming counterparts. 'A rather poor impression,' sniffed Struye; 'he speaks a mediocre French...rather vulgar (because he used colloquial Flemish in a telephone conversation while Struye was in his office), clicks his heels to salute us on departure. Basically, he appears to be afraid of offending the Germans.'[22] Despite Struye's stereotyping of Leemans as an upstart Flemish squirt, the impression was broadly in line with Leemans's actual conduct, with one caveat. Leemans might well have feared the Germans; but he also wanted to please them.

The resolution of the problem over the recruitment of railway staff was an exercise in combining an eventual demonstration of where power and authority lay in an inherently unequal collaborating relationship with the secretaries general, with the application of the Nazi 'leader principle'. The workings of the 'leader principle' also enabled the German military administration to control the Belgian labour market in the German interest, through their continued penetration of the Ministry of Labour and Social Welfare. The German takeover was made possible by the appointment in late 1940 of one Fritz-Jan Hendriks to head the employment agency that Verwilghen and Leemans had run. Formally a manager at the electrics firm Philipps, he was a Flemish nationalist and a member of the *Vlaamsch Nationaal Verbond* (*VNV*), who had convinced himself of the efficacy and social justice of the German Nazi labour and welfare system. Rebranded as the National Labour Office (*Office National du Travail* (*ONT*)) in April 1941, Hendriks's agency went completely rogue, acting independently and against the wishes of his superiors in the Labour Ministry. It applied all the available inducements and sanctions to direct the unemployed (and employed) towards work on German projects both inside and outside the country. Hendriks even tried to meet the military government's monthly targets for recruitment.

In March 1942, the secretaries general finally agreed, at the cost of the resignation–dismissal of Verwilghen, to the introduction of a compulsory labour service scheme in Belgium. Their agreement was as much the continuation of their lingering efforts to retain a modicum of influence over the national labour market as capitulation to pressure from the military administration. The scheme enabled the Labour department of the military administration to direct and assign labour to work projects in Belgium, and required Belgian employers and workers to use *ONT* offices for the hiring of labour. The secretaries general were horrified to find that they had already lost control of the ministry within the ministry that was responsible for the implementation of the scheme and, indeed, already monopolized the management of all employment matters in the country.

The Dutch secretaries general had previously mooted and then agreed to a compulsory labour service for work in the Netherlands as early as February 1941, as a way of absorbing high unemployment. It is tempting to explain the time lag between the introduction of similar schemes in the Netherlands and Belgium as a matter of the varying approaches to collaboration of the Reich Commissariat and the military government. Seyss-Inquart had certainly laid down clearer guidelines on the degree of officials' subordination to the will of the occupying authority. But, because the need was the same, to ensure a smooth and lasting cooperation among officials, he had worked out a strategy of collaboration that was similar to that of Reeder in Belgium.

Again, a rather subtle mix of alternately friendly and unfriendly pressure on the secretaries general and a canny application of the 'leader principle' produced the desired result. By early 1942, all the 160 officials who were also *NSB* members in the Dutch ministry of Labour and Social Welfare were concentrated in the central bureau of the Dutch employment service, which ran the labour exchanges throughout the country. These officials were all primed to introduce the 'national' form of 'socialism'. Their boss, the secretary general of the ministry, was Robert Verwey, a career official and conservative social Catholic, who moved from the Ministry of Public Works to become head of the Labour Ministry's office for unemployment insurance, where he was directly involved in the campaign to reduce unemployment in 1940. From this position, he was able to continue the policy that Dutch democratic politicians had dared to introduce to ease unemployment in the late 1930s—that is, penalizing the 'workshy' for refusing job offers by removing their unemployment benefit and welfare payments to family members, and placing them on public works schemes. Here, then, was at least part of the explanation for Dutch officials' acceptance of a compulsory labour scheme, well ahead of their Belgian counterparts. As in Belgium, an official who had impressed the Reich Commissioner with his willingness to cooperate with the Germans in relieving unemployment was 'recommended' to be the Secretary General of the Labour Ministry, where he was expected to be even more cooperative. It was a mark of Seyss-Inquart's continuing confidence in Verwey that he was one of three secretaries general in office in 1940 who were still standing when occupation partially ended in 1944.

It is important to realize that the confidence was reciprocal, and that this was the basis of a lasting relationship between the Reich Commissariat and the secretaries general. Seyss-Inquart was as keen as any occupying administrator to find ways of releasing Dutch labour for work in Germany. He was equally keen to carry Dutch officials with him. There was a long tradition of Dutch workers moving to Germany, even commuting to Germany, for work. The pre-war Dutch government had encouraged and facilitated such mobility in the 1930s, as the Nazi German economy emerged more rapidly from the Depression than in Western Europe. It was an easy decision for Seyss-Inquart to accept Verwey's conditions on his ministry's enabling of Dutch workers to go to Germany: that recruitment would be voluntary (even though actively promoted by both sides), that Dutch workers would not be employed directly in the war industries (in wartime conditions practically meaningless), and would enjoy normal pay and working conditions (in fact, they were usually better, to incentivize recruitment).

As in Belgium, the Dutch secretaries general responded adversely to German requests for the transfer of specific groups of skilled workers from late 1940. Seyss-Inquart conceded ground here to the arguments put forward by Verwey and the Reich Commissioner's favourite secretary general, Hirschfeld, that these workers needed to apply their skills to the delivery of German contracts lodged with Dutch factories, and that they would react badly to any coercive pressure on them to work in Germany. Hirschfeld, true to form, was simply applying to labour recruitment policy his obsessive linkage between economic collaboration and internal social and public order. Seyss-Inquart's reward for his self-restrained collaboration was Verwey's continued administrative centralization of all employment matters in the labour exchanges run by his ministry, which benefited both his and the German control of the labour market. He also, very significantly, gained Verwey's endorsement, after the usual token protests, and subsequent implementation of the February 1941 German decree on a compulsory labour scheme.

Across occupied Western Europe, the secretaries general had, by and large, protected the principle of voluntary recruitment to work in Germany. But they had, willingly in some cases, less so in others, also accepted the extension of state and German control over the labour force, which served to transform voluntary recruitment into a form of induced or constrained voluntariness, the classic Nazi totalitarian mix of consensual coercion, or coerced consent. At each point, German requests and demands had been accommodated within a still flexibly robust collaborative framework. The result was, as in the law-and-order arena, a more extensive and intensive collaboration, or, to put it another way, collaboration that had moved to a higher plane. This happened cumulatively, in the course of protracted negotiations and dialogue between the occupier and officials. It made the exceptional routine. It also opened up collaborating officials to challenges that would both test and strengthen that collaboration, and not only in the key area of the exploitation of the occupied countries' labour resources.

Potentially the greatest challenge to collaboration between the occupier and officials was the enactment of Nazism's ideological and political policies in the occupied territories. Anti-Semitic measures were introduced across the occupied territories of Western Europe in the early stages of occupation. This was something of real concern for the newly established German occupation authorities, especially the 'non-ideological' military administrations in occupied France and Belgium. Just bedded in and keen to establish working relationships with local officials, they feared that the imposition of measures that were likely to be unpopular would strain both the principle and the practice of collaboration.

Things were rather different in occupied Northern Europe. In Norway, as elsewhere, Jews were dismissed from public employment and banned from professional occupations. But this happened in mid-1941, not late 1940, as elsewhere. There was a census of Jewish businesses in the autumn of 1940, but the first German seizures of Jewish assets were in spring 1942. The invasion of the USSR led to the arrest and internment of some Norwegian and foreign Jews who lived in northern towns near the Russian border, who might, just, have constituted a security risk. It was the unsystematic and irregular pattern of persecution and discrimination that marks Norway out from occupied Western Europe. Even the deportation of Jews from Norway happened suddenly and quickly in October 1942, a few months later than elsewhere, and not apparently impelled by the launch of the 'final solution' in other countries. The decision to move against the Jews was provoked by the killing of a Norwegian border guard by the 'handler' of a group of Jews who were discovered trying to escape to Sweden. I can only speculate on the reasons for all of this. It does seem strange that the only occupied country to be under a fascist government came relatively late to anti-Semitism.

The Jewish 'question' was not a great one, numerically, and this might have induced the Reich authorities into some benign neglect, since not much attention was given to Norway at the Wannsee conference. Martin Luther, a Foreign Ministry official present at the conference to report on the potential diplomatic implications of anti-Jewish measures across Europe, told the meeting that there would be problems in Norway and Denmark, but not in France. The 'problems' were obvious enough in Denmark, the presence of an independent and democratic government. But it was not clear what the problems were in Norway. There were less than 2,000 Jews in Norway in 1940. Some of them were Germans, a small cohort of the many thousands of German Jews who fled Nazi Germany for refuge in other European countries during the 1930s. It was patently ridiculous to promote the usual trope about the disproportionate social, economic, and cultural influence of Jews in modern European societies. Mind you, it was absurd to do so in Belgium, as well, but that did not stop the introduction of measures by the military administration. The difference was the still small but more significant presence of refugee foreign Jews. Anyway, the minimal presence of Jews in Norway *might* have protected them from persecution; they were a 'threat' to nobody.

Terboven, the Reich Commissioner in Norway, always strained to check or moderate the flow of the intended Nazification of Norwegian society. He recognized that the agent of that Nazification, Quisling's *NS*, was unpopular as a party and as a government, and that an accelerated Nazification would provoke more civil disobedience and undermine the occupation. Terboven's concerns were perhaps greater but essentially no different from those of the occupation authorities in other countries, whatever the form and nature of the occupation. Anti-Jewish measures undoubtedly offended and alienated the local populations, which put at risk the prospect of a stable and 'peaceful' occupation resting on the minimum possible deployment of German resources and the maximum possible use of collaboration. These concerns were real ones, and in some cases affected the way the anti-Semitic measures were applied. But they were introduced, and early on, elsewhere, and it remains something of a mystery why they were not also introduced in occupied Norway. It might, nevertheless, be the case that, paradoxically, the very existence of an *NS* government in Norway 'protected' the Jews in the country.

With Denmark, the situation was clearer, and easier to explain. There were almost 7,000 Jews in Denmark, and uniquely in occupied Europe no action was taken against them until 1943. Here, collaboration in the other aspects of the occupation was ensured by non-cooperation in anti-Jewish measures. Their introduction would have put an end to collaboration per se in occupied Denmark. This was perfectly clear to both sides, and made perfectly clear by both sides, and was an integral and binding element of the agreement to collaborate, state to state. Renthe-Fink, the German Plenipotentiary in Denmark, and his superiors in the German Foreign Ministry, consistently took the line that they should not interfere in Danish domestic affairs, unless there was a perceived threat to German security, and applied this maxim specifically in relation to the Jewish 'question'. His replacement, Werner Best, the former administrator of occupied France and *SS* officer who had gone native, took exactly the same position. At stake here, also, was the German Foreign Ministry's rather desperate concern to hold on to its influence and power in the occupied territories, by now confined to control of Danish affairs, against the predatory expansion of the *SS* and other Reich agencies.

The Danish government, for its part, claimed from the Germans an automatic government veto on any suggestion of the occupier introducing anti-Semitic decrees in Denmark. This veto was a mark and guarantee of Denmark's continuing sovereign national independence, even though occupied. Or, as the pro-German Danish Prime Minister, Scavenius, said to the Germans in August 1942, at the point of the 'final solution' being applied elsewhere in occupied Europe, anti-Semitism was a 'denial of their ideals'.[23] The defence of their 'ideals' extended itself to the 1,400 or so German and now stateless Jews who were refugees in Denmark. They were treated as residents with the right to stay, and were not handed over to the German government. Elsewhere, lacking such protection, German Jewish exiles were early and obvious targets for arrest and deportation.

The agreement not to implement anti-Jewish measures in Denmark was an example of the virtuous circle of collaboration, demonstrating the mutual interdependence of occupier and collaborators. The Danish government collaborated in order to protect its form of government, laws, and institutions. The Germans did not insist on anti-Jewish measures in order to protect the otherwise productive collaborative relationship with the Danish government.

Anti-Jewish measures were applied from the start in occupied France. But it is still possible, and desirable, to compare the Danish and French situations because of the similarity in forms of occupation. German occupation coexisted with and rested on the cooperation of nominally sovereign and independent governments and state structures. The existence of a Danish government prevented the introduction of anti-Semitic measures in Denmark, while the existence of a French government accelerated the introduction of anti-Jewish measures in France. In the Danish case, state-to-state collaboration worked to the advantage of Jews; in the French case, to the detriment of Jews. This is not as wilfully paradoxical as it looks.

Discriminatory anti-Semitic measures were introduced unilaterally in France because the Vichy government was quite consciously a systemic political and ideological shift from a democratic Republic to an authoritarian state. Anti-Semitism was an integral element of the generally xenophobic outlook of the Vichy government and its National Revolutionary ideology. Vichy's major anti-Jewish laws were passed between July and October 1940. They included the first Jewish Statute, which, among other things, gave a racial, not religious or cultural, definition of 'Jewishness'; and the exclusion of Jews from the professions and the top levels of civilian and military officialdom. These laws, like all Vichy laws, were in theory meant to apply across all of France, since Vichy claimed to be sovereign in all of France. But obviously they needed the prior approval of the German occupying authorities for this to happen in practice. The laws preceded the first serious anti-Jewish measure introduced by the Germans in the occupied zone, which was a decree to 'Aryanize' the French economy in October 1940. The 'Aryanization' decree then triggered a kind of automatic sovereignty reflex, and set a pattern for a sort of competitive leapfrogging of Vichy and German measures against the Jews.

Since Vichy on its own initiative passed laws that effectively removed citizenship and a livelihood from Jews, and that it could apply itself in the unoccupied zone, we still have to establish a connection between anti-Semitic measures and Franco-German collaboration, at all levels. It cannot be assumed that Vichy started discriminating against Jews out of a desire to 'please' the Germans and so enhance the prospects of collaboration. Even less can it assumed that the Germans required Vichy to discriminate against Jews as a sign or pledge of further collaboration. Getting Vichy to promise concessions in advance of any German concessions was the usual way in which they came to conduct *donnant–donnant* collaboration; but it was not evident this early on, and not in this area of policy. The Germans generally affected an indifference bordering on disdain for the National Revolution, while the military administration in particular thought that even asking the French to implement German anti-Semitic decrees made unreasonable demands on Vichy's goodwill.

It was pretty clear that Vichy made anti-Semitic laws because they were steps towards transforming French society through the National Revolution. They were not even flattering the Germans by imitating the occupier's anti-Semitic policies. Vichy's criteria for identifying Jews were more racially rigorous than the German ones, for instance. This was the National Revolution, not Nazism. However, the connections between Vichy's collaboration with the Germans and anti-Semitic measures taken by the Germans in the occupied zone were made in the course of conversations and contacts in the summer of 1940 involving Laval, Abetz, and de Brinon. The outcome was an agreement that French authorities would—no, should—execute or help to execute German anti-Jewish measures in occupied France. In other words, French officials and police in the occupied zone would carry out German decrees against the Jews, as an exercise in and assertion of sovereignty.

More than this, it was accepted that such cooperation over the enactment of measures against the Jews was a basis, or a start in creating a basis, for further and more general Franco-German collaboration. Laval was clearly, even at this early point, and even before Montoire, working towards the realization of his vision of Franco-German reconciliation as the heart of a general European peace settlement. From what we know of him, Laval was no fervent anti-Semite, though Abetz and de Brinon undoubtedly were. He and his successor, Darlan, were indifferent to the Jews, which was probably worse. Both French leaders saw Jews and the Jewish 'question' as pawns in a far more important political and diplomatic game, to secure a place for France in the German New Order for Europe. Laval's position, shared by Darlan, was that Vichy France had no 'problem' about dealing with the Jews, and that the Jewish 'question' was not important enough to be allowed to disrupt or derail Franco-German collaboration. It was callousness for 'reasons of state'—that is, it was justifiable for a state to commit crimes against its own citizens in order to secure the very existence and survival of the state. How familiar that sounds.

The impact on officials was practically immediate. In late October 1940, the head of the Vichy government's representation in the occupied zone circulated to prefects in occupied France the German decree on 'Aryanization'. He instructed them to ensure that the registration of Jewish businesses took place so that 'Aryaniyation' ensued, and that sanctions were enforced for non-compliance with the registration process. It got worse, or better, depending on the perspective. In March 1941, the Vichy government set up the *Commissariat Général aux Questions Juives* (*CGQJ* (General Commissariat for Jewish Matters)), under Xavier Vallat, a conservative Catholic and authoritarian nationalist, who was both anti-Semitic and anti-German, a mark, then, of Vichy's concern to monopolize the handling of the Jewish 'question' in France.

The *CGQJ* was Vichy's response to German prompting and threats. If Vichy did not do so, then the Germans would establish their own office in the occupied territories to handle Jewish affairs and enforce the anti-Semitic decrees. The *CGQJ* was a Vichyite agency, with its headquarters in Paris, responsible to the Vichy government, which was allowed by the Germans to operate in the occupied zone, as well as in the 'free' zone. The corollary was that Vichy passed its own law on the 'Aryanization' of the French economy in July 1941. This law extended 'Aryanization' to the unoccupied zone, and made the *CGQJ* the agency for the enactment of 'Aryanization' in *both* zones, now applying a French law rather than a German decree.

Both sides had good reason to hug themselves, if not each other. The Vichy government had extended its practical sovereignty over French territory, and over the French economy. The hiving-off of uncongenial but necessary measures to a new governmental agency run by an ideologue not an official served to ease the pressure on the other officials required to apply anti-Semitic measures. The *CGQJ* recruited some staff from outside the civil service who were also often anti-Semitic themselves or opportunists prepared to become anti-Semitic in the course of their duties. As what today we would in the UK call a quango—that is, a publicly funded independent agency—the *CGQJ* emerged to be greeted with jealousy and alarm by career civil servants. Its staff were paid more than them, were more corruptible and blessed with greater opportunities for venality, and were not necessarily as competent as them because they had not jumped the competitive and meritocratic entry and training hurdles of conventional public service.

On the German side, the military government had successfully transferred an unpleasant and unpopular task to collaborating Vichy officials, while protecting the rationale behind collaboration, the minimal deployment of German personnel, and the maximum deployment of French officials. In reporting to their superiors in the Reich on how well the Jewish 'question' had evolved in France, the military administration did not hold back on its justified self-congratulation. Its 1942 report would have covered the 'final solution' in France, but it provided a suitable commentary on what had happened in 1940 and 1941 as well. It declared that we have

> managed to steer the French government's own impulses and those of the French police in the same direction [as us]. That way [we] not only saved effort. [We] also spared French self-respect and thereby brought even nationalist circles closer to the German positions. That reduced the odium of the use of force, since it was French force or left... at French doors.[24]

Vichy would have expressed things rather differently, but not necessarily from a different perspective. The point was that both sides of the collaborating relationship drew benefits and advantages from it. Collaboration seemed to work.

The German report mentioned the impact of collaboration on the conduct of the French police. We must now try to explain and understand how and why French officials implemented anti-Semitic policy in both the occupied and the unoccupied zones. French officials had to apply these measures not only against Jews, but also against themselves. We do not have much evidence of any significant internal opposition to the removal of Jews from public service employment, by way of walkouts or resignations, for instance. The exclusion of Jews, like that of communists and masons, was a serious attack on their professional integrity, the meritocratic basis of employment and promotion in public posts, and the right of officials to manage themselves without political interference. As such, it might have sparked into action the ethos of institutional solidarity that characterized the civil service. It might have been the case that officials responded in the rather shifty and embarrassed way the two retired *lycée* teachers, who were government employees, of course, remembered the sacking of Jewish colleagues, in *The Sorrow and the Pity*. At least one of them acknowledged that they had done nothing. But the sense of guilt and regret belonged to the interview, and their memory of events, rather than to when it actually happened.

It could be that, given the context, the *esprit de corps* worked in a different way when officials were faced with the loss of a colleague for ideological rather than professional reasons. The civil service was under general attack from the government that now employed them, as it attempted to purge the state administration it had inherited of officials who might not be fitted to continue under the National Revolution. The dismissal of Jews was part of a package of measures designed to streamline the civil service ideologically. Public employment under Vichy was now to be reserved for 'Frenchmen born of a French father'[25] (not 'mother' you will notice). 'Foreigners' were excluded, even those who might have been naturalized as French citizens, another aspect of the 'foreign' 'invasion' of France that Vichy was seriously reviewing. There was also a catch-all decree that allowed the government to remove *any* official deemed unsuitable to serve the new authoritarian state. Jewish public employees were, therefore, not treated as a singular case, in an odd anticipation of how Jews returning from the death camps after the war were handled. They were members of groups of undesirables in public employment, including socialists, communists, masons, and foreigners.

The state had given itself every right to control its employees. But it was also restoring the powers and standing of those who went on working for it. It was presumably advisable to roll with the purges, which did not affect most of them, and absorb things in a way that did not reflect on and preserved their professional duty to serve the state. Officials were not trained to be rebels, but to conform and obey. Even if an official felt none of these things, he would have been deterred from taking any action to defend his Jewish colleague by the draconian powers that his employer could use against him. If he spoke out against the dismissal of a fellow employee identified by his employer as an undesirable, then he risked being disciplined himself. The discretion that remained in the hands of the top officials applying anti-Semitic measures in their own departments was at the margins. Jardel, the director of the budget in the Ministry of Finances, corresponded with the Ministry of Education in June 1941 about the case of a Jewish professor who had been imprisoned for 'communist propaganda'. The question he was asked was whether the 'criminal' should be allowed to receive his pension under article 7 of the October 1940 law against Jews. This was typical of the kind of interpretation, and the kind of exemption, that were possible in the application of discriminatory laws, not only in government ranks, but in society at large. It was hardly the case that being able to do something small but important for an individual was what reconciled or compensated the official for implementing a distasteful law. It was simply an individual case that routinely emerged as a consequence of applying the law. There was, admittedly, something rather defensive about the acting ex-socialist mayor of Nantes in occupied western France exclaiming 'the law is the law', after sacking the three Jewish employees of the city council's 2,000-strong staff.[26] But the disruption to the council's work was minimal, and a man who had allowed himself to be co-opted by Vichy was not about to make himself vulnerable to the regime's retribution.

The argument, I hope, becomes less speculative when we turn to French officials applying Vichy's anti-Semitic measures in the country at large, in both zones. Discrimination against Jews was the law in Vichy France, and the job of officials was to apply the law in a professional—that is, competent— manner. The duty of the official, the essence of being an official, was to obey and enact the law. There was the possibility of interpretation and discretion in the working-out and framing of the regulations that would ensure that the law was applied on the ground. But, even here, you would be guided by and certainly supervised by your superiors. The proper place for the interpretation of law, if its enactment was challenged or posed unanticipated problems, was the courts, and also the *Conseil d'État*, or Council of State, which was both the government's legal department and a court of law for the public administration.

Doing the best that you could do as a professional civil servant probably lay behind what became, retrospectively, the most notorious cases of official collaboration in applying wartime measures against the Jews. One can pick up here on one of Hilberg's most telling points, that, once anti-Semitism had become policy and law, then it immediately became a bureaucratic process run and managed by officials, with its own inbuilt rationale and momentum.[27] If we extrapolate from Hilberg, it is plausible to say that this articulation of a law as a process divorced officials from the impact of the bureaucratic systems they had created in order to implement the law. How do you enact in practice a law discriminating against Jews? You define a 'Jew', and the law or related laws had already done this. You register Jews and put them on a list; you then take action against those you have identified and registered, and penalize and pursue those evading the registration process. This was the efficient and systematic way to do it. We know that this was how it happened, not only in France, but across the occupied territories, where it was officials who undertook or supervised the initial registration of Jews as Jews.

André Tulard, Vichy France's *fichier* supreme, who attended all the important logistical meetings between French and German SS officials over the enactment of the 'final solution' in the summer of 1942, was deputy director of the Office for Aliens and Jewish Affairs in the Paris Prefecture of Police, the equivalent of London's Met. He was responsible in October 1940 for ordering the records of those Jews resident in the department of the Seine who reported themselves to the French authorities for a census of Jews required by the German occupier in order to implement its own anti-Semitic measures, primarily the 'Aryanization' of the economy. He devised a brilliantly comprehensive filing system, using different sized and coloured cards to enter the personal and occupational details of all those Jews who registered in a city and region that contained the largest concentrations of Jewish inhabitants anywhere in France. The files enabled the alphabetical listing of all Jews living in a particular street, and the separating-out of foreign Jews from Jews who were French nationals. Addresses were recorded so precisely that it was possible for the police to locate the floor of an apartment block or the position round a courtyard where Jews resided.

The Germans were so impressed by this filing system that they requested and received duplicates from the Prefecture, for their own use. The files were found accidentally in 1991 by Serge Klarsfeld, the lawyer largely responsible for securing the indictment and trial of French officials held responsible for involvement in the 'final solution'. Tulard knew the purposes to which his filing system would be put, for the application of both Vichy and German anti-Jewish measures, and the arrest and internment of foreign and French Jews who violated the regulations implementing those measures. They were later used to identify Jews for arrest and deportation to the death camps in Eastern Europe from the spring and summer of 1942. But not even the SS contemplated the final 'final solution' in October 1940.

The second case is perhaps more harrowing, and in its own way more revealing, because it demonstrated the extent of authoritarian collaboration in 1940, and the way officials felt liberated to be more efficient by the German occupation of their country. Jacobus Lambertus Lentz was a Dutch career official in the population registry department located in the Interior Ministry, who had gained national and international recognition for his work on demographic registration before the war. He was also a founder member of the Dutch authoritarian grouping *Nederlands Volksgemeenschap*, whose members and ideas fed into the *NU*, the popular movement that collaborated in 1940–1.

His pre-war and wartime development of a rather sophisticated ID system that could have been used for wartime rationing was not taken up by the Dutch government because it was considered too invasively illiberal. No such frustrations met Lentz's concern to promote and implement his system once the government had gone into exile. The Germans knew about him and his work from pre-war days, and they characteristically pursued him as a 'leader' in his field. Lentz met SS officers in Berlin in August 1940, and put on a show for Friedrich Wimmer, the Reich Commissioner for Administration and Justice in Seyss-Inquart's Commissariat. He demonstrated how the system might work by compiling a list of Dutch surnames from his card indexes that could be used as a preliminary indication of Jewishness. The Germans soon concluded that Lentz's system was superior to their own.

His boss, the Secretary General for the Interior, Frederiks, knew of the unilateral German contacts and did not object to the Germans commissioning Lentz to work on a fully developed ID system. This was presumably because he realized that Lentz's work would also make his own ministry's policing of wartime Dutch society more efficient. Certainly, Lentz's ID card was made of fraud-resistant material, carried a photograph, fingerprint, and personal details that could be cross-checked against a duplicate central card index system. From late 1941, over seven million of these ID cards were issued. They were used by both Dutch and German police for spot checks, the issue of ration cards, the identification of Jews by the 'J' imprint, and, later, the labour draft. Lentz personally briefed local officials on how to register Jews and transfer their details to the central standardized register.

Lentz suffered for his perfectionism. He became a target for the Dutch Resistance, and ended the war a physical and mental wreck. He was tried after the war, and sentenced to three years' imprisonment for the various ways in which his population recording systems had equipped the German occupier to control and direct the Dutch people during the war. The apparent leniency of the sentence reflected the nuance that the post-war purges brought to the investigations of collaborators. He was culpable, but not as culpable as his superior, Frederiks, who had permitted Lentz to develop his systems and not provided appropriate guidelines to his subordinate. Frederiks, required at Lentz's trial to be a kind of character witness, came up with a portrait of a man with the attributes of an official he could be proud to manage, even though this was understandably not Frederik's intention. He was, said Frederiks, a workaholic and a self-absorbed perfectionist. He might well have been describing himself.

Lentz, having recovered his composure while in custody, put things in typically impersonal terms to the investigating police: 'as a civil servant, I felt it my duty to carry out my assigned tasks properly.'[28] This conventional statement of an official's daily grind rather deflected attention from the Germans' grooming of Lentz, and his willingness to be groomed. He was hardly politically neutral, given his NV connections. He was a political authoritarian, which reinforced his natural authoritarianism as an official. But he undoubtedly felt that his lenient sentence was still too severe for an official who had excelled at being an official. There was a technical problem to be solved, and he had solved it in the most efficient way possible, to the best of his professional ability.

In his memoir, the Dutch Secretary General for Internal Affairs, Frederiks, tried to explain his approach to the anti-Jewish measures introduced by the Reich Commissariat in the occupied Netherlands. He was clearly aware that he was responding to a situation that the 1937 guidelines had not anticipated, and that, to an extent, made them irrelevant. Both the guidelines and the Hague Convention expected the occupier to retain and respect national laws. Anti-Semitic measures clearly violated those laws, which was not the case in newly authoritarian Vichy France, and could be seen as part of Seyss-Inquart's plan to 'Germanize' and 'Nazify' Dutch society.

Frederiks, then, felt that he was on his own, and had to act cautiously and pragmatically, if only because in the early stages of the occupation it was important not to provoke the Germans or pose too great a test and challenge to a collaborating relationship that had barely begun. In his judgement, justified by events, the Germans would not compromise nor hold back on a policy that was so integral to the Nazi 'world view'. The conclusion Frededriks drew from this was that he had no possibility of persuading or influencing the Germans on anti-Semitic policy. The most, and the best, he could do was to disassociate himself from the policy and work at the margins of its implementation by, for instance, requesting exemptions. There remains the lingering suspicion, however, that Frederiks's attitude to the Jewish 'question' was influenced by a banal but nevertheless insidious anti-Semitism. He apparently expressed his distaste at the thought of his daughter marrying a Jew.

Retrospectively, of course, looking for exemptions was itself discriminatory. It could be regarded as another dereliction of the duty to protect all Jewish citizens under the law, rather than a practical step to salvage what could be salvaged. But, pragmatically speaking, it had a spectacular result. The Secretary General for Economic Affairs, Max Hirschfeld, was Jewish, the Dutch son of a German mother and a Russian businessman father who had moved from Germany to the Netherlands in the late 1890s. As was common practice, the family had assimilated both in pre-First World War Germany and the Netherlands by abandoning their Jewish religious practice and adopting Christianity.

According to De Jong, the Dutch historian of the occupation, Hirschfeld was so assimilated that he personally felt in no danger from the Germans' anti-Semitic policies, even though he was liable to discrimination under measures that defined Jews by race, not only by religion. This does seem rather odd. His democratically elected ministers and his superiors in the civil service feared that his Jewish background would affect his standing with German officials, with whom he negotiated intergovernmental trade agreements in the 1930s as head of department in the Dutch Ministry of Trade and Industry. It would have been Seyss-Inquart's decision on whether to apply his own discriminatory measures against somebody like Hirschfeld, though I must admit that I do not know whether Hirschfeld made the 'Aryan declaration' which the Reich Commissioner required of all civil servants. The point was that Seyss-Inquart effectively ignored Hirschfeld's Jewishness because of both his demonstrable willingness as a secretary general to collaborate in a crucial area for the occupier, the exploitation of the Dutch economy, and the trust and respect he enjoyed among Reich Commissariat officials for that collaboration.

Although he might have felt that his Jewishness was as irrelevant to him as it became to the Germans, Hirschfeld, like Frederiks, seemed to have a pretty clear idea that the Nazis were fighting an ideological and total war, and that they intended to work towards an incorporation of the Netherlands into the *Grossraumwirtschaft* and the future Greater Germanic Empire. This was why he regarded the 1937 guidelines and the Hague Convention as effectively sidelined by the kind of war the Germans were waging. Such awareness helps to explain his relaxed attitude to economic collaboration. In a 'total' war, it was useless to pretend that you could insist on Dutch companies only accepting German contracts for non-belligerent industrial production. There was something of the Bichelonne about Hirschfeld, not in the former's bumbling appearance and behaviour, but in the sense that he was a relatively young and dynamic technocrat with a commitment to a rationally organized *dirigiste* economy, and, more generally, to a modern meritocratic society run by its elites. Occupation had its attractions, from such a perspective.

So, like Frederiks, Hirschfeld took the calculated view that the Reich Commissariat would be immoveable on Jewish policy, and that it was pointless, in terms of preserving the essentials of collaboration, either to resign in protest at the policy or to seek to influence it, other than mitigate some of its effects. In Hirschfeld's wider view of things, resisting the occupier over its racial policy was divisive and a threat to public order, and, hence, to economic collaboration, which was of more significance to national cohesion and survival under conditions of occupation. One can only assume that Hirschfeld was intelligent enough to recognize that national solidarity and survival were being secured at the price of excluding from society a large minority of Dutch citizens. A kind of numbers game was being played here. Hirschfeld felt that, in the circumstances, callousness towards a minority protected the interests of the majority. He was acting not only rationally and realistically, but properly and patriotically.

The memoirs of these two Dutch secretaries general present their attitudes to anti-Jewish measures in the round, and as a finished and fully rationalized approach. You would not expect otherwise from experienced and expert civil servants. But we still need a sense of how this approach developed in response to actual demands being placed on them by the occupier, before the rough edges had been smoothed away in the coherent narrative of the memoirs. We need to assess how the secretaries general behaved in real time and in the sequence of events, not in the compressed and over-rationalized time of retrospect. Doing it this way, reconstructing decisions as they happened and were made, throws up some quite significant qualifications of the polished version of the memoirs, and, indeed, of the post-war inquiries into their conduct.

In the first place, the Dutch secretaries general found that they had to apply the occupier's anti-Jewish measures against themselves, against their own officials. This happened in Vichy France, of course, with the big difference that French officials were applying French laws, not measures coming from the occupier, which clearly violated Dutch law and practice. The Reich Commissariat went about introducing anti-Semitic measures in a well-choreographed and measured fashion. Their tactics drew the secretaries general into collaborating in a policy they objected to, and opened them up to further collaboration in a policy they continued to object to. You might say that the secretaries general should have realized that one thing would lead to another. They did; but, like everybody else, they could not have anticipated in 1940 that discriminatory measures against Jews would have the outcome of the 'final solution'. In the summer of 1940, it was implausible for them to respond in the awareness of what was, somehow but only in retrospect, bound to come.

In August 1940, the Reich Commissioner for Administration and Justice, Friedrich Wimmer, instructed the secretaries general to stop appointing Jews to civil service posts, and not to promote Jews who were already officials. This was presented as a purely administrative matter, for the secretaries general to implement in their own area of ministerial jurisdiction. They stated their objection to the instructions in principle, but agreed to them in practice. Frederiks, in his capacity as Secretary General for Internal Affairs, informed the local mayors and councils who were under his jurisdiction that they could no longer appoint Jews as officials, on 1 October 1940. His instructions included the definition of a 'Jew', which combined genetics and religious practice.

Within days, the softening-up process hardened into another German demand that Jewish officials be dismissed from public service. The demand was accompanied by an even more offensive and challenging test of the civil service's integrity. All Dutch public employees, including teachers, were required to declare their racial origin, and state whether they were 'Aryan' or not. They had to produce written documentary evidence of being 'Aryan'. The 'Aryan declaration' was the means by which the Germans intended to identify Jews in the civil service under a German decree that allowed the dismissal of public employees 'in disregard of existing laws'.[29] So, something even more crucial was being tested out here, Seyss-Inquart's claim that he was the only authority in the now-occupied country and that, as a result, officials had to obey him, rather than abide by the current laws of the country.

The secretaries general, meeting in committee, and as a 'cabinet', did not respond in a way that suggested that, having capitulated on a previous occasion, they felt bound to do so again. A majority of them wanted not only to object formally, but also to reject the demand and not carry out any dismissals. Hirschfeld's intervention in the debate was decisive in them collegially adopting a more nuanced response. It might have been the case that the others were swayed by Hirschfeld's apparent indifference, or neutrality, with regard to his own fate and that of his fellow Jewish officials. But we have no way of knowing this. What Hirschfeld came up with was, or became, the classic and oft-repeated defence or justification of the collaborating official across occupied Europe in 1940.

He argued that what was at stake was the future, let alone the present, of collaboration with the German occupier. To reject the German demand to purge the civil service of its Jewish officials was to reject collaboration with them altogether, at a point when it had barely been initiated. He also drew to his colleagues' attention the likely impacts of their refusal to comply on this relatively 'minor' specific issue. The Germans would simply dismiss 'refuseniks' or, as Hirschfeld put it, force them to resign, and that would result in 'general chaos in all areas'.[30] You can observe, here, all the complacency of the top officials at the time, the assumption that their skills and expertise were indispensable to hold the country and its public services together. He might have added, though he probably did not, that, with the NU in full rehearsal as the Reich Commissioner's chosen authoritarian collaborating force, any backtracking by officials would damage the NU and provide an opening for the NSB to pose as the occupier's loyal collaborators.

Hirschfeld argued, finally, that, in office, they could try to protect individual targets of the purge by requesting exemptions. This they could not do, if they were out of office. This was a familiar stance. Collaborating officials could not avert disaster, but they could draw things back to not being a complete disaster, which was better, or less bad, than disaster itself. This is my over-dramatization, since Hirschfeld would not have regarded the dismissal of Jewish officials as a disaster.

Hirschfeld was persuasive, and his view prevailed. He effectively drafted the committee's official reply to the Reich Commissioner, in November 1940, and took upon himself the task of explaining what it meant to the German authorities. They would have appreciated the subtleties of Hirschfeld's submission, especially when they knew that the substance of their demand had been met. The secretaries general agreed to dismiss Jews from public employment even though it was 'repugnant' to them 'as Dutchmen'. The measure would, they warned, have an 'unfavourable influence on the feelings of the Dutch people towards the occupation authorities',[31] a point emphasized by Hirschfeld in his personal briefings of Reich Commissioner Wimmer. He was, of course, proved correct in his assessment that the move, and moves like it, would cause protest and unrest, endangering the public order that both he and the Germans held dear, and hence posing a risk to the smooth running of collaboration in other areas. This was effectively the only leverage the secretaries general could bring to bear—the withdrawal of their collaboration—and Hirschfeld was looking ahead in his use of the lever at this point. In return for their collaboration now, Hirschfeld was expecting to influence later German policy in areas requiring their collaboration, in the hope that the Germans would not make demands that put too severe a strain on their willingness to collaborate.

Hirschfeld also expected small concessions in return for their collaboration. They would remove Jewish officials, but on the understanding that it was a 'temporary' measure, a wording ruled out by the Reich Commissioner in earlier meetings. This was little more than a face-saving formula, and was anyway rescinded. The secretaries general, rather than hoping that they could quietly lift any suspension and allow a later return to work, concentrated instead on gaining improved financial compensation for dismissed officials.

The 1937 guidelines did offer a kind of way out, both for historians and for secretaries general at the time, even though Hirschfeld rather questioned their relevance. They indicated that officials could consider resignation if remaining in office benefited the occupier in ways that outweighed the benefits they secured for the population by staying on board. Put yourself in Hirschfeld's position, and do the cost–benefit analysis on his behalf. It is not an easy thing to do, since it requires judgement of the relative weight of actual gains and losses and more imponderable benefits and disadvantages. As a historian, I would say that the determining element in Hirschfeld's decision-making was the context. At the start of a collaborating relationship, with both sides feeling their way, it appeared unwisely premature to test the resolve of the Reich Commissariat to a point where it might consider cutting back on the powers and responsibilities of officials in running and administering the country. Hirschfeld collaborated in this instance in order to protect the future of collaboration, generally.

In the event, about 2,000 Dutch officials were dismissed as 'non-Aryan', from a total public workforce of about 200,000. There were some very high-profile casualties. His fellow judges voted by a majority not to oppose the 'Aryan declaration', which meant the dismissal of the Jewish President of the Supreme Court, Lodewijk Visser. His 'Aryan' judicial colleagues apparently feared the consequences of not making the declaration for the continuation of the judiciary and its application of Dutch law for Dutch citizens. The overwhelming majority of public employees made the 'Aryan declaration.'

Further collaboration ensued in the enforcement of unpopular and unpalatable anti-Jewish measures. It included not only the registration of Jews for discrimination under German decrees, but also the repression of Jews. The protests and demonstrations in Amsterdam in March 1941 provoked by NSB incursions into the city's Jewish quarter, were put down by the German military police. Such was the dissatisfaction of the Reich Commissioner with the performance, or lack of it, of the Dutch police across the country in relation to the popular protests against the anti-Jewish measures that he removed mayors and police chiefs in the major cities, and appointed men like Tulp. He also pressed ahead with the centralizing reorganization of the Dutch police, something that the secretaries general agreed with, anyway. Dutch police participated in the round-up of young Jewish activists and vigilantes in the aftermath of the 1941 disturbances, which resulted in the imprisonment of 1,700 Jews in the German concentration camps of Matthausen and Buchenwald.

There are indications that the military government form of occupation in Belgium made a difference to the pace and timing of the introduction and enactment of common measures against the Jews, and to the extent of officials' collaboration in the process. As we have seen elsewhere, the capacity of officials to delay and mitigate the implementation of the occupier's measures was arguably a significant gain of collaboration. I must say that, in the Belgian case, some of these gains were marginal, and outcomes were not very different from what happened in the Netherlands.

The military administration in Belgium was very aware that requiring officials to collaborate in implementing anti-Jewish measures could undermine officials' continued commitment to collaboration as a whole. They were more sensitive about this than the Reich Commissariat in the Netherlands, and demonstrated that greater degree of sensitivity. In the Netherlands, the Reich Commissioner's outrider in Amsterdam had deliberately incited the local fascists to impose the petty day-to-day isolation of Jews in Dutch society, kicking them off public transport and out of public parks, and preventing customers from entering a Jewish-owned shop or café. No such provocation was encouraged by the military authorities in Belgium. When it did occur at about the same time as in Amsterdam, in April 1941, with *VNV* members invading the Jewish area in Antwerp, the city where most Jews lived, the military governor reported to Berlin that he would continue to oppose any such unauthorized vigilante action and retain control of the Jewish 'question' on his patch. He explained his position by referring to the need to implement anti-Jewish policy while preserving the secretaries general's collaboration in order to ensure a 'good' occupation. The concern was that local officials would become even more hesitant and passive in their collaboration than they were at the time. You can certainly detect a certain defensiveness of tone in the military government's reporting back to its Reich superiors. It knew that Berlin had concerns about the military administration enacting ideological measures and was suspicious of its commitment to them.

The military government's relative restraint might help to explain why there were no popular protests in Belgium against the application of the initial anti-Semitic measures, and why there was, for the moment anyway, no need to repress any disturbances of public order. But behind the scenes there was a good head of steam building up among officials, judges, and lawyers, who, if anything, were even more prickly about defending their own jurisdictions and the rights of their Jewish fellow-citizens than their counterparts in the Netherlands. It is worth remembering that, of the about 56,000 Jews eventually registered as such in occupied Belgium, most were European migrants and refugees residing and working in the country. The judiciary were standing up for the rights of residents who were not formally citizens and who were a small proportion of the population. But that was the point. You protected everybody by protecting the few, in defence of a principle of equal rights for all, citizens and residents. The judges were also trying to prevent what happened to those Central and East European Jews who had initially sought refuge from persecution in Belgium, and moved south into France during the German invasion, where they were arrested and interned by the French police, or handed over to German police in the occupied zone.

As in the Netherlands, the secretaries general and the judiciary had to resolve differences among themselves in order to arrive at an agreed and common response to the implementation of anti-Jewish measures. The Secretary General of the Interior Ministry, Jean Vossen, later forced to retire because of ill health but really because the Germans wanted to replace him, unequivocally presented to the military administration the secretaries general's principled objection to the first anti-Semitic measures. They violated Belgian law and the constitution, and the Hague Convention, which required the occupier to respect the laws of the occupied country. They referred the German decrees to their own advisory legal watchdog, the *conseil de législation*, or legislative council. It ruled that the decrees were illegal and unconstitutional, but offered what must have appeared to be the only way out. As officials bound to collaborate with the occupying power, they could not oppose the execution of the decrees. They had to accept the decrees, but did not have to participate in their execution, except in their own ministerial jurisdictions. They had, in other words, to apply the German decrees against themselves and dismiss Jews who were in public employment. In a cack-handed kind of way, the only way possible in the circumstances, applying the decree against their own colleagues preserved the secretaries general's right to administer their own departments, when the decree challenged and undermined that essential right under Belgian law and procedure.

The judgment went too far for some, and not far enough for others. The Germans did not have the resources to implement their own measures, and required the Belgian authorities to play some part in the operation. In his diary, Struye recorded a meeting of lawyers and judges who animatedly discussed the exclusion of Jews from public service. He himself fulminated against the measure, urging a judicial strike in solidarity with Jewish colleagues, on grounds that communist resisters would use a year later—that it would expose the Belgian people to what living under the Nazi New Order would be like.[32] You have to pinch yourself and remember that this was November 1940.

Struye had convinced himself that a majority of appeal court judges backed his stance. But, in the end, his was too bold and frightening a step at this stage of the occupation. Paul Veldekens, an appeal court lawyer and mayor of a Belgian suburb, said that any provocative response would endanger Belgium's future at a time of King Leopold's prospective meeting with Hitler. The president of the Brussels appeal court argued that opposition was pointless, since the Germans would enact the measures anyway; any opposition could lead to the dismissal of judges and their replacement by ones more acceptable to the Germans.

There could only be winners and losers in this situation. Ensuring that the defeat was not a humiliation was probably the best that could be expected. At least, there was no additional test of officials' integrity and loyalties in the shape of an 'Aryan declaration', imposed by the Reich Commissioner in the Netherlands. The Belgian secretaries general managed to disassociate themselves in principle from an illegal measure. They refused to have the German decree published as their own in the official government bulletin. It appeared only in the occupier's bulletin. But, as German, if not Belgian, decrees, they were still implemented, or partially so, by Belgian officials. The courts covered them, ruling that application of German decrees was not equivalent to 'participating' in them.

The secretaries general had to remove Jewish officials from their own ministries. Reeder, a good bureaucrat himself, allowed them to negotiate the modalities of the execution of the dismissals: Jewish officials were 'released' on full pay until their retirement came along. Other German decrees had to be enforced by Belgian officials. Local council offices had to register Jews, who were required to self-declare. They used a template card index file, which was sent to them as a 'German' document, when, in fact, it was designed by officials of the Brussels city council, apparently commissioned to do so by the Germans. The registration of Jews was carried out enthusiastically by the mayor and his officials in Antwerp, the start of a trend for officials in Flanders, but with apparent reluctance in Brussels. It was Romsée, the eventual successor to Vossen at the Interior, in April 1941, who instructed local officials to pass on those registers of Jews to the German authorities, yet another sign of the Germans' reliance on having the right man in the right place.

However, Belgian officials did not participate in what was the purpose of the registration of Jews, the 'Aryanization' of the Belgian economy. Most provisional administrators of confiscated Jewish businesses and property were German and appointed by the military government. They managed the liquidation of most Jewish assets by the spring of 1942. The Secretary General for Economic Affairs was, of course, Victor Leemans, a pro-German Fleming and a German recommendation for the job. The other secretaries general eventually accepted he could fill the post, on the rather specious grounds that his presence would serve to rally Flemish nationalists to 'Belgium', and that he would be a trusted intermediary between the committee and the Germans. The counter-argument, of course, was that Leemans would act not for 'Belgium' but for Flanders, would not be acceptable to the country's francophone establishment, and would use his powers of patronage and appointment to place more Flemings in the ministry under his jurisdiction. The same arguments passed to and fro among the secretaries general over the German recommendation of Romsée, first to be at Justice, and then, successfully, at the Interior.

Leemans was well disposed to get involved in the 'Aryanization' process, but collegial solidarity prevailed, and the most that he was allowed to do was not to object to the operation. It would be churlish to point out that the reason for official intervention in the process of 'Aryanization' in other occupied countries, to protect the country's economic patrimony against 'Germanization', did not really engage Leemans in Belgium. Most of the 'Aryanized' Jewish businesses belonged to foreign Jews, the refugees of the inter-war period, and were of little economic importance to anybody but themselves.

There had definitely been self-restraint on both sides in the enactment of anti-Jewish measures in occupied Belgium. The secretaries general did not push their principled opposition to the measures to the point of refusing to implement them. The military administration did not insist that officials organize and manage the 'Aryanization' of the economy, reflecting their awareness of the high levels of indignation emanating from the Belgian judiciary at the introduction of anti-Semitic measures. They took a more cautious and understanding line on the collaboration of officials, compared to the Reich Commissariat in the Netherlands, which had a more brazenly Nazi approach to collaboration. The absence of an 'Aryan declaration' for officials, and the absence of officials' involvement in bringing about economic 'Aryanization', were the only concrete outcomes of the different approaches of the different forms of occupation, and the only real gains of the greater degree of stroppiness shown by Belgian lawyers and judges. There seemed to be more that could be gained by collaboration. You could say that it was a matter of 'form', officials remaining true to Belgian laws and the constitution, over 'substance', the execution of Nazi Germany's discriminatory anti-Jewish policies, whether by German or Belgian officials, or both. The more contextually appropriate judgement would be that collaboration over the application of anti-Jewish measures kept collaboration going for the future.

The Dutch police were prevailed upon to arrest Jews after the March 1941 unrest because of the deliberate conflation of the Jewish 'question' with the maintenance of law and order. This occurred across occupied Northern and Western Europe. It was, I think, one of the main reasons why the police forces collaborated in measures against the Jews throughout the occupation. The police arrested Jews for breaking the law, not for being Jews, even though some of the laws they were breaking were in place precisely because they were Jews. This was, after all, how Western Europe's police had been required by their democratically elected political masters to handle the refugee 'crisis' of the 1930s. The 'crisis' was the result of an influx of Central and East European Jews fleeing state persecution, as well as political refugees from Germany and Austria, and affecting France, republicans crossing the border from Spain after their defeat in the Spanish civil war. The police were used to treating migrants and refugees, including Jews, as unwelcome aliens and foreigners who were, by their presence alone, potential and actual disturbers of the peace.

Henri Chavin, the secretary general for police in the French Interior Ministry, explicitly linked the presence of foreign Jews to 'criminal' activity in his orders to French prefects in the 'free' zone to proceed with a systematic internment of foreign Jews in the south of France, where some of them had congregated. This was in the spring of 1941. He stated in a circular to the prefects in July 1941 that the registration and census of Jews in the free zone was 'a measure of public order' and hence to be pursued comprehensively and rigorously.[33] Once again, the tone was set at the top. Vichy's Minister of Justice, Barthélemy, a man who prided himself on his dogged defence of liberal values in an authoritarian system, somewhat gratuitously condemned 'foreigners, naturalized or not, established in our country thanks to the weakness of previous governments . . . concerned only to exploit . . . resources created by Frenchmen'.[34] This was saloon bar xenophobia and anti-Semitism, loose talk at any time, and yet it appeared in a February 1941 circular the minister sent to state prosecutors in the appeal courts on the application of laws against the black market.

The extent to which such attitudes were rooted in the outlook of power-holders and decision-makers was revealed in the disingenuous way Maurice Gabolde, a leading state magistrate in the Paris region and later Vichy Minister of Justice, handled the stereotypical associations of Jewishness with crime, in a post-war testimony to the Hoover Institute. The French communist party, he said, was responsible for the development of 'political criminality' when it took up the armed struggle against the occupier, and Vichy, from the summer of 1941. He then noted that the first violent acts committed by communist resisters were perpetrated by Eastern European refugees and migrants in Paris, especially Jews. It was not true in the 1950s, any more than it was true in the early 1940s. But such attitudes left their mark. The prefect of Haut-Garonne, in a report of December 1941, echoed back at his superiors the same easy generalizations, congratulating himself on the arrest of various people implicated in 'Judeo-communist-anarcho-gaullist' plots.[35]

The association of Jews with foreigners, and with crime, both political and mundane, induced prefects to extend the use of one of their most significant administrative powers, a hangover from the 1939–40 period, that of internment. With no need to have recourse to the courts, the prefects could arrest and detain literally anybody they or their superiors deemed a threat to public order. This came to include people who were under suspicion of being Jewish. By early 1942, the Interior Minister, Pucheu, was telling prefects that internment was to be automatic for all stateless and foreign Jews in France who did not have the legal protection of their country of origin.

The rationale of public order was applied across the board to the official and police treatment of Jews, incorporating the depressingly familiar popular tropes about malingering and parasitic Jews. For officials, the influx and movement of Jewish migrants and refugees, which extended from the 1930s into the war years, 'caused' local unemployment, put an undue strain on already overstretched welfare systems, and took food from the mouths of decent working families because incoming Jews both supplied and were supplied by the black market. Marcel Ribière, the prefect of the southern French department of Alpes-Maritimes, was particularly keen to make these associations as a justification for his taking administrative measures against foreign and 'criminal' and 'suspect' Jews, largely because he was responsible for policing a region that had attracted a large number of well-off Jewish refugees from other parts of Europe as well as from the German-occupied zone of France.

His outlook was shared by prefects in other departments with a low number of Jewish incomers. There is no reason to assume that the police's association of the presence of Jews with criminality was a forced or convenient one, to deflect away concerns about the imposition of an ideological and inhumane policy. This was a well-established way of looking at things, based on their experience of policing foreigners in Western Europe in the 1930s. Jews were not a singular group; they were one army of an 'invasion' of foreigners who constituted a threat to social cohesion and public order.

The German occupiers required their collaborating officials and policemen to take action against both national and foreign Jews because they regarded them as a threat to their own security and that of the occupation. It was the job of local police and officials to make the occupiers secure. This was, of course, the way that the Nazis converted their Jewish victims into perpetrators. The Jews in Germany had resisted the application of anti-Semitic measures there, a dubious proposition in itself, and their racial kin would naturally disturb the occupation, elsewhere. Officials and police in the occupied territories could use this, the security of the occupier, as a justification for participating in anti-Jewish measures, and did so. But there was no need for them to do so. They were already persuaded that 'foreigners' were the most serious threat to the maintenance of order in the occupied territories. As a result, French police in Paris cooperated with German police in one of the early mass round-ups of about 4,000 Jews in August 1941. These raids were justified, in general, by all Jews posing an urgent security risk after the invasion of the USSR and, specifically, as reprisal and hostage-taking after the attacks on German military personnel in western France. The raid picked up both foreign and French Jews, some of them chosen deliberately because they were well-known figures. Most of them were kept in the camp at Drancy, in Paris, and helped to fill the first convoys to Auschwitz a year later.

We can observe the same unforced dissimulation of motives in how officials handled the 'Aryanization' of their national economies. The elimination of Jewish influence in the economy, which was policy in both the occupied and unoccupied zones of France, reached pitiful levels of implementation. The streets of eastern Paris, where thousands of impoverished migrants and foreign and national Jews resided, were stripped of their small-time traders and hawkers. The removal, and often internment, of Jewish stallholders and odd-job men left wives and families bereft of a bare livelihood. The provisional administrators appointed either to liquidate or to confiscate Jewish businesses found that there were no assets at all to dispose of. 'Aryanization' here had every appearance of being an operation to clean up the neighbourhood, which was probably how the French police saw the round-ups of foreign Jews in Paris in 1942, and certainly how they saw the ferocious trawl through the old port area of Marseilles, which they planned and conducted with the *Gestapo* in 1943.

The ministries of Finance and Industrial Production had a say in the nomination of these administrators, even when their agency body, the *Service de Contrôle des Administrateurs Provisoires* (*SCAP*), passed from the latter ministry to the *CGQJ*. But officials like Bichelonne did not involve themselves in the 'Aryanization' of enterprises that yielded nothing. Vichy's hasty passing of its own 'Aryanization' law was intended to catch up with and overtake the German decree in the occupied zone. The French government naturally feared that the occupier's 'Aryanization' would be the lever for the 'Germanization' of the national economy, with German businesses taking over the confiscated assets of the 'Aryanized' French companies. The military administration might well have intended this to happen. But, in the event, they were only too happy to exchange, as it were, the 'Germanization' of the French economy for the continued economic collaboration of Vichy and its officials, and their cooperation in the implementation of a difficult and uncongenial policy in their perceived patriotic and national interests.

How 'Aryanization' worked can be illustrated by the experience of a major French and Jewish shoes and boots manufacturer and retailer, *André Chaussures*. Everybody was interested in the 'Aryanization' of one of the main economic players in its sector. The Germans wanted to buy the firm's products, and at the same time make the sector more efficient by concentration, which was compatible with the aim of ridding the sector of its Jewish elements. The *CGQJ* wanted to eliminate Jews from the national economy in both zones, in a sector where Jewish businesses had a significant stake. The *CO* for the hides and leather industries wanted to dissolve a major company and distribute its plant, assets, stocks, and markets among the small and medium French-owned enterprises, which mainly made up the sector, and which were seen as the backbone of a National Revolutionary economy. The head of the *CO* for the banks was Henri Ardant, the conservative Catholic and anti-Semitic managing director of the *Société Générale*, a major deposit bank that was making excellent returns from handling some of the clearing transactions on Franco-German trade. He had a field day in removing the Jewish and foreign presence in the French banking sector, again in the interests of concentration and keeping out the Germans. In this case, Ardant, a powerful figure in France's collaborating economic establishment, intended to explore a different option, the transfer of the company's assets to a new and potentially bigger company to be expanded by fresh investment from his own and other banks.

The Ministries of Industrial Production and Finance wanted to 'Aryanize' in a way that advanced their schemes for the concentration and modernization of the French economy, and protected the nation's economic patrimony against German penetration. Ministerial officials usually encouraged the liquidation of Jewish businesses rather than their sale, so as to rationalize and concentrate business in French hands. The Ministry of Industrial Production was particularly keen to remove what it saw as excess capacity in inefficient and 'backward' sectors of the economy dominated by small and medium enterprises, which was where the Jewish presence was most marked. But they were very aware that, if the Germans wanted the closure of a French company, then they were expecting to shake out labour and raw materials that could then be deployed more efficiently elsewhere and in enterprises producing for the German war economy. Their concern to defend and protect their own management of the country's labour and raw materials resources in times of wartime shortages left them with an open mind about what to do in this particular case. Even the company's Jewish owners wanted 'Aryanization', a disguised or phoney one where the firm would be run by 'Aryan' proxies whose presence would protect it against both French and German predators.

The need to reconcile these ideological, national, and economic concerns made necessary weekly inter-ministerial and inter-agency meetings to decide on individual cases of 'Aryanization'. The economic importance of *André Chaussures* to both Vichy France and Nazi Germany, and to the economic collaboration between them, and its ideological importance for the *CGQJ* and the Germans, induced a very high-level meeting indeed of interested parties in March 1942. Bichelonne, for the Ministry of Industrial Production, attended, as did Ardant, Barnaud, head of the team negotiating Franco-German economic collaboration, the leader of the leather and hides *CO*, and representatives of the Ministry of Finance, *SCAP*, and *OCRPI*. This was a summit meeting to break the deadlock on what to do with the company. But it signally failed to deliver. The participants, or combatants, could only agree to differ, and, with no settlement, the company continued to operate under provisional administration up to the day of Liberation.

Many other cases of 'Aryanization' were unresolved at the end of the war, after months and years of procrastination. As for *André Chaussures*, it was probably the happiest possible outcome. At Liberation, the company was still formally in the owner's hands, and had not been sold or liquidated or dismantled. This happy ending is, of course, not the point of the story. The officials of France's economic ministries did not see the 'Aryanization' of the company as the enactment of Vichy's National Revolution, but as the enactment of their own 'modernizing' revolution, viewed exclusively in economic and material terms. Ardant, a *Pétainiste* banker, could see it as both economic and ideological, and 'patriotic' and 'national' in both senses.

It was, in one sense, amazing that economic officials, and a financier who was also an official, did not show any concern for the inviolable principle of a capitalist economy, the right to private property. But, from their perspective, they were putting in place a *dirigiste*, state-run, and state-directed economy in the national, collective interest, rather than protecting individual rights. This was 'politics' as administration, if you like. But the tendency of officials to be relatively unaware of and immune to the consequences for actual human beings of their rational and coherent policies was certainly a characteristic of their conduct as officials, both in peace and in war. An official acted, or thought that he acted, in a professional and impersonal manner, without fear or favour to individuals, in the national interest. He did not need to be an anti-Semite to enact anti-Jewish laws, though he might have done so with relish if he was.

One has, I suppose, to accept that the ministerial purge of Jews from the French educational system, with the highest numbers of Jewish employees in public service, was carried out in a different spirit by Jérôme Carcopino, a respected and prestigious academic and university administrator, and a moderate *Pétainiste*, who was Minister in 1941–2, from that of his successor, the anti-Semitic Bonnard. But Carcopino applied the anti-Jewish measures, nevertheless, liaising with the *CGQJ* as he did so, and, in his own retrospective and exculpatory words, 'I thought it was more useful to buckle down to the task'.[36] The professional performance of one's duty drove out ideology and made it irrelevant. Or it made the official ideologically technocratic.

The situation in Belgium, always exceptionally tense and febrile, became really combustible from March 1942. The fire had been lit some months earlier. Lawyers were heavily involved in creating and fomenting the crisis. But this was a legal storm that raised really fundamental issues about the continued legitimacy of Belgian law and the constitution under German occupation, and the powers of the secretaries general to run the country during the occupation. The two legal flashpoints were over administrative and institutional changes introduced by the secretaries general partly to facilitate a purposeful collaboration with the occupier.

There had been set up a national agricultural body called the *Corporation Nationale de l'Agriculture et de l'Alimentation (CNAA)*, the National Corporation of Agriculture and Food Supply, which was very much like the Reich Food Estate in Nazi Germany. The *CNAA* required all farmers to participate in a scheme that was intended to control and regulate the production, sale, and distribution of essential foodstuffs. It was an integral part of a general recasting of economic structures that enabled the secretaries general and the Germans to organize the wartime Belgian economy in an efficient, planned way. The organization of agricultural production in wartime was crucial everywhere. It was especially important in occupied Belgium because the country had previously relied heavily on agricultural imports to feed itself adequately. There was now a need to maximize domestic agricultural production and ensure that what was produced was distributed fairly among consumers. Farmers, as well as food wholesalers and retailers, hated the *CNAA* because it prevented them from making the most of very favourable wartime market conditions; their products were in huge demand. A lower court in a town in the province of Liège came to their aid. The local magistrate ruled that the establishment of the *CNAA* as a statutory public body was illegal under article 107 of the constitution. Since its institution was now invalid, farmers had no reason to continue their obligatory involvement with it, and could, for instance, refuse to deliver their production quotas for grain to the official granaries. The Germans arrested the magistrate, but the case passed through the higher courts. In March 1942, the Supreme Court confirmed that the decree setting up the *CNAA* was invalid, a decision that sparked a constitutional and legal explosion.

There was a parallel development. The secretaries general agreed to the creation of enlarged conurbations, or *grandes agglomérations*. Officials had planned for the establishment of big city administrations in the 1930s, but the Belgian government had not approved them. They were resurrected now, and strongly backed by the German military administration, on similar grounds of simplifying and streamlining the running of the country's major cities. The Germans had another motive, easily discernible. The *grandes agglomérations* were part of a wider scheme employed throughout the occupied territories, and not only in Belgium, to centralize administrative powers through the dismantling of the pre-war democratic and elective local government apparatus. So it was knowingly disingenuous for the new pro-German Interior Secretary General, Romsée, in office from April 1941, to argue that the *grandes agglomérations* were a necessary apolitical administrative reform. The secretaries general already knew that this kind of institutional change was beyond their remit from the government-in-exile, and probably beyond the powers they contentiously claimed to exercise under the 1939 and 1940 laws.

And yet the secretaries general had given an irresistible momentum to the process by agreeing to the appointment of a *VNV* member, Hendrik Borginon, as state commissioner for the *grandes agglomérations* in October 1941. Greater Antwerp had already been created the month before, without much fuss. Further steps were taken from the spring of 1942, overlapping with the storm brewing over the invalidation of the *CNAA*. It then became very clear that the German military government was not only interested in greater administrative efficiency. As with other centralizing administrative reforms, the intention was to dissolve existing bodies run by uncooperative or unreliable elected personnel and appoint rather more compliant officials to manage the new bodies. The new Antwerp was led by a Catholic mayor. Greater Ghent was temporarily placed under the *VNV*'s leader, Hendrik Elias. Greater Mons was administered by a Rexist council, while the new mayor of Greater Charleroi was a Rexist communal councillor. Later in 1942, Greater Bruges had a *VNV* mayor, and Greater Liège a Rexist majority council. The Flemish cities were being passed to the *VNV*, the Walloon cities to *Rex*.

There were big protests in July 1942 over the creation of a Greater Brussels, the capital city and neither a majority Flemish nor Walloon area. In December 1942, at the point when the reform had been largely implemented, the Brussels appeal court ruled that the original creation of a Greater Antwerp was illegal and unconstitutional. So, another legal bomb was exploded, a few months after the debris had been cleared up from the first bomb in spring 1942.

The Supreme Court decision on the *CNAA* not only declared its establishment invalid. It also invalidated the powers of the secretaries general to make and issue laws, and hence called into question all the decrees promulgated by them from the start of the occupation. At meetings of the secretaries general, it was reported that, as a result of the Supreme Court ruling on the *CNAA*, commissions putting in place the *grandes agglomérations* had suspended their work. The system of collaboration on which the running of the country under occupation was based was itself unravelling.

The military government had, like the Reich Commissariat in the Netherlands, always backed as full a delegation of powers to the secretaries general as possible, since indirect rule was regarded as the bedrock of occupation and alone made occupation viable. Such a fundamental challenge to the occupation precipitated decisive action by the German military administration. In May 1942, it decreed that the Belgian courts did not have the right to evaluate or review the legality or not of decrees issued by the secretaries general under the terms of the delegation of wartime powers to them. This dramatic move in defence of the powers of their proxies struck at the heart of Belgium's democratic constitution, and the hallowed principle of the separation of powers that placed the executive not above, but answerable to, the law and the judicial interpretation of the law.

Reeder's decree was not really a gamble, but a calculation. After some two weeks of anguished deliberations, the secretaries general eventually agreed to the publication of the German decree on their powers and those of the courts. His proposal to issue such a decree threw the onus for resolving the crisis of the occupation back onto the secretaries general and, you might say, the country's francophone establishment, where he knew opinion was divided.

This was immediately apparent when the committee of secretaries general met to discuss Reeder's 'proposal' to Schiund to issue the decree, in April 1942. Plisnier, the committee's president, took up a strict constitutional position: the courts must retain their right to review the legality of the secretaries general's decisions. Since the publication of the proposed German decree would destroy public confidence in the secretaries general, and induce a crisis of conscience among the officials themselves, it was, said Plisnier, up to Reeder to resolve the situation by withdrawing the threat to judicial review. This was, then, an attempt to call the occupiers' bluff, to test their resolve to keep collaboration going. Schiund, as Secretary General for Justice the official go-between with Reeder's department, basically agreed: the proposed decree was an attack on the magistracy and the authority of Belgian law.

Romsée assumed the role of pragmatist and authoritarian, arguing that it was the job of the judiciary not to encroach on the powers of the executive, but to cover the secretaries general when they had to invoke 'necessity' as justification for using the powers legally delegated to them. 'Above all', said Romsée, 'the country must be governed'[37]—precisely the German position. His was the minority view among the secretaries general. A majority did not support the publication of the German decree.

Later in May, Reeder made it clear to Schiund that he would remove or suspend judges and prosecutors who did not observe the decree, assuming that it would be published, and told Schiund to inform his judges that this would be the case. The threat was extended when Reeder made a speech, reported in the press, that, if the Belgian courts refused to take action against citizens violating the food supply regulations, then people using or operating the black market would be tried by German military tribunals, rather than in Belgian courts. The German courts would presumably remain beyond the jurisdiction of Belgian law and the judicial scrutiny of the secretaries general's measures. This new threat hit a number of sore spots, and required some secretaries general to rethink their positions on the principle at stake in the light of its specific and practical consequences.

Plisnier had to admit that the German administration of justice against food 'criminals' will be 'more rigorous than at present and the population will suffer for it'. De Winter, the Secretary General for Agriculture, already beside himself at the Belgian courts' refusal to allow arrest warrants for those suspected of illegal slaughtering, pointed to the way this kind of judicial leniency exposed and demoralized his officials in the CNAA. They were not only prevented from curtailing the black market in the interests of all. They had 'serious scruples of conscience', knowing that their inability to prosecute food crimes in the Belgian courts meant passing their fellow citizens over to German justice. His conclusion on the unpatriotic non-cooperation of the judiciary was that 'it is not permissible that the magistracy refuses to collaborate in the work that ensures the subsistence of our fellow-countrymen; in both its organization and its repression, this work has to be done by Belgians'.[38]

De Winter's concerns added a new ingredient to the debate, the sense that non-collaboration in one area of the country's administration could undermine the will to collaborate in another area. He was pointing to the effects throughout the administration of a rupture in the solidarity of collaborating officials. He was making a fresh appeal for cohesion, solidarity, and esprit de corps among all officials, around the principle of collaboration.

The debate among the secretaries general was echoed in their discussions and contacts with the judges and, more widely, among the Belgian elites.

Some lawyers and judges were for calling a judicial strike, extending the current paralysis of administration and justice. Others were more pragmatic, arguing that any further provocative acts by the judiciary would precipitate a German purge of the judiciary, and worse still, a move from a more or less consensual collaboration conducted with a more or less moderate military government to a much more severe and repressive form of occupation. Galopin, whose views mattered in this dispute, backed the secretaries general against the judiciary in the exercise of their powers, using the argument of unintended but hardly unforeseeable consequences. Judges who challenged the secretaries general would provoke more direct intervention in public affairs by the military administration and so undermine the continued running of the country by its top officials. Galopin wanted the secretaries general to remain in place, because he needed to renew the terms of economic collaboration, which had come under great strain during the winter of 1941–2.

Just in case the secretaries general were still not receiving the message, one of Reeder's colleagues told a delegation of them that the Germans would consider arresting those judges releasing prisoners charged with food crimes. If the current leniency persisted, then they would be obliged to envisage changes to the way the country was administered. This was undoubtedly an attempt to confront the officials with their own worst fears. In the circumstances, it was an extreme threat but not beyond the realm of possibility, given that the Belgian judiciary were effectively preventing the continuation of collaboration.

This unrelenting German pressure did not appear as such, since Reeder imposed no deadlines, put no limit on officials discussing the issues. The Germans could afford to wait, after all, applying a sublimely effective combination of cajoling and threat orchestrated so as to bring officials to their senses and confront them with the magnitude of the choices they had to make. In the end, all that was required of the secretaries general was to re-establish a working collaborative relationship, which was in danger of being ruined by the reckless provocations of the judiciary. It was no wonder they came round and concocted a fresh formula and procedure that allowed them to resume what had been disrupted.

The eventual compromise of June 1942 was formulated by Plisnier, the secretary general who thought that the initiative for a solution should come from the Germans, and that constitutional niceties enabling the judges to review the lawmakers should prevail. It was the result of angry and emotional exchanges between the secretaries general and the country's top lawyers and judges. You would not expect any of that anger and emotion to appear in the bureaucratic formulas that emerged. The 'new' approach was complicated enough to satisfy only lawyers and officials, and confuse everybody else, and needs some decoding for us ordinary mortals.

The secretaries general agreed that they would add a form of words to the preamble of their own decrees. This indicated that the decree had been issued 'taking into account the deliberations of the secretaries general of the ministries'.[39] Being interpreted, this denoted collegial or collective responsibility for decisions, with the committee behaving like a cabinet of ministers. No decree could be issued unless it had majority support in the committee. You could present this as an advance on previous arrangements. The requirement for a majority decision would be a restraint on any secretary general acting unilaterally in the area of his own ministerial jurisdiction. It would prevent any German divide and rule, exploiting their influence over men such as Leemans and Romsée.

All future decrees would carry the signatures of all secretaries general, to show that it was a collective decision for which each of them was responsible. So 'only' collegially agreed decrees were valid and legal, and therefore under the 'new' procedure, immune to review by the courts, as long as the decrees were not of a 'political' nature. Each decree would also contain a rationale for the measure, effectively explaining the secretaries general's right to take decisions under the powers delegated to them by the 1939 and 1940 laws. Mention of both laws could also be presented as a gain, since they allowed a more flexible interpretation of those powers being exercised as a matter of 'necessity'.

The concessions required of the judges were considerable. The High Court would have to approve the legality of the procedures, and recognize the validity of all the secretaries general's measures up to this point. In other words, the judiciary would have to forgo its right to retrospective evaluation and challenge of the executive. And, of course, the German military administration agreed to withdraw, or rather suspend, the May 1942 decree, now evidently irrelevant. This it could do without any apparent loss of face, because it had never actually had the decree published, only submitted it to 'approval' by the secretaries general. Everybody who mattered knew about it, of course. The Germans also agreed to release the judges they had arrested for organizing a strike in the courts, arrests that made its victims 'hostages' to a happy conclusion of the dispute.

As more than one secretary general commented, you provoked the Germans at your peril. What De Winter described as 'disloyal' acts of judicial sabotage and defiance were, to him, irresponsible, precisely because they were carried out in order to prick and challenge the occupier. The judges' behaviour during the crisis had, according to Claeys, the Secretary General for Transport, simply obliged the committee to concede more in order to rescue and restore the original state of play with the military administration.

The important thing to extract from the resolution of the crisis was that the secretaries general, as Belgian administrative authorities, were still running the country. As Leemans put it, and he was hardly a disinterested participant in the crisis, 'only a realistic (note the word) solidarity among the secretaries general will save the country from a solution which would not be a Belgian one'.[40] It would appear that the only thing that the secretaries general could agree on was that they should continue to administer the country.

The deal was a fudge, barely concealing a climb-down by the judiciary in face of the prospect of a more taxing and repressive occupation. Or was it? Given all the legal brains at work, the mention of the 1939 law as a legal cover for the secretaries general's measures might have been the pretext for a superbly timed intervention by the government-in-exile, which held fast to its interpretation of the 1940 law on the (lack of) legislative powers of the secretaries general. It was, however, more likely that, having had little influence on the resolution of the crisis, the government-in-exile simply wanted to remind its officials who their real masters were, in a gesture that indicated their sense of impotence and despair. Barely had the dust settled on the dispute when the Foreign Minister, Spaak, launched into a bad-tempered, abrasive, and sarcastic tirade on Radio London for the edification of the Belgian public, in August 1942. 'You want recognition of the right to make laws?' asked Spaak, rhetorically. 'Legal and public opinion has replied: never! And now, your leaders, we tell you, in turn: never! The rules which determine your duty have been outlined (a reference to the 1940 law). You don't want to understand them? Too bad!'[41]

This amounted to more than a public dressing-down. It was as close as you could get to a disavowal of the actions of your own officials and, therefore, of collaboration. Such an intervention, expressed in such a way, might well have reignited the judiciary's long-held scepticism about the powers of the secretaries general, more or less doused by the outcome of the spring 1942 crisis.

This might be fanciful. The question of the *grandes agglomérations* had a life of its own, after all. At least some of the secretaries general cared that such a major reform of big city administration appeared to modify pre-war statute, and pushed them into dealing with 'political' matters. The barely resolved crisis of legitimacy over the spring and summer of 1942 had certainly made the ongoing formation of the *grandes agglomérations* a red-hot 'political' issue. Part of the problem was that Romsée, as Secretary General for the Interior, was setting up the new city administrations unilaterally, exercising the power to handle matters that were under his ministerial jurisdiction. Some secretaries general backed the new arrangements on efficiency of service grounds, and so you could say that he was proceeding with their consent.

The military administration tried to take the heat out of the issue, which had been generated by the judicial crisis, by requesting in November 1942 that the appeal court delay for another two months its examination of the legality of Romsée's initial decree establishing Greater Antwerp. The German proposal provoked an action replay of what happened over the Supreme Court decision on the legality of the *CNAA*. Schiund seemed quite happy to reopen old wounds, and wind up the judiciary against the occupier. He told Reeder that, as a 'political' matter, it was beyond the remit of the secretaries general, and that it was something he had to clear up and take responsibility for, since the measure was illegal under current Belgian law. He also criticized Reeder for yet more interference in the Belgian judicial process and for disrespect of Belgian law and procedure. Plisnier went further, telling his colleagues that they should accept the appeal court decision on Greater Antwerp, knowing that it would be unfavourable. Some judges had gone even further, initiating a judicial strike affecting the appeal courts involved, itself, of course, delaying any appeal court judgment. The Germans had, once again, arrested the judges, pending the appeal court decision. Reeder, meanwhile, replied to Plisnier in kind, again masking the threat of worse with sweet reasonableness. In a classic negotiating manœuvre of focusing on a side issue created by the main issue, which, in turn, raised an even more important matter, he stated that, if the judges did not go back to work, then their refusal might well precipitate 'very severe measures which will undoubtedly have repercussions for all of the public life of the country'.[42]

Romsée appeared calm, as well he might be. He had a point when he remarked that Greater Antwerp had been a done deal for over a year, and that the committee had already accepted that its formation was a matter of administration, pure and simple. He repeated his view of the summer, this time rather more aggressively, since he realized that he could be isolated in the committee, and that the appeal court decision, when it came, would reopen disputes and conflicts soothed away by Plisnier's 'new' formulation on the process of their decision-making.

He forced his colleagues to think 'politically' about an issue that he continued to regard, deliberately, as apolitical. If Plisnier wanted, now, to reaffirm the right of the judiciary to review executive decisions, then that was inconsistent with his own formula and would discredit and weaken the authority of the secretaries general, particularly in their relations as a body with the judiciary. This was quite a subtle way of invoking collective solidarity to protect his personal position. He was well aware that he was a particular target of some of the judges for being the man in charge of the Interior Ministry, which was implementing fundamental changes.

The Brussels appeal court judgment in December 1942, that the setting-up of Greater Antwerp was illegal, was reiterated by the Supreme Court in February 1943. In between, there was another huge public row between the German military government and the judges, culminating in the equivalent of the occupier's May 1942 decree. In January 1943, the Germans did what Romsée had urged his colleagues to recognize: they required Belgian officials to continue applying their Belgian ministerial superior's decision on the *grandes agglomérations*.

The secretaries general, meanwhile, had dealt with the recurrence of the question of their legitimacy to act, by what we would now call 'kicking the ball into the long grass'. They decided to set up a commission of inquiry to 'clarify' the general legal position arising from the specific dispute over the city administrations. They calculated that this would take things back, or forward, to the summer 1942 'deal' with the military government. It would enable the judges to resume judging, the Germans to release the arrested judges, and the secretaries general to continue collaborating with the German occupier. This was a typically bureaucratic low-key conclusion to a highly charged situation, which decided nothing but allowed things to continue more or less as before. The tone had undoubtedly changed, however. The two crises in one, stretching from the spring of 1942 to early 1943, had soured relations between the country's administrative and judicial elites and, if anything, increased judicial scepticism about the merits of official collaboration. The government-in-exile now had so many doubts and anxieties about collaboration that it was consciously distancing itself from its practitioners. This was not new, but the extended judicial crisis had made things worse. These splits within the Belgian establishment over the point of collaboration clearly affected the secretaries general's collaboration from 1942 onwards.

As ever, it would appear that the occupation in Belgium was experienced more extremely and intensely than in any other occupied territory in Northern and Western Europe, in ways that tore the fabric of Belgian society, or at least of Belgian elite society. We still have to find some explanation for the compliance of the Dutch judiciary, which simply refused to offer a judgment on the legitimacy of indirect rule and the collaboration of the secretaries general, as compared to the combativeness of the Belgian judiciary, which contested both the standing of the secretaries general and the occupation. It cannot have anything to do with national temperament, surely—the idea that the Dutch were and are intrinsically more law-abiding. I only mention it here, because it has been adduced as one of the many reasons for the application of anti-Jewish measures in the Netherlands. Yet we know that some Dutch people protested publicly against those initial anti-Semitic measures. When opposition to the occupier was forced underground by the sheer repressiveness of the occupation, then some Dutch citizens organized secret networks that helped Jews and others to evade German measures as they intensified and escalated. We have, of course, to avoid eliding the response of citizens affronted by the occupier's measures with the response of officials whose job it was to facilitate the occupation. Officials were by their nature bound to be law-abiding in a way that citizens were not, and this had nothing to do with whether they were Dutch officials rather than Belgian.

The answer may lie in the differences between Belgium and the Netherlands as national states. Struye strongly backed the judiciary's stand against the secretaries general and the German occupier. The reasons for it became increasingly clear in his splenetic diary entries for 1941–2. Here, he constantly railed against the march of the Flemings under the German military administration. A particular target of his ire was Romsée, Secretary General for the Interior, sarcastically referred to as 'this good little fellow with the crafty smile'. Romsée *was* physically small and dainty, but, for Struye, he was achieving big, bad things, amounting to the destruction of the Belgian state. He had appointed 'the Nazi Elias', 'an agent of the enemy', to be mayor of Ghent, and '400' Rexist and *VNV* mayors throughout the country.[43]

Perhaps the prickly and defiant response of the Belgian judiciary was to be seen as the last stand of the francophone establishment against what it saw as the deliberate dismantling by the occupier of the pre-war political and communal settlement of how to govern Flemings and Walloons in a single, unified state. The secretaries general, who were increasingly less francophone and more Flemish in their composition, were, from this perspective, wilfully and knowingly complicit in the death of the Belgian state. A more objective view would be that the Belgian judges behaved exceptionally in an exceptional Belgian context. What perhaps needs highlighting was how identical positions on occupation and collaboration were reached by the judges and secretaries general in the Netherlands, and the secretaries general in Belgium. It just took a little longer in Belgium, and generated major crises on the way to a similar outcome.

In terms of officials collaborating with the occupier in Northern and Western Europe, Norway has always been something of a special case. This was because Reich Commissioner Terboven found himself running the country with an NS government, rather than through established elites. He aimed, like Seyss-Inquart in the Netherlands, to stimulate a bottom-up Nazification of society, so as to ease the country's full incorporation into a Greater Germanic Empire. It did not go well, precisely because the agency of Norway's putative transformation was an unpopular Nazi party and government. Unlike the German Nazi Party in the early 1930s, the NS in 1940 did not have the organizational grounding in society to effect change. Its understandably precipitate attempts to penetrate and win over Norwegian civil society met concerted opposition from that society.

Government officials refused to make declarations of loyalty to the new NS government, and, like fellow professional groups, teachers and doctors, they did not join the monopolistic NS associations set up to 'coordinate' them. There was what appeared to be an organized campaign of civil disobedience among many groups of Norwegians, culminating in a formal protest to the Reich Commissioner in spring 1941 at the enforced 'Nazification' of Norwegian life. Terboven applied the 'leader principle' in a ruthless way. He attempted to decapitate the organizations by arresting and interning the ringleaders of the protest, and appointing NS commissioners to run and 'coordinate' them. A teachers' strike a year later against being required to join the NS teachers' association resulted in the internment of 1,000 teachers.

As elsewhere in occupied Europe, local elected bodies gave way to central ministerial appointments of mayors and county governors, who became 'leaders' in the Nazi sense. NS membership was not a prerequisite for office, but 'loyalty' to the NS programme was. In this way, the NS government co-opted existing mayors, some of whom remained in office, and sidestepped the problem of a lack of competent party cadres to assume state positions. This was all very reminiscent of the situation in Fascist Italy and Nazi Germany, where a dominant fascist party occupying leadership positions confronted a largely 'unfascistized' government service. Party–state conflict appeared to contribute to the general disorderliness of the occupation, and make occupied Norway seem a 'resisting' rather than a 'collaborating' society.

However, there were other straws in the wind. We have already noted the way some NS mayors successfully intervened on their constituencies' behalf to restrain the occupier's recourse to a greater repressiveness. This resembled the way officials elsewhere in the occupied territories attempted to mitigate the impact of the Germans' counter-productive reprisal and collective punishment policies. We know that Terboven, as the occupying authority, recognized that a provocative and premature attempt to 'Nazify' Norwegian society would disrupt public order and, hence, the security of the military occupation, which it did. This kind of risk to the occupation was, after all, the reason why he had sought an authoritarian rather than an NS succession to the departing king's government. There undoubtedly needs to be more research on this. But we can at least indicate that the occupation was, in reality, more consensual than dissenting, at least at the level of officialdom.

By late 1942, over 80 per cent of the country's mayors and county governors were NS members, and many top officials at local government as well as the ministerial level were also NS. These were proportions never realized in the other occupied territories. But, given the shortage of suitable candidates in the ranks of the NS, these figures were achieved largely by co-option—that is, reappointing mayors who satisfied what were interpreted as very broad tests of political loyalty, and getting some of them to join the NS. The centralizing and authoritarian reforms of local government had gone through, but local government remained in the hands of many of its previous office-holders.

If you think about this, in the course of 1940–1, the NS government in Norway, advertently or not, had bedded down the occupation in the same way as it had occurred in the other occupied territories, through gaining the cooperation of local officials and mayors. You can imagine how local people in occupied Norway were reassured about the occupation, and even the attempted 'Nazification' of Norwegian society, by the familiar presence of the mayor and officials who continued to be responsible for the provision of public services. The mayors and officials were, in turn, reassured by the NS government's continued reliance on them, presumably because of their competence and experience. The abolition of elected local government and the rebranding of mayors as 'leaders' would have been rationalized by these officials as being necessary reforms improving the efficiency of the governmental administration in difficult wartime conditions.

Things did not remain quite the same. The NS Interior Minister, Albert Hagelin, now responsible for local government affairs rather than the Ministry of Justice, did begin to purge mayors and county governors whom he regarded as being politically unreliable, in 1941–2. Jonas Lie, the chief of police cultivated by the SS as a rival leader to Quisling, called on his patron's advice and guidance to reorganize the Norwegian police service so that it resembled and operated as a proper Nazi police force. These were not unusual developments. They ran in parallel with those in the other occupied territories, as the occupation continued.

One has to admit that I am left with the need to reconcile two rather divergent views of the occupation in Norway: a widespread civil disobedience in face of the attempted 'Nazification' of Norwegian society; a broadly consensual occupation based, as elsewhere, on the continuity of the state and its officials, and their willingness to collaborate in order to ensure an orderly occupation. Perhaps the reality was that both existed: a subterranean calm beneath a rather turbulent surface.

Over the course of the first two years of the occupation, collaboration synchronized with the need and desire of the occupying authorities to reap the advantages of indirect rule and ensure a relatively consensual occupation. In this sense, we can broadly say that the collaboration of 1940–2 developed with the grain of occupation. Collaboration between businessmen and occupier was relatively straightforward in this period, because it served the respective interests of both sides. Collaboration between officials and occupier was a far more challenging affair, even though it was, from the start, the dutiful thing for officials to do.

In Belgium, collaboration was a tumultuous affair, because of the communal divisions that even an 'apolitical' military administration was prepared to exploit and deepen, to the detriment of the survival of the Belgian state. Many of the country's francophone elites felt that collaboration came at too heavy a price, in relation to the integrity of the Belgium with which they identified. But Belgium's secretaries general, if not its top lawyers and judges, though widely disagreeing among themselves, nevertheless came together over what became the lowest common denominator, the perceived need to continue collaboration, almost at any cost. They, too, found ways of collaborating with the grain of occupation, as well as reasons for doing so.

Collaboration over policing and law and order was never really a problem, even when the Reich authorities required the occupying authorities to make occupation more repressive. Collaboration in the discriminatory treatment of Jews was eased by its conflation with the maintenance of law and order, the arena where collaboration, anyway, was readily forthcoming. The movement of labour to Germany posed the greatest challenge to the collaborating relationship between occupier and officials. The latter felt that they had just about held the line on this really contentious issue. But they were clearly perturbed by what was likely to happen in the future, the recourse to compulsion and deportation. From 1942, the direction and tenor of occupation shifted significantly, and induced yet more systematic and sustained questioning of the value and purpose of that continuing collaboration.

6

Collaboration against the Grain of Occupation, 1942–1944
The Deportation of Jews

In the course of 1940 and 1941, as both the occupying authorities and occupied elites experienced and tested out their collaborating relationship, there developed what could be called a 'logic' for collaboration, or, as I have put it earlier, a virtuous circle of collaboration. It was bound to be a difficult relationship, because of occupation. But it became a workable and working relationship. Both sides invested a lot of energy and effort in keeping the circle revolving, because they recognized that collaboration served convergent interests and mutual needs, and would continue to do so. There was something inherently self-validating about collaboration: the reward, or price, of collaboration was more collaboration. Maintaining the collaborating relationship was almost a mutually beneficial end in itself. What certainly sustained or facilitated collaboration in these early years of occupation was the shared sense of German current and future military domination, based on the near-certainty that Nazi Germany would win the war.

The war changed in its character and in its dimensions, and, as it did so, that certainty of a German victory waned. The changing fortunes of the military war transformed the context in which collaboration operated, and there emerged elements of constraint, reluctance, and uncertainty, which were not evident in 1940–1. So collaboration continued, but mutated according to the changing circumstances of war. It is possible in retrospect for the historian to find and justify what were the military turning points of the war. Those who lived through the war and occupation also did so after the Liberation in 1944–5, and, in a very short retrospect, rationalized away their behaviour during the occupation, as a result. But it is really quite difficult to be precise about these wartime military turning points and their impacts on people's conduct under occupation.

To put it another way, the turning points I can retrospectively refer to as a historian do not necessarily match the actual changes in attitude and conduct that occurred on the ground inside and outside the occupied territories. As that historian, I would tend to go along with the view of Struye, who recorded in his diary of 7 November 1942 the joyous private celebration of his circle of professional lawyers at the Axis's military reverses in North Africa, and at the gates of Stalingrad, and the military advances of US and Australian forces in the Pacific. 'It's the beginning of the end,' he wrote exultantly.[1] Struye and his group of friends were very well informed on international events, and were eternally optimistic about an eventual Allied victory, let alone heralding the global significance of the capture of Papua New Guinea from the Japanese. The optimism masquerading as fore-sight was Struye's way of consoling and steeling himself to the experience of an increasingly damaging occupation, where things only appeared to be getting worse. Struye's over-reaction alone would, for me, push on the real turning point of the war to the spring of 1943, when definitive defeats in North Africa and the USSR put Nazi Germany on a footing of defensive retreat. And Struye's choice of turning point, of course, made no difference to the way he thought about the occupation, or about collaboration; the one determined the other.

Gutt and Spaak, respectively the Ministers of Finance and Foreign Affairs in the Belgian government-in-exile in London, both thought that the war had shifted irrevocably towards the Allied coalition once the USA had entered the war in late 1941. This was prescience of a sort. But the Allies did not actually win the war in Europe until May 1945. In my view of what was feasible at this point of the war, to expect Galopin and the secretaries general to behave from late 1941 as if the Allies were going to win the war was a kind of madness. And yet both of them insisted on behaving like madmen, publicly criticizing Galopin et al. for being too subservient to the occupier, and requiring those administrative and economic elites currently collaborating with the German occupier to adhere to what the government-in-exile saw as the properly patriotic default position, which was resistance.

Similar vibes were transmitted by the Dutch government-in-exile; prob-ably a bit later, however. But, at least from 1942, both the Belgian and Dutch governments-in-exile emphasized, with growing confidence and expectation of being noticed, that they, rather than the German occupying authorities, were the officials' lords and masters. Along with everything else, the increasing assertiveness from a distance of the governments-in-exile exercised a growing and unwelcome pressure on how businessmen and officials collaborated for the rest of the occupation. They felt the heat of the changing fortunes of war from a point when the prospects of an end to German occupation were non-existent to remote. We need to remember that the context for the introduction of the most contentious and unpopular occupation policyies, the deportation of Jews and that of workers, was the Nazi German military and political empire being at the peak of its expansion in the summer of 1942. It is as necessary to remember that the continuation and extension of these policies took place in the occupied territories at a time in the spring and summer of 1943 when the Axis forces were being pushed back for good in both the Russian and North African theatres of war. This was bound to affect how officials responded over time to the challenge of the enactment of these policies.

At the opposite extreme to Gutt and Spaak were Laval, who returned to power in Vichy France in April 1942, and Bichelonne, the official he appointed as Minister of Industrial Production. The changing shape of the war, and the possibility, then likelihood, that Germany would lose the war, made no discernible difference to their commitment to collaborate with the Germans. Laval began to think about the possibilities for a compromise peace, and the contribution France could make to bringing it about. He also probably modified the advice he gave to those ministerial and prefectural officials who were directly responsible to him, and that was important. But his own public stance on collaboration never wavered, and he made sure that collaboration remained the policy of the Vichy government. For his part, Bichelonne ignored the advice of his friends and colleagues to do as they did, and leave government in 1942. Instead, he oversaw and encouraged an intensification of France's economic collaboration with the Germans in 1943–4, at the very time when the final defeat of the Axis powers appeared to be in sight.

Hovering unpredictably between these two pairs of would-be resisters and serial collaborators was Bernard Lecornu. We last met him as the sub-prefect of Châteaubriant, the official who was required by his minister, Pucheu, to get involved in the selection of communist internees to be shot by the *Gestapo* as reprisal for the killings of German military personnel in western France in autumn 1941. In his memoirs, Lecornu recalled that his own conversion from a life of sin as a collaborating official occurred on the road to Angers in the spring of 1942. Drink probably played a part. Lecornu shared a bottle of Cabernet Sauvignon with another official, Ivan Labry, the top economic official at the regional prefecture in Nantes. They met inadvertently on a drive that both of them were separately making to attend yet another ceremony where Pétain received the oath of loyalty from France's prefects. The two men began to think aloud and philosophize about the point and value of Pétain's collaboration, and their own experience of working with the occupying Germans.

For Lecornu, by his own account, it was a life-changing conversation, because it clarified for him an eventual decision to become a 'resister', or, rather, a collaborator who 'resisted'. One could say that his conversion really occurred in 1944, when Lecornu was prefect of the Corrèze department in rural and mountainous south-central France. Here, the *maquis* was well established and active, not least in the threats it made to inhibit the conduct of incumbent state officials. Be that as it may, Lecornu took up a role of 'resisting' collaborator, which was probably also assumed by some of his prefectural colleagues, but hardly in the spring of 1942. His decision to move from active collaboration to disguised resistance apparently owed nothing to the state of the war, which at the time would have encouraged continuing collaboration with the winning side. It was a personal decision, catalysed by a chance meeting, certainly rooted in his reflections on the occupation, but bearing no apparent relation to the war outside.

These cases have been chosen mischievously, to make a point. But, although apparently miscellaneous, they do indicate two significant shifts in the world of collaborating officials and businessmen from 1942 onwards. What officials saw as the carping external presence of the governments-in-exile was hardly new, but it was felt more often and more forcefully as time, and collaboration, went on. So not only were officials being reminded of whom, ultimately, they were responsible to; they were also being told off for continuing a policy of collaboration that their governments had entrusted them with, in the national interest—or so they thought. They had every reason to feel afraid of their own governments, and of what might happen to them once the war was over, and they were held to account for their conduct during the occupation.

The governments-in-exile also expressed their displeasure with collaborating officials in unpleasant ways that hit at the heart of what gave officials their cohesion and sense of purpose—that is, hierarchical obedience and collective solidarity and responsibility. As if this alone could vaporize the

Dracula of collaboration, the Belgian government-in-exile even reinvoked article 115 of the penal code, which threatened draconian penalties for certain kinds of collaboration. The Dutch government's revision of its 1937 guidelines in May 1943 strengthened the original injunction against officials resigning in the event of the occupier demanding that they undertake unpalatable measures. The government wanted to stem the bottom-up Nazification of Dutch society being gradually realized through the appointment of NSB members to official positions, something that was beginning to recur at the mayoral and communal level, especially. Instead of resignation, the official 'should refuse to implement the measure... while he remains carrying out his normal functions dutifully for as long as possible. Only in the case of dismissal, may he leave his post.' This was just incoherent. Who would replace the official dismissed for not collaborating with the occupier? Why, somebody from the NSB...

Dutch officials had staked their whole position on remaining in office through collaboration, in order to prevent the incursion of the NSB. They were the lesser evil, to the greater evil of the NSB. However much they might have to compromise and concede as collaborators, it was bound to be less demeaning and less damaging to the nation than what would be conceded by collaborationists. By their presence alone, officials felt that they were stalling the Reich Commissioner's intention and hope to Nazify Dutch society. For them, practically the only thing that would induce them to go was Seyss-Inquart installing a Quisling-like NSB government in the occupied Netherlands. There were many other good reasons why the Reich Commissioner checked the political aspirations of Mussert during the occupation. But one of them was certainly the prospect of alienating the officials who administered the country for him.

The 1943 guidelines specifically criticized the collaboration of higher officials, those 'who should have been an example, and who have not been consciously aware of their duty', those who 'have failed to demonstrate the correct attitude... by example and leadership'. In future, then, 'responsibility for following (the government's) instructions rests on the administration, and on each official individually and personally'. So the official was no longer bound by the orders of his superior, and, more importantly, perhaps, could no longer be covered by the claim that he was merely obeying orders. In place of collective responsibility was individual responsibility. Each official had to measure his enactment of any assigned task against 'his conscience, the law, and the instructions given to him by his legitimate government'.[2]

This was a bombshell. The new instructions threatened the cohesion and common action of departments, and the deference and loyalty of officials to their superiors, and were a challenge to the principles and practice of officialdom itself. At the very least, Frederiks and Hirschfeld would have started compiling their dossiers of defence for the post-war investigations and tribunals. Despite this governmental criticism, both secretaries general kept on collaborating—in Hirschfeld's case, right to the very end of the occupation. Their calmness and persistence would presumably have reassured their subordinates, by showing the kind of leadership that deserved their continued obedience. But the lower officials would also have been preparing themselves for the post-liberation purge commissions.

Even French officials eventually got their own troublesome government-in-exile. Developing from the Free French movement exiled in London, de Gaulle's shadow government acquired a territorial base in French North Africa after the Anglo-American invasions of November 1942. It took some time for the Allies to recognize formally that this was the legitimate French government. It gave itself this status by merging with the representatives of the major internal resistance groups, and declaring itself to be the Provisional Government of the French Republic just before the Normandy landings in June 1944. It was only at this stage that de Gaulle's government could regard itself as in any way near the legitimacy enjoyed by the other governments-in-exile.

This might explain why there were relatively few defections of officials from Vichy as a result of the German military invasion and occupation of the free zone in November 1942, in order to pre-empt a possible Allied invasion of southern France from North Africa. Pétain certainly considered abandoning ship, but decided he could do more for his country by staying on. Most officials appeared to feel the same. They undoubtedly felt demoralized by the full military occupation of their country, and might have conceded to themselves that some of the point of collaboration had been lost as a result of this negation of Vichy's quasi-independence. Since they were always interested in the formalities, they might have been reassured by Hitler's insistence that the Armistice and Vichy's sovereignty over all of France were intact. And their own government, which employed them and expected their loyalty, was carrying on, and, more importantly, was continuing to collaborate with the Germans as a matter of state policy.

In an odd way, the complete military occupation of the country from late 1942 enhanced their sense of national worth, and of being the only remaining representatives of the nation and its interests. Certainly, with the navy scuttled, the Armistice armed forces dissolved, and the empire lost, practically the only leverage the Vichy government possessed in its relationship with the occupier was the granting or withdrawal of the collaboration of its officials. The full military occupation of France overstretched German military and police resources. With more territory to cover and secure, the collaboration of French officials was even more necessary to the integrity and continuation of occupation. It could even be argued that the invasion of the southern zone affected the conduct of the German occupiers rather more than the Vichy government and its officials. The invasion enabled the direct extension of German policies and policing to the former 'free zone', and of the occupier's concern for ever tighter scrutiny, surveillance, and supervision of the French administration, as practised in the occupied zone. The occupier was becoming increasingly directive and interfering, tendencies accelerated by the greater demands being made of the occupied territories, and the vulnerability it felt in taking over yet more territory. So, although the country's power and standing had been diminished by the full occupation, those of Vichy's officials were not. Vichy's retention of the loyalty of the bulk of its officials after November 1942 meant that the nuisance posed by de Gaulle's Provisional Government was felt vicariously through the pressures exerted on them by its proxies inside occupied France, the resistance movements.

The growth of organized resistance in the occupied territories had a big impact on how collaboration continued from 1942. Driven underground by the occupier's repressiveness, non-communist resistance groups took time to coalesce. They needed the impetus provided by the increasing severity and unpopularity of the occupier's policies from mid- to late 1942. The most important, active, and ramified resistance network in the occupied Netherlands was the one that sheltered and protected those on the run from the measures directed at them by the occupier. Thousands of people tried to evade deportation to work in Germany. Many of them moved to find other work elsewhere, or, if they could, hunkered down to live and work on farms in the countryside. Some, also, found their way into resistance bands, which lived off the land, or commuted between a partisan and 'normal' existence. But all of them were treated as fugitive criminals and regarded as a security risk to the occupier. Their families came under official suspicion, and were often subject to reprisals by the occupier. All this increasingly strained the commitment and responsibility of officials and policemen to ensure a safe occupation.

Despite German military advances in the Soviet Union, the inability of German armies to knock Russia out of the war led over the winter of 1941–2 to a reappraisal of what was needed to win the war in the East. The agency for the mobilization of a total war economy was the Ministry of Armaments and Munitions, later called the Ministry of War Production, first under Fritz Todt, and then, after his death in a plane crash, Albert Speer. Nothing was ever definitive in an inherently chaotic Nazi polycracy, but Speer's ministry came closest to creating the mechanisms for the realization of a centralized and planned war economy in Germany. The military's own procurement agencies were steadily subordinated to Speer's civilian ministry, which imparted both control and dynamism to the war economy by empowering sectoral business group organizations run by industrialists and company managers straddling the worlds of enterprise and officialdom.

Hitler and the Nazi leadership continued to expect both 'guns and butter' from the war economy, if only to mitigate the strains imposed by total war on Germans as soldiers, producers, and consumers. The prolongation of the war, its transformation into total war, and the concern to protect German consumption as much as possible demanded a more extensive and systematic economic exploitation of the occupied territories. This included the transfer to the occupied territories of the Speer ministry's planning and organizational schemes, in order to incorporate them into a 'European' war economy. The one exception to the more intensive economic exploitation of the occupied territories was Norway, for reasons that will be made clear later in the chapter.

The effects of the transition to a total war economy were felt in the occupied territories from the autumn of 1942. They involved the partial integration of their industrial economies into the German planning system, and, as a result, even tighter German controls over them. These controls ran through the chain of production, with priority allocations of raw materials, energy, and labour to companies working on German contracts, and to the sectors of the economy that were not regarded as essential to the war effort.

Speer's reorganization of the German war economy naturally required more, not less, economic collaboration in the occupied territories of Western Europe, which became economically indispensable to the German war effort in the course of 1943–4. In some key industrial sectors, aircraft production, shipbuilding, mechanical and electrical engineering, construction, companies were supplying between 80 and 100 per cent of their production to Germany from late 1942 onwards. It cannot be said that West European industries did not rise to the challenge of greater and more intense economic collaboration. In late 1943, about 85 per cent of Dutch deliveries on German war contracts were on time; the figures were about 75 per cent for Belgian industries, and about 70 per cent for French industries. These were remarkable production and delivery levels, given the effects of increasingly felt shortages and bottlenecks of raw materials and energy, and of a disrupted transportation and distribution system, as the war wore on. We are left, then, with something of a puzzle with regard to economic collaboration in the occupied territories. Companies were increasing their industrial production for the German war effort from the very point when some of the apparently important leverages on collaborating conduct—the certainty that Nazi Germany would win the war, for instance—were weakening.

The invasion of the Soviet Union made the war 'total' in another sense. The war became ideological and 'European', and justified, from the German Nazi perspective, ever greater demands on the collaboration of the peoples of occupied Western Europe. They were expected to match the sacrifice of the blood of German soldiers on the Eastern Front in the European crusade against Bolshevism (and later in the defence of Fortress Europe against the same Bolshevik hordes) with the less onerous sacrifice of their products and their labour. The need and urgency of a 'final solution' to the greatest threat to the integrity and survival of European civilization, the 'enemy within', the Jews, were precipitated by the self-induced logistical problems of handling the hundreds of thousands of Jews falling into Nazi hands as the German armies moved east. The Wannsee conference of January 1942 served to clarify the dimensions of the Jewish 'question' in Europe, assert the supremacy of the SS over other Nazi bodies in its resolution, and to establish a framework for that 'final solution'. In the spring and early summer of 1942, labour and death camps in Eastern Europe were equipped to receive the mass deportations of European Jews, which began in the summer of 1942.

The Nazis' ideological warfare had mixed effects on the practice of collaboration in the occupied territories. On the one hand, it brought businessmen and officials into ever closer contact and cooperation with their German counterparts. This reinforced the mutually comprehensible and beneficial relationships between men who resembled each other and thought and acted in similar ways, which had developed in the early years of occupation. On the other hand, it exposed these same businessmen and officials to a breed of ideologically driven Nazi 'leaders' who thought and negotiated in very different ways from what they had become accustomed to. When Bichelonne met Speer, their eyes met and they together entered a kind of technocratic and European trance. When Laval met Fritz Sauckel, the Nazi labour plenipotentiary, or Theodor Dannecker met Jean Leguay, to 'discuss', respectively, arrangements for the deportation of workers and Jews in France, two worlds and cultures collided.

These collisions, together with the increasing uncertainty over the outcome of the war, eroded the previously established bases for a consensual occupation and collaboration. At the very points when Germany appeared to be losing the war, the Germans were intensifying their demands in the occupied territories. Both the occupation and collaboration with the occupier became unpopular. As a result, the occupying authorities became more distrustful of the reliability of their collaborators and ever more concerned to supervise and direct their activities. They began to press harder on the goodwill of the very people they depended on to sustain the occupation. The collaborators in turn became more reluctant to cooperate, as a natural reflex to the pressures on them. Far from completing a virtuous circle, collaboration was part of a downward spiral of diminishing returns.

Put this way, it seems remarkable that collaboration continued to the bitter end. One underestimated explanation for this lies in the occupier's steady weeding-out of officials, from secretaries general down to mayors and policemen, who were deemed inadequate or unsuitable, either a priori or on the basis of experience and the testing-out of their value to the occupation. Officials who had earned German trust and respect by the way they collaborated were retained. Others were replaced by men who were collaborationists or fellow-travellers. This process accelerated as liberation from occupation approached; some distrusted officials were arrested and sent to German concentration camps and prisons. But it was by no means a complete clear-out, and we still have to explain the continued willingness of most officials to collaborate during the dark years of the occupation.

Denmark was the only occupied country in Northern and Western Europe where the deportation of the Jews did not take place in 1942. It was only a postponement, but it was a crucial one. The eventual enactment of measures against the Jews in Denmark occurred in extraordinary and very different circumstances from those that pertained elsewhere in 1942. The Jews of occupied Western Europe had been isolated, segregated, deprived of their rights and livelihoods, according to a discriminatory pattern that resembled the process in Nazi Germany in the 1930s. None of this happened in Denmark, because of the Danish government's specific veto on anti-Semitic measures, in turn reflecting the German occupier's principle of non-interference in Denmark's democratic institutions, which was the basis of collaboration between the two governments.

There was a qualitative shift in the relations between the Danish and German governments in late 1942, although most commentators tend to emphasize that nothing really changed in practice. There was a dispute over nothing, or everything. Hitler took umbrage at the Danish king's habitual cool and formal 'thank you' to Hitler's rather more effusive birthday greetings to the king. It was only a ritual, and the protocols had been observed. Hitler certainly detested hereditary monarchs, and wanted nothing to do with them. He would have regarded this required exchange between two heads of state as obsequious and demeaning. But he did it, presumably because he recognized, or had been persuaded to recognize, that this was what heads of state did, and because, in this particular case, it reaffirmed in a symbolic way the state-to-state collaboration between Nazi Germany and Denmark.

It was possible, of course, that Hitler was having a bad day, made worse by receiving a telegram from the king of Ruritania that he regarded as being disrespectful of the ruler of the known world—and just exploded. But it was perhaps more likely that Hitler saw in his rage the opportunity to do something about an anomalous and contradictory situation where a 'Germanic' country was collaborating with Nazi Germany in order to protect its democratic parliamentary system of government. It was, after all, pretty clear that Denmark's collaboration was opportunistic and conditional, and that its commitment to a democratic constitution was a sign of it being anti-German and pro-Allied in the war. If this was the case, then Denmark should be treated as an enemy, not as a friendly country.

Foreign Minister Ribbentrop's overtures to the Danish government after the breaking of the 'crisis' indicated that Hitler was, in fact, giving some thought to Denmark's status, rather than acting on a dictatorial whim and a lost temper. Speaking to the Danish Foreign Minister, Scavenius, in Berlin in October 1942, Ribbentrop urged his counterpart to bring about a government reshuffle involving the inclusion of men from the Danish Nazi Party, the *Danmarks Nationalsocialistiske Arbejder Parti* (*DNSAP*). Scavenius replied carefully, arguing that if he, as Ribbentrop intended, became Prime Minister of a rejigged government, then it must not appear as if he was the anointed German candidate. The Danish government would forfeit the trust and support of its people, if that was the impression. Scavenius was on firmer ground when he claimed that the appointment of *DNSAP* members to be government ministers would provoke both derision and disorder in the country. But the point had been taken. If the Danes wanted to avoid the *DNSAP* in government, then they would have to accept changes to the government and a more pro-German stance.

Hitler and Ribbentrop decided to go for a more than halfway house in an attempt to resolve a crisis of their own making, and recast German–Danish relations. Scavenius became Prime Minister, as well as remaining as Foreign Minister, in November 1942. His government was not broadened out to include Danish Nazis, but some party men were replaced by non-political 'technocratic' ministers. The German diplomat plenipotentiary, Renthe-Finke, and the German military commander in Denmark were replaced by apparently 'more' Nazi and hard-line figures, Werner Best, the *SS* officer and veteran of the German military administration of occupied France, and General von Hanneken. In a subtle but quite significant change in status, Best, while still apparently responsible to the German Foreign Ministry, was plenipotentiary in, rather than to, Denmark, and no longer, like Renthe-Fink, a kind of ambassador representing one country to another.

The new appointments also presaged Hitler's personal and direct inter-vention in Danish affairs, on the new premise that Denmark was now to be treated as an occupied country. This, naturally enough, meant the exten-sion of Nazi occupation policies to Denmark, which effectively negated not only the Danish veto on anti-Jewish measures, but also Denmark's semi-independent status. Ribbentrop apparently instructed Best in April 1943 to plan for the 'final solution' in Denmark, and to suppress growing resistance activity there. The linkage of the two issues, Jews and public order and security, was the usual way in which the Nazis tried to induce officials and policemen to cooperate in applying measures against the Jews. Ribbentrop was telling Best to ensure that the Danish government made the appropriate connections in respect of the Jews that it had previously made in respect of the communists.

Best did nothing to prepare for the 'final solution' in Denmark. Barely a month before, he had allowed the Danes to hold free parliamentary elec-tions. Although some candidates stood on an anti-collaborating platform, the results nevertheless confirmed overwhelmingly the electoral support of the Danish people for the collaborating parties of the government coalition, and their lack of confidence in the *DNSAP*. This was not a coalition likely

Illustration 7. The Danish Foreign Minister and then Prime Minister, Erik
Scavenius, accompanies the German Plenipotentiary in Denmark, the SS officer
Werner Best, to an audience with the Danish king, late 1942.

to end willingly its veto on anti-Jewish measures; and nor was Best prepared
to rupture a collaborating relationship by disregarding that veto.

What changed everything, again, or apparently so, was the wave of
anti-German strikes and demonstrations that spread from the port of Odense
to most of the country's big towns and to the capital city, Copenhagen, in
August 1943. The agitation was, in part, probably impelled by news of
recent external events: the Allied invasion of Sicily, which precipitated the
fall of the Italian Fascist dictator, Benito Mussolini, and eventual abandonment of the Italo-German alliance by Italy's new monarchical government.
It now seemed much more likely that Germany would lose the war. The
spread of the unrest was also undoubtedly provoked by the German military
authorities' severely repressive approach to the initial acts of sabotage that
escalated into strike action, setting up a cycle of violence and reprisal that is

reminiscent of events in occupied France in late 1941. It is still slightly puzzling to see people taking to the streets and confronting German soldiers, who presumably only a few months before had voted for the government's policy of collaboration to continue. The 'Free Denmark' resistance movement was a cross-party affair with a solid core of illegal communist party members. They were clearly delighted by the way popular resistance had sprung up in response to the provocative and counter-productive policing of the strike in Odense. The heavy-handed repressiveness of the German authorities remains the most plausible explanation of the display of popular anger and outrage at the occupation, if only because it replicated what happened elsewhere in the occupied territories.

The Germans' political response to the agitation certainly indicated that Hitler was itching for a fight in Denmark, and that nothing had changed his mind about how best to react to popular resistance to occupation. Best was summoned to Berlin and told by Hitler to issue an ultimatum to the Danish government, which was held responsible for the breakdown in law and order. A fine was to be levied on the town of Odense as reprisal for the death of a German officer there. The government had to get a grip on sabotage and resistance by banning strikes and demonstrations and the possession of arms, imposing a curfew, and enabling the death penalty to be applied to saboteurs and those in possession of arms. The death penalty was a long-standing issue between the two governments, and the Danish government had in the past made it, like the veto on anti-Semitic decrees, a condition of continuing collaboration. It was an ultimatum that was designed to be rejected, or one that could be accepted only by a newly formed government. The ultimatum was intended to change the way the country had been administered and occupied up to this point.

When the rejection of the terms of the ultimatum came, the Germans declared martial law, which meant the suspension of parliamentary government and of the operation of Danish law. These suspensions continued until the end of the occupation, even though the state of emergency was lifted after some weeks. The king behaved in a very smart way. Although the government was clearly in abeyance, it did not actually resign, or, rather, the king did not accept its resignation. This would have precipitated the formation of a new government, or no government at all. Instead, the king advised his ministers to take a well-deserved break and retire from the fray for a while. The administration of the country could continue, since the secretaries general would take over the running of the ministries from the elected politicians. This was a coolly taken manœuvre. After all, the cabinet of ministers could carry on meeting informally, out of the public eye. But it was not a manœuvre that was likely to worry or wrong-foot the Germans. The country would continue to function, under its top officials, while the political tune would be called by Germans under current emergency rule, which removed the previous Danish constitutional and governmental checks on the Germans acting unilaterally. The Nazis revelled in creating and taking advantage of *de facto* situations, because it allowed them to frame a new reality by doing. As a result of the state of emergency, from August 1943 Denmark came reasonably close to the situation of occupied Belgium and the Netherlands in the summer of 1940, with Best as a kind of albeit reluctant Reich Commissioner governing the country with the help of the secretaries general.

We should remind ourselves that Best had gone native while working at the German military administration in Paris, which probably explained his transfer to Denmark. He continued to believe in what he had theorized about as an 'expert' in occupation regimes. It was highly unlikely that he would have done what he had to do in August 1943, unless directly instructed by Hitler himself. In his view, 'indirect rule' was the best way to secure a consensual and productive occupation; direct rule, involving repression and the imposition of Nazi policies on a cowed and resistant population, made for an insecure occupation and the wasteful expending of German resources in keeping down peoples used to governing themselves. The consistency of this vision of how best to run occupied countries alone makes sense of the incredible way Best handled the 'final solution' in Denmark. The Central Office of Reich Security (*Reichssicherheitshauptamt* (*RSHA*)), the SS police headquarters in Berlin, probably sensed Best's reluctance to act against a small Jewish population who did not constitute a 'problem' for him. They got Hitler's personal authorization for the deportation of Jews from Denmark. Realizing that the Danish police would probably not cooperate, and that Best would not want to ask them, SS police and staff were sent over to carry out the arrests, which were planned to take place early in October 1943.

Best then undermined the whole operation by getting a German economic official at the embassy with good Danish contacts to tip off those contacts so that the Jewish community could evade the round-ups and arrange flight across the water to neutral Sweden. Some of the escapes were organized through resistance networks, some through personal and group deals with individual fishermen. As with most evasions across Nazi-occupied Europe, they were paid for.

So it was certainly the case that no Danish official knowingly collaborated in the planned deportation of Jews from Denmark. In fact, their cooperation was neither expected nor desired by the German and SS authorities. The operation to deport the Jews was derailed because of Best's deliberate sabotage of it. He had the *chutzpah* to let Berlin know, on 2 October 1943, that Denmark was *Judenfrei*, which, of course, it was. He thought this warranted the release of interned Danish soldiers, a return on the Danish people's cooperation in ridding the country of its Jews. The whole charade was seen by Best as a way of re-establishing the collaborative relationships alone capable of sustaining the German occupation of the country. You could not make this Danish story up: a German SS officer 'saves' the Jews in order to salvage collaboration.

It is difficult to generalize from the abortive implementation of the 'final solution' in Denmark, which is why it has been treated as a special case. But we should try. The deportations in Denmark failed because of Best's lack or loss of will. There was no such lack of will on the part of those Nazi officials who ran the *Gestapo* Jewish offices in the other occupied territories, and who implemented the plans of Adolf Eichmann, the official in the Berlin *RSHA* who was in charge of the deportations of Jews to the death camps. Quite the reverse; as we shall see.

Best did not seek to involve Danish officials and policemen in the operations against the Jews, which, again, probably contributed to their ineffectiveness. Nazi officials could organize the deportations, making use of census data usually gathered for them by local officials for the application of earlier discriminatory measures against Jews. But they still lacked the manpower and resources to do everything themselves. In France, for instance, there were about 2,500 SS police, both *Sipo Sicherheitspolizei* (SIPO (state security police)) and *Sicherheitsdienst* (SD (the investigative and intelligence branch)). They could call on the presence of about 3,000 more German 'order police'. This, to cover a country with a total Jewish population of about 330,000, many of whom, however, especially foreign Jews, were concentrated in Paris and its region. They needed the collaboration of local officials and policemen to carry out the round-ups of Jews, intern them in holding camps, and transport them to the frontier. They also needed help on the ground to track down and detain those Jews who evaded the round-ups. So, to be completely effective, the whole operation required both Nazi and local officials and policemen to be efficient in the way they carried out the tasks assigned to them. To a great extent, the success of the operation depended on the Nazi officials impressing their own will on their collaborators—official to official, as it were.

After the Wannsee conference in January 1942, Eichmann went into full bureaucratic mode. The 'final solution' became logistics, planning, and execution, the embodiment of what Hannah Arendt memorably called 'the banality of evil' after observing Eichmann at his trial in Israel in 1961. It is important to grasp this. Genocide was no longer a matter of special police squads murdering Jews in the wake of German armies invading the Soviet Union, but an impersonal bureaucratic process.

Eichmann had to work really hard to persuade the *Reichsbahn* and the Minister of Transport to make available the convoys of trains required to ship Jews from Germany's western borders, and to find a slot for them in Europe's railway timetables. In itself, this logistical exercise set up very tight schedules, which had to be met all the way down the line to the occupied territories. The execution of the 'final solution' became an affair of logistical and bureaucratic, as much as ideological, imperatives. Eichmann exerted all the pressure he could muster on his subordinates in the occupied territories, most of whom were friends and colleagues from the *RSHA*, so that they met the deadlines for the supply of Jews to the convoys of trains. He was literally terrified of losing face with the *Reichsbahn* if the schedules for deportation were not kept to, or the trains had to be cancelled or leave below capacity because of the unavailability of Jews to fill them. He knew that performance and execution were all to a Nazi 'leader', and that not filling the convoys at the right times would make it more difficult for him to secure *Reichsbahn* cooperation in the organization of future convoys.

All these arrangements were apparently in place by the time Eichmann briefed the *SS* officials responsible for Jewish affairs in occupied Western Europe, in June 1942. In this meeting, initial overall targets were agreed and set for the deportation of Western Europe's Jews to Auschwitz: 100,000 from both zones in France, 15,000 from the Netherlands, 10,000 from Belgium. They were to be deported over a period of eight months, at a rate of three convoys of 1,000 Jews each per week. The targets shifted, as they always did for the Nazis, but not as haphazardly as when Göring made up figures for economic production for the occupied territories in the heat of that meeting with Nazi leaders in August 1942. Eichmann later reduced the period of execution of the deportations to three months, to squeeze them into the summer and autumn months before a winter break. He also raised the Netherlands target to 40,000, presumably because he thought that this could be managed on the ground: 70,000 of the country's 140,000 Jews lived and were practically ghettoized in Amsterdam. He raised the Belgian target to 20,000 in August, despite Reeder's consternation at the original figure. The 100,000 target for France had apparently been set by the RSHA's man in Paris, Theodor Dannecker. It pretty much included each and every able-bodied adult Jew in both zones.

Setting a target at the very limit of what was possible was a mark both of his zeal and enthusiasm for the task, and of his belief, shared by Eichmann, that deporting Jews from France would be a relatively easy thing to do. However, his SS police superiors, Karl Oberg and Helmut Knochen, not for the last time, had to persuade Dannecker that the original 100,000 target was unrealistic and could not be achieved. Nazis were used to dealing with unrealistic targets; they saw meeting them as a test of their will and expertise. But there was nothing worse than failing to meet your target. Dannecker came up with a new figure of 39,000 Jews to be deported from France—that is, thirty-nine convoys over a phase of three months, which Eichmann agreed to. He told his colleagues that their job was to arrange the arrest and transfer of Jews to holding camps, ready for the first convoy departures on 13 July 1942.

The schedules, deadlines, and pressures placed by Eichmann on his Nazi colleagues were then transferred by German officials onto their counterparts in the occupied territories. This led to some challenging confrontations with national officials. Some aspects of the collaboration in the deportation of Jews, however, were pretty plain sailing. In France, the SNCF was commissioned to transport Jews from camps in the provinces to the one at Drancy in Paris, and from there to the border. In a recent civil case, the railway company tried to hide behind its state ownership, arguing that it had been forced to cooperate with the German occupying authorities. But it was a straight commercial transaction, the cattle truck transportation being categorized as third-class tariff and charged to the German government.

Officials and police were ready to arrest and intern foreign and stateless Jews for deportation. They represented significant proportions of the resident Jewish populations, just over half in France, over 90 per cent in Belgium, and about 17 per cent in the Netherlands. These Jews were mainly interwar immigrants and 1930s refugees from Germany, Eastern and Southern Europe, and Russia. They were usually perceived by both police and host populations as unwelcome incomers who were a burden on local welfare and support services, and a threat to employment, security and order, and their way of life. The police in occupied West European countries saw their involvement in the deportation of foreign Jews as the final settlement of a troublesome pre-war refugee crisis, exacerbated by wartime displacements of people, and an opportunity to restore peace and order to disrupted societies.

Foreign Jews also became the 'give' of *donnant–donnant* style collaboration, in return for the 'take' of national Jews. The same went for the many Jews in France who had been naturalized as citizens in the interwar period, only to find their status under constant review in the Vichy National Revolution. Officials and police were prepared to collaborate in the deportation of foreign Jews, because it postponed or prevented the recourse to Jews who were national citizens, who were French or Belgian or Dutch. They also arrested and interned, and hence facilitated the deportation of, national Jews who had broken the law, joined the resistance, or violated the many punitive regulations governing their lives, or were suspected of and charged with doing so.

Officials and police in occupied Belgium were not expected to participate in the process of deporting Jews from the summer of 1942 and, with a few exceptions, did not do so. However, officials and police in the occupied Netherlands were expected to cooperate in the deportations, and did so, for about a year, by which time most of the country's relatively large Jewish population had been deported to the death camps. The Germans knew that the policy would be unpopular and would test the collaborating relationships built up from 1940. They adjusted the logistics of their genocidal operation, but never compromised on the ultimate aim of ridding Europe of its Jews, so as to suit the circumstances of occupation and the dynamics of collaboration. They acted in a way that was designed to deliver the Jews of the occupied territories, as well as preserve the collaboration of officials, which they continued to recognize was necessary to sustain occupation.

One would expect the German occupying authorities, whether they were a Reich Commissariat or a military government, to take this approach, since they were responsible for occupation as a whole and for maintaining it with as little local turbulence as possible. But the SS leadership, which had asserted at Wannsee its control and direction of genocide, was also flexible as to the mode of its enactment, while remaining committed to the ultimate realization of its ideological mission. In considering the 'final solution' in occupied Western Europe, you have to start from the German perspective and approach. It was a Nazi policy, a programme that the Nazis initiated, and how they implemented it would both determine and be determined by the reaction of those who were collaborating in the occupation. A flexible approach was almost bound to find a more accommodating or less hostile response.

How the 'final solution' was enacted did, clearly, in part depend on how these two countries were occupied. The Reich Commissariat had been installed in the Netherlands because the Dutch were regarded as a 'Germanic' people who over a period of time could be both 'Germanized' and 'Nazified'. Purging the Netherlands of its Jews was a way of raising the Dutch people to a proper consciousness of their racial identity, and a step towards realizing the eventual incorporation of the country into a Greater Germanic Empire. The Reich Commissariat and the SS engaged in what one might call a friendly rivalry in implementing the 'final solution'. But ultimately, the control by the SS of the process was recognized, and there was never any doubt about the ideological unity of purpose between the two Nazi bodies that impelled the realization of the 'final solution' in the Netherlands.

The military administration of occupied Belgium was deliberately non-ideological, a safe bet while the Nazi leadership considered its options on the future of a bilingual country. It was improbable that Reeder was as ideologically anti-Semitic as Seyss-Inquart. But too much can be made of this. The military government was obliged by Hitler himself and the Reich authorities to carry out ideological and political policies in the country it ran. Its deliberate stimulation of Flemish pro-German feelings and its appointment of Flemish fascists and nationalists to positions in the Belgian administration were evident signs of its obedience to mandatory instructions coming from Berlin.

Reeder ran a tight ship, and clearly resented the way the SS exploited its control of race policy to extend its political influence in the country and infiltrate its police forces. The presence of German military police in the operations to arrest and deport Jews in Belgium was part of a long-running struggle to contain the activities of the *Gestapo* on his patch. But Reeder's overriding concern was not to block the 'final solution', only to ensure that its implementation did not shake the collaboration of Belgian officials, which he had nurtured and protected through a turbulent and contested occupation. On past and present experience alone, he realized that the Belgian judiciary, at the very least, would not take easily to any local involvement in the arrest and deportation of Jews.

So, in my view, the level and extent of collaboration in the deportation of Jews in occupied Belgium and the Netherlands were largely determined by the occupier's assessment of what was bearable in the current circumstances of occupation. The decisions about collaboration, or not, were made by the Germans, not officials, for which, you could say, the officials were immensely grateful. You get a sense of this dynamic working in the first round-ups of Jews organized in occupied Belgium. In Antwerp, with a small but evident Jewish population, the mayor enabled municipal police to participate in the process, under *Gestapo* direction. They delivered the individual summonses to Jews to report for 'labour' duty, and helped to transfer Jews to the holding camp at Malines. This conformed to a pattern. Previous anti-Semitic measures, including the obligation for Jews to wear the yellow star affirming their identity as Jews, had been applied and received in 'Germanic' Flanders rather more readily than in Walloon or mixed areas of the country.

The Antwerp operation had to be followed up, because not all Jews responded to the call, and the search for evaders was bound to attract public attention and concern. There were obvious organizational reasons for mounting a few large-scale, mass arrests of Jews for deportation, rather than an infinite series of small-scale incursions into residential areas. The police possessed quite precise data on who the Jews were and where they lived, which permitted the staging of big and, at the same time, targeted raids. A progression of small raids on Jews obviously warned the rest of the Jewish community as to what was to come, and hence both encouraged and facilitated evasion. But, big or small, police operations to pick up and detain Jews hardly took place in secret, however carefully planned and staged they were. People came out to see what was happening. Few arrests took place without at least the observing and witnessing presence of neighbours, who usually expressed sympathy for the victims and anger at the perpetrators. The gathering of often hostile and critical groups necessitated yet more uncongenial policing of ordinary people.

Reeder had already attempted to get the secretaries general onside, promising them that initially the targets would be foreign and not Belgian Jews. He was alarmed, then, by Plisnier's remarks at a committee meeting expressing concern at the presence of a few Belgian Jews in the first consignment of Jews sent from Antwerp; and even more so by the secretaries general's informal protest after a round-up in Brussels, where local police help, as was the norm in the capital city, was not as forthcoming as it had been in Antwerp.

Reeder moved decisively to head off the threat to collaboration overall posed by a hostile popular and officials' reaction to the first round-ups for deportation. With the endorsement of Himmler himself, and that of Romsée, the Secretary General for the Interior, who was responsible for some, if not all, Belgian police forces, he categorically reaffirmed the focus on foreign, not Belgian, Jews; ensured that as far as possible mass arrests and round-ups were avoided; and banned the German police, whether military or SS, from calling on the services of the Belgian police in the deportation process.

Between June and October 1942, about 17,000 Jews were deported from Belgium, practically two-thirds of the total figure for the occupation period. In September 1942, Reeder reported with some relief to his superiors that the 'final solution' was being implemented in Belgium with a minimum of fuss and unfavourable popular comment. As an official reporting upwards on his own activity, you would hardly expect him to say otherwise. But Reeder always made it clear where he felt that other agencies were interfering with the priority of ensuring as trouble-free an occupation as possible. It was unnecessary at this point because Himmler had shown a flexible understanding of the needs of occupation, a position he also assumed at about the same time in relation to the deportation of Jews from France.

The reasons for Reeder's confidence in the effectiveness of the implementation of the 'final solution' so far were also self-evident. It was difficult for anybody, except perhaps the Resistance, to generate much steam over the removal of relatively so few people, who were, after all, foreigners, not Belgian citizens. However inhumane the measures against foreign Jews, they were being carried out by German police and officials with practically no involvement of Belgian police and officials. This was a German policy being enacted by Germans and their natural ideological allies, auxiliary volunteer policemen recruited from the fascist and collaborationist militias sponsored by the occupier. Reeder's stance enabled the secretaries general to adopt a position that complemented his own. They opposed the deportations, on principle, but not in practice, since, while they allowed the deportations to occur, they were not required to take part in them. Reeder ensured that the 'final solution' took place, but not at the price of Belgian officials withdrawing their wider cooperation in running the country, his main concern.

The one and only formal protest by the Belgian secretaries general came in October 1943, when the military administration was instructed by the Reich authorities to complete the 'final solution' in Belgium, and arrest all remaining Jews in the country. This order required Reeder to break the terms of his tacit agreement with the secretaries general, and stage mass round-ups in Antwerp and Brussels, which netted about 1,000 Jews, many of them Belgian citizens. He had sought assurances from Berlin that Belgian Jews would be targeted only if they had broken laws and regulations. But, since most of them were in hiding, anyway, this was no real restraint on the extent of the round-ups. Most foreign Jews had already been deported, and the secretaries general confined their condemnation of this violation of human rights to the fate of captured Belgian Jews. As was usual, the raids were conducted by German military police, the *Gestapo*, and Flemish SS and Rexist auxiliaries, not the regular Belgian police forces.

The protest did provoke a response. Reeder released some Belgian Jews from Malines into a form of house arrest. But the SS did not feel they owed anything to the secretaries general, and the Belgian Jews they arrested were duly deported. It was unlikely that the secretaries general seriously considered going any further in their protest. Reeder's response and his evident detachment from the SS would have reminded them of the lesson learned earlier in the occupation, that collaboration with the military government was the country's best defence against Berlin.

Reeder and the SS in Belgium also 'bought' the continuing overall collaboration of Belgian officials by allowing exemptions to the mass deportation of Jews. He gave the secretaries general themselves a stake in these exemptions, which enabled them to demonstrate to their own people that collaboration was worth the effort. It has to be emphasized that exemptions were permitted across the occupied territories, whatever the kind of occupation regime. They served a common purpose and function. Exemptions clearly eased the acceptance by officials of the bulk of deportations, and made them complicit in the process. You could not claim an exemption without first recognizing the rule from which you were requesting an exception. More than that, while exemptions might well slow down the completion of the process, they were never allowed to stall the process altogether. The exemptions were contingent and temporary.

In occupied Belgium and the Netherlands, national citizens were initially exempted from deportation, as were Jews in mixed marriages, and 'Protestant' Jews. Exemptions were extended to Jewish workers whose skills and employment the Germans, and, of course, the officials, wanted to retain. The Jewish diamond cutters and polishers of Antwerp and Amsterdam carried on working, and, as they did so, were obliged to shorten (or extend?) their own lives and livelihoods by passing on the skills of their trade to disabled

German SS veterans. In Eindhoven, the Dutch electrical giant Philips, thriving on German aircraft components contracts, effectively did a Schindler and exempted from deportation a batch of Jewish workers by guaranteeing them employment, even when some of them later worked from a special factory unit set up in a concentration camp where they had been imprisoned. Again, as for Schindler, nothing was quite what it seemed. The Jewish workers were retained to work on German contracts at German insistence, and the company secured the backing of the resistance for using the labour of inmates of a concentration camp, because it averted, or rather delayed, their deportation. Officials in Belgium rather imaginatively used labour mobilization regulations to deport Jewish workers to the Todt Organization's Atlantic Wall construction projects in northern France. This move prevented, or at least postponed, their deportation to the death camps. Since they also helped to meet the quota of workers demanded by Sauckel, some other Belgian workers were thereby 'saved' from deportation to work in Germany.

Exemptions were also granted to the officials who ran the Jewish agencies set up at German instigation to manage the affairs of persecuted Jews and, then, to help to select the targets of the round-ups. Their families became exempt, too. Foreign Jews who were citizens of countries at war with the Axis were usually exempted, as were Jewish nationals of Axis or friendly countries, at least until the necessary diplomatic approaches had been made, and met. In the Netherlands, Frederiks and his colleague, the pro-German university professor J. van Dam, who ran the education ministry, were allowed to select a few hundred of the great and good Dutch Jews deemed worthy of survival. They were holed up in a castle for safe keeping, somewhere between being hostages and honorary citizens. Hardly surprisingly, the secretaries general chose establishment figures like themselves: ex-parliamentarians, ex-ministers, ex-officials, ex-university professors. In this case, the privileging of certain Jews worked, to the extent that many of them survived the Holocaust. When deportation came, late on, they were sent to Theresienstadt concentration camp, almost a kind of refugee camp for elderly Jews and others, or to Bergen-Belsen, for the SS to 'exchange' for captured Germans. This was the camp where Anne Frank and her sister died of illness and deprivation.

In their own way, exemptions enabled the momentum of deportations to be maintained, or picked up again, from the spring of 1943 onwards. By this time, most Jews had been deported, and the progressive erosion of exemptions helped to fill the remaining convoys. What was effectively the final round-up in the Netherlands took place in September 1943, with the deportation of the members of the especially compliant Jewish Council and their families, a sure sign that the Germans felt that the job was practically done. But the defence of exemptions, and their haphazardly cumulative rather than synchronized destruction over time, group by group, helped to keep the rationale for collaboration alive right up to the end of the occupation.

Reeder (and the SS in Belgium) had very early on decided that the arrest and deportation of Jews were a matter for them. The Belgian police and judiciary were unreliable, partly because the centralizing and simplifying reforms of the police forces were incomplete, and the influence of the SS on the personnel and conduct of policing in the country had been contained by Reeder. Reeder (and Himmler) also agreed that requiring Belgian police and legal officials to participate in the deportations would simply reignite their hostility to the occupation, and threaten, once again, the generally good and productive relations between Reeder and the secretaries general.

No such limitations existed in the occupied Netherlands. Rauter, the Reich Commissioner for Security, was a Higher SS and Police Leader, and, from 1942, was acknowledged by Seyss-Inquart as the Nazi leader responsible for racial policy in the Netherlands. He fully shared the SS vision for the incorporation of the Dutch people into the Greater Germanic Empire and, for this reason, cultivated the Dutch SS, and Rost von Toningen as a rival to Mussert in the NSB. In the wake of the popular protests against anti-Semitic measures in early 1941, the Reich Commissariat had appointed men like Tulp to be the police chiefs of the major cities. Rauter knew that Tulp would commit his 2,500 policemen to the arrest and deportation of Jews in Amsterdam, where 60 per cent of the country's Jews lived. Rauter had also made considerable progress in reorganizing the Dutch police at both state and municipal levels, and in imbuing the police with the outlook and methods of the SS. It was not only the case of the recruitment from May 1942 of an auxiliary paramilitary force, drawn from the Dutch SS and NSB members, who later took action against the Jews in their home towns. Specifically, to facilitate the deportations, Rauter formed special police units at the central RHSA headquarters in The Hague, to which he attached selected Dutch police officers. Other Dutch officers were seconded to work with the Gestapo in the major cities.

We get some sense of what it was like to be a Dutch policeman required to take part in operations against the Jews from the summer of 1942 by observing how Tulp ran things in Amsterdam. Tulp, who regarded Rauter as both his mentor and his superior, had set up anti-Jewish police teams, often Dutch SS or NSB members, the most obvious way of ensuring the loyalty and reliability of his force. Large, attention-grabbing raids were avoided, as far as possible. The mini-raids were meticulously planned and prepared for, and the officers carefully and precisely briefed. The raids on individual houses and apartments usually took place at night, after the curfew. Tulp himself selected men whom he thought were capable of seeing them through. Naturally enough, he tended to veer away from the older career officers and chose from among the younger newly trained officers at his disposal, who were expected to operate in their home neighbourhoods. We have already seen that such small-scale raids were regarded as undesirable and ineffective in Belgium. They were presumably adopted in the Netherlands because of the greater reliability and more intense preparation of the police involved, allied to their local knowledge.

Tulp not only organized the raids on the houses of Jews. He often also participated in them, a touch that undoubtedly endeared the officers to their chief, and bound leader and followers together in a common enterprise where responsibility was shared. This cultivated camaraderie among policemen was buttressed by an unforgiving disciplinary regime. The small teams of policemen carrying out the individual round-ups were made personally responsible for each designated arrest. Officers perceived as being reluctant or critical were deliberately involved in raids, and subject, therefore, to the considerable internal peer-group pressure to be solid and unified in the professional performance of their jobs.

Any officer who refused to lead a raid was reported and dismissed. Dutch police disciplinary matters were dealt with by a German SS special court, a practice objected to by Frederiks, to no avail. The disciplining of an officer often involved sanctions and reprisals against his family, especially in the case of dismissal. One should not underestimate the deterrent effect of potential dismissal on the conduct of Dutch policemen during the period of the deportation of Jews. It was not just the loss of income and status; it was isolation from your colleagues and the denial of the solidarity and protection afforded by belonging to the police 'community'. Dismissal in conditions of occupation meant dropping out of life and, effectively, going underground. One can begin to see the appeal of resistance calls from spring 1943 for serving officers to defect to them, and bring their weapons. It was risky, but so was risking dismissal, and at least the risks of life under occupation were now, again, shared and mitigated by membership of a group with a common purpose and solidarity.

A combination of Tulp's brand of charismatic leadership and the activation of peer-group solidarities worked wonders. Tulp could report to Rauter in September 1942 that his police had rounded up in a week about 450 Jews each night, which he passed off as nothing very special. But his report also observed that police raids had been witnessed by groups of angry and compassionate neighbours, and that he was obliged to deploy men from his special units to police them, since the 'regular' police found this so uncongenial and demoralizing. Tulp's presence and initiative were clearly crucial to the effectiveness of the Amsterdam force—both the strength and the weakness of a system based on the 'leader principle'.

Tulp became ill in early October 1942 and died later in the month. The city *Gestapo* reported on the declining morale and commitment of Dutch policemen when he was absent from the fray. By this point, much of the damage had been done: 12,000 Jews were deported in October, the peak monthly figure, and the last month where Tulp's charisma had its direct personal effect. Very noticeably, the Germans relied increasingly, and then exclusively, on the collaborationist auxiliaries and the trusted officers of the special anti-Jewish units, in order to carry out the later deportations.

It was probably from the spring of 1943 that the Dutch police's commitment to taking action against Jews seriously began to waver. Their growing reluctance was undoubtedly linked to a more general disaffection at the kind and extent of unpalatable policing required of them by the Germans. They began to realize just how unpopular and isolated they were as a result of their policing of the occupation. In April 1943, for instance, Dutch police were obliged to arrest and re-intern POWs so that they could be deported to work in Germany. But, again, by this point, much of the work had been done. No longer regarded as reliable, the police were spared the task of hunting down Jews in hiding, arresting previously exempted groups, and deporting Jews already held in camps and prisons for the violation of regulations or for further investigation of their cases.

The Dutch secretaries general must have felt as impotent to do anything about the Dutch police's involvement in the deportation of Jews as their Belgian counterparts did when confronted by the loss of ministerial control over the national labour offices. Frederiks did what he could, asking in vain that the Germans did not make use of the municipal police, still under his ministerial jurisdiction, for the round-ups of Jews. Perhaps the sense of impotence was intentionally self-induced, a way of making palatable the lack of control over the Dutch police. Frederiks addressed his protest-cum-request through the strictly appropriate channels, contacting Wimmer, the Reich Commissioner for Internal Affairs. In my view, to make any difference, he should have gone directly to Rauter, who was actually in charge of policing affairs and using his office to extend SS rather than NSDAP power and influence in the occupied Netherlands.

This may be rather harsh on Frederiks. His powerlessness was real enough. It was little use him tackling the Secretary General for Justice, whose ministry controlled the state police, since he was an NSB member. Frederiks retreated behind the line that was typical of the secretaries general: they could safely deny any responsibility for the deportations, and wanted no part in them, but had to accept that they would happen, if only because the Germans had managed to 'turn' the Dutch police and bypass its established career officers. Frederiks was apparently incensed and appalled by the government-in-exile's May 1943 guidelines on how to respond to measures against the Jews. Not only was the 'advice' rather too late to affect things, coming after the Dutch police's full involvement in the 1942 deportations. As such, it was a judgement on him, not guidance for future behaviour. It merely endorsed a line of inaction that the Germans had unilaterally decided on, intending to rely henceforth for the execution of anti-Jewish policy on themselves and their Dutch fascist militiamen. The advice was, in other words, just superfluous in the current situation, since it stated the obvious— that the deportation of Jews was illegal under Dutch and international law, and that any cooperation in it was prohibited. Frederiks must have been puzzled, as well as frightened and angry. If, as the guidelines indicated, obeying orders that could not be disobeyed was no longer a safe refuge for officials and their collaboration, past, present, and future, then was more expected, like resistance?

Hirschfeld, if his post-war rationalizations are anything to go by, was more calm and collected than Frederiks, and metaphorically shrugged his shoulders at the 1943 guidelines and its strictures on non-cooperation in the deportation of Jews. He thought, anyway, that the Dutch Jewish Council was more culpable than the secretaries general in cooperating with the deportations, though the word he used was not 'culpable' but 'naive'. For him, the 'final solution' was a German fait accompli that could not have been prevented. In the light of the Nazi commitment to get rid of Europe's Jews, it was futile to think that you had to save what could be saved, even when, as was the case with the Jewish Council members, you were saving yourselves. From Hirschfeld's high-ground perspective, it was more important to secure the interests of the bulk of the population, and the only guarantee of that was the continued collaboration of officials with the occupying authorities.

In retrospect, it is just about possible to ask why the French response to the 'final solution' could not have been the Belgian response to the 'final solution'. The Belgian position was essentially this: the deportations were a Nazi German policy, which officials were opposed to, but could not prevent; as a German policy, it had to be carried out by German agencies and police, not involving Belgian officials or police; the most that officials could do was to ensure that the Germans acted initially against foreign rather than Belgian Jews, the concession that the Germans were prepared to make in order to protect collaboration in other areas of occupation.

In context, however, the question cannot be asked seriously, even though some elements of the Belgian equation reappeared in the French case. Vichy officials and police served an authoritarian, anti-communist, anti-Semitic, and xenophobic regime. From late 1940, French prefects and police had interned most foreign and some French Jews in both zones, sometimes at German instigation, sometimes on their own account, usually on the basis that Jews were 'criminals' or a threat to security and law and order. Prefects and police, by the time of the start of the 'final solution', had experienced nearly two years of applying legal discrimination and persecution of Jews, and equipped themselves with the policing apparatus to do so, especially advanced in the Prefecture of Police for Paris and its region, where most Jews resided.

The German SS leaders in France stressed the less ideological as much as the more ideological elements of the 'final solution', realizing that, from the perspective of the security of the occupation, continued French police cooperation and compliance could be expected and induced. When, for example, High SS and Police Leader Karl Oberg renewed in April 1943 the Franco-German police agreement of July 1942, made at the start of the implementation of the 'final solution', he told the regional prefects and chiefs of police that together the Vichy and German police were acting against 'terrorists' and those 'agencies' behind 'terror' attacks and sabotage— that is, Jews, Bolsheviks, and the Anglo-Americans.

The availability of the French police to undertake anti-Jewish measures must have fed Eichmann's and Dannecker's belief that ridding France of Jews would be a relatively painless job. Of course, arresting Jews for deportation and death was different from arresting Jews for internment. But, once Oberg and Laval had agreed in September 1942 that the publicized destination of the deported Jews was to be labour camps in the East, in a deliberate attempt to reassure both international and internal opinion, then officials and police felt that they knew all they needed to know about the ultimate fate of those they were arresting.

For both Bousquet, Vichy's chief of police, and Laval, Vichy's Prime Minister, Interior Minister, and Foreign Minister, involvement in the 'final solution' became part of a wider collaborating game they were separately and jointly playing. For both men, the deportation of Jews was a happening that was secondary to the real thing, which was the existence and survival of Vichy as a sovereign state, and its place in the European New Order. In my view, this had an evidently dehumanizing impact on their attitudes to the 'final solution'. They saw the 'Jewish question' as an instrument of policy, a means towards the achievement of a higher purpose.

One would not expect Vichy leaders to have any inherent respect for universal human rights, even a lapsed Republican like Laval, since the state's perceived interests would always be put before those of the individuals who made it up. But Laval sometimes produced aggressive, gratuitously contemptuous, and brutal justifications of Vichy's treatment of foreign Jews during the Holocaust, in very frank conversations with, say, US government and relief agency representatives, or with Catholic and Protestant church leaders, all of whom were intervening to save Jews from genocide. Laval knew that his remarks would go the 1940s equivalent of 'viral', but did not seem to care. Although apparently not an ideological anti-Semite, he had already ceased to regard foreign Jews as human beings, or the 'final solution' as a humanitarian disaster in the making. This can be the only plausible explanation for his comments, that he was deliberately and in a calculated way distancing himself and the Vichy regime from the fate of those Jews who had sought refuge from persecution in France. They were the tools, not the determinants or ends, of policy, a lever of collaboration that took that collaboration onto a higher and more productive plane.

When Bousquet was confronted in September 1942 by a Protestant pastor protesting about the round-ups of Jews for deportation, he came up with a chilling response that aligned him to those other top Vichy officials who had made similar remarks about their standing and activity in different areas of collaboration. 'Having taken the decision it must be implemented,' he said, arguing that 'the role of public opinion is to be agitated, that of the government is to choose'. It was not as if Bousquet was avoiding responsibility for the 'decision'; 'the current unpopularity of the government', he concluded, 'will be one of its most glorious attributes in the future'.[3] The unpopularity of the round-ups did, in fact, affect the process of deportations, even if it did not end them, in ways that Bousquet was unwilling to acknowledge here. You would think he would have taken the opportunity to placate or reassure his interlocutor, with words, if not actions. A politician might have done. But Bousquet responded as the official of an authoritarian state, secure in his rectitude and service to what he saw as a higher national cause.

When Laval returned to power in April 1942, the military situation in North Africa and the USSR was promising enough for him to retain his belief in and commitment to a German victory in the war, and hence to the dream of Franco-German reconciliation as the basis of the European New Order. He thought, or calculated, that an Allied victory would entail the Bolshevization of European countries, not, as it turned out, such a wild assessment of what might happen in Europe in the event of Nazi Germany's defeat. Laval made several famous, or notorious, public statements and radio broadcasts to the French people on how they must contribute to the Nazi war effort in order to save Europe from Bolshevism. To his own cronies and contacts, Laval passed off the speeches as merely confirmation of his cleverness in dealing with the Germans. Words, after all, were cheap. The cost to his reputation in expressing such pro-German sentiments was worth it, since words could serve the purpose of reassuring the Germans without requiring the concession of anything rather more concrete. As he said in respect of the Nazi plenipotentiary for labour Sauckel's scheme to get foreign workers to work in Germany, 'I prefer to pay them in words rather than deeds... In return for a bit of politeness on the radio, I can deny that lout Sauckel hundreds of thousands of the workers he's asking for.'[4] Laval was always too clever by half. His anti-communism was sincere and consistent, and actions, of course, did accompany the words. The mobilization of French workers to work in Germany was propagandized as France's patriotic contribution to the future security of Europe against Bolshevism.

Laval continued to believe in *donnant–donnant* collaboration as the most productive way of ensuring that France secured as independent and powerful a place as possible in a Nazi-dominated Europe. What he really wanted during the war was for Hitler and the Nazi leadership to commit themselves to the prospect of a comprehensive political and territorial settlement—a Franco-German peace treaty, in other words. Laval communicated more with Hitler, usually by letter, with no guarantee of return of correspondence, given Hitler's unbureaucratic ways, and, more importantly, his ingrained reluctance to agree to anything that would tie Nazi Germany's hands both now and in the future. Laval also tried the head-to-head summits, because he trusted his own powers of persuasion and knew that personal contact with Hitler was the usual way of getting what you wanted in the Nazi system.

The meeting between Hitler and Laval in December 1942 was a kind of action replay of previous meetings between the two leaders, down to the civility that Hitler always accorded to Laval. This time, Laval did have something new to propose: the revival of a small Vichy armed force, dissolved with the full German military occupation of France in November 1942; and a single Lavalian party to buttress the Vichy regime internally. This resembled the Pucheu–Bénoist–Mechin proposal for a serious ideological realignment of the Vichy regime during Darlan's previous government. But it denoted, not Laval's conversion to fascism, but rather his intention to strengthen his own and the regime's position internally. The plan was to dissolve all the existing fascist and collaborationist parties into a government-supporting single party.

Hitler, as usual with Laval, was amicable and welcoming, but, again as usual, sidestepped all the substantive individual issues raised by Laval in the meeting. He simply repeated the mantra that Vichy France had to convince him of its will to collaborate, if it sincerely wanted to replace a traditional hostility with the mutual trust that would enable Nazi Germany to consider a place for France in the New Order. Perhaps in order to spare Laval's feelings during the actual meeting, and to give the impression that he was ready to consider his proposals, Hitler replied to the points of substance in a letter shortly afterwards.

While Hitler was sympathetic to Laval's appeal for Vichy to have some military forces of its own, he could not really move on this, without taking into account his ally, Mussolini, who would not be too happy about the re-emergence of a French navy. There could be no removal of the demarcation line, even after the full occupation of France, nor any change to the status of the French northern departments attached to occupied Belgium. French POWs in German camps would not, *en masse*, become civilian workers free to move and work on proper labour contracts, though they would have the prospect of some leave in France. A single party was fine by Hitler, as long as it did not involve the disappearance of a fascist party like the *PPF*, which, as later events were to demonstrate, remained a useful counterweight to Vichy.

These were the usual scraps from the table, and Laval must have felt peeved at the poor returns from his meeting with Hitler. In a letter to Hitler in March 1943, Laval expressed himself very directly, to the effect that, if Hitler wanted him to propagandize and promote Franco-German collaboration to the French people, then he, Laval, needed some indication of the place France would occupy in the New Order. This correspondence, significantly, came after the publication of a so-called European Charter in February 1943. This at least indicated that Hitler was responding to the pressures and appeals of his Axis partners, including Fascist Italy, as well as Laval, and Goebbels and Ribbentrop among the top Nazi leaders, for a statement of Nazi war aims that would give a reason for continuing to support and promote the German war effort. Was there enough for Laval in a rather conventional and generic declaration of a future New Order that 'guarantees a secure existence to all European peoples in an atmosphere of justice and collaboration, liberated from all Jewish-plutocratic dependence, encouraged and stimulated in their activity and in the safeguarding of their mutual interests within the safe boundaries of the great European living space'?[5] Probably not, since in his letter Laval still posited a federated Europe, anchored on a Franco-German axis, to keep the USA (and the USSR) out of the continent's affairs, an almost exact foretaste of de Gaulle's post-war enactment of the European idea.

For his part, Hitler expressed to Ribbentrop his very realistic view of the value of Laval's collaboration, when discussing with his Foreign Minister the point of yet another meeting with Laval, in May 1943. Hitler was clearly impatient with Vichy's persistent 'demands' that Nazi Germany make concessions to secure their cooperation when he could get what he wanted from France, anyway, without the need for or expectation of concessions. This was a significant assessment, reflecting the greater call on the resources of occupied Western Europe at a time when the military situation was deteriorating, and an intensified cycle of repressiveness and resistance in the occupied territories. At this point, Hitler felt that Laval's fear of a Europe under Bolshevism would keep him collaborating with the Germans, whatever happened. In his mind, this excluded the need even to pretend that collaboration would generate concessions from Germany.

It would appear that Laval picked up Hitler's effective disavowal of the virtues of *donnant–donnant* collaboration, and realigned and lowered his expectations of Franco-German collaboration, accordingly. It did not stop him trying again with Hitler, when they met in his East Prussian bunker in early 1944. His claim that the French workers working in French and German factories were Vichy's contribution to Nazi Germany's defence of Europe against Bolshevism was undoubtedly sincere. But he knew now that Germany could not win the war, and the best hopes for Vichy France's survival lay in some sort of compromise peace. His words did not evince any positive reaction from Hitler regarding France's place in a future Europe, whatever its shape, which merely confirmed their respective stances on the value and benefits of Franco-German collaboration assumed in 1943. If the point of collaboration was no longer the prospect of negotiating a long-term future for France in the European New Order, then at least it was still useful in the sense of mitigating and channelling the greater repressiveness of the occupation. Collaboration might be sufficient to delay or head off direct German Nazi rule in France, or a more likely combination of the occupying authorities working through fascists and collaborationists, rather than Vichy officialdom. If this is a plausible rendering of the change in Laval's thinking, then it shows that Vichy's collaboration in 1943-4 more closely resembled that of the secretaries general in Belgium and the Netherlands from 1940.

The consequences of this shift in the character of Laval's collaboration can be observed in his own and his government's behaviour between 1942 and 1944. From spring 1942, when Laval returned to power, to spring 1943, Vichy cooperated with the Germans over the 'final solution', and what overlapped it, the German demand for labour, in the continuing expectation that it would receive something in return. From the spring of 1943 until the liberation in August 1944, Vichy began to clam up on cooperation on the deportations of Jews and workers. In turn, this affected the way the Germans occupied the country, and again, as a reflex, the extent and commitment of Vichy's collaboration.

Laval was nothing if not consistent. The rather more reluctant and guarded collaboration of 1943-4 was matched by his growing sense, however illusory it was, that, while only a German victory would save Europe from Bolshevism, the best hope for France was the negotiation of a compromise peace in Western Europe. France, in such circumstances, could hang on to some standing and power, and Germany could continue fighting Europe's war in the East. The interesting thing to observe was whether, and how, Laval's reorientation of collaboration was communicated to collaborating officials and replicated in their behaviour on the ground.

Laval appointed René Bousquet as secretary general for police in the Interior Ministry on his return to power in April 1942. Bousquet was then a regional prefect, and had been Vichy's youngest prefect in 1940. In essence, he was a Republican official, on a conventional career path distinguished by a meteoric rise through prefectural and ministerial ranks, down to his abilities and the usual Republican political patronage, in Bousquet's case, of Republican politicians close to Laval who themselves served as officials and ministers in Laval's pre-war and wartime governments. In turn, Bousquet appointed his friend and colleague Jean Leguay to be the Interior Ministry's representative in the occupied zone, effectively one of the Vichy government's most important links to both the German occupation authorities and prefects in the occupied zone. Leguay was a kind of Bousquet clone or double, enjoying a similar career progression to Bousquet, though always a few steps behind him. Their paths had last crossed when Leguay was Bousquet's subordinate colleague in the Marne prefecture in 1940.

Both men serially denied any direct involvement in the deportation of Jews from France, and in the light of the lawyer Serge Klarsfeld's meticulous reconstruction of the Holocaust in France, had simply lied about it in any public forum. Bousquet deployed his own version of the usual disclaimer of the obedient but not responsible official at his High Court trial in 1949: he 'administered a police force which he did not lead'.[6] Both men were eventually successfully prosecuted for crimes against humanity in the late 1980s and early 1990s, on the basis of Klarsfeld's exhaustive trawl of the archives.

Bousquet operated as chief of police within the framework of collaboration set by his minister, Laval. From the start, he wanted to establish the bases of Franco-German policing collaboration in a clear, comprehensive, and linear way. He aimed to disassociate French police from the damaging and counter-productive German repression of resistance activity in the occupied zone in late 1941, and to extend operationally as well as nominally the French police's remit in both zones. As police chief, he intended to assert and exercise the sovereignty of the Vichy state over all French territory.

The outcome of his negotiations with Oberg, now in charge of policing in occupied France, was a formal police agreement that was publicly revealed to prefects, police chiefs, and their SS counterparts in August 1942. The Oberg–Bousquet agreement established the operational independence of the French police in a collaborating partnership with the German police authorities. Both sides pledged themselves to a struggle against common enemies, 'communists, terrorists, and saboteurs'. Jews were not specifically identified as a common enemy, but the agreement also promised that both German and French police forces would cooperate in the repression of all enemies of the Reich.

The point for Bousquet was that the French police would wage this common struggle independently and in parallel to the German police. Intelligence and information would evidently be shared, and there was to be 'close collaboration', presumably mutual notification, between the forces in the execution of policing measures. But the French police would act under their own responsibility and procedures, which the German authorities had to respect. The German police could not simply give orders to the French police. 'As far as possible', they had to communicate beforehand to Bousquet himself any big measures they intended to take against their common enemies. Unless the situation was really urgent, any instructions to the French police had to pass through their hierarchical channels.

The two major principles enshrined in the agreement were that the French police would play no part in German hostage-taking, and no German reprisals could be taken against people arrested by the French police; and that, while German police and courts dealt with crimes committed by Frenchmen against the occupying troops and authorities, all other crimes, political and common, would be a matter for French police for judgment in French courts under French law and procedure.

In an attempt to make the French police more efficient and effective, and capable of policing all of France, and to draw on SS experience and expertise, there was a general agreement to arm and equip the French police better, and to set up special police training schools. There was a specific agreement to create a paramilitary flying squad, the Groupes Mobiles de Réserve (GMR ('mobile reserve force')), a kind of special operations shock force.

It was quite an achievement for Bousquet to persuade the Germans to allow the greater arming and militarization of the police of a defeated, occupied, and enemy country, and to enable the GMR to operate in the occupied zone. It was clearly part of Bousquet's plans to demonstrate to the Germans that the French police were perfectly capable of keeping law and order and making the occupation secure, in their own country. The SS regarded all their opponents as ideological, and were naturally pleased that they had managed to secure the cooperation of the French police in what the agreement called the 'current struggle for the liberation of Europe'.[7] There were sufficient letouts in the wording of the agreement ('as far as possible', 'generally speaking', 'as a matter of principle', 'urgency') not to inhibit the way Nazi agencies habitually operated, which was, uninhibitedly, creating and re-creating situations that required urgent, improvised interventions. Nazi officials were not trained to stick to the rules. But at least the French police and judiciary had some formal reference points and principles for their own and the Germans' conduct, rather like a country's written constitution.

The revelation and promotion of the agreement were preceded by some important meetings that set the tone, as it were, for the French police's involvement in the 'final solution'. In May 1942, Heydrich himself, Himmler's deputy and factotum, visited Paris, in order to introduce Oberg as SS and Higher Police Officer, and get the lie of the land. He met Bousquet for a wide-ranging and amicable conversation, which lasted for five hours. It was a kind of love-in; the two men were each evidently impressed with the other. Nazi leaders, at whatever level, always set great store by face-to-face meetings and exchanges with their counterparts. They were a kind of enactment of the 'leader principle', a means through which you established the personal and, therefore, binding relationships that enabled you to get things done when you wanted them to be done.

Heydrich clearly thought that he had found his man. Bousquet, in his estimation, was not only capable but dynamic, in the Nazi mould, with a combination of energy and ability that made him a likely prime mover and shaker in Vichy politics, and, as such, definitely worth cultivating. The 'Jewish question' was not a major topic of conversation, and the fact that it was referred to almost in passing in a heady atmosphere of mutual intoxication might have induced Bousquet to make his unguarded, inadvertent, and anyway opportunistic remarks. Picking up on Heydrich's mention of their readiness for the 'evacuation' of stateless Jews from the occupied zone, Bousquet apparently asked about the possibility of including in those first transportations foreign Jews who had been interned for some time in French camps in the free zone. He phrased the request in a way that would have resonated with the *modus operandi* of his Nazi audience. They were long-standing internees who were an administrative and welfare burden to the French state, and here was a chance to ease that burden and solve that problem. Bousquet's request was not followed up in the conversation, but it remained in the record of the meeting and in the minds of the Nazi officials who heard it. In later meetings, Bousquet would be reminded of his apparently voluntary commitment to the 'final solution'. His attempts to row back on the request made it appear that he was reneging on a promise and a pledge, and certainly exposed his vulnerability to German pressure to deliver Jews from the free zone.

In late June 1942, the young upwardly mobile career official, and Bousquet's friend and colleague, Jean Leguay met Theodor Dannecker, the young upwardly mobile *SS* official, and Eichmann's friend and colleague, who was head of the *RHSA*'s Jewish section in Paris from 1940. It was improbable that Leguay had come across an official like Dannecker. One of a crop of dynamic and driven *SS* officials who staffed the *RHSA*'s offices in Berlin and abroad, Dannecker was in charge of anti-Jewish policy in occupied France. He had proposed the setting-up of a compliant French Jewish council to manage the affairs of persecuted Jews, and of what became the special agency for anti-Semitic measures, the *CGQ J*. His proposals, as intended, practically obliged the Vichy government to establish these bodies themselves as pre-emptive measures to retain some control over Jewish policy in occupied France. By the time of this meeting, the *CGQ J* was run by one Louis Darquier de Pellepoix, a totally obnoxious ex-Parisian city councillor who combined an ideological anti-Semitism with corruption and opportunism. The *CGQ J* was a close ally of the Germans, moving from enforcing the 'Aryanization' of the economy and Vichy's racial laws to assisting in the implementation of the 'final solution'. For a short while, Darquier was actually in charge of the policing operations for the arrest and deportation of Jews.

Dannecker was a pest of an official, to put it mildly, constantly biting at the heels of recalcitrant French officials to ensure that the first convoys were filled up. He treated the 'final solution' as Hitler's personal mandate for him to remove all Jews from France, and literally believed that he was performing the best of services to France in emptying the country of its Jews. This was why he was constantly exasperated by and critical of what he saw as French officialdom's deliberate obstruction and delaying of a process that would liberate them from the greatest menace to European civilization. He would turn up at Drancy, in Paris, the main holding camp for deportees, and initially run by the French police, and demand to see the lists of imminently departing Jews, assess the exemptions, make more selections, and insist on the compilation of a reserve list, just in case. Although he organized the first deportations from Drancy, he did not witness them, having secured Bousquet's

THE DEPORTATION OF JEWS, 1942–1944

permission to tour the French internment camps in the free zone, searching for the Jews 'promised' by Bousquet. There he found fewer Jews interned than he had expected or wanted, but was glad to find French prefects and heads of police who apparently were only too supportive of his desire to remove Jews from their departments.

Dannecker was not party to the Oberg–Bousquet negotiations over the respective roles of the French and German police. Even if he had been, it is unlikely that he would have felt constrained by any formal agreement. The fact that it enshrined Franco-German police cooperation would have been sufficient incentive for him to push on and ensure that there were no boundaries to that cooperation. He came to the meeting with Leguay armed with quite specific plans, and detail, on how and whom he expected to be arrested and deported to meet a target of 39,000 Jews in thirty-nine convoys in three months, concentrating on adult males and females between 16 and 45 years of age. He anticipated the arrest of 22,000 from Paris and its region, 60 per cent foreign Jews, 40 per cent French Jews, and of 10,000 foreign Jews from the free zone, as a first stab at reaching that 39,000 target. Typically, Dannecker was trying it on, seeing what he could get away with. His insistence that four out of ten Jews from the occupied zone be French nationals was a real leap in the dark. He evidently hoped to involve the French police in the round-up and deportation of French Jews from the very start, and saw that initial participation as a sign of Vichy officials' willingness to implement the 'final solution' to the point of removing all Jews from France. He even had a suggestion for how French officials could meet the 40 per cent target of French Jews, which was the denaturalization of Jews who had emigrated to France after the First World War and become citizens after a period of residence. He was pointing the finger at Jews who were, in other words, not really 'French' at all.

Leguay held his nerve, and did what any decent career official would do in a difficult, dangerous, and unpredictable situation. Dannecker clearly thought that he was approaching a French official more or less at his level of operational responsibility, and expected an immediate and binding response to his approach for French help in arresting and deporting Jews. This was the common task and, official to official, leader to leader, they would sort it out, or, rather, Leguay would agree to do what Dannecker wanted him to do. Leguay, instead, simply refused to make any decision, let alone any commitments. He said that he would refer the approach to his superior, Bousquet, who would, of course, pass it on to Laval, intimating that the decisions and arrangements to be made were of such importance that he lacked the rank and responsibility to make them. He did point out that, since the internment camps in unoccupied France were full of foreign Jews, it would be easier to deport them from the free zone than Jews from the occupied zone. This amounted to a restatement of Bousquet's opportunistic remark to Heydrich, even though Dannecker was insistent that German security required arrests of French Jews in the occupied zone. We can understand why Dannecker apparently exploded when Leguay informed him the next day that Bousquet was cooling off on the idea of finding 10,000 Jews from the free zone, and would discuss it with Oberg. Whether he realized it or not, Dannecker's demands on Leguay stretched the agreement on policing that Bousquet and Oberg were finalizing, especially Dannecker's expectation that the French police in the occupied zone would be directed by the Germans to arrest and deport Jews.

Dannecker had, in effect, isolated himself. He had offended and misread Leguay and his superiors, assuming that Leguay could take these decisions rather than act as a kind of shuttle between the Vichy government and the Germans. He had offended his own superiors, both for his lack of tact and circumspection in dealing with collaborating French officials, and for exceeding his brief. After the war, Leguay milked these meetings with Dannecker, boasting that his firmness and respect for bureaucratic forms had provoked the 'fall' of Dannecker. There is at least a glimmer of truth in this claim. He was transferred from Paris in late July 1942, and for the rest of the war served the 'final solution' in Bulgaria, Hungary, and, finally, occupied northern Italy.

The only plausible explanation for his transfer was the realization of Oberg and his deputy, Helmut Knochen, that Dannecker's zeal and enthusiasm for the job were straining the collaboration of French officials, whose continuing collaboration was necessary not only for the implementation of the 'final solution', but also for collaboration in all other areas, including policing. His removal was itself a statement that the German authorities were prepared to concede and make changes of their own in order to protect the principle and practice of collaboration. Knochen, as the SS officer who did Oberg's negotiating for him, was committed to both implementing the 'final solution' and securing Vichy's overall collaboration.

It must be said that the SS colleague who took over from Dannecker the organizing of the convoys of Jews from France, Heinz Röthke, was as tenacious in his harrying of French officials to meet Eichmann's targets, and as critical of their performance in doing so. One can only assume that he did his job with sufficient charm to reassure Knochen that collaboration itself was not at stake. Leguay could later claim that he had got rid of Dannecker, as if that was enough to get rid of the 'final solution', or at least his involvement in it. What happened, of course, was that, after Dannecker's approach, Leguay found out from his superiors the extent of Vichy's support for the carrying-out of the 'final solution'. He participated in planning meetings with Röthke and others in order to organize the arrests to fill the convoys, and demanded, in turn, that prefectural officials and police cooperated in the round-ups that took place at the local level.

Dannecker's confrontational approach might well, nevertheless, have influenced the outcome of another meeting, which helped to clarify Vichy's policing role in the 'final solution'. Early in July 1942, Bousquet, on his own, met a formidable team of German SS officers: Oberg; Knochen, effectively his assistant and deputy as head of the SD intelligence section of the SS police in France; Kurt Lischka, a French speaker, previously head of the SS police in Bordeaux, and now head of the Gestapo in Paris; and Herbert Martin Hagen, another young Nazi official on Knochen's staff, a Jewish 'expert' and ex-colleague of Eichmann at the Reich RHSA. Maybe it was the company he was keeping, but Bousquet again behaved rather like a Nazi official, agreeing to things on his own initiative and his own interpretation of his brief, which only later had to be condoned by Laval and the Vichy Council of Ministers. The meeting, even before the publication of the Oberg–Bousquet police agreement, showed that Vichy's involvement in the deportation of Jews was intended to be part of Bousquet's strategy to extend and exercise state sovereignty in France. Bousquet committed the French police to cooperate *in both zones* in the arrest, confinement, and transportation of those foreign Jews wanted by the Germans for deportation to Auschwitz. The agreed figure was 52,000 Jews, 10,000 of whom were to come from the free zone. This figure was, in fact, increased later, after Bousquet had informed Knochen that he now had governmental approval for the deportation of all foreign Jews in both zones.

Something of the dynamism that Dannecker sought to impose on Vichy's officials was reflected in Bousquet's and Laval's subsequent behaviour. Bousquet exerted his full personal and institutional authority over the prefects who would actually have to organize and supervise the round-ups of foreign Jews in the departments from July 1942. These were his instructions to the regional prefects in August 1942: you must take personal charge

Illustration 8. A grinning and relaxed René Bousquet, Vichy's Chief of Police, smokes among German SS officers during the round-up of Jews in Marseilles, January 1943.

and responsibility for the round-ups; you must crush any popular opposition to the round-ups; you must discipline and keep on task officials who are indiscreet, passive, or act in bad faith, and, hence, hinder operations; after the round-ups have taken place, you must hunt down those evading them. Your aim, Bousquet stated, is 'to liberate your regions totally of all foreign Jews'.[8] You can read these instructions in only one way: Bousquet was determined to demonstrate to the Germans that his police forces were so efficient in tracking down Jews that they could be trusted to police all French territory.

Klarsfeld's documentation allows us to move even further down the chain of command, and gives us some insight into what it was like for French policemen required to carry out the arrests of Jews in Paris in July 1942. Some 4,500 policemen were mobilized for the raids of 16–17 July, and they arrested nearly 13,000 men, women, and children, short of the 22,000 target. The French police had taken action against Jews for some time now, but their very detailed instructions revealed the extent of official sensitivity to the tasks they faced during the raids. The emphasis was on the round-ups being conducted efficiently and impersonally. Police were to make the arrests rapidly and without engaging unduly with their charges, by refusing to respond to any 'observations' made to them by the Jews being arrested, not discussing their state of health, and avoiding any 'useless words and derogatory remarks'.

The small teams of officers were provided with a big list of exemptions, and fixed criteria on who were to be arrested. Doubtful cases were to be sorted out by the teams once the Jews were gathered at the assembly points, and people whose cases could not be resolved were to 'follow the same path as the others'.[9] It was clear that the teams were individually responsible for marking targeted arrests. They had to record the arrests; the files of both arrested and evading Jews were to carry the names of the officers carrying out the raids, and, in the event of no arrest, reasons had to be provided in the files. Röthke typically blamed evasions on the prior warnings of policemen to Jews, but there is not much evidence of this being widespread in the July round-ups. The detailed instructions and the meticulous planning clearly indicated that police were to have no excuse for not doing their duty.

When deportations resumed in early 1943, things were probably more difficult for participating policemen. The mass round-ups had given way to even more precisely targeted smaller raids on individual homes, hospitals, orphanages, temporary foster and care homes, as the SS began to pick up groups of Jews exempted or spared deportation in earlier round-ups. There was, also, self-evidently, knowledge of earlier round-ups and deportations, which made everybody more wary. Here, there was a stronger emphasis in the instructions on police doing their unavoidable duty with 'tact' and 'humanity'.[10] That meant, among other things, making prior medical checks on those Jews liable to arrest who were in hospital, and the transfer to hospital for those too old or too ill to face the internment camp at Drancy.

Evidently, there were far more poignant, not to say harrowing, individual cases to handle. One team had to revive a Russian Jewish refugee who had tried to gas herself behind the locked doors of her home, and then take her to hospital. One policeman recorded the experience of arresting an elderly Polish couple, the wife guiding her partially sighted husband. The unit had to convince themselves that the couple were fit enough to be detained. They were, after all, not completely blind, they could dress themselves, they were not incapacitated, and did not protest at the arrest. The clincher, apparently, was the old man lighting a cigarette, dropping it, and then retrieving it, 'which proved that he could see clearly'.[11] There was nothing like the sense of a job well done.

Bousquet's instructions to the prefects also urged no exemption for children in the round-ups, which certainly encouraged the arrest of *French*

Jews, since many of the children of arrested foreign Jews had been born, raised, and become citizens in France. This was a delicate area in which Laval opportunistically intervened, taking the initiative in July 1942. The round-ups were provoking considerable popular antipathy to the arrests and sympathy for those being arrested. At the points of arrest, and transfer to the holding camps, children were often forcibly separated from their parents, so that the parents could be deported and the children taken into care. It must be said that parents were subject to almost unbearable strain on these occasions, torn by their love and concern for their children in the shocking realization that it was probably best that their children did not accompany them and share their fate. Whatever that might be, it would not be pleasant.

For Laval, these separations were an affront to the dignity and cohesion of family life, at the heart of the cosy world of the National Revolution, and the cause of considerable *angst* to arresting policemen and officials, and of a greater administrative and welfare burden for the French state, now required to care for distressed and abandoned children. So it was in a cynically humanitarian spirit, to keep Jewish families together and ease the consciences of his own officials, that Laval proposed to the Germans that in the free zone children should accompany their parents to the holding camps. It might later have occurred to Laval that including children also moved them closer to meeting targets on the arrest and deportation of Jews.

This was clearly an unexpected move to the Germans, who realized as well as Laval that, if children departed with their parents, it would be difficult to protect the reassuring fiction that Jews were being sent to labour rather than death camps in the East. The matter was referred to Eichmann in Berlin, who eventually endorsed the non-separation of Jewish families being deported, presumably because it widened the range of candidates to fill the convoys, and was a more final 'final solution'. For those children who had already been separated from their parents, the decision imposed its own additional humanitarian cost. These children were transferred to the holding camps, and then deported, unaccompanied.

Popular indignation at the round-ups made the French police as well as the occupier unpopular, and undermined consensual policing and occupation. This was bound to affect the outlook of both the Vichy government and the SS. In September 1942, it was agreed between them that the pace of the deportations should be eased. The SS promised not to keep confronting Vichy with numerical targets that were unrealistic and too challenging to Vichy's goodwill and collaboration. Round-ups would concentrate on foreign Jews, which Vichy was prepared to accept, and which ensured their continuing cooperation in the process. Himmler's approval was sought and given to this 'deal', allowing the resumption of deportations, which had been suspended because there was no guarantee in practice that the convoys could be filled. Once again, the Germans had displayed the necessary flexibility to keep collaboration on course.

After the winter break, round-ups and deportations restarted in spring 1943. Things were apparently auspicious. Himmler met Bousquet in April 1943, and confirmed the now-deceased Heydrich's earlier glowing references on Bousquet, who was then, as now, Germany's 'precious collaborator'.[12] The Oberg–Bousquet police agreement was formally and publicly renewed, though this might have been deemed necessary to quieten anxieties about the strains that threatened its continuation. But Laval and Bousquet were clearly rethinking their positions, downgrading in their own minds what could now be expected to be the fruits of continuing collaboration. The crunch came over German efforts to move more decisively on to the next stage of the 'final solution' in France, which was to deport French Jews as 'Jews', rather than as violators of regulations and disturbers of order.

A self-evident way of releasing more French Jews for deportation was to revive Dannecker's proposal of June 1942—that is, denaturalize immigrant Jews who had been granted French citizenship by residence after the First World War. The 'negotiations' centred on the date from which naturalization should be revoked. Bousquet and Laval were for 1933, which would expose about 20,000 Jews to the prospect of deportation. Knochen and the CGQ J were for 1927, which would net a prospective 50,000. Laval and Gabolde, the Vichy Minister of Justice, got as far as signing off a draft law for the removal of citizenship from those who had received it from 1927. Laval backtracked, on the grounds that the SS was trying to force his hand and was already planning to deport soon-to-be-but-not-quite-yet denaturalized French Jews (which it was). This was deliberately disrespectful pressurizing of an independent government. Vichy, thought Laval, was collaborating, but could not be seen so nakedly exposed as such, since it appeared that the government was passing a law that allowed the Germans to move against French citizens.

Knochen put Laval's reticence down to the worsening military situation in North Africa and the USSR, as if a few good German victories would restore Laval's equilibrium. This undoubtedly had an effect; it was now increasingly uncertain that Germany could win the war. But it was more likely that Laval's stance sprang from a more profound sense on his part that collaboration with Nazi Germany was now never likely to yield the expected longer-term benefits for Vichy France.

The row over denaturalization in spring 1943 was a kind of watershed in Vichy's collaboration in the 'final solution'. Knochen certainly concluded that the French government was no longer committed to the 'final solution', and French officials and police could no longer be relied on to cooperate in the round-ups and deportations. The Germans moved towards doing things themselves. They took over the running of the Drancy camp in July 1943, and called in an SS troubleshooter, Alois Brunner, who had just cleared the Greek city of Salonika of its 40,000 Jews. The round-ups he organized in the autumn of 1943 on the Côte d'Azur, where many well-off foreign and French Jews had congregated, were conducted by German police on their own. The inverse of the virtuous circle of collaboration occurred: French reluctance to help fed into and enhanced German self-reliance.

Increasingly, the pattern became the use of French police where cooperation was forthcoming at the local level, and a reliance on German police supported by the CGQ J police force and collaborationist and fascist militias. Bousquet had been quite aware of the dangers inherent in the Franco-German police agreement at the time of its inception, confirmed with the passage of time and experience of how it worked on the ground. In demonstrating their repressive efficiency and independence, the French police ended up doing the Germans' business, which had consequences both for consensual policing and for the morale and commitment of the forces. Bousquet had drawn the attention of the SS to the demoralizing impact of involvement in the round-ups and arrests of Jews on French policemen, who were becoming 'passive' rather than active custodians of law and order. This was one reason for Bousquet to press the Germans for a formal renewal or relaunch of the 1942 agreement.

Both Laval and Bousquet seized on opportunities to cool their commitment to helping the German police. When the Italian authorities in their occupied zone in south-eastern France refused to allow Vichy officials and police to apply measures against resident Jews, and even secured the release of foreign Jews arrested by Vichy's police, Laval cried foul, on the sovereignty issue. How could the French police be expected to do one thing in German-occupied France, and another thing in Italian-occupied France? If the Italians protected foreign Jews from Vichy arrest in their zone, how could Vichy allow or enable the arrest of French Jews in the rest of France? This alibi worked at least until the September 1943 armistice that took Italy out of the Axis war, and led to the German takeover of the Italian zone. In the autumn of 1943, Bousquet went as far as instructing individual prefects not to release to the Germans information on French Jews liable to arrest and deportation, a stance that finally convinced Oberg and Knochen that he was no longer such a 'precious collaborator'.

At their behest, Bousquet was replaced as chief of police in December 1943 for not collaborating in the same 'spirit' as before. His successor, Joseph Darnand, was a collaborationist and leader of the *Milice*, a paramilitary force formed primarily to combat the Resistance. He had earlier hatched a 'plan' for transforming Vichy into a single-party police and fascist state, the single party springing from the *Milice*, which would supply the cadres to replace 'hostile', meaning 'passive', state officials. He encouraged *miliciens* to volunteer for service in the *Waffen SS* on the Eastern Front, and took a personal oath of loyalty to Hitler as an officer of the *SS*. He was one of the signatories of a petition or motion in July 1944 that was effectively an attempted coup against Laval and anticipated the installation of a fully collaborationist and pro-German 'revolutionary' government. All Frenchmen knew their revolutionary history, and this was his 1793 moment.

Darnand was, of course, still responsible to Laval as his governmental and ministerial superior, both as chief of police and as head of the *Milice*, and, while he personally had little compunction about arresting French Jews, he had to respect the Vichy 'deal' on foreign before French Jews. However, his presence as chief of police did make a difference to possibly the final significant round-up of Jews under Vichy involving the French police. It occurred in January 1944 in the Bordeaux region in occupied south-western France, where Maurice Papon was the top prefectural official responsible for managing Jewish affairs for the regional prefect.

In his research into the holocaust in France, Klarsfeld had deliberately pursued Papon for his part in arresting and deporting Jews because he was a typical career official serving the Vichy state; his role was seen as representative of how Vichy officials behaved throughout the country. Employed as a civil servant in various Republican ministries of the late 1930s, including the centre-left Popular Front governments, he was reunited with his political patron, Maurice Sabatier, in the Interior Ministry in late 1940. He moved to Bordeaux when Sabatier was appointed by Laval to be the regional prefect in May 1942. Between 1942 and 1944, Papon cooperated with the Germans over racial policy, including the deportations; he planned and discharged police operations to arrest Jews and transfer them to Drancy.

Illustration 9. Maurice Papon, the French official at the prefecture in Bordeaux who was involved in the deportation of Jews in 1942–3, is here pictured being released from prison in Paris on the grounds of poor health in September 2002, after serving thirty months of a ten-year sentence for complicity in crimes against humanity following his trial in 1998.

Some have portrayed Papon as a chancer and risk-taker. But, while we would expect Papon to depict himself at his trial as an obedient official doing his duty, this is also the impression emerging from Klarsfeld's documentation. He was by all appearances a very scrupulous and cautious official. He carefully checked with his ministerial superiors on the validity of each operation to arrest and transfer Jews, in order to 'cover' himself. The local *SS* commander sought French prefectural and police support for the raids planned in early 1944. Papon duly reported the matter upwards to the regional prefect and police chief, and thence to the Interior Ministry and the Vichy government. It became a confusing and confused situation, where nobody on the French side really wanted to assume responsibility for a reply to the German request, or demand. Eventually, beyond the eleventh hour, Laval literally handed over the telephone to Darnand, who, on the grounds that the Germans were unyielding and would go ahead anyway, gave the all-clear to French cooperation.

This is a sorry and tragic tale. Vichy's involvement in the 'final solution' was seen by Bousquet as a golden opportunity to demonstrate by their efficiency the independence and sovereignty of the French police. The outcome was Bousquet's removal and replacement by Darnand and reliance on the collaborationist *Milice*, and the end of independent French policing of French territory. For Laval, the Jews in France were something that Vichy had and the Germans wanted, which meant that a collaborating deal, with concession and counter-concession, was feasible. The outcome was a quite significant change in Laval's approach to, and expectations of, collaboration, which undoubtedly affected the collaboration of officials and police on the ground from late 1943 and early 1944.

For once, it may be worth asking a counterfactual question, if only to illuminate the explanation for Vichy's collaboration in the arrest and deportation of Jews. This may not be the counterfactual question you want to ask. But it is one that fits the context, and relates to the actual conduct of officials elsewhere in occupied Western Europe. We have to accept that helping Jews to escape arrest and deportation was not really an option considered by most French officials. So, my counterfactual question is, what might have happened if the Vichy government had taken the position of the Dutch and Belgian secretaries general, and allowed but not cooperated in the enactment of the 'final solution'? Well, the 'final solution' would have happened, with or without Vichy France's involvement. Vichy's non-involvement, however, would have ruled out Bousquet's opportunity, and stymied Laval's efforts to extract both immediate and longer-term concessions from Nazi Germany. They were not the only political leaders to justify the means by the end. The question is historically pointless, like most 'what if' history.

7

Collaboration against the Grain of Occupation, 1942–1945
The Deportation of Workers

The continuing war in the USSR, which precipitated the moves towards a total and European war economy, created a huge demand for civilian labour in Nazi Germany. Heavy losses on the Eastern Front necessitated the military call-up of German workers and led to a shortage of skilled labour in the German war industries. It was evident to Speer that more men and more arms production could be extracted from the occupied territories to fill the current and future gaps in German war production. Foreign workers could be exploited for the German war effort in two ways. They could be employed directly in German factories, both to replace conscripted German workers, who might then be permanently lost to the German labour force through death or injury, and to release German workers for transfer to priority war production. They could also be employed in factories at home in order to increase military production there, or work on consumer goods contracts to service the German civilian population and, again, free up German workers for work in German war industries.

The demand for labour was urgent and pressing enough for the Reich to resort to a characteristically Nazi kind of appointment, that of a 'leader'. 'Fritz' Sauckel was made plenipotentiary for labour in March 1942, mandated by Hitler with full powers to mobilize the labour resources of the occupied territories for the German war effort. Recently, attempts have been made to portray Sauckel as a technocrat. This is on the rather specious grounds that he owned, ran, and expanded an arms and vehicle manufacturing business in central Germany, and made it one of the core elements of the regional war economy, which he organized as a Reich Defence Commissioner, a kind of regional economic supremo.

However, this son of a postal clerk and seamstress had been a merchant seaman in foreign mercantile marines before the First World War, worked in a ball bearings factory after the war, and had a year of technical college training without graduating before his life was consumed by his political activities in the Nazi movement. He became the *Gauleiter* or regional Nazi Party boss of Thuringia, later its State Governor, the positions from which he came into possession of the arms company, a Jewish family business he expropriated in a *de facto* 'Aryanization'. Sauckel was almost a parody of the lower-middle-class *parvenus* who became local and regional Nazi Party leaders. Making a virtue of his lack of formal qualifications and learning, he had advanced politically by being a fixer and an organizer who got things done. Like all Nazi Party leaders, he was inspired by Hitler's personal mandate to perform and achieve. He brought to the job of labour plenipotentiary that lethally effective blend of ruthlessness, energy, drive, proven organizational ability and experience, and ideological conviction, which characterized Nazi officials who had Party origins and pedigree. As we shall see, Laval, who regarded Sauckel as an unsophisticated lout, found him unmanageable and largely immune to his personal charm and smooth, nuanced negotiating skills. Laval did, in fact, succeed in piercing Sauckel's implacable persona just once, managing to extract something for POWs once he had found out that Sauckel had himself been a POW in France during the First World War. But, although he was the last to admit it, Laval met his match in Sauckel.

Because he was used to it, Sauckel very quickly improvised his own small bureaucratic apparatus and staff, who were dispatched to rove the occupied territories seeking out surplus labour. In the Netherlands, he quite deliberately bypassed the Reich Commissioner for Economic Affairs, and co-opted and worked through the Commissioner for Political Affairs, Schmidt, who was a Party man and representative like himself. As Hitler's mandated plenipotentiary, he could direct and instruct other German authorities, including the occupation regimes, or simply ignore them and go over their heads. In practice, Sauckel usually set up his own labour staff to work in and through the existing German administration in the occupied territories, and also established offices in various parts of the occupied countries.

Sauckel was never a natural fit with Speer's attempts to bring rationality, order, and coordination to the German war economy. But it is important to realize that they worked in harmony for some time, until the mutual contradictions of their respective policies became all too evident. Both men, after all, wanted to increase production for the German war effort, and intended to exploit to the full the economic resources of the occupied territories, especially their labour, in order to do so. Their roles could initially even be regarded as complementary. Sauckel's job was to recruit the workers to work in Speer's German arms factories.

It is difficult to keep track of and distinguish the various labour recruitment campaigns, or 'Actions', launched by Sauckel, since he ran one campaign into another, setting additional targets even though, or because, earlier targets had not been met. The occupied territories were under constant pressure to perform, as a result. As with the deportation of Jews, the deportation of workers became a huge bureaucratic exercise, protracted in its own right, since the process involved the selection, designation, and combing-out of workers from across the industrial economy, medical checks, and assessment of their suitability to work in one or another German factory. The process was also deliberately drawn out, in the hope that at least some intended deportations could be delayed or prevented.

Both German and national officials tended to inflate the numbers of those notionally going to work in Germany, the almost inevitable outcome of a target culture. Given the amount of bureaucracy necessarily involved, Sauckel's targets were breathtaking, as were the official figures on the supply of workers to Germany. It is unlikely that they reflected the reality on the ground, especially when many workers often declined to return to Germany to complete their contracts after spending time at home on leave. But, nevertheless, hundreds of thousands of workers in occupied Western Europe were obliged to work in Germany between 1942 and 1945. The scale of the operation made it a very different beast from the deportation of Jews, who were a relatively small and persecuted minority of the population in the occupied territories. Sauckel's 'Actions' reached into the homes and family life of millions of people, and their effects resonated throughout the national economies.

Sauckel, for instance, insisted that workers' pay could not be increased in the occupied territories, in order to maintain a pay differential that would apparently make employment in Germany more attractive. This was very much against the advice and wishes of both national officials and the German occupation authorities, who recognized the need to sustain family livelihoods and social peace against the impact of food shortages and the inflation of prices caused by shortages. Hours of work were increased (to fifty-three hours a week in the Netherlands), both to shake out workers for deportation and to meet the shortfall, temporary or permanent, of their departures. The combing-out of workers meant short time, even closures and mergers, for some businesses in sectors considered non-essential to the war effort, where the workers were needed but their products were not.

More and more people were drawn into the maws of the process, as Sauckel's demands eroded the initial exemptions to labour service. In Belgium and the Netherlands, veterans of the 1940 military campaigns, POWs but enabled to live 'normally', were recalled and reconscripted for employment in Germany, a move that provoked particular resentment and hostility in the population and among officials and police expected to oversee the recall. Women, university students, agricultural and forestry workers, professional people, officials themselves, forfeited their initial exemptions. The biggest losses of labour were incurred in the artisan sectors of the industrial economy, as well as in the services sector, where towns were stripped of their shop assistants, waiters, and hotel staff. Sauckel remarked contemptuously in one of Speer's central planning committee meetings in Berlin that France had a considerable underlying surplus of overemployed labour and could easily forgo the 'luxury' of small bistros with twenty-five piece orchestras and two waiters for each table.[1] The deportation of labour to Germany made the deepest cuts of the occupation to the economies and societies of the occupied territories, and left the deepest scars.

Overall, apparently, in occupied Western Europe and northern Italy, only 10 per cent of Sauckel's targets were met, and that, of course, was bad enough. Since the labour recruitment schemes required compulsion and enforcement, they invited sabotage and evasion, and set in motion the law of diminishing returns, the unavoidable cycle of coercion necessitating yet more coercion. The more you forced things, the less you obtained; the less you obtained, the more you had to force the issue, and so on. From, perhaps, the spring of 1944, Sauckel's 'Actions', in pursuit of a 1944 target of 1,000,000 more workers from France and 250,000 more from Belgium and the Netherlands, did not even pretend to be systematic. Men and women were picked up in the streets by German police and their local auxiliaries, around cinemas, restaurants, cafés, and air-raid shelters, in random, indiscriminate raids that were both cause and effect of a more general breakdown of order towards the end of the occupation.

Two countries escaped the coruscating effects of labour deportations. On Hitler's orders, there was no compulsory labour scheme in Denmark, in the same way as there was no initial deportation of Jews, respecting the special status of the collaborating Danish government. In the summer of 1944,

Sauckel turned to end this last exemption, at a time when Denmark was simply another occupied territory. But Best managed to head off its belated implementation in the country, arguing successfully that imposing it would threaten the continuation of Danish food supplies to Germany, the guarantee of which was collaboration.

The situation in Norway reflected its anomalous economic position in occupied Northern and Western Europe. Developing the Norwegian economy to fit into the *Grossraumwirtschaft* required the input of imported foreign labour from the USSR and Eastern Europe. Occupied Norway could ill afford to release skilled workers to the Reich, and, while Norwegian workers did work in Germany, their presence remained 'voluntary'.

Hitler's only other reticence in backing Sauckel to the hilt was over the deportation of women workers. As in Nazi Germany itself, labour mobilization was extended to women in Belgium and the Netherlands with reluctance. It is important to recognize that Hitler and Sauckel shared the same Nazi Party distrust of the occupied populations and their willingness to collaborate with the Germans. If something was not given voluntarily, or was unlikely to be provided voluntarily, then compulsion was the only (Nazi) answer. Compulsion also required no give and take. You took what you wanted without making any binding or constraining concessions or promises in return. And, if your measures provoked resistance, then again, the recourse to repression and coercion was immediate and necessary. The law of diminishing returns meant nothing to Hitler and Sauckel, when the overriding and urgent need was for ever more workers, to be met by all means possible. If the target was 100 workers, and you obtained 50, that was a result and its own justification of coercive methods.

Both Hitler and Sauckel were, in this sense, victims of their own stereotypes. They believed that German contracts being delivered by factories in the occupied territories were inherently at risk from the sabotage and low productivity of reluctant employers and workers. They were bound to be more productive working in German factories where the necessary work discipline was directly imposed by German managers and Party bosses. In this way, the disputes between Speer and Sauckel over the deployment of foreign labour became 'ideological' as much as economic, at least on Sauckel's side. Speer, along with the German occupation authorities and collaborating national officials, took what they saw as the rational stance. It made good sense to employ more workers on more German contracts in the occupied territories themselves, now that the industrial zones of Germany were subjected to heavy and sustained Allied bombing campaigns. Workers employed *in situ* were bound to be more willing and productive, simply because they were living in their homes and with their families, and working on machines under managers they understood and respected. Forcing them to leave to work in Germany was actually counterproductive: it provoked hostility, opposition, disruption, evasion, and resistance.

All this was evident on the ground. Employers were understandably reluctant to put at risk the production and continuity of their businesses by agreeing to the departure of a quota of skilled workers. Workers, especially those married and with families, naturally responded to a forcible departure to work in Germany with dismay, and evasion. We know, or can surmise, that sometimes workers decided to go because they realized that, by refusing to go, they placed another perhaps more vulnerable worker at risk. Whichever way the decision went, it was divisive and likely to cause bad feeling in the workforce and among the local community, as exemptions also did. In some places, Sauckel's 'Actions' revived collective and organized labour agitation, disrupting the social order that lay at the heart of economic collaboration and the security of the German occupation. In the Netherlands, the reinternment of POWs in April 1943 provoked strikes of solidarity in some factories, a remarkable attempt to assert some kind of collective muscle against the occupation. The Germans responded in the most draconian way possible. They arrested and executed strikers, and then issued a new decree extending the call-up of Dutch male workers to three specific age groups of younger workers, which was meant to yield another 148,000 workers. Only 8,000 of the 300,000 demobilized POWs actually turned up. But the whole episode was a sure sign of an intensifying cycle of resistance and repression. This was the real fear and threat experienced by employers, officials, and occupation authorities, that the 'Actions' would undermine what had been so carefully built up and protected in the previous two years, a relative degree of 'order' that enabled factories to produce, and made collaboration feasible and the occupation secure.

In occupied Belgium and the Netherlands, the deportation of workers was illegal and unconstitutional under both national and international law. For what it was worth, the governments-in-exile explicitly ruled out any official cooperation in the process—in the Dutch case, well into Sauckel's second or third 'Action' in spring 1943. These bans on cooperation specifically referred to Labour Ministry officials, who were not meant to provide lists of workers for possible deportation, or indeed any information on the 'available' labour force. They were not to assign people to work nor supervise the recruitment of workers liable to compulsory labour schemes. It was just impossible for Dutch officials to respect these guidelines. Part of the problem was the fact that the Dutch administration, like the Belgian one, had steadily increased its own bureaucratic controls over the national labour market in response to earlier German requests for voluntary labour to work in Germany. By the time deportation came, Dutch and Belgian officials had in place labour service schemes for the assignment of unemployed and part-time workers to jobs in Germany or to public works projects in their respective countries.

You could not wish all this away, nor could you withdraw the information on the national labour force that had already been officially registered. As an official, you would not want to wish it away, since it was, in part, anyway, pre-emptive, the way you retained some modicum of direction over the national economy during the occupation. You could, in other words, use your own apparatus to affect and influence the implementation of German decrees on labour and ensure that their application was, to some degree, dependent on that administrative machinery. So, Dutch and German labour officials who had cooperated in voluntary recruitment carried on cooperating in the compulsory mobilization of labour.

Frederiks, poor soul, had the worst of all possible worlds. He instructed the mayors not to release data to facilitate the German labour draft, and insisted that the local police should not be required to arrest any Dutch person for any alleged breach of a German decree that violated Dutch law. This stance was as much to do with asserting his declining central ministerial authority over areas nominally within his administrative jurisdiction at the Interior. But he could not do very much about his subordinate colleague, Lentz, head of the Inspectorate for Civil Registration, telling mayors that it was acceptable to hand over to the Germans information on the age groups of workers liable to deportation.

Verwey, like Hirschfeld, stayed on as secretary general until the end of the occupation. Officials in his Ministry of Labour authorized the release of data on workers to the Germans and deployed themselves and their subordinates on the bureaucratic tasks involved in the process of deportation. They won, in return, the exemption of their own staff from the labour draft and earned for Verwey the resistance's soubriquet of Germany's 'number one bootlicker'. Verwey took the view, shared by his officials, that the compulsory labour scheme was an extension rather than a rupture with labour schemes on which they were already cooperating.

Hirschfeld, in his memoir, recalled that he had opposed the strikes of March 1943 staged in protest at the reinternment of war veterans, opening them up to deportation to work in Germany. The strikes were backed by the government-in-exile. He castigated the government-in-exile for its irresponsibility in supporting the strikes, saying that it deliberately induced chaos and disorder, which would rebound against the people's interests and security. His comments, written in retrospect, might have been the result of hindsight, given his (and his audience's) knowledge of the German reprisals in response to the strikes. But, knowing as we do Hirschfeld's obsession with order above all things, it was undoubtedly also his view at the time that strikes would set off a chain reaction leading to a German 'terror', and a German reliance on collaborationists to aid and abet that 'terror'. This was to the detriment of the administration of the country by secretaries general and officials who were duty bound to act in the people's interests. Hirschfeld was 'right' and was proved to be 'right.' This sense of rectitude went some way towards explaining his imperturbable and consistent behaviour as Secretary General for Economic Affairs, at a point when Frederiks was demonstrably feeling the strain of facing all ways at once, towards the Germans, the government-in-exile, the resistance, and his own officials.

It was Hirschfeld, rather than Frederiks, who was apparently behind one of the most controversial decisions taken by officials during the occupation. There is some evidence to suggest that the secretaries general delayed their approval of this particularly contentious matter, in order to enable the resistance to sabotage it. Rauter's new ration and ID card scheme was mooted in the summer of 1943, but not approved by the secretaries general until the end of the year. But, given Hirschfeld's view of the resistance movements as inveterate disturbers of good order, this was, perhaps, again a retrospective and out of context judgement of his conduct.

The German authorities intended to identify and trap people who were using false IDs to evade deportation and other occupation measures by issuing a new set of ID cards, for which people would have to apply anew, and on which was dependent essential aspects of daily life, like the food ration. Despite pressure from the resistance and the government-in-exile, Hirschfeld eventually signed off the new card issue in December 1943, and coupled it with a word to his officials that they should stand firm in the face of resistance threats and certainly not stop working and go underground. He knew why the Germans were resorting to a new more foolproof card scheme and took a similar view to that regarding the deportation of Jews. The Germans, he thought, would proceed with the card reissue, whatever he, the government-in-exile, or the resistance said about it. Since the measure was unavoidable, the point was to influence the process and the outcome, and preserve as much executive control as they could over the much more important issue of food supply and rationing. Its equitable and smooth running was threatened by resistance attacks on labour offices and the destruction of official documents, including ID cards.

In late 1944, Sauckel's men required Dutch officials to cooperate in the registration of workers for deportation, now extended to adult males aged between 16 and 40, under whatever number 'Action' it now was. Again, the resistance and government-in-exile told officials not to participate in a round-up of an intended 50,000 workers in Rotterdam, the country's major industrial port city. Again, Hirschfeld formally opposed the measure but told his officials to comply, on the grounds that, if they were not involved in the process, the Germans would do it themselves and, by using more force, accelerate the cycle of resistance, repression, and reprisal. Hirschfeld also told employers that compliance would enable his officials to negotiate exemptions for workers who were essential to safeguard food supplies for the Dutch population. In the event, the round-ups did not occur. The Germans lacked the manpower to carry out the raids, and the Reich Commissariat disagreed with Sauckel's representatives over the opportuneness as well as the practicality of the measure.

Such an outcome reveals that Sauckel's measures could be stymied by the lack of resources at the Germans' disposal. But it is also evident that absent or inadequate local support was not the problem. In this instance, officials' cooperation was forthcoming, though the Reich Commissariat's doubts about the operation came from its concern about the impact on the population, the security of the occupation, and the strain placed on collaborating officials. Hirschfeld appreciated that the German need for collaboration gave him some room for manœuvre and leverage. But he had to balance some small tangible gains (a modicum of control over the process, in order to secure exemptions serving the population's more general interests), against what, exactly? What advantages could he expect to gain from adopting the government-in-exile's position? At the time, of course, he could argue quite plausibly that his line of conduct had been vindicated by events. He had not offended the Germans to the point of them breaking off relations with him, which would have removed whatever capacity he had, or could extract, to affect the implementation of German measures. The round-up of Dutch workers had been called off, precisely because of the argument he put to his own officials and to the Reich Commissariat, that the initiative would make the occupation even less secure.

The greatest pressure regarding the implementation of the deportation measures was probably felt at the base point of the Dutch administrative system, as indeed it was elsewhere in the occupied territories. The communal mayors helped to run the local police and rationing offices, and held the records of the local population, many of whom they would know personally. Their own behaviour was always under popular scrutiny. Would they, for instance, exempt or register their own children for the deportation programme? Would they instruct the local police to hunt down evaders of the deportation decrees? Would they enforce, or turn a blind eye to shop keepers', butchers', and their customers' infractions of food supply regulations? These were hardly easy choices to make, and taking the 'wrong' path could result in local people losing confidence in their administration of local affairs and make them as unpopular and isolated as the occupiers were becoming. The tendency, overall, was for mayors to try to remain in office, even well into 1944, and what ensured that they remained in office was, of course, continuing to collaborate with the Germans. But at least in office, rather than out of it, mayors could expect to influence the enactment of occupation decrees and so keep on the right side of popular sentiment or tolerance. Certainly, nobody else aspired to do the job in 1943–4, except perhaps NSB members, who by the summer of 1944 were mayors of communes containing about half of the Dutch population.

In occupied Belgium, the mark of Sauckel was felt in the adoption of a compulsory labour service scheme in October 1942, which affected all adult males between 18 and 50 years old, and unmarried women between 21 and 35, who were liable to be called up for work in Germany. The secretaries general, or a majority of them, did not want to get involved in a compulsory scheme, even though they had cooperated in the labour service decree of March 1942, which directed unemployed workers to work in Belgium.

Labour mobilization on the scale envisaged by Sauckel could not proceed without some cooperation from officials and employers. Factory owners and managers were expected to provide lists of available staff, and therefore select them, once the Germans had decided on the quotas of workers to be deported for work in Germany. The national labour offices, as they had already done under the previous scheme, would register the chosen workers, set up medical examinations, draw up work contracts, and arrange departures. Leemans had used his good standing with the Germans to extract a concession that he anticipated would help to reconcile employers to collaborating in the process. It was perfect pain: employers could not only select workers for deportation, but also, provided they did so, choose the workers to replace those being deported. This was the classic way of delegating misery and was and is practised by austerity-minded governments everywhere. Employers, as collaborators, were given some sense of ownership of the process, which was close to being rational and therefore acceptable. Employers had the power to select deportees and find their replacements according to their view of how best to manage and maintain the factory's productive capacity. They could replace like with like, or not, depending on the needs of the company in deploying its labour, but obviously had to take account of who was actually available, and, it must be said, whether anybody else was available. Some of the replacements might need reskilling or training up, another disruption to the smooth running of the factory. But, then, there was nothing very smooth about running a factory in 1943–4.

The onus for meeting Sauckel's deportation targets lay with the German military administration of occupied Belgium, which was as keen as the secretaries general to keep a degree of control over the country's labour market. Reeder, true to form, wanted and needed the cooperation of the secretaries general over this particular issue, and on all issues, generally. But, as he must have expected, the labour draft reignited, or rather kept going, the long-running triangular conflict between himself, the secretaries general, and the judiciary. Again, as Reeder wearily realized, the deportation of labour, serious enough in its own right, raised the usual questions about the respective legal and *de facto* powers of officials as opposed to the military government. Since there was yet another German decree requiring enforcement, it was once again a matter of deciding who policed, who judged, and according to whose laws.

As it happened, Reeder thought that he had reached a kind of *modus vivendi* on policing that coincided with the October 1942 labour mobilization decree. The tacit agreement resembled in some ways the Oberg–Bousquet arrangement in France and had much the same outcomes. Reeder clearly wanted and expected the Belgian police and judiciary to be in charge of law and order, so that he could co-opt them to combat their common enemy, resistance, now increasingly threatening the security of the occupation. The problem was that the Belgian judiciary just would not accept the validity of the position reached by the Reich Commissariat in the occupied Netherlands—that German decrees should be enforced by Dutch policemen, and such enforcement should not be subject to judicial review as to whether this violated Dutch law, or not. The Belgian secretaries general went some of the way with the judiciary, in their concern to protect the operational independence of the Belgian police and judicial process. The analogy with Bousquet is now evident.

The secretaries general and Reeder agreed on higher penalties for gun possession and use, and recognized that it was practically impossible to distinguish acts of violence and sabotage against the occupation, a matter for the German police, from, say, attacks on Rexist mayors and communal officials, a matter for the Belgian police. It was all 'resistance'. This acknowledgement of a common enemy, resistance, was really quite significant, as we shall see. The authority of the police to act was to be respected. The prosecuting magistrates would continue to investigate cases and make arrests through the judicial police, on condition that the occupying authorities did not intervene in or take over Belgian cases. So, as in France with the Oberg–Bousquet agreement, the Belgian police and judiciary would act independently against resistance, not at German direction, and would apply Belgian laws according to Belgian legal process.

The agreement unravelled as soon as it met actual cases on the ground. In November 1942, for example, the Brussels state prosecutor arrested two Belgians under suspicion of writing anti-Rex slogans on walls that castigated Rexists as 'traitors' for backing the German occupation, and for possession of arms and explosives. The German military police 'requested' that the two prisoners be passed over to them, since they were about to be released after investigation. The Belgian magistrate refused to do so. But the prisoners were, nevertheless, transferred to German custody, and a couple of months later were shot as hostages without trial before a German military tribunal, let alone a Belgian court. That formality was at least assured in a later, more publicized case. The notoriously pro-German editor of a collaborationist newspaper, Paul Colin, was murdered in April 1943. The suspect, a Belgian student, was sought by the Belgian police under a Belgian arrest warrant. But the German police found him first, arrested him, put him before a German military court, and executed him. What price an independent Belgian police and judiciary? The Belgian police had, willy nilly, been drawn into the repression of acts of resistance, 'political' crimes, and ended up doing some dirty policing against Belgian citizens.

It was this effective devaluation of the October 1942 agreement that provides the setting for a kind of *dénouement* over the enforcement of the labour deportation process. The specific point of issue was whether Schiund, the Secretary General for Justice, the official in charge of the prosecuting and investigative magistrate system in Belgium, should be required to pass on, and hence endorse, Reeder's directives on the enforcement of the deportation measures to the Belgian police. These included police being encouraged to use their weapons in arresting Belgian suspects. The wider issue was, evidently, who policed Belgium, and how.

The debate in the secretaries general committee in September 1943 was prolonged, difficult, and divisive. It highlighted what had become almost a breakdown in collegial behaviour, with pro-German secretaries general confronting the rest. Even before this apparently decisive meeting, Plisnier and Schiund had ganged up on Romsée, who was attempting to gear up and strengthen the Belgian police for the repression of 'terrorism'. He and the Germans managed to identify their very own Belgian 'Tulp' in the person of Armand Tilman, the former head of the paramilitary force attached to the fascistic and Flemish *VNV*, who was put in charge of special anti-communist teams located in the *gendarmerie*, the police force responsible to Romsée at the Interior.

To Plisnier and Schiund, Romsée and the Germans were counterproductively exacerbating the security situation in the country by appointing unpopular collaborationist Rexist or *VNV* mayors, who immediately became natural targets of the resistance, and embarking on a campaign of 'counterterror' to resistance 'terror'. Romsée confirmed a long-held approach in the tumultuous September meeting: 'terrorism'—that is, resistance—was not patriotic, and should be ruthlessly repressed by all means, Belgian as well as German. Schiund countered by insisting that the Germans must stick, in practice, to the policing agreement of the previous autumn. The Belgian police and judiciary should be permitted to police Belgians under Belgian law and procedure. Plisnier drew attention to the key issue: the police and judges should not be required to hand over Belgian citizens for judgement in German military courts. He warned that magistrates and police would simply refuse to execute Reeder's instructions on the implementation of the labour drafts, even if they were passed on by Schiund; the outcome would be 'real anarchy'.[2]

Schiund's position, backed by a majority of his colleagues, was intransigent enough to secure his dismissal as secretary general and being placed under house arrest by the Germans. This precipitated a crisis in relations with the military administration, or, one should say, a potential crisis, which the subsequent deal resolved, or put off, yet again. Schiund had not resigned; he had been dismissed, which gave the secretaries general a bit of leverage. They had now to appoint his successor. While that would clearly have to be someone acceptable to Reeder, they could threaten collective resignation if his successor was obliged to enact the measures that had led to Schiund's dismissal.

Schiund's removal and succession therefore became part of the deal. Robert de Foy, a senior police official in the Interior, replaced Schiund as Secretary General for Justice. A policeman occupying a legal position was a sign of how constitutionally separate executive and judicial functions were merging in an authoritarian direction. But Plisnier's point was met: in cases involving the possession and use of firearms where there was no direct German interest and reason to intervene, the Belgian police and judiciary could act independently and see through their own investigations. It was back to October 1942, since Reeder had secured the repression of resistance by the Belgian police at the 'price' of them being enabled to do it independently.

Schiund's removal had an interesting private postscript. It induced Struye's grudging respect and acknowledgement of the secretaries general's position throughout the occupation. He described Schiund's dismissal as 'a good departure' for him,[3] a remark that showed that Struye realized that there was something, after all, in the secretaries general's claim that they were the 'lesser evil'.

It was very noticeable that labour deportations were subsumed into a wider and serious conflict over who policed Belgium under occupation. It was a sign, in itself, of how the deportations soon turned into a policing rather than an administrative matter, as people evaded the obligation to work in Germany. This required Reeder, not Sauckel, to negotiate and reach a deal with the secretaries general, in a repeat show of collaboration. It was just as well that the secretaries general did not have to negotiate with Sauckel. They tried, of course. Leemans and De Winter, pro-German both of them, met the labour plenipotentiary in August 1943, in an attempt to persuade him to soften his demands on the supply of Belgian workers to the German war economy. Sauckel aped the *Führer* and spoke uninterrupted for two hours, saying that Hitler expected 10 per cent of the Belgian population, or 800,000 people, to be involved in the labour draft, and set new eye-watering quotas for the rest of 1943. The Belgian deputation pointed out quite reasonably that the 800,000 figure would entail the move to Germany of practically all the country's industrial workers, and that the new quotas would undermine both the industrial and the agricultural economy, would not allow workers to produce what was necessary to sustain the Belgian people, and, hence, threaten social and public order.

All that Sauckel was prepared to concede, and this did amount to something, was the exemption of agricultural workers from the labour draft. He also promised not to extend, as he had originally intended, the period of obligatory work in Germany to eighteen months, which did not amount to much. Finally, he agreed that there would be no further call-up of age groups, which amounted to nothing, since it was extended in September. Sauckel was absolutely immoveable on the new targets for workers: 40,000 by mid-September 1943, and 150,000 by the start of 1944.

The continuing constitutional and legal conflicts between the German military government and the Belgian secretaries general and judiciary were serious enough, and a constant challenge to the principle and practice of collaboration. But, in the case of labour deportations, there was a certain amount of shadow boxing in Reeder's position. The factor that really facilitated the deportations in occupied Belgium was the military government's earlier successful turning and co-option of the Belgian national labour offices under Hendriks.

The secretaries general agonized long and hard over how to handle the defection of their own rogue department. After the fall of Verwilghen, no less than four short-term appointments as Secretary General for the Labour Ministry between April 1942 and September 1944 could not find a way of bringing the ONT to heel. They eventually even thought of cutting the national labour office adrift and divorcing it from the state administration, which would have eased their responsibility for the organization's willing cooperation in the labour schemes, but put it beyond their influence, for good. In March 1943, when the Germans called up all the young males of three age groups, a typical escalation of German demands across the occupied territories, the secretaries general not only protested, as was expected, at the damage being inflicted on the national economy. They also tried to reassert their administrative control over the labour offices, by insisting that the Germans could not unilaterally commission local offices to find workers for departure to Germany, something that had been happening up to now. They tried to restrict *ONT* involvement to working out exemptions to labour service on welfare and family grounds, and even to deny them a say in allocating workers to German firms operating in Belgium. It was common practice to reassign to work in Germany workers designated to work in Belgium.

Finally, in July 1943, the *ONT* budget was cut; and finally, finally, the decision was taken in February 1944 to make the *Warenstellen* rather than the *ONT* responsible for placing labour under the drafts, and to insist that the *ONT* communicate exclusively through the appropriate secretary general, not directly with the German military administration. Since this would effectively cut off the source of labour, Reeder, informed of the move by Hendriks, intervened to arrest Olbrechts, the current Secretary General for Labour, and told the secretaries general to find a successor. This provoked a Custer's last stand in the secretaries general committee. Plisnier told his colleagues that the arrest made it 'morally impossible'[4] to continue collaboration. This was not as threatening as it sounds, because they intended to carry on with routine administration. But they would not meet again as a committee and decision-making body until Olbrechts had been released. In the event, the committee decided not to make Plisnier's threat their own. Instead, Leemans was dispatched to speak to Reeder, and calm was restored. The deal was that Olbrechts would be released, which presumably made collaboration 'moral' once more, while the secretaries general would appoint a new colleague to run the Labour Ministry. *Plus ça change…* All this was rather late and ineffectual. The Germans, quite understandably, went on using the national labour offices to comb out workers for jobs in both Belgium and Germany.

So the secretaries general did not cooperate in the labour drafts, or tried not to, while the *ONT* did, willingly. This, when you think about it retrospectively, was quite convenient for the secretaries general. They were officially against the implementation of the labour call-ups, but unofficially they could do little or nothing to restrain their own officials from complying. It was a kind of solution to an intractable problem. They covered themselves with formal protests against the policy, while the Germans got what they wanted without too much strain on the collaborating relationship. That came when the labour issue was transformed into yet another confrontation over policing and law and order in occupied Belgium. The secretaries general's attempts at the time to manage their renegade department showed that they were trying to rectify the situation of impotence in which they found themselves, rather than use that powerlessness to affect things as a convenient screen.

This makes the behaviour of the military government all the more interesting. The Germans could quite happily work through the national labour offices and their productive relationship with local military commands in order to secure workers for Germany. Reeder, nevertheless, constantly looked for ways of engaging the secretaries general in the process. He proposed, for instance, that the *ONT* manage the labour draft in respect of work in Belgium, which the secretaries general rather liked, because they could see that it was a way of preventing or scaling down deportations to work in Germany. The initiative came to nothing, and negotiations broke down over the secretaries general's demands that no women should be considered for the labour draft, and that no worker assigned to work in Belgium should then be reassigned to work in Germany. But the initial move had been made by Reeder, not the secretaries general, an indication that he still wanted and felt the need to secure their collaboration, both on this specific policy, and, of course, generally. The spirit of collaboration was still alive in Reeder, while it could scarcely be detected as ever having existed in Sauckel. Reeder's demonstrable commitment to collaboration with the secretaries general was, perhaps, the only positive outcome of the implementation of labour policy in occupied Belgium.

As a nominally independent and semi-occupied country, Vichy France could insist on state-to-state negotiations over Sauckel's drive for labour. Laval certainly treated it as an opportunity to exercise *donnant–donnant* collaboration, as he did over the deportation of Jews. There was never any question about whether French officials (and then French policemen) would carry out plans to send French workers to Germany. The point, as elsewhere in the occupied territories, was for the Vichy government and its officials to retain control of the running of the national economy, and of the policing of sovereign French territory.

The June 1942 agreement was itself negotiated beyond the deadline set by Sauckel for the delivery of the first huge batch of French workers. At its heart was the idea of an exchange between Vichy France and Nazi Germany. It was an unequal one, certainly; Laval had wanted a one-for-one exchange. It reflected the natural power imbalance between defeated and victorious countries, but it was an exchange, nevertheless, that suggested that France and Germany were partners in a common enterprise. The idea was contained in the term given to the labour recruitment scheme *Relève*, or 'relief', as in the replacement of one military watch by another. For every three skilled workers sent to work in Germany, France would receive in return one French POW held in camps in Germany, as long as the overall targets were met. The repatriation of the over 1.5 million still in captivity, most of them put to work in Germany, had been a demand, or a hope, of the Vichy government since the signing of the Armistice. France was the country that Germany had defeated and occupied in 1940 that did not see a significant return home of POWs.

Since the *Relève* was to be administered by the French authorities in order to pre-empt any compulsory scheme imposed by the Germans, Vichy had to promote and induce voluntariness among French employers and workers. Even when a compulsory scheme was formally applied from February 1943, the Vichy government and its officials continued to use the term *Relève*, both to preserve the idea of there being an exchange and to disguise the compulsion. The operational planning and work for the scheme were undertaken by Ministry of Industrial Production officials, and Bichelonne played a significant role in negotiating and implementing the scheme.

Ministry officials channelled their efforts through the already existing apparatus for managing the national economy. They urged the heads of the *Comités d'Organisation* to promote and organize recruitment among member companies, as well as approaching some big companies individually. They suggested a form of quota, with teams of staff, including managers, technicians, and workers, to be assembled by individual firms for departure to Germany, where they would work together in German factories that were to be regarded as partners. The hope was also that French POWs, converted into civilian workers with proper contracts, would be transferred to German factories to join their compatriots. The idea turned out to be an additional complication that burdened the scheme. For this to happen, German economic agencies and employers would have to adapt themselves to choices on destination and location made by French officials and employers. But that, after all, was what an exchange partnership entailed.

Laval also intended the *Relève* to be a practical illustration of the benefits accrued to France as a result of the official policy of collaboration. To induce participation in the scheme and gain popular approval for it, Vichy heavily propagandized the *Relève* on the radio, in the newspapers, and through rallies and gatherings of factory employees. The prefects were instructed to launch recruitment campaigns in their departments, and to

Illustration 10. A Vichy propaganda poster from the summer of 1942 for the government's *Relève* scheme tells French workers that it is their patriotic duty to collaborate, since they 'hold the key to the camps', and 'by working in Germany...will liberate French Prisoners of War'. The *Relève* typified the hope behind Vichy's collaboration with the Germans—that, by giving something, something would be gained in return.

ensure that both employers and their workers took part in the scheme. This was, for the Vichy regime, an exercise in authoritarian, if not totalitarian, mass mobilization and propaganda. It was made necessary by the self-evident fact that it was a very hard sell to both employers and workers. Companies, naturally enough, wanted to retain their corps of skilled workers for the current and future integrity of the business; while workers, naturally enough, preferred to work from home and family and support them directly rather than through some kind of migrant remittances.

The *Relève* was sold in the Ariège, a poor, depopulated, rural department near the Spanish border, as an opportunity to repatriate peasant POWs and, hence, revive abandoned farms and improve local agricultural production. That became an empty promise of economic revival, once, from early 1943, previously exempted agricultural and forestry workers were obliged to go, joining those already combed from the small local textile firms and mines. More local peasants left the land, either for Germany or hiding out, than peasant POWs returned.

Since the *Relève* made little economic or social sense to employers and workers, the appeal was largely made on the basis of self-sacrifice for the patriotic interest. By 'volunteering' for the *Relève*, workers would benefit the nation, ease the burdens and injustices of occupation, and restore good Frenchmen to their homes and families. Later on, workers were told that, by contributing with their labour and skills to the European-wide struggle against Bolshevism, they were also constructing the new Europe where France would have a prominent and integral place.

The response to the *Relève* and subsequent campaigns was, shall we say, mixed. An appeal based on self-sacrifice when people felt that they were already suffering enough from war and occupation was unlikely to strike home. You can sense the popular reluctance that Laval was trying to overcome in the rather testy tone of one of his radio broadcasts to the 'free zone' in October 1942, which emphasized obedience and duty before will as the road to national redemption: 'overcome your selfishness. You have the chance to recover with your tools what France has lost by arms. For yourselves, for the prisoners, for France, you must obey the government's orders.'[5]

Employers, to promote the scheme, often gave the mistaken impression that the *Relève* would facilitate the repatriation of POWs who were family members of those who 'volunteered' for work in Germany. This false promise both raised and confused expectations. When such an exchange did not happen, and could not happen, the alienation and distress were evident in a general popular disaffection with the scheme. Officials implementing the *Relève* recognized the economic rationality of the case employers made against compliance, even as they complied, grudgingly. Berliet, our irascible and single-minded *patron*, not slow in provoking the ire of both Vichy and German officials, supplied about 570 workers under Vichy's labour schemes, not a bad return, even though the Germans apparently wanted 1,500 from his factories, overall. Berliet supplied lists of workers to the mixed commissions of French and German labour officials who came to 'visit' his factories, and here his selection was honed to safeguard the core of his skilled workers. The final selections were made by the officials from his lists.

Interestingly, Berliet became more cooperative as time went on. In autumn 1942, he allowed a team of workers to leave for a 'partner' company in Germany under the scheme, and included two of his sons in the group, presumably to ensure that his workers were treated well, and also to observe German production and management methods at first hand. This led to a rather more formal relationship with the German 'partner' company, with the latter now the so-called godfather of his French business. That a *patron* like Berliet was prepared to allow a German stake and involvement in his company indicated that the prospect of a voluntary partnership that suited both sides economically might well have reconciled employers to a partial compliance with Vichy's labour recruitment scheme.

Peugeot, a strongly *Pétainiste* company, took a similar line to Berliet. It would comply, but managers were careful to tell their workforce that they would not select workers for the scheme, which was the responsibility of the officials. This was compliance and non-compliance at the same time, with the managers clearly trying not to cross a line with behaviour that alienated their workforce or the Vichy government. Peugeot's attitude certainly hardened when the *Relève* became a compulsory scheme, which, in Peugeot's case, led to German soldiers entering the factory at Sochaux to seize recalcitrant workers who had not been fingered by their managers nor had responded individually to the call-up.

One senses that most employers, in order to save what could be saved, demonstrated some compliance without ever committing themselves enthusiastically to the scheme. They did enough to get by, in all senses. But it is difficult to generalize about this. Georges Villiers, the Vichy-appointed mayor of Lyons and later a resistance leader, remembered a big launch for the *Relève* staged by the regional prefect and attended by members of the city's chamber of commerce, Bichelonne, and a German deputation. The speeches were apparently received in 'glacial silence' by the assembled employers, leaving the Germans very angry and Bichelonne ashen-faced. The prefect snarled at Villiers, 'you industrialists have understood nothing'.[6]

As the Peugeot managers realized, the workers themselves were unlikely to accept the scheme willingly, which was why they refused to select any of them. In October 1942, a Vichy official from Marion's Ministry of Information, no less, organized a meeting at a locomotive factory in Nantes to explain and promote the *Relève* to the workforce. Only a minority attended, and the star turn, a returning POW who had worked in Germany, was heard in a silence punctuated by some mild heckling, enough, anyway, to make him later withdraw his backing from the scheme. A manager unwisely revealed to the men who were there that the company had already got its little list of seventy-five workers and eight technical staff who were bound for Germany. When, after the meeting, the list was published, the workers went on strike. The German military command threatened to arrest all those who did not answer the call-up. The agitation spread across the department and its neighbours, involving over 5,000 workers. In a nearby aircraft factory, the German military police arrested workers in the factory and imprisoned them until they signed their already drafted labour contracts. German officials demanded fresh names from the management to replace those on the original list who were not responding to the call of their patriotic duty.

Laval himself attended the first ceremonial changeover of returning POWs and departing workers at Compiègne railway station in August 1942. But Lecornu, then a sub-prefect, recorded the events at Saint Nazaire, a shipbuilding port on the west coast, where a delegation of German officers from the regional military command turned up at the specially decorated

Illustration 11. In the presence of Rudolf Schleier, German ambassador to the Vichy government, on the far left, Pierre Laval, Vichy Prime Minister, preaches on his familiar theme of national and European solidarity at the railway station of Compiègne, to the north-east of Paris, the place where the armistice of June 1940 was signed and now a symbol of Franco-German cooperation in more ways than one. This ceremony marks the crossover of a train carrying 'volunteer' French workers to Germany with one repatriating French POWs, in August 1942. It was also the place from where Jews and others imprisoned in the town's internment camp were deported to German camps and Auschwitz.

railway station with a military band, to celebrate the departure of all of two French workers. The German officers and soldiers did not wish to risk further humiliation by actually accompanying the workers on the train, as intended, and the two men took advantage of the lack of a military escort to hop off at the next station and go into hiding.

It was hardly incidental that these events occurred in the occupied zone, and involved workers who were barely reconciled to the *Pétainisme* of their employers. But they showed how very quickly a scheme of induced voluntariness could become one of *de facto* compulsion. The prefects had their work cut out in mediating an end to the strike action, diverting the threat of German reprisal for non-compliance, and restoring order to a situation that compromised the day-to-day collaboration between government officials and local German military commanders. Some prefects never quite managed to straddle the line between compliance, which invited unpopularity, and non-compliance, which invited dismissal. When the system became compulsory in early 1943, some of them cracked. It was the end of the regional prefect of Marne-et-Loire, Jean Roussillon, in July 1943, who had been regarded by the Germans as an exemplary official up to this point. Apparently no longer reliable because of his reluctance to promote the compulsory call-up of workers, and for not wanting to waste police time on catching protesters and evaders, he had still done enough in his previous service to be condemned as a 'collabo' by the local resistance. The rates of evasion, if that is the way to put it, varied greatly from place to place. But one of the most important variables that helped to determine whether evasion occurred and whether the evader evaded recapture was undoubtedly the stance and decision-making of office-holders, the prefects and mayors, above all.

In the circumstances, it was hardly surprising that the *Relève* did not enable the recruitment of a sufficient number of skilled workers to meet Sauckel's initial targets. One has to say that official figures showed that it was a close-run thing. Of the 150,000 skilled workers demanded by Sauckel in his first 'Action', lasting from June to September 1942, officially over 137,000 were found. But it was pretty clear that the limits of available labour susceptible to mobilization under a nominally voluntary scheme had already been reached. The law of diminishing returns kicked in. In the recurrence of workers' opposition to the call-ups, there was the knowledge or realization of what the 'Action' and the *Relève* actually entailed.

So both Sauckel's and Vichy's recourse to a compulsory labour scheme in August and September 1942 reflected the reality that a voluntary scheme would not enable the regime to meet the next 'Action' target, eventually agreed at 250,000 additional workers. Sauckel's compulsory labour decree, applying across the occupied territories, provoked Laval's one and only threat to resign. He told Sauckel that the Germans were treating France as if it was Poland. In recognition of Laval's importance to Franco-German collaboration generally, Sauckel was prepared to accept that a compulsory scheme would be run by Vichy, not by himself. Laval must have realized that the threat of resignation and of the withdrawal of cooperation, could be played only once in his case.

Sauckel's decree was immediately trumped by the Vichy law setting up the *Service du Travail Obligatoire* (*STO* (Compulsory Labour Service)), clearly pre-emptive, and applying, of course, to both zones. It envisaged the compulsory registration for 'national' work in both France and Germany of all adult French males between the ages of 18 and 50, and all unmarried adult females aged 21 to 35. It led to the mobilization of three age groups for two years of assigned work, a quite significant change in the selection of workers for compulsory labour.

The *STO*, formally operative from February 1943, allowed the retention of the exchange element of the *Relève*, just. Laval wanted to improve the exchange ratio to 2:1, but Sauckel 'conceded' that there would be an unchanged 3:1 ratio. It became the practice to convert POWs in Germany to the status of civilian workers, which meant they received regular work contracts and a contractual right to a period of leave in France, from which they often did not return. When they did not, Sauckel demanded the missing numbers be made up by further recruitment in France.

Laval was also able to reassert the principle of *donnant–donnant* collaboration, and reaffirm, to himself anyway, the high stakes of Franco-German collaboration. Perhaps in a tacit recognition of how rough a negotiator Sauckel proved to be, Laval expressed his thinking in a pretty explicit and downbeat way, as if he was approaching the end of his tether. How much simulated toughness was there in his blunt message to Sauckel in January 1943? He told Sauckel that, as a result of their negotiations on labour recruitment, what had been a policy of Franco-German collaboration was becoming the German enforcement of its policy on France, and something had to be done to redress the balance. He thought that it was time for Germany to step up and honour Vichy's collaboration by rewarding it. This was an implied threat to withdraw that collaboration, and again Laval must have smelt the burning of negotiating bridges as he lit yet another cigarette on the tip of what remained of the previous one. It was, Laval stated categorically, 'materially and morally impossible...to send a quarter of a million French workers to Germany, *unless the necessary climate to do so is created...*'.[7] These were the words highlighted in the report on their meeting. The 'climate' meant two interconnected things for Laval: popular opinion that was in favour of collaboration and would therefore facilitate collaboration; and a German propensity to make the concessions to France that would encourage opinion to favour collaboration.

Sauckel was not impressed or moved by such arguments, even though he saw that Laval was staking the very permanence of the Vichy regime on collaboration. He was not interested in courting French public opinion; what Nazi Germany wanted could not be qualified or conditioned by the views or needs of the population of a defeated and occupied country. He, like Hitler, always acknowledged that Laval's presence as Vichy's head of government was essential to the prolongation of Franco-German relations. But he did not want to, nor did he need to pay any price for Laval's collaborating presence. The matter of what Vichy France could hope to gain from collaboration was not Sauckel's concern, anyway; it was beyond his remit and his decision-making powers. It would be settled by Hitler, at a moment of Hitler's choosing. He did not really care whether French workers were delivered by compulsion or cooperation, as long as they were delivered. And delivered they were. The 250,000 French workers of Sauckel's second 'Action' were apparently signed up for work in Germany by April 1943, an agreed month later than the original deadline. Laval might portray this fulfilment of a target as a triumph of collaboration. For Sauckel, it was vindication of a policy of compulsion.

Laval reached the point of what appeared to be actual, rather than calculated, despair after a meeting with Sauckel, also attended by Bousquet and Bichelonne on the French side, which lasted from 4.45 in the afternoon to 10.30 in the evening on 6 August 1943. All of Laval's meetings with Sauckel were difficult and prickly. This one was even more bruising and turbulent than usual. In the course of 1943, Sauckel had submitted demands for yet more French workers, which even the *STO* was unable to satisfy. In the August meeting, Sauckel wanted yet another half a million workers by the end of 1943. This was how a sympathetic journalist and *confidant* of Laval remembered in the early 1950s what Laval said to him in August 1943 after his confrontation with Sauckel. Laval described Sauckel as a 'dreadful brute. He wants 100,000 workers within a week. I discussed it all day, but he didn't want to listen to anything. I said that I would give him an answer tomorrow morning.' Laval then apparently left Paris for Vichy, to avoid having to see Sauckel again. In his confidences to the journalist, anyway, Laval conceded that all he could negotiate now was a delay in proceedings. He also tried to reduce the numbers of workers required to work in Germany, or at least divert some of them to work on Todt Organization projects in France. 'I couldn't refuse him,' said Laval, 'because a "no" would provoke violent reprisals. They are exasperated by my inaction.'[8]

In fact, Laval ended up agreeing in principle to another 500,000 workers by late 1943, after initially refusing to accept Sauckel's demands, if only to get Sauckel off his back and avoid another face-to-face meeting. He was able to recover from the shock of the meeting and his encounter with Sauckel, because he had no intention or desire to meet the new target. He felt confident enough to stall on meeting Sauckel's 1943 demands, now that he had an alternative policy. Laval's rejection of Sauckel and a process of enforced collaboration on labour led to intensified and relatively unforced economic collaboration of a different and more congenial kind. Sauckel also seemed to regard the August 1943 meeting as a kind of watershed, referring to Laval's reluctance to accept future targets as sabotage, and telling his own people that he would now have to inform the *Führer* that France was no longer prepared to contribute to the German war effort.

That was hardly the case, of course. Vichy wanted to contribute in another way, as did the rest of the occupied territories. It soon became clear after Sauckel's 'Actions' had started that there were obvious contradictions between Speer's and Sauckel's respective policies. Sauckel was calling on the workers who were needed to fulfil German contracts in the occupied territories, and that included the huge defence projects like the Atlantic Wall, as well as deliveries of war materials. The deportation of workers to Germany also hindered Speer's plans to devolve more consumer goods production to firms in the occupied territories. Speer's approach, promising rational and planned economic collaboration conceived on a European scale, and conducted through organizations that brought together officials and businessmen, was always the more attractive package; compared to Sauckel's compulsive and coerced asset stripping.

This was evident in Bichelonne's overtures in July 1943 to Elmar Michel, the former head of the economic section of the military administration in occupied France who was now in charge of the whole show. The approach took full advantage of the now evident conflict between Speer and Sauckel, and the military government's own despair at the impact of Sauckel's 'Actions' on the security situation in occupied France. Bichelonne's programme for increased and protected French production for Germany in the framework of a 'European war economy' was more than enough to gain him a meeting with Speer in Berlin, from which emerged the famous Speer–Bichelonne agreement of September 1943. Speer had first secured Hitler's permission to meet Bichelonne, and to treat France as a friendly partner.

It was an almost perfect convergence of personalities, economic approach and outlook, and mutual needs and benefits. Both men clearly thought that they had found a way for France to contribute more intensively and productively to the German war effort, while also forging an economic partnership that put France at the manufacturing hub of Europe and raising the prospect of an integrated European economy, a *Grossraumwirtschaft*. It was the latter vision that allowed the two men to fantasize a little and entrance themselves. Speer recalled almost wistfully in his memoirs the 'utopian thoughts in which Bichelonne and I lost ourselves for a while at that time—a token of the world of illusions and dreams in which we moving'.[9] It was only an 'illusion' in retrospect; it seemed within their grasp while Germany was still in the war.

The late-night conversations might have dealt with illusions, or aspirations, but the deal, duly approved by Hitler, resonated throughout the French economy, and indeed, throughout the economies of the occupied territories. Bichelonne committed the Vichy government to find the additional French workers needed to increase production on additional German contracts to be completed in French factories. This commitment, as intended by both sides, would rule out any further labour drafts forcing workers to move to work in Germany. Bichelonne was effectively guaranteeing Speer that 70 per cent of French productive capacity would be dedicated to the German war effort. So, for instance, there would have to be more miners in French coalfields to increase production there; 30,000 men registered for the *STO* could be employed as miners. More French-produced coal and iron would have to go French industries working on German war contracts, which meant the diversion of raw materials and energy away from some French businesses. The deal could be met only by closures and declining activity in sectors deemed not essential to the war effort.

The two existing categories of 'protected' factories were rolled up into a new single category of *Speerbetriebe* factories, which had absolute priority in the supply of raw materials, labour, and energy. Workers in *S-betriebe* factories were exempted from Sauckel's labour sweeps. The *S-betriebe* spell would be cast not only on companies working on German contracts, but also on railways, road and water transport, mines, forestry, and electricity generation. It would include factories and utilities in the two northern departments attached to occupied Belgium, the restoration of a notional national economic union in a notional wider European economic union.

Bichelonne felt that he had secured a really good deal. In his view, this agreement enabled France to develop a stronger and more resilient post-war peacetime economy, since France would increase its capacity for consumer goods production, while Germany concentrated on military-related production. Speer made the same point in October 1943 to the most unsympathetic audience possible, a room of Nazi Party *Gauleiters*, whose concern was to protect the German home front in both war and peace. They were not enamoured by the prospect of French consumer goods industries clothing, booting, and feeding German workers and furnishing their homes after the war had been won. The deal, as you might expect, given that Sauckel belonged to them, met with their resentment and disapproval.

The essential elements of the Speer–Bichelonne agreement were extended to occupied Belgium and the Netherlands, for the same reasons and to meet the same needs. They were not required in Denmark, since economic collaboration continued as before to provide what Germany needed, even though the special relationship had broken down and Denmark resembled in its occupation the other West European occupied countries. The ripples from the Franco-German agreement certainly helped to ease relations between Reeder and the secretaries general in the autumn of 1943. The latter showed themselves willing to cooperate in the compulsory allocation of labour in *Belgium*, when it was made clear to them that more workers on German contracts there would compensate for a reduction in the numbers of workers required to work in Germany. This was almost the equivalent of the Speer–Bichelonne agreement.

Galopin's 'policy of production' still broadly met the needs and interests of the country's economic and official establishment, and certainly ensured that the country was fed, even if it displeased the government-in-exile. It was tailor-made for the Speer strategy of diverting more production from Germany to the occupied territories, and found an unanswerable justification in stemming the outflow of skilled Belgian workers to factories in the Reich under the Sauckel 'Actions'. Employers, workers, and officials throughout occupied France and the Low Countries clamoured for categorization as *S-betriebe*, to save themselves from Sauckel. By March 1944, in France, about 13,000 factories employing 1.4 million staff were *S-betriebe*, and there were plans to exempt 600,000 more workers. The biggest increases in industrial production came in the ex-free zone in southern France, as the Germans eventually tapped into the potential of the whole national French economy. In Belgium, by February 1944, over 850 factories employing over 550,000 people were 'protected' under the scheme. By May 1944, in the Netherlands, the figures were over 300,000 workers in nearly 2,000 factories. And the inter-company 'partnerships' promoted by Speer blossomed. By late 1943, over 700 French companies were 'twinned' or patronized by over 200 German 'godfather' firms.

Sauckel, it must be said, thrived on conflict and competition. He condemned the *S-betriebe* factories as the 'legal *maquis*',[10] since, with the backing of both the occupation authorities and national officials, factories actively recruited back to work all those who had moved homes and jobs, or gone into hiding, in order to evade the call-ups. He also took his case to Hitler, and, in what was meant to be a clear-the-air meeting with Speer, in Hitler's presence, in December 1943, things rebalanced in his favour. Hitler restated his support for the compulsory labour drafts, which encouraged Sauckel to urge his men on the ground to raid even the protected factories for workers to deport, and fed his expectation that all workers released by closures or part-time working should be scooped up for work in Germany. Sauckel was also allowed to solicit the help of all German agencies, including the SS, in order to reach his labour targets, another step on the road to outright compulsion and requisition. This must have been sweet news to Sauckel, since he had felt constrained in his meeting with Laval in August by Oberg's warning that there were insufficient German police and soldiers available to round up the growing army of draft evaders. What Oberg said was objectively the case, but it also reflected the concern that all German authorities in the occupied territories had about the impact of the 'Actions' on the security of the occupation and popular tolerance of it.

Speer did not seem to be prepared for the Sauckel onslaught on his position, after he had secured Hitler's endorsement of his agreement with Bichelonne. But at least, and at last, he did what he could to retrieve the situation, catching Hitler just after the meeting had ended and securing his verbal support for a continuation of the *S-betriebe* arrangement. Hitler had, as usual, said 'OK' to the last person he had spoken to. This was a characteristic outcome of the Nazi system of rule. A meeting called to decide between conflicting strategies and personalities had ended up by endorsing both sides and enabling both sides to carry on, under Hitler's personal mandate. Hitler evidently felt that both sets of policies could be made to work; any conflicts could be sorted out by the balance of forces and will on the ground.

Sauckel certainly returned to his ongoing negotiation with Laval on the 1944 targets like a new man. In January 1944, he demanded a fresh law from Laval that called up all men between 16 and 60, and all single childless women between 18 and 45; a longer working week and lower wages in French factories; the execution of officials who sabotaged the labour drafts; and the removal of more exemptions from compulsory labour service. Laval held out on wages and the execution of 'saboteurs', but conceded the law, with the proviso that women should do their compulsory labour in France alone. He was also reassured by Sauckel that, if significant steps in recruitment were made, then he would consider making no further labour demands on France, depending, of course, on the military situation. Even Laval must have smiled or grimaced at the newly negotiable Sauckel, and the incongruity of both the target and the promise.

With the suspension of parliamentary government and the imposition of direct German rule from August 1943, Denmark became, for the first time during the war, like any other occupied territory. Since it was no longer the anomaly, Denmark should therefore be included in a general assessment of how steadily worsening conditions in the occupied territories from late 1943 affected the practice of occupation and collaboration.

The convergence between the German occupation authorities and officials lay in their common concern and responsibility for ensuring a peaceful and secure occupation, to be achieved through collaboration. This natural alliance persisted to the very end of the occupation. But it became increasingly ineffective, even irrelevant, in terms of maintaining the occupation, as collaboration gave way to compulsion and collaborationism. There was an inherently self-destructive cycle to German Nazism and its systems of conquest and rule. Its methods and policies induced and exacerbated problems that, from the Nazi perspective, required more coercion and repression to resolve them, undermining the principle and practice of collaboration. The crisis of occupation from late 1943 was largely a self-induced one. It was Reich leaders and agencies, not the occupation authorities, who imposed policies in the occupied territories that provoked both passive and active opposition and hostility, and made occupation unpopular, dangerous, and insecure.

By early 1944, across the occupied territories, most things were a matter of repressive policing, whether it was combating the activities of resistance groups and Allied agents; enforcing food supply regulations against farmers, traders, and consumers; hunting down Jews and evaders of labour deportation decrees, and their accomplices in evasion. In some areas, you could say that there was a breakdown of law and order from the summer of 1944. In some parts of France, where the *maquis* was particularly assertive and violent, and in large parts of Belgium, there was incipient civil war. Everything was more extreme in occupied Belgium. Even from the spring of 1943, what looked like a rural insurgency gripped the Belgian countryside. The resistance, encouraged by the government-in-exile, attacked *CNAA* offices, dairies, cheese factories, and agricultural depots, and threatened farmers with violence unless they both avoided German and official requisitioning, and sold and distributed food to consumers at 'fair' prices. In Belgian towns and cities, especially in francophone regions where Rexist mayors had been installed by Romsée and the Germans, collaborationists and resisters fought and killed each other.

Collaborators and collaboration were this war's casualties and victims, literally so. The architect and guarantor of economic collaboration in Belgium, Galopin, was himself murdered with his wife in February 1944 by paramilitaries under the command of the head of the Flemish SS and the secessionist Flemish political organization sponsored by the German SS. Like all good fascists, the Flemish SS were anti-establishment and hated the 'plutocratic' elites; and, like all good Flemish fascists, they wanted to remove one of the most eminent of francophone Belgians, who, they told themselves, was collaborating with the German military government, not the SS. Galopin's victimization for being a collaborator was confirmed by the shameful silence of the government-in-exile at the news of his death. Their concern was not to make a patriotic martyr of a man whom they condemned for the policy of economic collaboration. Galopin died to the excoriation of the Belgian government-in-exile, the Belgian resistance, and Flemish collaborationism. For some time before his death, Galopin had dedicated himself to defending the 'policy of production', and advising all who were prepared to listen on what to do in the post-liberation period to facilitate the country's recovery and reconstruction. Not unsurprisingly, he took up the authoritarianism prevalent among officials in 1940-2, arguing, like Bichelonne, that a provisional post-war government with exceptional powers over the economy should adapt rather than dismantle the wartime economic agencies run by officials and businessmen, so as to ensure an efficient and planned transition to a peacetime economy and polity.

In the occupied Netherlands, Frederiks was advised by his own officials to remove himself from the fray of the competing claims on his loyalty and service, and absent himself from work. From September 1944, he lived in a kind of self-imposed internal exile in his own house, though that was not exactly a safe haven, since it was burgled by people who could have been either collaborationists or resisters. At least he was able to avoid attending a special ceremony to receive a decoration for his occupation service from the Germans, the receipt of which would have amounted to a probable death sentence. The Reich Commissariat always knew how to look after one of its most trusted collaborators.

The deteriorating security of the occupation made collaborating officials less willing to collaborate, because what was increasingly demanded of them was not cooperation, but obedience and repression, and the Germans less trusting of their collaboration and less willing to rely on it. It was yet another self-reinforcing and self-justifying twist to the transition from collaboration to compulsion. This nullified what might have been one of the consequences of a steadily worsening situation, that collaborators could expect and demand more in return for that collaboration. There was little leverage available when your offices were no longer being called on by the occupier.

This was evident at all levels. It was probably not coincidental that, in the days after Laval's bruising and apparently inconclusive confrontation with Sauckel in Paris in August 1943, the *Gestapo* arrested several top officials in Vichy's economic ministries, including men from the cabinets of Bichelonne and Pierre Cathala, a long-time stooge of Laval, then the Minister of Finance. Both ministers, good collaborators both, used up time, energy, and collaborating credit in appealing for their release. Some were released, and then hidden away in obscure corners of the ministerial administration; others were deported to imprisonment in Germany.

This became a regular feature of the final year of occupation, and not only in France. The Germans removed or insisted on the removal of officials they perceived as being unreliable, and appointed, or had appointed, more reliable collaborators, drawn from lists and intelligence on potential replacements they had been accumulating for just such an eventuality. Almost inevitably, repressive policing in the occupied territories in 1944–5 was carried out by new collaborationist police forces, superseding the professional career services and usurping their repressive powers. Under the new police chief, Darnand, the *Milice* instituted a 'revolutionary' terror in France, setting up special courts for the summary judgment and punishment of 'terrorists'. In Clermont-Ferrand, in south-central France, in the summer of 1944, the real power was with the *Gestapo* and the *Milice*, not the prefect and the *gendarmerie*. In the Netherlands, the Germans disarmed the Dutch police, coinciding with the Allied liberation of the south of the country and the continued German occupation of the north, including Amsterdam, over the autumn and winter of 1944–5. In Denmark, the appointment of Günther Pancke as Higher *SS* and Police Leader in November 1943 practically inaugurated the terror and counter-terror cycle of repression, resistance, and reprisal. Pancke overruled Best's softly-softly approach and took over policing in Denmark, with the internment and disarming of the regular Danish police in September 1944, moving to a reliance on Danish *SS* and *DNSAP* auxiliaries.

The recourse to fascist paramilitary police forces sponsored by the *SS* in the occupied territories was an affront to the professional integrity of the regular police forces. They were ceding the state's monopoly of coercion to irregulars whom they regarded as gangs of ideological fanatics who were more like armed vigilantes than policemen. This was undoubtedly demoralizing, as shattering as the loss of policing by popular consent consequent on a more repressive role in enacting the will of the occupier. The police would probably not have seen things in this way, but the occupier's reliance on their own police and fascist militias in 1944 got them off the hook of collaboration. Confined by their unreliability to 'normal' and nondescript policing anyway, they might well have been bored at their inactivity, but it aligned them with the resistance, willy-nilly. It was certainly the case that resistance groups by the end of the occupation wanted policemen to defect to them and go underground. But the inertia of 1944, whether induced by the occupier's suspicion or by the resistance's threats, had provided a kind of alibi for their conduct during the previous years of the occupation. It counted as 'passive resistance' and eased the transition to life and service after the Liberation.

State officials faced choices throughout the occupation, of course, but such choices became acute at a time when the occupation was increasingly repressive and unpopular, as was officials' collaboration with it. Popular sympathies, even tolerance, drained away from the occupying and state authorities, sometimes into open hostility and certainly into more law-breaking. People came to perceive that those in authority were the reason for, rather than the solution to, the deteriorating conditions of occupation, and pursued personal and often selfish strategies for survival in straitened circumstances.

Officials could resign, though that was the nuclear option. The instruc-tion from their superiors, after all, was that they could not resign, only be dismissed. Resignation offended their sense of hierarchy and duty. It put themselves and their families at considerable personal risk. Resignation would be taken as a hostile act by the occupying authorities, and by their superiors, and require them to go underground or into hiding once they had left office. This was the unequivocal message conveyed by Jean-Pierre Ingrand, the Vichy government's long-standing official liaison with the German occupier, to a prefect who wanted to resign because Ingrand had instructed him to notify the people in his department that recent acts of sabotage would be punished by German reprisals. 'If you don't withdraw your resignation immediately,' warned Ingrand, 'you will be arrested and sent to a concentration camp'.[11] Resignation also exposed the people they were meant to serve to a replacement who was likely to be worse and com-mitted to the repressive ways of the occupier. In the event, most resignations in 1944 occurred at the local level of officialdom, among mayors whose office had only just lost its popular and electoral legitimation, and who understandably found it next to impossible to mediate and balance the con-trary pressures and demands on them, from their superiors, the occupiers, the resistance, and the population.

Some officials decided not to resign, but to retire hurt, as much a sign of their sense of impotence as resignation. This was the case with the belea-gured Frederiks, who was particularly sensitive to the criticism levelled at him by the government-in-exile and the Dutch resistance. One senses that his self-imposed house arrest was the only way he felt he could protect his own life and head off a personal breakdown. It happened in an even more calculated way to the mayor of Angers, Victor Bernier, the man who had opened the gates of the city to the German army in 1940 and was regarded as a saviour for doing so, since he had prevented a German military bom-bardment and attack. In March 1944, the *Gestapo* wanted to replace him, but in the light of the impact this would have on the Angevins, his officials persuaded the Germans to allow him to remain in office, but not to go to work. An enforced sabbatical was, one supposes, a compromise that suited neither side, and both sides, at the same time.

If most officials decided to stay on and avoid dismissal, then the spirit in which they did their duty obviously mattered. You could do so in a spirit of resistance, and this was not as odd as it sounds. There was a distinct resistance organization in France that recruited officials and fostered resistance among officials. This was the *Noyautage des administrations publiques* (*Nap* (Infiltration of Public Bodies)), aimed at senior level officials, with a special section, *Super-Nap*, for prefectural officials. They were selected for membership, and there were not many of them, perhaps 1,500 fish in an ocean of about 1,000,000 officials, for obvious reasons. To be effective resisters, you had to remain in post and not expose yourself as such. You had to act surreptitiously to avoid detection, and the sensitivity of your position meant that your range of resistance activity was confined to what might be called 'passive resistance'. That involved losing files, delaying bureaucratic process, turning a blind eye, not following up an investigation, passing on information to resistance groups operating in your area, meekly surrendering when resisters raided offices to seize and destroy documentation, telling your subordinates to do nothing. The possibilities to resist within the framework of your daily activities as an official were endless, but limited. 'Passive resistance' in the final throes of occupation was also the perfect alibi for officials facing the post-war purge commission for acts of collaboration committed in the earlier stages of occupation. Such 'resistance' was undetectable, often unprovable, but probably there, as a matter of benefit of the doubt. It also served to protect the official's anonymity and lack of responsibility for his actions, since the real motivation for being passively resistant was impossible to discern and could only be assumed. It was also, shall we say, easier to resist in this way, and certainly carried less risk than being with the *maquis* or going underground.

Some strongly *Pétainiste* and authoritarian officials in occupied France excelled in their collaboration during 1944, regarding the resistance, as did all officials, as the real disturbers of order, and to be violently repressed. The new chief of police in Toulouse, in southern France, from April 1944, willingly embarked on joint operations with the German police against the local *maquis*, and very pointedly deployed the *Milice* and other auxiliary militias while sidelining the *gendarmerie*, which he regarded as unreliably hostile to undertaking anti-resistance activity. One could perhaps say that the *gendarmes* were not, in the end, unhappy about their exclusion. The new prefect of Tours, Ferdinand Musso, eagerly met a demand from the German regional military for him to provide a group of workers to clear up the damage caused by Allied bombing to the local railway station and airfield. This was in June 1944, with invasion imminent; he even arrested those workers who did not turn up.

Most officials decided to stay put, and to continue to collaborate in a way that took account of the changing and worsening circumstances of occupation. This involved coming to terms with, and having contact with, the resistance. Prefects in France were always well attuned to shifts in the political profile of their departments, and were required to adapt to them, as the representatives of the periphery to the centre, and the centre to the periphery. This might appear to be a cynical and opportunist changing of sides, but to the official it was a seamless transfer of loyalty to the coming power in the land. Papon exemplified the transition perfectly. He not only established his resistance credentials by harbouring a resistant colleague on the run, but also liaised beforehand with the Gaullist commissioner who took over and provisionally ran his region after the Allied liberation of France. This ensured that he was promoted prefect for the transitional post-liberation period, which proved to be the basis for a blossoming career in public service in the post-war period.

Lecornu remembered having several elliptical conversations with his minister, Laval, about his posting as a prefect to Corrèze, where the *maquis* was active, in July 1943. Laval's advice, as far as it could be discerned, was for Lecornu to try to stem the flow of violence in his new department and to restore a kind of order, implying that the use of the *Milice* and a counter-terror was probably not the best way to do it. Lecornu took the hint. He liaised with all sides, the local *maquis* (who were communist), the German military command, the *Gestapo*, and his own police chief, and eventually a *modus vivendi* was reached that would at least slow down the cycle of violence and counter-violence.

The communist resisters agreed to stop attacking the police, in return for the police chief withdrawing from a planned sweep of the countryside to root out the *maquis*. This was clearly meant to be an ongoing arrangement. Lecornu told the resistance leaders that he would not pass on information about police movements, if that intelligence resulted in resistance attacks on the *gendarmerie*. This might be a gloss on his own cleverness, but Lecornu portrayed himself as the man in the middle, keeping the peace and restoring order to his department by engaging with both the *Gestapo* and the *maquis*. To the *Gestapo*, he argued that he had to restrain the *Milice* because, otherwise, their deployment against the resistance and the complicit local population would rachet up the counterproductive cycle of violence and repression, and make the occupation even more insecure. To the *maquis*, Lecornu's advice was to abandon certain planned attacks on certain targets, since they would damage the interests of the local people who harboured them in their midst, if only by provoking German and *Milice* reprisals.

When Lecornu revealed this plague-on-all-your-houses strategy to Laval, the Interior Minister lit up another cigarette and said, 'You've got it right!'[12] Lecornu was, of course, 'collaborating' and 'resisting' simultaneously, but he was, above all, behaving as a prefect should, aligning himself to the forces that had power in his department in order to create and maintain an order that would allow the population to live more normally.

This was a matter of instinct and training for officials, who saw themselves as the only remaining embodiments of order in an increasingly chaotic situation. There was, of course, still plenty to do as the occupation came to an end. Hirschfeld, as ever true to what he considered to be his primary role as secretary general, to bring order where there was chaos, busied himself with practical, organizational humanitarian work after the country was split in two, part-liberated, part-occupied, throughout the quite dreadful winter of 1944–5.

Seyss-Inquart blockaded the liberated south, and directly diverted food supplies to meet the needs of the occupying German troops and officials. Hirschfeld not only protested against the Reich Commissioner's deliberate impoverishment of the Dutch population, but did something about it. He improvised a new body that commissioned and requisitioned available river and canal transport, in an attempt to ensure that scarce food and fuel supplies reached as many as possible. His attempt to re-create a centrally controlled and equitable food distribution system made him pretty unpopular with some mayors who were desperately seeking local emergency solutions to the problem of feeding their constituents. Hirschfeld's last stand won him the praise of the resistance, which scarcely helped his standing with the *Gestapo*. He continued to be contemptuous of the resistance and the disorder it generated by its activities, and continued to be true to himself as an impartial and competent official.

The only place to close this excursion into the outlook and mentality of officials in the latter stages of the occupation is occupied Belgium, where, arguably, officials experienced the worst of times throughout the occupation. In July 1944, the Nazi *Gauleiter* Josef Grohe replaced the German military governor as Reich Commissioner, and, in the following month, a Higher SS and Police Leader was appointed to run the policing of Belgium. It was all too late to make much difference, and Grohe sensibly retained the services of Reeder, to keep the secretaries general onside. Even so, the greater evil from which the secretaries general had spent the occupation claiming to protect the Belgian people had finally arrived.

At least one of the secretaries general, the pro-German De Winter, at the Ministry of Agriculture, wanted to resign over the Germans' direct requisitioning of foodstuffs to feed themselves. He was prevented from doing so by his colleagues: if you go, there will be total rather than relative chaos in food supply and distribution for the Belgian people; if you stay, there will be a modicum of order to the process. So, the deal is, you can contemplate resigning again, once the harvest is in. The prevailing majority view of the Belgian secretaries general was that they must stay on and collaborate.

And the justification? 'We must always act prudently', said the record of Plisnier's presidential address to a special meeting of the secretaries general committee on 21 July 1944, 'having in mind the general interest which we, more often than not, are the only ones capable of appreciating seriously'.[13] And then, with the Germans leaving Belgium in September 1944, the secretaries general again reassured themselves that they, alone, 'ensure the continuity of national life'.[14] The secretaries general were back in 1940 and at the same time, looking ahead to the period after Liberation. That certainty, that arrogance, of office, simultaneously the most and least attractive attribute of the top official, had carried them through and beyond the occupation. Nobody was better suited than they were to manage national emergencies and transitional upheavals.

This being Belgium, there was always an additional edge to things. The secretaries general were determined to stay on during the latter stages of the occupation because they had several points to prove to the government-in-exile, who, in fact, suspended them when the country was liberated. The government-in-exile had already, in May 1944, made its judgement on collaboration during the occupation. It ruled that the secretaries general had abused their powers under the 1940 legislation, and that all measures taken by them under those powers were illegal, unconstitutional, and invalid. This was more than the government-in-exile reclaiming its legitimacy. The secretaries general were furious, and responded in kind, arguing that the High Court judgment of March 1942 had vindicated their interpretation of the use of powers under the 1940 laws. Their final meetings as a committee spent some more time on their self-defence, and the stage was set for the prolongation of the bitter disputes between the government-in-exile and themselves over collaboration into the post-war years.

The point has been made that in 1944 officials who were regarded as unreliable were bypassed by the Germans, who increasingly relied on collaborationists to compel when before they had relied on officials to collaborate. This process went furthest in occupied France, where fascists and fellow-travellers actually entered Laval's government in key positions, Darnand as head of police, Déat as Minister of Labour, and Philippe Henriot as Minister of Information and Propaganda, and the *Milice* tackled the repression of the resistance. Being sidelined was not an option for industrial employers and their workers. Economic collaboration continued and intensified in 1943-4, as a result of Speer's production programmes. Through the protected factories scheme, employers could not only hold on to their skilled labour force, but also secure essential supplies of raw materials and fuel necessary to maintain production. The overall context, you might say, was against collaboration, since the war was being lost by Germany and occupation was becoming more repressive. But, economically, the will to collaborate remained strong on both sides, even though the ability to fulfil German contracts was constantly buffeted by the impact of Allied bombing raids and of the resistance's sabotage of plant and infrastructure. The decline in production levels in 1944-5, after they had peaked in spring 1944, was not down to a reluctance to collaborate, but rather to the disruption to supply and delivery caused by a broken distribution and transportation network.

How to continue production in the face of Allied bombing and sabotage was the problem that faced many employers dependent on military and military-related contracts. Peugeot was groomed by its German 'partner' or 'patron', *Volkswagenwerk*, for the uncongenial production of V1 rockets, the bright new weapon that was going to win the war for Germany. The management prevaricated over this, and nothing was ever done to develop the rocket in Peugeot factories. But, working almost exclusively on military contracts, the company was a natural target for bombing raids; one on its Sochaux factory killed and wounded over 250 workers. Company managers then agreed to what became common practice among some industrial employers, a deal with Allied agents and the resistance. The factory would allow or enable the sabotage of plant and machinery, in return for no more Allied bombing raids. There can be no doubt that production suffered as a result. In the year before Liberation, there were eighteen sabotage attacks on the factory, and on one occasion production was halted for three months. Any stop in production, of course, exposed workers to the Sauckel labour drafts. Peugeot, like other employers in the same position, kept paying the wages of redundant workers, and disguised the excess of workers by putting them on repair and maintenance tasks. Sometimes, they received reimbursement from the government after the end of the war for the additional costs incurred in keeping their workforce together and shielding them from deportation to Germany. It certainly earned the companies concerned some invaluable resistance credit.

Eventually, *Volkswagenwerk* abandoned the factory at Sochaux in May 1944, but dismantled machinery and transferred it to Germany. This was a big price to pay, the loss of the means of production, and one wonders whether this eventuality was factored into the management's calculation of risk. The deal over bombing and sabotage was one component of Peugeot's wider involvement in resistance. The company fed and clothed the *maquis*, provided resistance groups with vehicles, for which it again received payment, and gave information to the British secret service on *Volkswagenwerk* plans for V1 rocket production at Sochaux. It also placed workers evading the STO in other factories, or employed them as gardeners on factory allotments, and provided false IDs and work certificates.

Not all employers were open to such deals. Michelin refused to play, as did, of course, Berliet, twice. His factory was duly bombed in May 1944. We have here cases of major employers who willingly collaborated economically between 1940 and 1944, some of whom 'resisted' not so willingly in 1943–4. They were simultaneously 'collaborators' and 'resisters'. What are we to make of this? The first point is that collaboration and resistance were clearly *choices* made by each employer. Interestingly, the measurable and discernible element of constraint, of enforced choice, resided not in 'collaboration' but in 'resistance'. Again, all choices were made in a context. Employers clearly could not do away with Allied bombing or resistance sabotage. They were the inevitable consequences of Nazi Germany moving towards military defeat, and of the forthcoming, soon imminent, Allied liberation of occupied Western Europe. Just as German occupation was the reality to be adjusted to in 1940; so, now, in 1943–4, the coming end of occupation was the reality to be adjusted to. What determined the conduct of employers was the productive integrity of their companies, both now, and certainly in the circumstances of 1943–4, in the future.

So employers continued to produce for the Germans, since the fulfilment of these contracts guaranteed some continuity of production and, as important, the maintenance of productive capacity, in the form of a skilled workforce, machinery and plant. This was the easy choice to make. No employer thought that, because the Allies were winning the war, it was sensible to stop producing for the Germans. How an employer responded to the threat to production and productive capacity, the ability to produce in the future, posed by the Allies and the resistance, involved a fine consideration and calculation of alternatives and risk.

All employers were law-and-order men, and were natural authoritarians who regarded armed resistance as a disruptive force of disorder in society and in their factories. Berliet intransigently stuck to this view, and he was not about to be pushed around by anybody. He was not prepared to allow the resistance into his factories, and employed a *milicien* as his head of security to keep his workforce disciplined and on the job. He regarded bombing as inevitable, anyway, and estimated that it would require a lot of destruction to render his factories inoperable. The impact of a bombing raid was likely to be more haphazard than targeted internal sabotage of machinery and plant. Peugeot made the same calculation and reached a different conclusion. In their view, 'supervised' internal sabotage of the factory would do less permanent damage than 'guided' bombing. Again, they shared with Berliet the perception that the resistance would attempt to sabotage production, with or without the knowledge and connivance of employers and workers. Peugeot thought it was better with; Berliet thought that it was worth trying to keep the workforce disciplined and the resistance out. In his view, the resistance threat to his factory, and to his management of it, was greater than the bombing threat, the enemy within than the enemy without. More of his factory was likely to survive a bombing raid than sabotage.

As Berliet's painful post-war trial for economic collaboration demonstrated, his decision was, ultimately, not a wise one, and was, in terms of the future integrity of his business, disastrous. The second approach for a deal came from someone who claimed to be acting on behalf of the French provisional government in North Africa, who told Berliet that he was seen as a collaborator by this Gaullist shadow government in waiting. To survive the transition to the post-war Gaullist future, he needed to acquire some resistance credentials. This was something that struck a chord with all employers engaged in economic collaboration with the Germans.

The resistance could not be ignored; coming to an understanding with it, which they had to do, anyway, given its presence inside and outside the factory gates, provided an alibi that enabled employers to redeem their economic collaboration. The examples of this happening were legion. Take Henri Ardant, a white-collar employer as a banker, who both collaborated and resisted. A very visible collaborator, he was a regular presence at the Ritz meals laid on by the German military government in Paris to bring together in convivial surroundings German and Vichy ministers, officials, and businessmen. It was the ostentatious and public nature of his collaboration that seemed to annoy his investigators most in the post-war trials. Bousquet suffered in the same way because he and his wife had enjoyed nights out with SS officers. Ardant was the active 'Aryanizer' of the French banking profession, as the head of the CO for banks. But he also gave money to resistance organizations, sheltered resisters and evaders in his company, and again, as CO chief of banking, negotiated exemption of bank employees from the STO and Sauckel's labour conscriptions, eventually revoked by Déat in April 1944. As with Bousquet, his 'resistance' compensated for his collaboration, resulting in three non-lieux verdicts in post-war High Court trials and purges.

Businessmen and financiers were 'patriots' in 1940 by collaborating to get the national economy back on its feet. They were 'patriots' in 1944 by resisting to rid the country of its foreign occupier, and by being in a position to contribute to post-war recovery and reconstruction. When the Belgian and Dutch governments-in-exile began to finance selected internal resistance groups in 1943, they did so on credit, using the banks in situ to forward cash to the resistance on the promise of repayment after the war. Many employers funded resistance groups and individual resisters on their own account, of course. But the government-in-exile's initiatives to foster resistance gave firms and financial institutions a direct material stake in liberation, and made resistance, like collaboration, a commercial transaction. They also provided political and patriotic credibility to the employers' acts of resistance, which ensured the latter's economic standing in the post-war world.

In a real sense, the categories of 'collaboration' and 'resistance' are simply redundant here, in terms of understanding why people behaved as they did. All the terms do is camouflage what happened. Many employers helped their workers to avoid the Sauckel labour drafts, in order to retain their own productive capacity. This was 'resistance', and certainly counted as such after the war. But those same workers were then reintegrated into their workforces when the employers' factories became *S-betriebe*, and working on German contracts was, of course, 'collaboration'. Peugeot and Berliet conducted themselves throughout as employers, which meant they collaborated and resisted, or not, depending on their calculation of what best served the interests of the company, both currently, and especially in the future.

In the end, this was what connected the conduct of officials and employers during the war. They were, throughout the occupation, consistently true to themselves and to their professions. They were really 'patriotic' about their office and their business, and the continuity and worth of their office and business. Papon and Peugeot made different choices to Bichelonne and Berliet, with very different consequences for the future, but they all made those choices on the same ground and from the same perspective.

Conclusion
Officials Will Be Officials

In his final radio broadcast to the French people in August 1944, as he was being taken by the Germans into protective custody in Germany, Pétain made an eloquent, dignified, and disingenuous defence of his collaboration. 'If I could not be your sword,' he said, 'I tried to be your shield...I held off from you some certain dangers; there were others...I could not spare you'.[1] The analogy was developed in a statement made at his trial in 1945: 'I used my power as a shield to protect the French people...every day, a dagger at my throat, I struggled against the enemy's demands...While General de Gaulle carried on the struggle outside our frontiers, I prepared the way for liberation by preserving France, suffering but alive.'[2] It is hardly any wonder that the 'sword–shield' combination has been used to justify collaboration, generally. The 1960s historiography of the occupation in Norway was very much based on a view of collaborating officials as auxiliaries of the resistance movement, since they were collaborating in order to resist, and to resist in the only way open to them, which was 'passively'. Even de Gaulle found the argument compelling.

The problem is that Pétain's self-defence provides no explanation, let alone justification, of Vichy's collaboration with the Germans, nor of the National Revolution. We know that Pétain had fewer expectations of collaboration than Laval and Darlan. But his final words do not illuminate the collaboration mooted at Montoire, nor the collaboration embarked on by the Laval and Darlan governments. They collaborated willingly with Nazi Germany in order to secure an independent and imperial France a proper place in the Nazi New Order. Laval and Darlan, anyway, waved their swords, rather than buckling on their shields. They always saw collaboration as an offensive weapon, not a defensive one.

Pétain's sword and shield imagery might apply better to the collaboration practised in the occupied territories where officials administered countries in the name of absent governments. Belgium was admittedly the extreme case of a contested occupation. But it is difficult to see how the Belgian government-in-exile would ever have seen the secretaries general and Galopin as the Belgian 'shield', when they entertained the damaging expectation that these officials should actually be Belgium's 'sword'. We can, at least, dispel the illusion built into the analogy, of collaboration being the product of compulsion or constraint. There was no 'dagger at the throat'. The only constraint that existed was occupation, and it was certainly possible to arrive at choices in such an unavoidably constrained situation. Within the framework of occupation, officials and businessmen collaborated willingly and for a definite and rational purpose. And where exactly was the constraint to collaborate when the Vichy government ran the 'free zone' up to late 1942, and the Danish government ran all of Denmark until late 1943?

One has to say that, if collaboration is to be judged by its outcomes, then it certainly delivered. This is admittedly a difficult argument to make in respect of Vichy France. Pétain gave the impression that he had saved France from being treated like Poland. Some Nazi leaders considered the possibility, even the likelihood, of erasing France as a European and global power. But that realization gave yet more impetus and point to Vichy's attempts to find a place for itself in a world dominated by Germany, and to do so through state-to-state collaboration. The stakes of collaboration were so high in Vichy France, higher than anywhere else in occupied Western Europe, as to make their aims unrealizable in a Nazi-run Europe. But that did not stop Laval and Darlan from trying, even if the only really tangible gain of collaboration was the recognition by at least some German leaders that France could become a valuable and functioning partner in the *Grossraumwirtschaft*.

The Danish government collaborated in order to retain its independence and the political system that defined that independence, for as long as it was possible. The results were spectacular, especially when compared to the other occupied territories where collaboration occurred on a different basis. Denmark's democratic parliamentary system survived more or less intact until late 1943, despite the political pressures exerted on the government by a nominally hands-off German occupier. There was no 'final solution' in Denmark until late 1943, and its less than 'final' outcome was largely down to the lateness of its implementation. There was no deportation of labour in Denmark at any point of its occupation, and economic collaboration proceeded breezily along even after the late 1943 shenanigans.

With their governments in exile, officials in occupied Norway, Belgium, and the Netherlands adopted the view that by their very presence alone they could prevent worse. The worse amounted to the imposition of a Nazi revolution and incorporation into a Greater Germanic Reich through German proxies, the national fascist parties and movements. The NS came to power under the Reich Commissariat in Norway. But this was more the unintended result of Terboven's botched attempts to mange the transition to occupation. The NSB got no further than an advisory role to the Reich Commissariat, while, in Belgium, the German military government gave way only at the last moment to a Reich Commissioner.

The Galopin committee defended its activities in a final report submitted to the government-in-exile, which had given it so much grief throughout the occupation, in October 1944, after the Liberation. It referred to what might have happened if the 'policy of production' had not been followed, and if it had obeyed the government's eventual injunction to repeat the First World War experience and 'abstain'. In their judgement, being present rather than absent prevented the total 'Germanization' of the Belgian economy, and indeed the dissolution of the Belgian state. This was actually the case, just. They might have added that, without economic collaboration, the Belgian people would not have been fed.

This kind of judgement is always open to the counter-argument that economic collaboration kept the war going, and kept the occupation going, with all the possible, or likely, consequences for the livelihood and security of the occupied peoples, and for the very survival and integrity of occupied countries in the event of Nazi Germany winning the war. Governments and top officials knew and acknowledged what was at stake, in choosing whether to collaborate or not. In Belgium, especially, officials and businessmen who had lived through the experience of German occupation in the First World War knew what the 'greater evil' was, and the appalling consequences for the Belgian people of the refusal to collaborate with the occupier. In the Belgian case, I would say that it was understandable that the government-in-exile, initially, and the country's administration, throughout the occupation, decided to collaborate. Most of them saw collaboration as a way of avoiding, or mitigating, not a hypothetical but an actual or imminent national catastrophe.

The same perceptions were shared by officials in the other occupied territories, and similarly determined their decision to collaborate, and to continue to collaborate. They realized that they had some leverage with the Germans, largely deriving from the occupier's sense that local collaboration was necessary and desirable in order to carry out occupation policies. When the Germans decided to take what they wanted, anyway, or threatened to do so, then the officials' response was usually to abandon any responsibility for the measures, but exercise what influence they could over the process, by, for instance, applying for exemptions to the measures. Being able to do this was dependent on continuing collaboration.

We can, perhaps, after the event, be critical of those perceptions, and argue that they were an exaggerated view of reality. But, at the time, the circumstances and sense of what would happen if they behaved differently, which shaped those perceptions, seemed 'real' enough. We do also have to accept that, in some cases, the 'worse' that collaboration was intended to prevent eventually occurred. In other words, collaboration was futile. Officials knew this, too, and took the view that it was, in these circumstances, their duty to stay in office and attempt to delay, deflect, and mitigate the consequences of the 'worse' happening. From the perspective of officials, when the 'worse' happened, collaboration was demonstrably achieving less, but the small gains possible were worth the continuation of collaboration.

The occupier's response to the difficulties of enacting measures that were unpalatable to officials and the occupied populations was, increasingly, to move the execution of such policies from those who collaborated to mitigate to those who were collaborationist; and there were *some* collaborationist officials. This explains why both governments-in-exile and state officials continually invoked the argument of the 'lesser evil'. It was demonstrably the case that it was 'better' to entrust the administration of the country to collaborators rather than to collaborationists. If, however, you think that the default mode of officials and businessmen should have been, not collaboration, but resistance, given the nature of Nazism and what was likely to happen if Nazi Germany won the war, then these explanations of collaborating behaviour must be incomprehensible.

These explanations do not suffice, when applied to the Vichy government's handling of the 'Jewish question' in France. Here, the Vichy government instructed its officials and policemen to enact discriminatory anti-Semitic laws and regulations. It then required their participation in the process of arresting and deporting foreign Jews and 'criminal' French Jews, as part of a wider strategy of collaboration, through which it intended to secure a place for an independent France in the Nazi New Order. There was no official will to protect foreign and refugee Jews from the 'final solution'. Vichy even denaturalized immigrant and refugee Jews who had become national citizens. It baulked only at the large-scale deportation of French Jews, once it became evident that the expected gains of that wider strategy were not forthcoming. French officials collaborated in the persecution of Jews because it was state policy to do so, and they were dutiful servants of the state.

Some readers will have found this book rather repetitive, but that is because collaboration was repetitive, even addictive. The approach has been to deal with collaboration as a series of set pieces, or tableaux, in order to ensure that we can evaluate the point and purpose of collaboration in a changing context. We have to realize that officials made decisions in real time and in real circumstances, on issues as they arose, and that, on each occasion, they had to balance out the arguments for and against collaboration. What becomes clear was that, even as the context changed, officials (and governments), after considerable deliberation and, in the Belgian case, sometimes agonized debate and discussion, came to the conclusion that more was to be gained and less was to be lost by continuing to collaborate.

One must emphasize that collaboration was a relationship between collaborators and occupier. It was an unequal relationship, because of defeat and occupation, and its imbalances led to officials doing the dirty work of the occupier, as with the deportation of Jews and workers. It is usually around these issues that moral judgements about officials' conduct are made, both then and now. Visser was removed as president of the Dutch High Court for being a Jew early in 1941, and complained to his fellow Jew, David Cohen, about the lack of response to his dismissal, arguing that, in respect of illegal and evil measures, 'resistance . . . was a moral duty even if it did not affect the outcome'.[3] Cohen was the wrong person to speak to; he was co-director of the Jewish Council in the Netherlands, which was almost totally compliant in its handling of the German deportation of Dutch and foreign Jews. But officials *did* do their 'moral duty' in protesting against what they regarded as illegal and unconstitutional measures against Jewish citizens, even though they knew that their objections would hardly affect what the Germans intended to do. When, quite rightly, the default position of officials was collaboration, not resistance, the need then was to ensure that their protests on a matter of principle did not prevent them from continuing to collaborate in practice on a whole range of other issues. As officials, that was how they interpreted their 'moral duty'. It was at least on a par with how those guardians of public morality, the Catholic Church, responded to the deportation of Jews.

The collaborating relationship worked and persisted because the occupying authorities themselves recognized its value and purpose. In other words, collaboration was willed by the occupier, as it was by the collaborators, and this made a difference to what happened. Natural alliances formed between officials on both sides, often working together to mitigate the impact of policies that Reich agencies wanted to impose on the occupied territories. Even the SS in France compromised on the pace and direction of the 'final solution', if never on the finality of the aim. They acknowledged the strength of the argument constantly put to them by the military governor and French officials that even the 'final solution' should proceed in a way that did not put at risk the continuation of the occupation through collaboration. It was this dual commitment to the process of collaboration that ensured that it continued.

Practically every testimony in the Hoover collection is laden with retrospective self-justification and denial. But when Elmar Michel, the career Economics Ministry official who ran the military government of occupied France's economic department and then, from September 1942, the military administration itself, recalled that he had overseen 'a productive collaboration determined by shared practical tasks',[4] you feel that he actually meant it, and he had got it at least partly right.

The argument about collaboration in this book rests on treating officials and businessmen as members of a group with a group mentality, not as individuals. Criminal gangs can be analysed and understood in the same way, of course. This generalizing approach not only makes manageable the writing of their history during the occupation. Otherwise, one would be left with trying to make sense of an accumulation of individual sets of motivation. It also corresponds, I think, to what lay behind their behaviour.

The overwhelming majority of top officials collaborated, which at the very least indicates that they did so for general rather than individual reasons. These officials had a well-developed *esprit de corps*, their own shield and security when times were hard, and their choices difficult. The secretaries general often disagreed with each other, and, in the Belgian case, to the point of near rupture. This was because many of their decisions straddled the Fleming–Walloon divide and affected the present and future of Belgium as a country and a state. One cannot dispute the judgement that Schuind ran his Ministry of Justice in a very different way from Romsée at the Interior. Nevertheless, the line held. The committees of the secretaries general in both Belgium and the Netherlands evolved into a form of cabinet government, where something approaching collective responsibility prevailed. Even when they differed sharply during their committee meetings, the airing of their differences acted as a kind of catharsis. They usually arrived at a common position, even if it was to procrastinate and discuss things further, and, in effect, do nothing. Whatever their internal disagreements, they cohered around a policy of continuing collaboration. When the Belgian Secretary General for Agriculture, De Winter, wanted to resign towards the very end of the occupation, he was persuaded by his colleagues to stay on, in order that the government administration could demonstrate sufficient unity of purpose to see the country through the transition to another occupation, and then the coming of peace.

Employers were more individualistic in outlook. But, again, most of those whose products were wanted by the Germans decided to collaborate economically. Even the few big names that did not produce for the Germans arguably did not do so for what they regarded as good business reasons. For all their individualism, employers mixed and networked with each other, both informally and through formal mechanisms such as the cartel, the employers' association, and the wartime bodies that regulated their conduct and economic activity. They were aware of each others' concerns, if only because of a need to match their competitors. They were accustomed to operating together and protecting common interests in both the relative freedom of peacetime markets, and the unavoidable restrictions (and opportunities) of wartime economic regulation.

The undeniable fact that most officials and businessmen acted in the same way during the occupation, and collaborated, shows that each group shared common and collective interests and aims, and acted more or less in unison to protect those interests and realize those aims. With officials, I would say that this was both self-evident, and natural to them, integral to their sense of themselves as state and public officials. It was not that they were automatons, or ceased to be single men, or married men with families, or Catholic or Protestant, or right wing or left wing. But the determining elements of their conduct as officials during the occupation was their way of looking at the world, and rearranging it, which they developed as trained and practising officials.

In a sense, this meant that officials and businessmen had their choices during the occupation narrowed down by the nature and responsibilities of their professions, to what they perceived as service to the public interest, and to the future and integrity of their enterprises. Arguably, individual citizens had more options available to them in the course of the occupation. When the priority was survival for themselves and their families in dangerous and penurious circumstances, they could, and did, act inconsistently (both 'collaborating' and 'resisting'), and extraordinarily (both consumers and providers in a black market). They could even, sometimes, choose to do nothing at all, in order to survive.

As I hope is evident from the way I have quoted and analysed some of the top officials' more authoritarian and technocratic rationales for their behaviour, I do find in the occupation experience a historical validation of democratic politics over authoritarian administration by an enlightened and expert elite. Those who want to drive the 'politics' out of government, and this is a stance usually found among people on the right of the political spectrum, would do well to consider what rule by officials entailed during the occupation.

Officials and businessmen behaved during the occupation as officials and businessmen. Bichelonne was not the kind of official who could heed the advice of his friend and colleague Lehideux to the effect that there were problems that even he could not resolve. Their behaviour was to be expected, and they did not disappoint; this was how they behaved. Perhaps it was too much to expect that they behaved otherwise, as human beings.

Notes

PREFACE

1. Michael L. Smith, 'Neither Resistance nor Collaboration: Historians and the Problem of the *Nederlandse Unie*', *History*, 72 (1987), 251–78.

INTRODUCTION: DEALING WITH THE PAST

1. See Philippe Burrin, *Living with Defeat: France under the German Occupation, 1940–1944*, pt II, 'Accommodations' (London: Arnold, 1996). Also, Jan Gross, 'Themes for a Social History of War Experience and Collaboration', in István Deák, Jan Gross, and Tony Judt (eds), *The Politics of Retribution in Europe: World War II and its Aftermath* (Princeton: Princeton University Press, 2000), 31, and p. 35 n. 48.
2. See Uffe Østergård, 'Swords, Shields, or Collaborators? Danish Historians and the Debate over the German Occupation of Denmark', in Henrik Stenius, Mirja Österberg, and Johan Östling (eds), *Nordic Narratives of the Second World War: National Historiographies Revisited* (Lund: Nordic Academic Press, 2011), 33.
3. Quoted in Richard Overy, 'Business in the *Grossraumwirtschaft*: Eastern Europe, 1938–1945', in Harold James and Jacob Tanner (eds), *Enterprise in the Period of Fascism in Europe* (Aldershot: Ashgate, 2002), 172.
4. See István Deák, 'Introduction', in Deák, Gross, and Judt (eds), *The Politics of Retribution in Europe*, 7.
5. Quoted in Simon Kitson, 'From Enthusiasm to Disenchantment: The French Police and the Vichy Regime, 1940–1944', *Contemporary European History*, 11/3 (2002), 382.
6. Burrin, *Living with Defeat*, 207.
7. The speech is mentioned in Wendy Burke, 'A Dutch Occupation: The Representation of World War II in Films from the Netherlands, 1962–1986' (Ph.D. dissertation, King's College, London, 2009), 106–7; included in *Images of Occupation in Dutch Film* (Amsterdam: Amsterdam University Press, 2017), ch. 1.
8. See Pieter Lagrou, *The Legacy of Nazi Occupation: Patriotic Memory and National Recovery in Western Europe, 1945–1965* (Cambridge: Cambridge University Press, 2007), especially ch. 1.
9. Quoted in Colin Nettlebeck, 'Getting the Story Right: Narratives of the Second World War in Post-1968 France', in Gerhard Hirschfeld and Patrick Marsh (eds), *Collaboration in France: Politics and Culture during the Nazi Occupation, 1940–1944* (Oxford: Berg, 1989), 268.

10. See Burke, *Images of Occupation*.

11. Pascal Ory, *Les Collaborateurs, 1940–1945* (Paris: Éditions du Seuil, 1976), 10.

12. See Václav Havel, 'The Power of the Powerless', in John Keane (ed.), *The Power of the Powerless: Citizens against the State in Central-Eastern Europe* (London: Hutchinson, 1985), 23–96.

1. STARTING AT THE END: LIBERATION AND THE POST-WAR PURGES OF COLLABORATORS

1. Quoted in Martin Conway, 'Justice in Post-War Belgium: Popular Passions and Political Realities', in Deák, Gross, and Judt (eds), *The Politics of Retribution*, 146.

2. The figure used by Tony Judt, 'The Past Is Another Country: Myth and Memory in Postwar Europe', in Deák, Gross, and Judt (eds), *The Politics of Retribution*, 301.

3. See Peter Novick, *The Resistance versus Vichy: The Purge of Collaborators in Liberated France* (New York: Columbia University Press, 1968), 26–7.

4. Novick, *The Resistance versus Vichy*, 187.

5. See Luc Huyse, 'The Criminal Justice System as a Political Actor in Regime Transitions: The Case of Belgium, 1944–50', in Deák, Gross, and Judt (eds), *The Politics of Retribution*, 162; Richard Overy, 'Scandinavia in the Second World War', in John Gilmour and Jill Stephenson (eds), *Hitler's Scandinavian Legacy: The Consequences of the German Invasion for the Scandinavian Countries, Then and Now* (London: Bloomsbury, 2014), 32.

6. Henri Rousso, *The Vichy Syndrome: History and Memory in France since 1944* (Cambridge, MA, and London: Harvard University Press, 1991), 8.

7. Henry L. Mason, *The Purge of Dutch Quislings: Emergency Justice in the Netherlands* (The Hague: Martinus Nijhoff, 1952), 101.

8. Mark Van den Wijngaert, *L'Économie belge sous l'occupation: La Politique d'Alexandre Galopin, gouverneur de la Société Générale* (Paris-Louvain-la-Neuve: Duculot, 1990), 126; Jacques Willequet, *La Belgique sous la botte: Résistances et collaborations, 1940–1945* (Paris: Éditions Universitaires, 1986), 68.

9. Harald Espeli, 'The German Occupation and its Consequences for the Composition and Changes of Norwegian Business Elites', *Jahrbuch für Wirtschaftsgeschichte*, 2 (2010), 121–2.

10. François Rouquet, *L'Épuration dans l'administration française: Agents de l'état et collaboration ordinaire* (Paris: CNRS Éditions, 1993), 114–15.

11. Marnix Croes, 'The Dutch Police Force and the Persecution of Jews in the Netherlands during the German Occupation, 1940–1945', in Bruno de Wever, Herman Van Goethem, and Nico Wouters (eds), *Local Government in Occupied Europe (1939–1945)* (Ghent: Academia Press, 2008), 76–8.

12. Carl Christian Givskov, 'Danish "Purge Laws"', *Journal of Criminal Law and Criminology*, 39/4 (1948), 458.

13. Pierre Vermeylen, 'The Punishment of Collaborators', *Annals of the American Academy of Political and Social Science*, 247 (1946), 77.

14. Espeli, 'The German Occupation', 119.
15. Peter Romijn, '"Restoration of Confidence": The Purge of Local Government in the Netherlands as a Problem of Postwar Reconstruction', in Deák, Gross, and Judt (eds), *The Politics of Retribution*, 188.
16. Lagrou, *The Legacy of Nazi Occupation*, 54.
17. See Burrin, *Living with Defeat*, 460.
18. Hoover Institute, *La Vie de la France sous l'occupation (1940–1944)*, 3 vols (Paris: Librairie Plon, 1957).
19. Per H. Hansen, 'Dealing with the Problem of Business and German Hegemony, 1939–1945', in Joachim Lund (ed.). *Working for the New Order: European Business under German Domination, 1939–1945* (Copenhagen: University Press of Southern Denmark and Copenhagen Business School Press, 2006), 175.

2. THE NATURE OF THE BEAST: THE NAZI NEW ORDER, AND THE NAZI OCCUPATION OF NORTHERN AND WESTERN EUROPE

1. From the record of a meeting in July 1941, reproduced in Walter Lipgens (ed.), *Documents on the History of European Integration*, i, *Continental Plans for European Union, 1939–1945* (Berlin and New York: de Gruyter, 1985), 85.
2. Göring to Funk, August 1940, in Jeremy Noakes and Geoffrey Pridham (eds), *Nazism, 1919–1945: A Documentary Reader*, iii. *Foreign Policy, War and Racial Extermination* (Liverpool: Liverpool University Press, 2014), 282–3.
3. Quoted in Alan Milward, *The New Order and the French Economy* (Aldershot: Gregg Revivals, 1993), 77.
4. Noakes and Pridham (eds), *Nazism*, iii. 902.
5. Quoted in Alan Milward, *The Fascist Economy in Norway* (Oxford: Clarendon Press, 1972), 134–5.
6. Noakes and Pridham (eds), *Nazism*, iii. 894–5.
7. Quoted in Robert E. Herzstein, *When Nazi Dreams Come True* (London: Abacus, 1982), 5.
8. Quoted in Norman Rich, *Hitler's War Aims*, ii. *The Establishment of the New Order* (New York: W. W. Norton, 1974), 198.
9. See the German Foreign Ministry report on Denmark, October 1942, reproduced in Margaret Carlyle (ed.), *Documents on International Affairs, 1939–1946*, ii. *Hitler's Europe* (London: Oxford University Press, 1954), 220–1.

3. COLLABORATION WITH THE GRAIN OF OCCUPATION, 1940–1942

1. Robert Gildea, *Marianne in Chains: In Search of German Occupation, 1940–1943* (London: Macmillan, 2002), 381.
2. Paul Struye, *L'Évolution du sentiment public en Belgique sous l'occupation allemande* (Brussels: Les Éditions Lumière, 1945), 17.

3. Struye, *L'Évolution du sentiment public*, 17.

4. Struye, *L'Évolution du sentiment public*, 20.

5. Henri Frenay, *The Night Will End* (London: Abelard, 1976), 106.

6. Quoted in Gerhard Hirschfeld, *Nazi Rule and Dutch Collaboration: The Netherlands under German Occupation, 1940–1945* (Oxford: Berg, 1988), 55.

7. Quoted in Geoffrey Warner, *Pierre Laval and the Eclipse of France* (London: Eyre and Spottiswoode, 1968), 190.

8. See Dominique Veillon, *La Collaboration: Textes et débats* (Paris: Librairie Générale Française, 1984), 72.

9. Quoted in Veillon, *La Collaboration*, 74.

10. Henri du Moulin de Labarthète, *Le Temps des illusions: Souvenirs (juillet 1940–avril 1942)* (Brussels: La Diffusion du Livre, 1947), 289.

11. See Veillon, *La Collaboration*, 77.

12. Reproduced in Veillon, *La Collaboration*, 80–1.

13. Quoted in Veillon, *La Collaboration*, 75.

14. Quoted in Warner, *Pierre Laval and the Eclipse of France*, 232.

15. See article by Peter Bradshaw in the *Guardian 2*, 20 June 2014.

16. Quoted in Veillon, *La Collaboration*, 74.

17. See Bouthillier's testimony in Hoover Institute, *La Vie de la France sous l'occupation*, iii. 1421.

18. du Moulin de Labarthète, *Le Temps des illusions*, 43.

19. See Carlyle (ed.), *Documents*, ii. *Hitler's Europe*, 125.

20. Quoted in Veillon, *La Collaboration*, 74.

21. du Moulin de Labarthète, *Le Temps des illusions*, 43.

22. See Jules Gérard-Libois and José Gotovich, *L'An 40: La Belgique occupée* (Brussels: CRISP, 1980), 220–3.

23. You can follow the crisis in his diary entries for the May to November 1940 period, in Paul Struye, *Journal de guerre, 1940–1945* (Brussels: Éditions Racine, 2004), 62–167.

24. Quoted in Hirschfeld, *Nazi Rule and Dutch Collaboration*, 59.

25. See Hirschfeld, *Nazi Rule and Dutch Collaboration*, 70–1; Smith, 'Neither Resistance nor Collaboration', 255–8.

26. Quoted in Gerhard Hirschfeld, 'Collaboration and Attentism in the Netherlands, 1940–1', *Journal of Contemporary History*, 16 (1981), 480.

27. Quoted in Hirschfeld, 'Collaboration and Attentism', 481.

28. See, e.g., clause 15 of these instructions, reproduced in Johannes Jacobus van Bolhuis (ed.), *Onderdrukking en verzet: Nederland in Oorlogstijd (Oppression and Resistance: The Netherlands in Wartime)*, i (Amsterdam: Van Loghum Slaterus, 1955), 387–94 (translated by Wendy Burke and Rob Riemsma).

29. Quoted in Marc Olivier Baruch, *Servir l'état français: L'Administration en France de 1940 à 1944* (Paris: Fayard, 1997), 225.

30. Quoted in Baruch, *Servir l'état français*, 215; see Bouthillier's circular to officials, reproduced in the appendix to Baruch, *Servir l'état français*, 646.

31. Quoted in Baruch, *Servir l'état français*, 215.

32. See article 3 of the Armistice, on the Avalon Project <http://avalon.law.yale.edu/wwii.frgarm.asp> (accessed October 2009).

33. See Carlyle (ed.), *Documents*, ii. *Hitler's Europe*, 202.

34. See Carlyle (ed.), *Documents*, ii. *Hitler's Europe*, 202–4.

35. See Carlyle (ed.), *Documents*, ii. *Hitler's Europe*, 203.

36. See the text of the Hague Convention on the Avalon Project <http://avalon.law.yale.edu/20th_century/hague04.asp> (accessed October 2009).

37. Carlyle (ed.), *Documents*, ii. *Hitler's Europe*, 204.

38. See van Bolhuis (ed.), *Onderdrukking en verzet*, i. 388, 395.

39. van Bolhuis (ed.), *Onderdrukking en verzet*, i. 394.

40. van Bolhuis (ed.), *Onderdrukking en verzet*, i. 396.

41. See exchange of letters in Jean-Léon Charles and Philippe Dasnoy (eds), *Les Secrétaires généraux face à l'occupant: Procès-verbaux des réunions du Comité des Secrétaires généraux (1940–1944)* (Brussels: Lucien de Meyer, 1974), 35–8.

42. Charles and Dasnoy (eds), *Les Secrétaires généraux*, 43.

43. Quoted in Van den Wijngaert, *L'Économie belge sous l'occupation*, 13.

4. ECONOMIC COLLABORATION, 1940–1942

1. See his testimony in Hoover Institute, *La Vie de la France sous l'occupation*, i. 194.

2. Quoted in Peter F. Klemm, 'La Production aéronautique française de 1940 à 1942', *Revue d'Histoire de la Deuxième Guerre Mondiale*, 27/107 (1977), 38.

3. See Burrin, *Living with Defeat*, 28.

4. See Joachim Lund, 'Business Elite Networks in Denmark: Adjusting to German Domination', in Lund (ed.), *Working for the New Order*, 123.

5. See Gérard-Libois and Gotovich, *L'An 40*, 179.

6. Quoted in Pietro Melograni, *Gli industriali e Mussolini: Rapporti fra Confindustria e Fascismo dal 1919 al 1929* (Milan: Longanesi, 1972), 45.

7. Quoted in Renaud de Rochebrune and Jean-Claude Hazera, *Les Patrons sous l'occupation*, i. *Face aux allemands: Collaboration, résistance, marché noir* (Paris: Odile Jacob, 1995), 160.

8. Quoted in Rochebrune and Hazera, *Les Patrons sous l'occupation*, i. 64.

9. Quoted in Rochebrune and Hazera, *Les Patrons sous l'occupation*, i. 121.

10. Quoted in Michel Margairaz, 'L'État et la décision économique: Constraintes, convergences, résistances', in Jean-Pierre Azéma and François Bédarida (eds), *Le Régime de Vichy et les français* (Paris: Fayard, 1992), 339.

11. See Joachim Lund, 'Building Hitler's Europe: Forced Labour in the Danish Construction Business during World War II', *Business History Review*, 87/3 (2010), 493.

12. Quoted in Philip Giltner, *'In the Friendliest Manner': German–Danish Economic Cooperation during the Nazi Occupation of 1940–1945* (New York: Peter Lang, 1998), 76.

13. See Henning Poulsen, 'Le Danemark: Une collaboration d'état sans idéologie', in Azéma and Béderida (eds), *Le Régime de Vichy et les français*, 720.

14. Quoted in Giltner, *'In the Friendliest Manner'*, 118.
15. Quoted in Jacques Benoist-Méchin, *De la défaite au désastre*, i. *Les Occasions manquées, juillet 1940–avril 1942* (Paris: Abin Michel, 1984), 322.
16. Quoted in Patrick Facon and Françoise de Ruffray, 'Aperçus sur la collaboration aéronautique Franco-Allemande (1940–1943)', *Revue d'histoire de la Deuxième Guerre Mondiale*, 27/108 (1977), 90.
17. See Benoist-Méchin, *De la défaite au désastre*, i. 89.
18. Quoted in Benoist-Méchin, *De la défaite au désastre*, i. 102.
19. See Struye, *Journal de guerre*, 172, entry for 19 December 1940.
20. See Struye, *Journal de guerre*, 246, entry for 13 November 1941.
21. See his report of June 1941, in Struye, *L'Évolution du sentiment public*, 69.
22. Quoted in Jean-François Crombois, 'Les Limites de la "gestion conservatoire": Les Divergences entre Londres et Bruxelles sur la collaboration économique en Belgique occupée', in Olivier Dard, Jean-Claude Daumas, and François Marcot (eds), *L'Occupation, l'état français et les entreprises* (Paris: ADHE, 2000), 44.
23. From the testimony of Pierre de Calan, in Hoover Institute, *La Vie de la France sous l'occupation*, i. 31.

5. THE COLLABORATION OF OFFICIALS, 1940–1942

1. Quoted in Nathalie Carré de Malberg, 'Les Inspecteurs des finances sous l'occupation: Les Passages de l'entreprise à l'état', in Dard, Daumas, and Marcot (eds), *L'Occupation, l'état français et les entreprises*, 274.
2. See René Belin, *Du secrétariat de la CGT au gouvernement de Vichy* (Paris: Éditions Albatross, 1978), 135.
3. Belin, *Du secrétariat de la CGT*, 147.
4. Quoted in Warner, *Pierre Laval and the Eclipse of France*, 246.
5. Belin, *Du secrétariat de la CGT*, 137.
6. The story comes from the acid memoir of Joseph Barthélemy, *Ministre de la Justice: Vichy, 1941–1943: Mémoires* (Paris: Pygmalion and Gérard Watelot, 1989), 622.
7. See Barthélemy, *Ministre de la Justice*, 622.
8. Pierre Pucheu, *Ma vie* (Paris: Amiot-Dumont, 1948), 255.
9. See Meindert Fennema, 'Max Hirschfeld, Secretary-General of a Decapitated Ministry (1940–1945)', in Madelon de Keizer, Mariska Heijmans-van Brugen, and Erik Somers (eds), *Onrecht: Oorlog en rechtvaardigheid in de twintigste eeuw* (Zütphen: Walburg, 2001), 155.
10. Quoted in Baruch, *Servir l'état français*, 190.
11. Quoted in Baruch, *Servir l'état français*, 337.
12. Quoted in Jean Mièvre, 'L'Évolution politique d'Abel Bonnard (jusqu'au printemps 1942)', *Revue d'histoire de la Deuxième Guerre Mondiale*, 27/108 (1977), 23.
13. Quoted in Hirschfeld, *Nazi Rule and Dutch Collaboration*, 149.
14. See van Bolhuis (ed.), *Onderdrukking en verzet*, i. 387.

15. See Charles and Dasnoy (eds), *Les Secrétaires généraux*, 123.

16. Quoted in Niels Aage Skov, 'The Use of Historical Myth: Denmark's World War II Experience Made to Serve Practical Goals', *Scandinavian Studies*, 72/1, 2000, 93.

17. Quoted in Barthélemy, *Ministre de la Justice*, 245.

18. See du Moulin de Labarthète, *Le Temps des illusions*, 335–6.

19. du Moulin de Labarthète, *Le Temps des illusions*, 334.

20. See Charles and Dasnoy (eds), *Les Secrétaires généraux*, 119.

21. See Charles and Dasnoy (eds), *Les Secrétaires généraux*, 60.

22. See Struye, *Journal de guerre*, 145–6, entry for 12 October 1940.

23. Quoted in Jørgen Glenthøj, 'The Little Dunkerque: The Danish Rescue of Jews in October 1943', in Michael D. Ryan (ed.), *Human Responses to the Holocaust: Perpetrators and Victims, Bystanders and Resisters* (New York and Toronto: Edwin Mellen Press, 1981), 96.

24. Quoted in Michael R. Marrus and Robert O. Paxton, *Vichy France and the Jews* (New York: Basic Books, 1981), 77.

25. See Baruch, *Servir l'état français*, 118.

26. See Gildea, *Marianne in Chains*, 231–2.

27. See Raul Hilberg, *Perpetrators, Victims, Bystanders: The Jewish Catastrophe, 1933–1945* (New York: Harper Collins, 1993), ch. 7.

28. Quoted in Bob Moore, 'Nazi Masters and Accommodating Dutch Bureaucrats: "Working towards the Führer" in the Occupied Netherlands, 1940–1945', in Anthony McElligot and Tim Kirk (eds), *Working towards the Führer: Essays in Honour of Sir Ian Kershaw* (Manchester: Manchester University Press, 2003), 198.

29. See Bob Moore, *Victims and Survivors: The Nazi Persecution of the Jews in the Netherlands, 1940–1945* (London: Arnold, 1997), 56.

30. See Hirschfeld, *Nazi Rule and Dutch Collaboration*, 144.

31. See Hirschfeld, *Nazi Rule and Dutch Collaboration*, 139–40.

32. See Struye, *Journal de guerre*, 155, entry for 8 November 1940.

33. See Marrus and Paxton, *Vichy France and the Jews*, 100.

34. See Barthélemy, *Ministre de la Justice*, 508.

35. Quoted in Jean-Pierre Azéma, Nicole Racine-Furland, and Dominique Veillon, 'Certitudes et hesitations des préfets de Vichy', in Jean-Pierre Azéma, Antoine Prost, and Jean-Pierre Rioux (eds), *Le Parti Communiste français des années sombres, 1938–1941* (Paris: Seuil, 1986), 160.

36. See Marrus and Paxton, *Vichy France and the Jews*, 151.

37. See Charles and Dasnoy (eds), *Les Secrétaires généraux*, 138.

38. Charles and Dasnoy (eds), *Les Secrétaires généraux*, 140, 146.

39. Charles and Dasnoy (eds), *Les Secrétaires généraux*, 149.

40. Charles and Dasnoy (eds), *Les Secrétaires généraux*, 141.

41. Quoted by Marc Van den Wijngaert, 'Le Comité des secrétaires généraux', in Charles and Dasnoy (eds), *Les Secrétaires généraux*, 29.

42. Charles and Dasnoy (eds), *Les Secrétaires généraux*, 156–7.

43. See Struye, *Journal de guerre*, 232, entry for 4 September 1941.

6. COLLABORATION AGAINST THE GRAIN OF OCCUPATION, 1942–1944: THE DEPORTATION OF JEWS

1. See Struye, *Journal de guerre*, 337, entry for 7 November 1942.
2. For these extracts from the 1943 guidelines, see van Bolhuis (ed.), *Onderdrukking en verzet*, i. 395–7.
3. See Baruch, *Servir l'état français*, 399.
4. Quoted in François-Georges Dreyfus, *Histoire du Vichy. Vérités et légendes* (Paris: Perrin, 1990), 629.
5. See Philip Morgan, 'The Italian Fascist New Order in Europe', in Michael L. Smith and Peter Stirk (eds), *Making the New Europe: European Unity and the Second World War* (London and New York: Pinter, 1990), 39.
6. Quoted in Baruch, *Servir l'état français*, 389.
7. For the text of the police agreement, see Serge Klarsfeld, *Vichy-Auschwitz: Le Rôle de Vichy dans la solution finale de la question juive en France*, i. *1942* (Paris: Fayard, 1983), 315–16.
8. See Baruch, *Servir l'état français*, 399–400.
9. See Klarsfeld, *Vichy-Auschwitz*, i. *1942*, 251.
10. See Serge Klarsfeld, *Vichy-Auschwicz: Le Rôle de Vichy dans la solution finale de la question juive en France*, ii. *1943–44* (Paris: Fayard, 1985), 254.
11. See Klarsfeld, *Vichy-Auschwitz*, ii. *1943–44*, 253.
12. See Klarsfeld, *Vichy-Auschwitz*, ii. *1943–44*, 54.

7. COLLABORATION AGAINST THE GRAIN OF OCCUPATION, 1942–1945: THE DEPORTATION OF WORKERS

1. See Milward, *The New Order and the French Economy*, 116.
2. See Charles and Dasnoy (eds), *Les Secrétaires généraux*, 203; also, Rudi van Doorslaer, 'La Police Belge et le maintien de l'ordre en Belgique occupée', in E. Dejonghe (ed.), *L'Occupation en France et en Belgique, 1940–1944*, i, special issue of *Revue du Nord* (1987), 87.
3. See Struye, *Journal de guerre*, entry for 27 September 1943, 420.
4. See Charles and Dasnoy (eds), *Les Secrétaires généraux*, 262.
5. Quoted in Warner, *Pierre Laval and the Eclipse of France*, 310.
6. See de Rochebrune and Hazera, *Les patrons sous l'occupation*, i. 516.
7. See Milward, *The New Order and the French Economy*, 120.
8. See Hoover Institute, *La Vie de la France sous l'occupation*, iii. 1213.
9. See Albert Speer, *Inside the Third Reich* (London: Weidenfeld and Nicolson, 1970), 310.
10. Quoted in Guy Sabin, *Jean Bichelonne, Ministre sous l'occupation, 1942–1944* (Paris: Editions France-Empire, 1991), 76.
11. See Baruch, *Servir l'état français*, 547.
12. See Bernard Lecornu, *Un préfet sous l'occupation allemande* (Paris: Éditions France-Empire, 1984), 194.

13. See Charles and Dasnoy (eds), *Les Secrétaires généraux*, 287.
14. Charles and Dasnoy (eds), *Les Secrétaires généraux*, 291–2.

CONCLUSION: OFFICIALS WILL BE OFFICIALS

1. Veillon, *La Collaboration*, 111–12.
2. Veillon, *La Collaboration*, 135–6.
3. See Werner Warmbrunn, *The Dutch under German Occupation, 1940–1945* (London: Oxford University Press, 1972), 182.
4. Hoover Institute, *La Vie de la France sous l'occupation*, iii. 1765.

Select Bibliography

GENERAL AND COMPARATIVE

Arendt, H., *Eichmann in Jerusalem: A Report on the Banality of Evil* (New York: Viking, 1964).

Deák, I., Gross, J. T., and Judt, T. (eds), *The Politics of Retribution in Europe: World War II and its Aftermath* (Princeton: Princeton University Press, 2000).

Dear, I. C. B., and Foot, M. R. D. (eds), *The Oxford Companion to the Second World War* (Oxford: Oxford University Press, 1995).

Dejonghe, E. (ed.), *L'Occupation en France et en Belgique, 1940–1944*, 2 vols, special issues of *Revue du Nord*, 1987–8.

de Wever, B., Van Goethem, H., and Wouters, N. (eds), *Local Government in Occupied Europe, 1939–1945* (Ghent: Academia Press, 2008).

Fein, H., *Accounting for Genocide: National Responses and Jewish Victimization during the Holocaust* (Chicago and London: University of Chicago Press, 1984).

Gilmour, J., and Stephenson, J. (eds), *Hitler's Scandinavian Legacy: The Consequences of the German Invasion for the Scandinavian Countries, Then and Now* (London: Bloomsbury, 2014).

Grant, W., Nekkers, J., and van Waarden, F. (eds), *Organizing Business for War: Corporatist Organization during the Second World War* (New York and Oxford: Berg, 1991).

Griffioen, P., and Zeller, R., 'La Persécution des Juifs en Belgique et aux Pays-Bas pendant la Seconde Guerre Mondiale: Une analyse comparative', *Cahiers d'histoire du temps présent*, 5 (1999).

Griffioen, P., and Zeller, R., 'Anti-Jewish Policy and Organization of the Deportations in France and the Netherlands, 1940–1944: A Comparative Study', *Holocaust Genocide Studies*, 20/3 (2006).

Hilberg, R., *Perpetrators, Victims, Bystanders: The Jewish Catastrophe, 1933–1945* (New York: Harper Collins, 1993).

Housden, M., '"Banal Evil" and "Cogs in the Machine": Exploring the Relationship between Atrocity, Bureaucracy, and Modernity', *SATH: History Teaching Review Year Book*, 20 (2016).

James, H., and Tanner, J., *Enterprise in the Period of Fascism in Europe* (Aldershot: Ashgate, 2002).

Kossmann, E. H., *The Low Countries, 1780–1940* (Oxford: Clarendon Press, 1988).

Lagrou, P., 'Victims of Genocide and National Memory: Belgium, France, and the Netherlands', *Past and Present*, 75/1 (1997), 181–222.

Lagrou, P., *The Legacy of Nazi Occupation: Patriotic Memory and National Recovery in Western Europe, 1945–1965* (Cambridge: Cambridge University Press, 2000).

Lipgens, W. (ed.), *Documents on the History of European Integration*, i, *Continental Plans for European Union, 1939–1945* (Berlin and New York: de Gruyter, 1985).

Lund, J. (ed.), *Working for the New Order: European Business under German Domination, 1939–1945* (Copenhagen: University Press of Southern Denmark and Copenhagen Business School Press, 2006).

Moore, B., *Survivors: Jewish Self-Help and Rescue in Nazi-Occupied Western Europe* (Oxford: Oxford University Press, 2010).

Nissen, H. S. (ed.), *Scandinavia during the Second World War* (Minneapolis: University of Minnesota Press, 1983).

Petrow, R., *The Bitter Years: The Invasion and Occupation of Denmark and Norway, April 1940–May 1945* (New York: William Morrow, 1974).

Rings, W., *Life with the Enemy: Collaboration and Resistance in Hitler's Europe, 1939–1945* (New York: Double Day, 1982).

Ryan, M. D. (ed.), *Human Responses to the Holocaust: Perpetrators and Victims, Bystanders and Resisters* (New York and Toronto: Edwin Mellen Press, 1981).

Smith, M. L., and Stirk, P. (eds), *Making the New Europe: European Unity and the Second World War* (London and New York: Pinter, 1990).

Stenius, H., Österberg, M., and Östling, J. (eds), *Nordic Narratives of the Second World War: National Historiographies Revisited* (Lund: Nordic Academic Press, 2011).

Stirk, P. (ed.), *European Unity in Context: The Interwar Period* (London: Pinter, 1989).

Winter, J., and Sivan, E. (eds), *War and Remembrance in the Twentieth Century* (Cambridge: Cambridge University Press, 1999).

Wright, G., *The Ordeal of Total War, 1939–1945* (New York and London: Harper Torchbooks, 1968).

THE NAZI NEW ORDER AND OCCUPATION

Carlyle, M. (ed.), *Documents on International Affairs, 1939–1946*, ii. *Hitler's Europe* (London: Oxford University Press, 1954).

Frøland, H.O., 'Nazi Planning and the Aluminium Industry', in F. Guirao et al. (eds), *Alan S. Milward and a Century of European Change* (London: Routledge, 2012), 168–88.

Herzstein, R. E., *When Nazi Dreams Come True* (London: Abacus, 1982).

Hirschfeld, G., 'Nazi Propaganda in Occupied Western Europe: The Case of the Netherlands', in D. Welch (ed.), *Nazi Propaganda: The Power and the Limitations* (London: Croom Helm, 1983), 143–60.

Lemkin, R., *Axis Rule in Occupied Europe* (Washington: Rumford Press, 1944).

Mazower, M., *Hitler's Empire: Nazi Rule in Occupied Europe* (London: Allen Lane, 2008).

Militärgeschichtliches Forschungsamt (ed.), *Germany and the Second World War*, v. *Organization and Mobilization of the German Sphere of Power*, pts 1–2 (Oxford: Clarendon Press, 2000, 2003).

Noakes, J., and Pridham, G. (eds), *Nazism, 1919–1945: A Documentary Reader*, iii. *Foreign Policy, War, and Racial Persecution* (Liverpool: Liverpool University Press, 2014).

Overy, R. J., and Cate, J. H. T. (eds), *Die Neuordnung Europas NS-Wirtschaftspolitik in den Besetzten Gebeiten* (Berlin: Metropol, 1997).

Rich, N., *Hitler's War Aims*, ii. *The Establishment of the New Order* (New York: W. W. Norton, 1974).

Speer, A., *Inside the Third Reich: Memoirs* (London: Weidenfeld and Nicolson, 1970).

Tooze, A., *The Wages of Destruction: The Making and Breaking of the Nazi Economy* (London: Penguin, 2007).

BELGIUM

Aron, P., and Gotovich, J. (eds), *Dictionnaire de la Seconde Guerre Mondiale en Belgique* (Waterloo: André Versaille editeur, 2008).

Baudhuin, F., *L'Économie belge sous l'occupation, 1940–1944* (Brussels: Emile Bruylant, 1945).

Charles, J.-L., *Les Dossiers secrets de la police allemande en Belgique* (Brussels: Lucien De Meyer, 1972).

Charles, J.-L., and Dasnoy, P. (eds), *Les Sécretaires généraux face à l'occupant: Procès-verbaux des reunions du Comité des Sécretaires généraux (1940–1944)* (Brussels: Lucien De Meyer, 1974).

Conway, M., *Collaboration in Belgium: Léon Degrelle and the Rexist Movement, 1940–1944* (New Haven and London: Yale University Press, 1993).

Garfinkels, B., *Les Belges face à la persécution raciale, 1940–1944* (Brussels: Édition de la l'Institut de Sociologie de l'Université Libre de Bruxelles, 1965).

Gillingham, J., *Belgian Business in the Nazi New Order* (Gent: Jan Dhondt Foundation, 1977).

Gillingham, J., 'The Baron de Launoit: A Case Study in the "Politics of Production" of Belgian Industry during Nazi Occupation', *Revue belge d'histoire contemporaine*, 5 (1979), 1–59.

Gérard-Libois, J., and Gotovich, J., *L'An 40: La Belgique occupée* (Brussels: CRISP, 1980).

Gérard-Libois, J., and Gotovich, J., *Léopold III: De l'an 40 à l'effacement* (Brussels: Pol-His, 1991).

Hanquet, R., *Les Pouvoirs des Sécretaires généraux pendant l'occupation* (Brussels: Goemaere, 1946).

Hansen, E., 'Hendrik de Man and Economic Planning', *European Studies Review*, 2 (1978), 234–57.

Klem, P., *German Economic Policies in Belgium from 1940 to 1944* (Ann Arbor: University Microfilms, 1973).

Knight, T. J., 'Belgium Leaves the War, 1940', *Journal of Modern History*, 41/1 (1969), 46–67.

Struye, P., *L'Évolution du sentiment public en Belgique sous l'occupation allemande* (Brussels: Les Éditions Lumière, 1945).

Struye, P., *Journal de guerre, 1940–1945* (Brussels: Éditions Racine, 2004).

Van den Wijngaert, M., 'Les Sécretaires généraux et la mise au travail obligatoire (1940–1944)', *Cahiers d'histoire de la Seconde Guerre Mondiale*, 1 (1970), 7–23.

Van den Wijngaert, M., *L'Économie belge sous l'occupation: La Politique d'Alexandre Galopin, gouverneur de la Société Générale* (Paris-Louvain-la-Neuve: Duculot, 1990).

Verhoeyen, E., 'Les Grands industriels belges entre collaboration et résistance: Le moindre mal', *Cahiers d'histoire de la Seconde Guerre Mondiale*, 10 (1986), 57–114.

Vermeylen, P., 'The Punishment of Collaborators', *Annals of the American Academy of Political and Social Science*, 247 (1946), 73–7.

Warmbrunn, W., *The German Occupation of Belgium, 1940–1944* (New York: Peter Lang, 1993).

Willequet, J., *La Belgique sous la botte: Résistances et collaborations, 1940–1945* (Paris: Éditions Universitaires, 1986).

DENMARK

Albrecht, R., 'La Politique danoise au cours de la première année d'occupation', *Revue d'histoire de la Deuxième Guerre Mondiale*, 96 (1974).

Anderson, W. D., 'The German Removal of the Danish Cabinet in 1943', *Scandinavian Studies*, 49/4 (1977), 119–21.

Giltner, P., '*In the Friendliest Manner': German–Danish Economic Cooperation during the Nazi Occupation of 1940–1945* (New York: Peter Lang, 1998).

Givskov, C. C., 'Danish "Purge Laws"', *Journal of Criminal Law and Criminology*, 39/4 (1948), 447–60.

Kirchhoff, H., 'Denmark: A Light in the Darkness of the Holocaust? A Reply to Gunnar S. Paulsson', *Journal of Contemporary European History*, 30 (1995), 465–79.

Lund, J., 'Denmark and the "European New Order", 1940–1942', *Contemporary European History*, 13/3 (2004), 305–21.

Lund, J., 'Building Hitler's Europe: Forced Labour in the Danish Construction Business during World War II', *Business History Review*, 87/3 (2010), 479–99.

Nissen, M., 'Danish Food Production in the German War Economy', in F. Trentmann and F. Just (eds), *Food and Conflict in Europe in the Age of the Two World Wars* (Basingstoke: Palgrave Macmillan, 2006).

Paulsson, G. S., 'The Bridge over the Oeresund: The Historiography on the Expulsion of the Jews from Denmark, 1943', *Journal of Contemporary History*, 30 (1995), 431–64.

Sorensen, N. I., 'Narrating the Second World War in Denmark since 1945', *Contemporary European History*, 14/3 (2005), 295–315.

Voorhis, J. L., *A Study of the Official Relations between the German and Danish Governments in the Period between 1940–1943* (Evanston, IL: Northwestern University Press, 1968).

FRANCE

Andrieu, C., *La Banque sous l'occupation: Paradoxes de l'histoire d'une profession, 1936–1946* (Paris: PFNSP, 1990).

Azéma, J.-P., and Bédarida, P. (eds), *Le Régime de Vichy et les français* (Paris: Fayard, 1992).

Azéma, J.-P., Racine-Furland, N., and Veillon, D., 'Certitudes et hésitations des préfets de Vichy', in J.-P. Azéma, A. Prost, and J.-P. Rioux (eds), *Le Parti Communiste français des années sombres, 1938–1941* (Paris: Seuil, 1986), 150–73.

Barthélemy, J., *Ministre de la Justice: Vichy, 1941–1943: Mémoires* (Paris: Pygmalion and Gérard Watelot, 1989).

Baruch, M. O., *Servir l'état français: L'Administration en France de 1940 à 1944* (Paris: Fayard, 1997).

Baudot, M., 'L'Épuration: Bilan chiffré', *Bulletin d'Histoire de l'Institut du Temps Présent*, 25 (1986), 37–53.

Belin, R., *Du secrétariat de la CGT au gouvernement de Vichy* (Paris: Éditions Albatros, 1978).

Beltran, A., Frank, R., and Rousso, H. (eds), *La Vie des enterprises sous l'occupation* (Paris: Belin, 1994).

Benoist-Méchin, J., *De la défaite au désastre*, i. *Les Occasions manquées, juillet 1940–avril 1942* (Paris: Albin Michel, 1984).

Burrin, P., *Living with Defeat: France under the German Occupation, 1940–1944* (London: Arnold, 1996).

Buss, R., *The French through their Films* (London: Batsford, 1988).

Cahill, C., *Bad Faith: A Forgotten History of Family and Fatherland* (London: Jonathan Cape, 2006).

Dard, O., Daumas, J.-C., and Marcot, F. (eds), *L'Occupation, l'état français et les enterprises* (Paris: ADHE, 2000).

Davies, P., *France and the Second World War: Occupation, Collaboration, and Resistance* (London: Routledge, 2001).

Dejonghe, E., 'Pénurie et repartition charbonnière en France', *Revue d'Histoire de la Deuxième Guerre Mondiale*, 102 (1976), 21–55.

D'Hoop, J.-M., 'La Main d'œuvre française au service de l'Allemagne', *Revue d'histoire de la Deuxième Guerre Mondiale*, 81 (1971), 73–88.

de Rochebrune, R., and Hazera, J.-C., *Les Patrons sous l'occupation*, i. *Face aux allemands: Collaboration, résistance, marché noir* (Paris: Odile Jacob, 1995); ii. *Face à Vichy: Pétainisme, intrigues, spoliations* (Paris: Odile Jacob, 1997).

Doueil, P., *L'Administration locale à l'épreuve de la guerre, 1939–1949* (Paris: Recueil Sirey, 1950).

Dreyfus, F.-G., *Histoire de Vichy: Vérités et legends* (Paris: Perrin, 1990).

du Moulin de Labarthète, H., *Le Temps des illusions: Souvenirs (juillet 1940–avril 1942)* (Brussels: La Diffusion du Livre, 1947).

Facon, P., and de Ruffray, F., 'Aperçus sur la coopération aéronautique franco-allemande, 1940–43', *Revue d'histoire de la Deuxième Guerre Mondiale*, 27/108 (1977), 85–102.

Fishman, S., et al. (eds), *France at War: Vichy and the Historians* (Oxford: Berg, 2000).

Fogg, S. L., *The Politics of Everyday Life in Vichy France: Foreigners, Undesirables, and Strangers* (Cambridge: Cambridge University Press, 2008).

Footitt, H., and Simmonds, J., *France, 1943–1945* (Leicester: Leicester University Press, 1988).

Fox, J. P., 'How Far Did Vichy France "Sabotage" the Imperatives of Wannsee?', in D. Cesarani (ed.), *The Final Solution: Origins and Implementation* (London: Routledge, 1994), 194–214.

Frenay, H., *The Night will End* (London: Abelard, 1976)

Gildea, R., *Marianne in Chains: In Search of German Occupation, 1940–1945* (London: Macmillan, 2002).

Golsan, R. J. (ed.), *The Papon Affair: Memory and Justice on Trial* (New York and London: Routledge, 2000).

Gordon, B. M. (ed.), *Historical Dictionary of World War II France: The Occupation, Vichy, and the Resistance* (London: Aldwych Press, 1998).

Hewitt, L. D., *Remembering the Occupation in French Film: National Identity in Postwar Europe* (London: Palgrave-Macmillan, 2008).

Hirschfeld, G., and Marsh, P. (eds), *Collaboration in France: Politics and Culture during the Nazi Occupation, 1940–1944* (Oxford: Berg, 1989).

Hoover Institute, *La Vie de la France sous l'occupation (1940–1944)*, 3 vols (Paris: Librairie Plon, 1957).

Jackson, J., *France: the Dark Years, 1940–1944* (Oxford: Oxford University Press, 2001).

Jones, A., 'Illusions of Sovereignty: Business and the Organisation of Committees of Vichy France', *Social History*, 2/1 (1986), 1–31.

Kitson, S., 'From Enthusiasm to Disenchantment: The French Police and the Vichy Regime, 1940–1944', *Contemporary European History*, 11/3 (2002), 371–90.

Klarsfeld, S., *Vichy-Auschwitz: Le Rôle de Vichy dans la solution finale de la question juive en France*, i. *1942*; ii. *1943–44* (Paris: Fayard, 1983, 1985).

Klemm, P. F., 'La Production aéronautique française de 1940 à 1942', *Revue d'histoire de la Deuxième Guerre Mondiale*, 107 (1977), 53–74.

Knapp, A. (ed.), *The Uncertain Foundation: France at the Liberation, 1944–47* (Basingstoke: Palgrave-Macmillan, 2007).

Kuisel, R., 'The Legend of the Vichy Synarchy', *French Historical Studies*, 6/3 (1970), 365–98.

Kuisel, R., 'Vichy et les origines de la pianification économique', *Le Mouvement social*, 98/1 (1977), 77–101.

Laurens, A., 'Le STO dans le department de l'Ariège', *Revue d'histoire de la Deuxième Guerre Mondiale*, 95 (1974), 53–74.

Lecornu, B., *Un préfet sous l'occupation allemande* (Paris: Éditions France-Empire, 1984).

Loubet Del Bayle, J.-L., *Les Non-Conformistes des années 30: Une tentative de renouvellement de la pensée politique française* (Paris: Éditions Seuil, 1969).

Marcot, F., 'La Direction de Peugeot sous l'occupation', *Le Mouvement social*, 189 (1999), 27–46.

Marrus, M. R., and Paxton, R. O., *Vichy France and the Jews* (New York: Basic Books, 1981).

Mièvre, J., 'L'Évolution politique d'Abel Bonnard (jusqu'au printemps 1942)', *Revue d'histoire de la Deuxième Guerre Mondiale*, 27/108 (1977), 1–26.

Milward, A., *The New Order and the French Economy* (Aldershot: Gregg Revivals, 1993).

Novick, P., *The Resistance versus Vichy: The Purge of Collaborators in Liberated France* (New York: Columbia University Press, 1968).

Paxton, R. O., *Vichy France: Old Guard and New Order, 1940–1944* (New York: Columbia University Press, 1982).

Pucheu, P., *Ma vie* (Paris: Amiot-Dumont, 1948).

Rémond, R. (ed.), *Le Gouvernement de Vichy, 1940–1942: Institutions et politiques* (Paris: PFNSP, 1972).

Rouquet, F., *L'Épuration dans l'administration française: Agents de l'état et collaboration ordinaire* (Paris: CNRS Éditions, 1993).

Rousso, H., 'L'Organisation industrielle de Vichy', *Revue d'histoire de la Deuxième Guerre Mondiale*, 116 (1979), 27–44.

Rousso, H., *The Vichy Syndrome: History and Memory in France since 1944* (Cambridge, MA, and London: Harvard University Press, 1991).

Sabin, G., *Jean Bichelonne, Ministre sous l'occupation, 1942–1944* (Paris: Éditions France-Empire, 1991).

Shennan, A., *Rethinking France: Plans for Renewal, 1940–1946* (Oxford: Clarendon Press, 1989).

The Sorrow and the Pity: A Film by Marcel Ophuls, film script translated by Mireille Johnston (New York: Outerbridge and Lazard, 1972).

Sweets, J. F., *Choices in Vichy France: The French under Nazi Occupation* (Oxford: Oxford University Press, 1994).

Veillon, D., *La Collaboration: Textes et débats* (Paris: Librairie Générale Française, 1984).

Vinen, R., *The Politics of French Business, 1936–1945* (Cambridge: Cambridge University Press, 1991).

Vinen, R., *The Unfree French: Life under the Occupation* (New Haven and London: Yale University Press, 2006).

Warner, G., *Pierre Laval and the Eclipse of France* (London: Eyre and Spottiswoode, 1968).

Wellers, G., Kaspi, A., and Klarsfeld, S. (eds), *La France et la question juive, 1940–44* (Paris: Éditions Sylvie Messinger, 1981).

THE NETHERLANDS

Burke, W., *Images of Occupation in Dutch Film* (Amsterdam: Amsterdam University Press, 2017).

De Jong, L., *The Netherlands and Nazi Germany* (Cambridge, MA, and London: Harvard University Press, 1990).

Fennema, M., 'Max Hirschfeld, Secretary-General of a Decapitated Ministry (1940–1945)', in M. de Kaizer, M. Heijmans-van Bruggen, and E. Somers (eds),

Onrecht: Oorlog en rechtvaardigheid in de twintigste eeuw (Zutphen: Walberg, 2001) (translated from the Dutch by E. Velthoen).

Fijnault, C., 'The Police of the Netherlands in and between the Two World Wars', in C. Emsley and B. Weinberger (eds), *Policing Western Europe: Politics, Professionalism, and Public Order, 1850–1940* (Westport, CT, and London: Greenwood Press, 1991), 237–53.

Hirschfeld, G., 'Collaboration and Attentism in the Netherlands, 1940–41', *Journal of Contemporary History*, 16 (1981), 467–86.

Hirschfeld, G., *Nazi Rule and Dutch Collaboration: The Netherlands under German Occupation, 1940–1945* (Oxford: Berg, 1988).

Maass, W. B., *The Netherlands at War: 1940–1945* (London, New York, and Toronto: Abelard-Schuman, 1970).

Mason, H. L., *The Purge of Dutch Quislings: Emergency Justice in the Netherlands* (The Hague: Martinus Nijhoff, 1952).

Meershoek, G., 'The Amsterdam Police and the Persecution of the Jews', in M. Berenbaum and A. J. Peck (eds), *The Holocaust and History: The Known, the Unknown, the Disputed, and the Reexamined* (Bloomington and Indianapolis: Indiana University Press, 2002), 284–300.

Moore, B., 'The Netherlands', in J. Noakes (ed.), *The Civilian in War: The Home Front in Europe, Japan, and the USA in World War II* (Exeter: Exeter University Press, 1992), 126–49.

Moore, B., *Victims and Survivors: The Nazi Persecution of the Jews in the Netherlands, 1940–1945* (London: Arnold, 1997).

Moore, B., '"Goed en fout" or "grijs verleden": Competing Perspectives on the History of the Netherlands under German Occupation, 1940–1943', *Dutch Crossing*, 27/2 (2003), 155–68.

Moore, B., 'Nazi Masters and Accommodating Dutch Bureaucrats: Working towards the Führer in the Occupied Netherlands, 1940–1945', in A. McElligot and T. Kirk (eds), *Working towards the Führer: Essays in Honour of Sir Ian Kershaw* (Manchester: Manchester University Press, 2003), 186–203.

Romijn, P., 'Frederiks' Op de Bres—an Official Apology', in *Oorlogsdocumentatie '40–45: Tiende jaarboek van det Nederlands Instituut voor Oorlogsdocumentatie* (Amsterdam: Walberg, 1999), 140–64 (translated from the Dutch by E. Velthoen).

Smith, M. L., 'Neither Resistance nor Collaboration: Historians and the Problem of the *Nederlandse Unie*', *History*, 72/235 (1987), 251–78.

Smith, M. L., 'Ideas for a New Regime in the Netherlands after the Defeat of 1940', in M. Winter and P. Vincent (eds), *Modern Dutch Studies: Essays in Honour of Peter King* (London: Athlone Press, 1988), 175–85.

Sniffen, B. G., 'Forced Labour Drafts and the Secretaries-General during the Nazi Occupation of the Netherlands, 1940–1941', *Societas*, 3 (1973), 129–41.

van Bolhuis, J. J. (ed.), *Onderdrukking en verzet: Nederland in oorlogstijd*, i (Amsterdam: Van Loghum Slaterus, 1955).

Warmbrun, W., *The Dutch under German Occupation, 1940–1945* (London: Oxford University Press, 1972).

NORWAY

Andenaes, J., Riste, O., and Skodvin, M., *Norway and the Second World War* (Oslo: Johan Grundt Tanum Forlag, 1966).

Espeli, H., 'The German Occupation and its Consequences for the Composition and Changes of Norwegian Business Elites', *Jahrbuch für Wirtschaftsgeschichte*, 2 (2010).

Frøland, H. O., and Kobberrød, J.T., 'The Norwegian Contribution to Göring's Megalomania: Norway's Aluminium Industry during World War II', *Cahiers d'histoire de l'aluminium*, 42–3 (2009), 130–47.

Milward, A. S., *The Fascist Economy in Norway* (Oxford: Clarendon Press, 1972).

Wicken, O., 'Industrial Change in Norway during the Second World War: Electrification and Electrical Engineering', *Scandinavian Journal of History*, 8/1–4 (1983), 119–50.

Picture Acknowledgements

1. © Robert Capa / International Center of Photography / Magnum Photos.

2. Cartoon by David Austin, from *The Guardian*, June 1994. British Cartoon Archive, University of Kent, <www.cartoons.ac.uk>.

3. © MPI / Stringer / Getty Images.

4. © Image Bank WW2 - NIOD.

5. © Image Bank WW2 - NIOD.

6. © CEGES / SOMA.

7. © Danish Royal Collection.

8. Bundsarchiv, Bild 101I-027-1475-37. Photo: Wolfgang Venneman.

9. © Michel Euler / AP / REX / Shutterstock.

10. © FPG/Getty Images.

11. © akg-images.

Publisher's Acknowledgements

We are grateful for permission to reprint extracts from the following in this book.

Simon Kitson: 'From Enthusiasm to Disenchantment: the French Police and the Vichy Regime', *Contemporary European History*, Vol 11 issue 3 (2002), citing Roger Chevrier, French broadcaster, reprinted by permission of Cambridge University Press via Copyright Clearance Center.

Michael R. Marrus and **Robert O. Paxton**: *Vichy France and the Jews* (Stanford University Press, 1995), copyright © 1981 Calman-Levy, from a German administration report of 1942, reprinted by permission of Stanford University Press, sup. org. All rights reserved.

Albert Speer translated by Richard and Clara Winston: Inside the Third Reich (Weidenfeld and Nicholson, 1970 / Phoenix 2003), copyright © 1970 by The Macmillan Company, New York, reprinted by permission of the Orion Publishing Group, London.

We have made every effort to trace and contact all copyright holders before publication. If notified, the publisher will be pleased to rectify any errors or omissions at the earliest opportunity.

Index

Abetz, Otto 136, 143, 145, 197–8
Actions, by Sauckel, *see* Sauckel, Fritz
administrative collaboration, *see* officials
Agnelli, Giovanni 118
Allied liberation (1944–5) 1, 13–31
amnesty 27
André Chaussures 218–20
anti-Bolshevism 42, 303
Anti-Comintern Pact (1941) 41–2, 132
anti-communism, post-war 16, 42
anti-Semitism 193–5, 210–15, 234
    Belgium 210–15, 234
    Denmark 195–6, 244–5, 248
    France 196–200, 215–17, 270
    Netherlands 203–11, 215
    Norway 193–5
    Vichy France, *see* France
    see also deportation, of Jews; final
        solution
Ardant, Henri 218–19, 220, 325
Arendt, Hannah 251
Armistice Commission 104
Aryan declaration 205, 208, 210,
    213, 214
Aryanization
    of Jewish property 37
    of occupied economies 127, 197
    see also *individual countries*
Atlantic Wall 47, 258
autarky principle 35, 105
authoritarian collaboration 63, 69–97,
    110, 154–235

Barnaud, Jacques 129, 136, 156, 161–2, 219
Barthélemy, Joseph 157, 178, 215
Beel, Louis 25
Belgium
    amnesty proposal 15
    anti-Semitism 210–15, 234
    Aryanization of 213–14

banking crisis 94
Belgian law, legitimacy of 220–1
Belgian lawmaking powers 97–100
civilian food supply 147–52
communist resistance 167–8
completion of purges 18
deportation
    of Jews 252, 253, 254, 256–9, 263;
        see also deportation, of Jews; final
        solution
    of workers 284–90, 300, 311
economic collaboration 21–2, 100,
    102–53
First World War occupation 100–1
German fragmentation of 93–4
German military occupation 43, 46,
    55–7
government
    evacuation 56
    -in-exile 56, 239, 321, 329
    restructuring, in New Order 78–9
and greater evil 329
imprisonment for collaboration 19–20
incipient civil war 314
industrial cooperation with
    Germany 40, 94
intellectual debate 60
international trade 105
judicial crisis 94
judicial disloyalty 227
judiciary/courts and wartime
    legislation 97–100, 220–31, 296,
    321–2
jurisdiction clashes 168
king's collaboration 69–72, 94
military defeat 56
military government 50–1, 54
military purge tribunals 18–19
ministerial delegation 94
national dishonour 24–5

Belgium (*cont.*)
  non-collaboration 224
  occupation guidelines 86–101
  official appointments 151
  officials as collaborators 23–6, 134–5,
    154–231, 233–4, 239
  police
    recruitment 172–3
    and repression 296
  political conflict, post-war 14–16
  post-war defences 328
  POW conscription 287
  and pre-war political systems 56–7
  public opinion 55–6, 57
  racial/linguistic communities 46, 93,
    95–6
  Rexist party/officials 41, 131, 166, 222,
    230, 314
  socialist left policy 59–60
  Société Générale de Belgique 100,
    110, 131
  SS activities 50–4, 97, 314
  steelmaking 119
  steel manufacturers and German
    consortiums 130
  Supreme Court and occupier's rights
    90–2
  trade agreement with Germany 111
  transfer of powers legislation 94
  transition to occupation 93
  and worker migration 187–94
  see also officials
Belin, René 112, 156–8
Benoist-Méchin, Jacques 136–7, 143, 145
Berliet 122–5, 326
Berliet, Marius 122–5, 303–4, 324–5
Bernier, Victor 317
Berthelot, Jean 85, 161
Best, Werner 170, 195, 246–7, 248,
    249, 316
Bichelonne, Jean 122, 134, 153, 156–9,
    162, 218, 219, 237, 244, 304, 308,
    309, 310, 311, 315, 326
black market 115, 334
Bolshevism threat 40
Bonnard, Abel 161, 220
Borginon, Hendrik 222
Bousquet, René 29, 264–5, 269–83,
    294–5, 308, 325
Bouthillier, Yves 64–6, 85, 140, 143–4,
    155, 161

Brauschitsch, Field Marshal Walther
    von 104
Brice, Pierre-Louis 129
Broersen, Leo 172
Brufina 126
Brunner, Alois 280
Buhl, Vilhelm 175
Burrin, P. 161
businessmen
  attitudes as owners 120–1
  as collaborators, *see* economic
    collaboration
  collective interests 333
  post-war preparations 152–3

Carcopino, Jérôme 220
Carles, Fernand 178
Cathala, Pierre 315
centralized war economy 109
CGQJ (*Commissariat Général aux
    Questions Juives*) 198–9, 218, 219,
    220, 272
CGT (*Confédération Générale du Travail*)
    union federation 156
Chartres, and collaboration 5–7, 17
Châteaubriant interment camp
    179–81, 237
Chavin, Henri 215
Chevalier, Maurice 9
Chevrier, Roger 4–5
Chirac, Jacques 9
Christian X, king of Denmark 61, 245, 248
cinema, and wartime history 9
civil servants, *see* officials
Claeys, Gaston 190, 227
Clermont-Ferrand, collaboration 8–9
CNAA (*Corporation Nationale de
    l'Agriculture et de l'Alimentation*)
    221–3, 224, 228, 314
coal cartel 130
Cohen, David 331
Colijn, Hendrik 73–4
Colin, Paul 295
collaboration 1940–2
  alternative terms for 1
  and collaborationism 2
  and competing German agencies
    53–4
  extent of 3–4
  German acceptance of 34
  as inertia 10

and Jewish deportation, *see* deportation, of Jews
  logic for 146, 235
  and Nazi polycentrism 53–4
  and occupation symmetry 55
  of officials, *see* officials
  post-war views of 4
  premeditated 55
  and purges 13–31
  rationalizing after Liberation 235
  use of term 1–2
collaborationism 2–3
  German mistrust of 34, 41
collaboration penalties 19
collaborators, post-war purges of 13–31
communist party (Denmark) 62
communists, as enemies of fascism 2, 164
company sales, to Germans 128
consensual law-and-order policy 170
construction boom, in occupied territories 103
corporate socialism 70
CO (*Comité d'Organisation*) 112, 123, 127, 142

Dannecker, Theodor 244, 252, 263–4, 272–83
Darlan, Admiral Jean-François 64, 104, 137, 143–5, 158, 198, 327, 328
Darnand, Joseph 281–3, 316, 322
Darquier de Pellepoix, Louis 272
Dautry, Raoul 156
death sentences 19, 20
Déat, Marcel 59–60, 322, 325
De Brinon, Fernand 161, 178, 197–8
de Foy, Robert 297
de Gaulle, General Charles 4, 47, 63, 116, 240, 327
Degrelle, Leon 41, 145
De Launoit, Baron Paul 30, 126, 130–1
Delhaye, Raymond 96–7
De Man, Hendrik 59–60, 69–72, 78, 149
democrats, as enemies of fascism 2
Denmark
  acceptance of German occupation 44, 61
  anti-Semitism 195–6, 244–5, 248
  authoritarian collaboration 61–86
  collaboration
    definition 134
    in 1–2, 22, 313
    policy 22

collaborator internments post-war 16
cooperation
  with Germany 44, 61–2
  as term for collaboration 1
death penalty for resistance 176
deportation
  of Jews 244–50; *see also* deportation, of Jews; final solution
  of workers 287–8, 329
diplomatic relations with Germany 82–3
economic collaboration 102–53
fascist paramilitaries 316
food supplies 135–6
formal relationship with Germany 44
German bureaucratic supervision 82–3
German–Danish relations 246
government semi-independence 136
imprisonment for collaboration 19–20
international trade 105
martial law in 248–9
military occupation 43
neutrality status 177
occupation 86–101, 245–9, 313
occupied territory status 313
officials
  as collaborators 23–6, 134–5, 154–235
  resignations 317
parliamentary institutions 51
police disarmament 316
policing in 175–6
policy of negotiation 134
political union, post-war 15–16
post-war
  defences 328
  government and resistance movements 14
repression in 316
reprisals 175
resistance
  collaboration polarization 176
  outlawing 177
and saboteurs 176
shipbuilding contracts 119, 135
sovereignty 176–7
and Soviet Union 42
SS and Jewish arrests 249
Study Group 114
wild purge 17–18
see also officials

denunciation 17
deportation
    of Jews 9, 12, 27, 29, 48, 244, 249–83,
        331; *see also* anti-Semitism; final
        solution
    of workers 12, 21, 27, 120, 244, 266–7,
        284–326
De Winter, Emile 148, 151, 224, 227, 297,
        321, 333
displacement policy 115
District Commanders 50
*DNSAP (Danmarks Nationalsocialistiske
    Arbejder Parti)* 245–7
donnant–donnant, see give-and-take
        collaboration
Drancy deportation camp 272, 280
du Moulin de Labarthète, Henri 66,
        158–9, 163, 181, 182
Dutch Jewish Council 262–3

economic collaboration 11, 21–2, 30, 31,
        60–1, 100–1, 102–53, 243, 329,
        333–4
economic planning 37–8, 47
economic targets 36–7
Eichmann, Adolf 251, 252, 263–4, 272, 275
Elias, Hendrik 222, 230
enemies of fascism 2
Europe, postwar re-shaping 40
European Charter 267
European New Order 32–54
extra-legal purge commissions 28–9

false ID cards 291–2, 323
fascism, and parliamentary democracy
        58–9
fascistized Europe 2
FFI (Forces Françaises de l'Intérieur) 6
FIAT 118
Field Commanders 50
final solution 27, 202–3, 210, 217, 243,
        246, 251, 253–4, 256, 258, 263–4,
        271–2, 274–5, 278, 283, 328, 332
Four Year Plan Office 35, 39, 51,
        106, 107
France
    adminstrative resistance claim 103
    Alsace/Lorraine annexation 48
    anti-Semitism 196–203, 207,
        215–17, 270
    Armistice 138, 142, 145, 241

Aryanization of 197–8, 202, 218–20,
        272, 325
authoritarian collaboration 63–87
collaboration against resistance 9
colonization by Germany 3
completion of purges 18
denaturalization 279–80
deportation
    of Jews 9, 29, 48, 244, 250, 252,
        263–83, 331; *see also* deportation,
        of Jews; final solution
    of workers 9, 244, 266–7, 287,
        300–12, 323, 325–6
deterrence by terror 169
division of 47
economic collaboration 21, 102–53,
        322, 325
economic recovery 102
ethnic cleansing 48
and final solution 275
final solution meetings 202–3
forbidden coastal zone 47
government
    evacuation 56
    -in-exile 240
    restructuring 78–9
high-profile trials 27
imprisonment for collaboration
        19–20
incipient civil war 314
Infiltration of Public Bodies 318
intellectual debate 60
lynching 16
Milice paramilitaries 281, 283, 316,
        318, 322
military demarcation in 102
military government 50–1, 54, 240
military industry 122–5, 137–45
modernization of economy 128
national dishonour 24–5, 29
Nazi reprisals 168–9, 175, 179–83
neo-socialism 59
occupation
    forces reduction 164
    guidelines 86–101
officials
    as collaborators 11, 20, 23–6, 59,
        134–5, 154–235
    resistance 318
    see also officials
organized resistance 241

Parti Socialiste de France 59
planned future of 47–8
police
    and collaboration 5, 29, 199–200
    and Jewish deportation 276–8, 280
    repressiveness 158
policing in 175, 184, 269–70
post-war defences 327–8
and pre-war political systems 56–7
protected factories 310–11
Provisional Government 240
public works to stimulate economy
    102–3
rubber industry 121
sexual relations with Germans 5–7
skilled labour shortage 185
socialist left policy 59–60
special section courts 180
SS
    activities 50–4
    civilian killings 48
    policing 171, 178, 270
steel manufacturers and German
    consortiums 130
unemployed workers 184–5
vehicle production 122–5
vigilantes 16
wild purge 16–18
worker migration 184–7
and worker migration 187
workers' weekly hours 187
see also Vichy government
Franco, Francisco 65, 181
Franco-German relations 136–45, 160,
    198, 267, 307
Francolor takeover 128
Frederiks, Karel Johannes 25, 26, 80–1,
    93, 203–7, 240, 258, 260–2, 290–1,
    315, 317
Free Denmark movement 248
Freedom Council, Denmark 15–16
Free French 4, 5, 47, 63, 116–17, 240
free unions 113
Frenay, Henri 57
French Algerians settlers 184
Funk, Walter 35–6, 107

Gabolde, Maurice 216, 279
Galopin, Alexandre 100, 101, 110, 111,
    117, 119, 128, 131, 147–51, 152, 225,
    236, 311, 314

Galopin doctrine/committee 111, 117,
    118, 126, 131, 146, 147, 150, 151,
    152, 329
Gauleiters 45
German–Danish relations 246
Germanization 4
Germany
    anti-Semitism 217
    and Bolshevism 42
    Business Groups 105–6
    colonization 3
    currency overvaluation 37–8
    economic planning 37–8, 47
    German authorities and
        collaboration 87
    industrial competitors in occupied
        countries 107–8
    industrial plundering 107
    military alliance with Italy 42
    mistrust of collaborationists 34, 41
    occupation
        aims 50–1
        of Northern Europe 32–54
    Soviet Union invasion (1941) 3, 4, 37,
        105, 116, 164, 243
    worker migration to 184–94
    see also Nazism
Gildea, Robert 55
give-and-take collaboration 128, 137,
    139, 141, 143, 144, 253, 265,
    300, 307
GMR (*Groupes Mobiles de Réserve*) 270
Goebbels, Josef 33, 267
Goods Offices 109–10
Göring, Hermann 35–6, 39, 45, 106, 107,
    108, 139, 145, 149–50, 251
Goris, René 70
government officials, *see* officials
governments-in-exile 14, 56, 86, 116,
    236–9, 262, 292–3, 321, 329, 330
    and economic collaboration 116–17,
        147, 150
grandes agglomérations 221–2, 227–8
Greater Antwerp 228–9
Greater Netherlands 41
    idea 41
Grohe, Josef 321
Grossraumwirtschaft (large economic
    area) 11–12, 32–54, 78, 113, 114,
    121, 122, 129, 132, 135–6
Guardian Hitler cartoon 32–3

Guérard, Jacques 160
Gutt, Camille 100, 117, 119, 149, 152, 236

Hagelin, Albert 233
Hagen, Herbert Martin 275
Hague Land Warfare Convention
    (1907) 86–91, 94, 98, 99, 104, 167,
    204, 212
Hanneken, General Hermann von 51, 246
Hendriks, Fritz-Jan 191, 298, 299
Henriot, Philippe 322
Heydrich, Reinhard 170, 271, 274, 279
Himmler, Heinrich 34, 41, 51–2, 97, 170,
    171, 256, 259, 279
hindsight/retrospect, and collaboration 31
Hirschfeld, Max 105, 109, 111, 119, 159,
    165, 168, 205–10, 240, 262–3,
    290–2, 320
Hitler, Adolf
    and colonization 3
    and European New Order 32–54
    and forced labour 287–8
    Guardian cartoon 32–3
    and king of Denmark 245
    meets Darlan 143–4
    meets Laval 67–9, 141, 144, 266–8
    meets Leopold 71–2
    meets Pétain 1, 64–9
    meets Speer 312
    mistrust of military 44
    and motorway network 132
    negotiations with 143–4
    and reprisals 168–9
    views on occupation 43
Holocaust, see anti-Semitism;
    deportation, of Jews; final solution
horizontal collaboration 5–6
Huntziger, General Charles-Léon 104,
    139, 141

ideological affinity 2
ideological bureaucracy 80
IG Farben 122, 128
indirect rule 50
Infiltration of Public Bodies 318
Ingrand, Jean-Pierre 178, 179, 317
interwar economic relationships 130
Italo-German alliance 247
Italy
    economic collaboration 118

military alliance with Germany 42
resistance/reprisals cycle 247–8

Jardel, Jean 160
Jewish Council (Netherlands) 331
Jewish deportation, see deportation,
    of Jews
Jewish genocide, see final solution
Jews, as enemies of fascism 2
Junker 140
jurisdiction clashes 168

Klarsfeld, Serge 202–3, 269, 276, 281–2
Knochen, Helmut 252, 274, 279, 280–1

Lacombe, Lucien 9, 11
Laval, Pierre 20, 63–4, 65, 67, 93, 139, 140,
    157, 160, 161, 197–8, 237, 244, 264,
    265–9, 275, 278, 279–80, 282–3,
    285, 300–3, 305, 307–9, 313, 315,
    319, 327, 328
    meets Hitler 67–9, 141, 145, 266–8
law-and-order, and officials 164–70, 183
leader principle 79–84, 110, 140, 173,
    190, 191, 261, 271
League of Nations 43
Le Chagrin et la pitié (The Sorrow and
    the Pity) 8
Lecornu, Bernard 180, 181, 237–8, 305,
    319–20
Leemans, Victor 190, 191, 214, 226, 227,
    294, 297
Leguay, Jean 29, 244, 269, 272, 273, 274–5
Le Havre, and collaboration 17
Lehideux, François 103, 131, 132, 136, 162
leniency, by post-war governments 14
Lentz, Jacobus Lambertus 203–4, 290
Leopold, King of Belgium 69–71, 78, 213
liberals, as enemies of fascism 2
Lie, Jonas 52, 174, 233
Lischa, Kurt 275
logic of collaboration 146, 235
Low Countries, see Belgium; Netherlands
Luther, Martin 194
Luxembourg, steel manufacturers and
    German consortiums 130
Lyngstad, Frida 6, 17

Malle, Louis 9
Marion, Paul 136, 304

masons, as enemies of fascism 2
Michel, Elmar 309, 332
Michelin 121–2, 125
military occupation 43
military production 119
military turning points 236
Mitteleuropa (Central/Eastern economic
    zone) 35
Monnet Plan 153
Montoire meetings 64–9, 140, 198, 327
mushroom companies 103
Mussert, Anton 41, 77, 145, 239, 259
Musso, Ferdinand 319
Mussolini, Benito 247, 266

national dishonour 24–5, 29
national economic patrimony 125, 128
National Front movement
    (Netherlands) 73
nationalism, among fascist groups 2
National Offices 111
    Netherlands 111
national unity, post-war 7
National Unity *Nasjonal Samling* 2
nation
    of collaborators theory 10
    of resisters myth 8, 10–11, 16, 26, 30
Nazism
    and Eastern Europe living space 34–5
    and European New Order
        (*Grossraumwirtschaft*) 11–12,
        32–54, 78, 113, 114, 121, 122
    as ideological system 7
    polycentrism policy 53–4
    post-war rejection of 8
    racial purification 34
    racial superiority 34
    SS in occupied territories 51–4
    SS supremacy 243
    Waffen SS 53
    see also final solution; Germany
Netherlands
    anti-Semitism 203–11, 215
    authoritarian collaboration 63–88,
        239
    and communism 75
    completion of purges 18
    compulsory labour 191–3
    construction work 105
    deportation

of Jews 252, 255, 257–63; *see also*
    deportation, of Jews; final solution
    of workers 287, 289–90, 292–5, 311
Dutch seen as traitors 36
economic collaboration 21, 102–53
German bureaucratic supervision 82–3
German occupation 48–9, 58, 165
government
    -in-exile 56, 86, 262, 292–3, 329
    restructuring in New Order 78–9
ID system 203–4
imprisonment for collaboration 19–20
industrial cooperation with
        Germany 40
intellectual debate 60
interwar political system 72
Jewish harassment 168
military production 119
national dishonour 25
occupation guidelines 86–101
official appointments 151
officials as collaborators 23–6, 134–5,
        154–235, 239–40
police
    collaboration 23–4, 88, 215
    and deportations 293
    disarmament 316
policing by SS 88, 173
POW conscription 287
and pre-war political systems 56–7
purge tribunals 19, 20
railway workers' resistance 7–8
Reich Commissioners 49–50
religious pillars 72–3, 74
resistance 165
self-Nazification 75, 77
socialist left policy 59–60
SS policing 172–4
Supreme Court and occupier's
        rights 89–90
see also officials
New Order in Europe, *see* Nazism
NG (*Nederlandse Gemeenschap*) movement
        73–4
Night and Fog decree 169
Nordic Union 41
Norway
    anti-Semitism 193–5
    authoritarian collaboration 62–86,
        231–3

Norway (cont.)
  bottom-up Nazification 231
  collaboration in 2–3, 12, 44–5
  deportation
    of Jews, see deportation, of Jews
    of workers 288
  economic collaboration 21, 102–53, 233
  German bureaucratic supervision 82–3
  and German economic planning 38–9
  and German police 171
  government-in-exile 116, 329
  government restructuring in New
    Order 78–9
  imprisonment for collaboration 19–20
  military occupation 43
  Nazification
    of police 233
    of society 195, 231–3
  occupation guidelines 86–101
  officials as collaborators 23–6, 231–5
  pardons 27
  political purges 233
  Reich Commissioners 49–50
  as special case 231
  SS policing 174
  Supreme Court and occupier's
    rights 90
  teacher internment 231
  wild purge 17–18
  see also officials
Novick 19
NSB (Nationaal-Socialistische Beweging)
    party 41, 52, 72, 74–7, 80, 81, 92,
    112, 133, 168, 172, 173, 208, 239,
    259, 293, 329
NS (Nasjonal Samling) government/
    officials 2, 20, 21, 45, 174–5, 195,
    231–3
NU (Nederlandse Unie) movement
    73–8, 208

Oberg, Carl-Albrecht 171, 252, 263,
    269–70, 271, 273, 274, 275,
    279–81, 294–5, 312
occupation
  authorities, pressures by 82
  /collaboration symmetry 55
  guidelines 86
OCRPI (Office Central de Répartition des
    Produits Industriels) 112, 219

offensive collaboration 22
officials
  anonymity of 155
  anti-communist activities 164–5
  anti-resistance stance 164–6, 169–70
  and anti-Semitism 196–220
  as collaborators 11, 20, 23–31, 59, 60–1,
    134–5, 154–235, 238, 330, 332
  education of 155–6
  group mentality of 332–3
  and law-and-order 164
  ministerial functions 162
  negotiation with Germany 163
  over-bureaucratization 162–3
  as political appointees 160
  politics as adminstration 163
  as problem-solvers 163
  purge commissions 18, 22–3, 24–31
  and repression 175
  resignations by 317–18
  rule of law suspension 166–7
  sabotage/resistance proclamations 166
  solidarity between 154
  and state continuity/sovereignty
    159–60
  technocratic 156
  see also deportation, of Jews;
    deportation, of workers
Olbrechts (Secretary of Labour) 299
ONT (Office National du Travail) 191,
    298–9, 300
Ophuls, Marcel 8
order displacement policy 107
Ougré-Marihaye 131
ownership/management separation 120

Pancke, Günther 316
Papon, Maurice 29–30, 281–2, 326
pardons 27
Paris Protocols 145
parliamentary democracy, and fascism
    58–9
passive resistance 318
patrimony 125, 147, 186
Pétain, Marshal Philippe 20, 55, 63–6, 85,
    124, 139, 145, 181, 183, 184, 238,
    240, 327
  meets Hitler 1, 64–6, 71
  sword and shield imagery 327–8
Petit, Lucien 156

Peugeot
  as employers 326
  and *Relève* scheme 304
  and VI rockets 322–4
Peyrouton, Marcel 83
Philips, and Jewish workers 258
Pierlot, Hubert 95–6, 99
Plan for a New Order in France 136
Plisnier, Oscar 151, 189, 223–4, 225–6,
    229, 255, 296, 297, 299, 321
Poland
  occupation of 4
  resistance in 4
police
  Belgium 172–3, 296
  Denmark 175–6, 316
  France 5, 29, 158, 199–200, 276–8, 280
  and *Gestapo* 20, 24
  Netherlands 23–4, 88, 173, 215, 293, 316
  Norway 233
  Vichy 5, 29
policy
  of negotiation 134
  of production 146, 147, 152
political conflict, post-war 14
political criminality 216
POW conscription 287
PPF (Parti Populaire Français) 64, 136,
    161, 267
pre-emptive arrest 166–7
private property rights 220
PTT (Postes, Télégraphes et Téléphones)
    postal/telecommunications
    workers 23
Pucheu, Pierre 84, 136, 157, 158, 161, 178,
    179, 180, 181–4, 216
purges of collaborators, post-war 13–31
purge targets 20

Quisling, Vidkun 2–3, 20, 38, 41, 44–5,
    52, 62, 63, 145, 174, 233

Raeder, Admiral Erich 45
Rauter, Hans Albin 165, 172, 173, 259–61
Reeder, Eggert 97, 98, 147–8, 150–1, 152,
    167, 190, 213, 223–4, 225, 228, 252,
    254–7, 259, 294–9, 300, 321
regional economic unions, post-war
    40–1
Reich Commissioners 49–50, 51, 54

Relève relief scheme 301–3, 306, 307
Renault 124
Renthe-Fink, Cécil von 51, 113, 176, 177,
    195, 246
resistance
  as legal defence 29
  while collaborating 238
resisting nations, *see* nation, of resisters
    myth
Ribbentrop, Joachim 33, 133, 245, 246, 267
Ribière, Marcel 216
Rijksbureau 111, 112, 127
*RNP (Rassemblement National
    Populaire)* 59
Romier, Lucien 183–4
Romsée, Gérard 166–8, 213, 214, 222,
    223–4, 226, 228, 229, 230, 256,
    296
Rosenberg, Alfred 45, 133
Röthke, Heinz 274–5, 277
Rouquet, François 23
Roussillon, Jean 306
RSHA (Reichssicherheitshauptamt) 249,
    251, 259, 272
rule of law, suspension of 167
Russia, *see* Soviet Union

Sabatier, Maurice 281
Sauckel, Fritz 51, 244, 265, 284–90, 292–4,
    297–8, 300, 306–13, 315, 325
*SCAP (Service de Contrôle des
    Administrateurs Provisoires)* agency
    body 218, 219
Scavenius, Erik 61–2, 113, 133, 196,
    245–7
Schleier, Rudolf 305
Schlotterer, Gustav 39–40
Schmidt, Fritz 75
Schmidt, Paul 66
Schrieke, Jacobus 165, 172
Schuind, Gaston 166–8, 223–4, 228,
    296–7, 333
Seyss-Inquart, Arthur 48–9, 52, 58, 73,
    74, 75, 77, 81, 82, 87–92, 114, 167,
    168, 173, 175, 191, 192, 204, 205,
    231, 239, 254, 259
shipbuilding contracts 119
Sicily, Allied invasion of 247
*SNCB (Société Nationale des Chemins de
    Fer Belge)* state railway 188–9

SNCF (*Société Nationale des Chemins de Fer Français*) railway employees 23, 85, 252
South Tyrol 3
Soviet Union, German invasion of (1941) 3, 4, 37, 105, 116, 164, 243, 284
Spaak, Paul-Henri 100–1, 227, 236
special section courts 180
Speer, Albert 37, 108, 134, 242–3, 244, 285–8, 309–10, 311, 312, 322
SS policing 171–2
steel manufacturers, and German consortiums 130
Steinbrinck, Otto 130
STO (*Service du Travail Obligatoire*) 307, 308, 310
Struye, Paul 55, 57, 147, 148–9, 190, 213, 230, 236, 297
Stülpnagel, General Otto von 170, 180
Sybelac (*Syndicat Belge de l'Acier*) 127, 131

Terboven, Josef 45–6, 62–3, 77, 90, 108, 174–5, 195, 231–2
third-way thinking 60
Tilman, Armand 296
Todt, Fritz 242
Todt organization 51, 115, 129, 132, 185, 242, 258, 309
Toningen, Rost von 133, 259
top-down economic structures 109
total war economy 242–3
treason trials 28
Tulard, André 202
Tulp, Sybren 173–4, 210, 259–61

USSR, *see* Soviet Union

VI rockets 322–3
Vallat, Xavier 198
Van Acker, Achille 15
Veldekens, Paul 213
Verwey, Robert 26, 192, 290–1
Verwilghen, Charles 189, 190, 191, 298
Vichy government xv, 5
  anti-Bolshevism 42, 178, 182
  and anti-Semitism 196–203, 207
  characteristics of 64
  and coal mine owners 130
  collaboration 22–3, 48, 55, 64–9, 84–5, 135–53, 237, 308
  Darlan government 64, 104, 137
  defection from 240
  deportation
    of Jews, *see* deportation, of Jews; final solution; France
    of workers, *see* deportation, of workers; France
  economic collaboration 102–45, 184
  and German industrial demands 106, 122–45
  Gestapo arrests of 315
  and Jewish question 330
  and law-and-order crisis 175
  legitimacy of 63
  loyalty of officials 241
  National Revolution 24, 64, 78, 196, 197, 218, 220, 253, 278
  in Nazi New Order 121
  post-war defences 328
  repression by 178, 179
  and sovereignty 80, 91, 175, 177–8, 240, 264
  special sections 178
  state authority conceptualization 83–4
  see also France
Villiers, Georges 304
Visser, Lodewijk 210, 331
VNV party/officials 191, 211, 222, 230
Vossen, Jean 212

Wannsee conference (1942) 53, 194, 243, 251, 253
Warenstellen 111, 112, 127
Wassard, Matthias 113
wild collaboration 106
wild purges 16–18, 106
Wimmer, Friedrich 203, 207
Wolff, Otto 131
worker pay differential 286
workers, as exempt from investigation 21

ZAST (*Zentralauftragstelle*) 108, 109, 127